UK Law and Your Rights For Dummies

The UK's Top Ten Rights

- The right not to be tortured, treated inhumanely, condemned to death, or executed
- The right to free elections
- The right to a fair trial
- The right not to be discriminated against
- The right to National Health Service treatment
- The right to an education
- The right to marry or register a civil partnership and build a family
- The right to be paid at least the minimum wage
- The right not to be sacked unfairly
- The right to at least 20 days' paid holiday each year

When You're Most Likely to Need Legal Advice

- You're involved in a dispute with your employer.
- You and your spouse or partner are splitting up.
- You may lose your driving licence for a traffic offence.
- You're in debt and could lose your home.
- Your builder has botched up the job but won't put it right.
- You've bought something faulty, but the shop won't return your money.
- You're buying or selling your property.
- You need to make a will.
- You've committed an offence that can land you in prison.
- You want to claim compensation for a personal injury.

For Dummies: Bestselling Book Series for Beginners

UK Law and Your Rights For Dummies®

Cheat Sheet

Your Best Sources of Help and Advice

The **Citizens Advice Bureau** is a free, independent, and impartial service of information, advice, and support. Look in your phone book for the details of the bureau nearest to you or find them online at www.adviceguide.org.uk.

You may have a **Law Centre** in your area. Look in the phone book or contact **The Law Centres Federation** on 0207 387 8570 or at www.lawcentres.org.uk for details. **The Scottish Association of Law Centres** is on 0141 4402503 or www.govanlc.com/salc. **Law Centres Northern Ireland** is on 02890 244401 or www.lawcentreni.org.

Mediation is a good way to try to resolve most disputes. Ask your nearest Citizens Advice Bureau if a service is in your area, try **Mediation UK** – 0117 904 6661 or www.mediationuk.org.uk.

Victim Support is an organisation that offers support and advice and can help you through the emotional and practical aspects of crime. Call 0845 3030900 for details of your local branch.

The Law Society can give you lists of solicitors. Call 0870 606 6565 in England and Wales, 0845 1130018 in Scotland, and 02890 231614 in Northern Ireland. If you want to complain about a solicitor or the bill, talk to the Law Society on 0845 6086565 or have a look through the Web site at www.lawsociety.org.uk.

The **Advisory, Conciliation, and Arbitration Service (ACAS)** can give advice on your rights at work. Contact ACAS through the Web site at www.acas.org.uk or through Equality Direct at ACAS 08456 003 444.

Trading Standards can help on all aspects of consumer law. Try www.tradingstandards.gov.uk. The new phone and Internet-based consumer advice service Consumer Direct is operating in most parts of the UK – call 08454 040506 or visit www.consumerdirect.gov.uk.

NHS Direct can help you find a GP and advise you if you feel unwell and aren't sure whether you need to see a doctor. Call 0845 4647 or see www.nhsdirect.nhs.uk.

If you need help on money, you should talk to independent financial advisers. You can reach **The Association of Independent Financial Advisers** at 0207 6281287 or at www.unbiased.co.uk.

Just about any query you may have about UK law is likely to be covered on the Government's own Web site at www.direct.gov.uk. It's a very useful source of information.

For Dummies: Bestselling Book Series for Beginners

UK Law
and Your Rights
FOR
DUMMIES®

by Liz Barclay

JOHN WILEY & SONS, LTD

UK Law and Your Rights For Dummies®

Published by
John Wiley & Sons, Ltd
The Atrium
Southern Gate
Chichester
West Sussex
PO19 8SQ
England

Email (for orders and customer service enquires): cs-books@wiley.co.uk

Visit our Home Page on www.wiley.co.uk or www.wiley.com

Wiley also publishes its books in a variety of electronic formats. Some content that appears in print may not be available in electronic books.

British Library Cataloguing in Publication Data

A catalogue record for this book is available from the British Library

ISBN-10: 0-470-02796-7

ISBN-13: 978-0-470-02796-7

Printed and bound in Great Britain by Bell & Bain, Ltd, Glasgow

10 9 8 7 6 5 4 3 2 1

WILEY

About the Author

Liz Barclay has worked as an adviser, trainer, and manager with the Citizens Advice Bureau and still advises small businesses and sole traders on relationship management with staff and customers. Liz is well connected within the media; she presents *You and Yours*, a factual radio programme on Radio 4, and has worked on a wide range of business and finance programmes for the BBC both on TV and radio. As a writer, Liz specialises in personal finance. She has written for the *News Of The World*, *The Express*, *Moneywise*, *Family Circle*, and *Save Money* and is currently working on the *Mail On Sunday* personal finance magazine.

Dedication

This book is dedicated to Jean Goodwin – a wonderful friend and my first boss at Citizens Advice Bureau. She gave me encouragement, support, confidence, the occasional dressing down, and the desire to fight injustice and somehow change the world. She was the most enthusiastic, dedicated, motivated fighter for the rights of the individual that I've ever come across. Jean, you have my eternal admiration and gratitude. It wouldn't have happened but for you.

Author's Acknowledgments

Thank goodness for the expertise of my friends! Marion Wright from Citizens Advice Bureau has spent many hours checking to make sure that this book is as legally correct and up to date as it possibly can be. Thank you, Marion, for being my Technical Adviser and for teaching me so much when I first joined the CAB. Thanks to Employment lawyer Dave Jones, business consultant Alistair Tait of TEDL, Elizabeth Manford from Trading Standards Institute, and tour operator and travel writer Neil Taylor for their help and expertise.

Publisher's Acknowledgments

We're proud of this book; please send us your comments through our Dummies online registration form located at www.dummies.com/register/.

Some of the people who helped bring this book to market include the following:

Acquisitions, Editorial, and Media Development

Development Editor: Kelly Ewing

Executive Project Editor: Martin Tribe

Content Editor: Steve Edwards

Commissioning Editor: Samantha Clapp

Proofreader: Kim Vernon

Technical Reviewer: Marion Wright

Executive Editor: Jason Dunne

Cartoons: Ed McLachlan

Composition

Project Coordinator: Jennifer Theriot

Layout and Graphics: Carl Byers, Andrea Dahl, Heather Ryan

Proofreaders: Susan Moritz, Brian H. Walls

Indexer: TECHBOOKS

Publishing and Editorial for Consumer Dummies

> **Diane Graves Steele,** Vice President and Publisher, Consumer Dummies

> **Joyce Pepple,** Acquisitions Director, Consumer Dummies

> **Kristin A Cocks,** Product Development Director, Consumer Dummies

> **Michael Spring,** Vice President and Publisher, Travel

> **Brice Gosnell,** Publishing Director, Travel

> **Suzanne Jannetta,** Editorial Director, Travel

Publishing for Technology Dummies

> **Andy Cummings,** Vice President and Publisher, Dummies Technology/General User

Composition Services

> **Gerry Fahey,** Vice President of Production Services

> **Debbie Stailey,** Director of Composition Services

Contents at a Glance

Table of Contents

Introduction

....

Welcome to *UK Law and Your Rights For Dummies*. The law in the UK gives citizens their rights and the means of protecting and enforcing those rights. Unfortunately, the law is extremely complicated and changes all the time.

With rights come responsibilities. If you have rights, so do other people, and you have a responsibility to respect their rights as well as your own. Sometimes that means compromising. If you use this book to increase your knowledge of your own rights, you'll be more aware of your responsibilities, too.

About This Book

This book gives you a good basic knowledge of how UK law is made. Not all of the law is exactly the same in all parts of the UK. In particular, the law on some issues can be quite different in Scotland as opposed to the rest of the UK.

The law is a collection of pieces of legislation that have been on the statute books for many years, new laws devised by the current Government, and directives coming from Europe. The law is also evolving constantly because of cases brought before the courts and tried or heard by judges and juries. Their decisions clarify how the law, as it is written, should be interpreted.

In this book, I cover how the law is enforced and what you should do if you feel that your rights have been infringed. Remember, no matter how hard I tried, there is absolutely no way to fit all of UK law and your rights into a book this size. I have shelves and shelves full of law books, and I still can't find details of some aspects of the law when I need them. Forgive me if there's something you would like to read about here that I haven't covered.

Conventions Used in This Book

To help you navigate this book, I used a few conventions:

- ✔ *Italic* is used for emphasis and to highlight new words or terms that are defined for the first time – including a lot of the 'legalise' and names of different pieces of legislation you'll come across.
- ✔ `Monofont` is used for Web addresses.
- ✔ Sidebars (the shaded grey boxes) contain information that, although helpful, may not apply to all readers.

Foolish Assumptions

I know – you should never assume – but I had to! Otherwise, I'd never have been able to decide where to start! I assumed that:

- ✔ You aren't a law student or a lawyer! This book is written for people who aren't legally trained, don't have a library full of legal tomes at their disposal, and don't have barristers for parents.
- ✔ You aren't very familiar with how the law is made or how it works, simply because you haven't had many dealings with it.
- ✔ You've bought this book because you'd like to know where you stand so that you can avoid being ripped off or breaking the law.
- ✔ You will heed my warnings that a book of this size can't contain all the information every individual may need in any given situation and that you will take additional advice as necessary.
- ✔ You realise that you have rights, and the other person in a dispute does, too, and that the best solution is often an amicable settlement.

How This Book Is Organised

UK Law And Your Rights For Dummies is divided into six parts. The chapters in each part cover specific topics in as much detail as possible, given the limitations of space and without being overly technical.

Part 1: Living with the Legal System

Chapter 1 deals with the basics of how the law is made and who makes it; the roles the courts play in the system; and who's who in the legal profession. The rest of Part I covers the basic issues of life in the UK, such as your rights to live and work and carry a British passport, use of the UK's public services such as the NHS, and to buy or rent a home and live in harmony with your neighbours.

Part II: Keeping on the Right Side of Family and Friends

Part II is possibly the most important part of the book in that it's likely to apply to most people. It covers all aspects of living together and getting married or registering a civil partnership, as well as building a family and having children. If you want to know if you can keep the engagement ring despite the wedding not going ahead, or if you're worried about the paperwork to complete when your baby arrives, this part provides the answer.

Part III: Making Enough to Live On – Legally!

The chapters in this part look at where the money comes from and your rights in each of those situations. If someone else employs you, you're paid for the work that you do, but you also have a lot of protection under UK law. Employment law is very complex, and if you do get into a dispute with an employer, Chapter 9 can help you decide what steps to take to resolve it.

This part also covers working for yourself, living on welfare benefits if you can't work, or living on retirement income if you're at the age where you have better things to do in life than work!

Part IV: Spending Your Hard-Earned Cash

Wherever your income comes from, you probably find it goes out again fairly quickly. This part deals with your rights as a shopper or as a consumer if you're paying someone else to do work for you, such as building an extension. This area of law gives rise to a large proportion of legal disputes. It helps to be armed with the information about your rights before you set out to make a complaint, and a huge range of organisations can help settle consumer disputes. This part also looks at what happens if you do a bit too much shopping and get behind with your essential bills.

Part V: Getting Out and About

This part deals with your movements outside your home. If you want to take to the roads and buy a car, this part explains all you need to know relating to your car and your right to drive.

This part also covers your rights as a paying customer of the trains, buses, and planes, including the misery of delays, cancellations, and missing luggage, as well as what you need to travel outside of the UK.

Part VI: The Part of Tens

Every *For Dummies* book has a Part of Tens. This part covers the kinds of insurance policies that can buy you peace of mind and explains the best ways of protecting your rights.

Icons Used in This Book

When you flick through this book, you'll notice little icons in the margins. These icons highlight suggestions and cautions when it comes to the law.

This icon is something that may make life easier in general or a dispute easier to avoid or resolve.

This highlights important information that may be useful to you in the future.

Not all of these are dire warnings – but if you read and apply the information in them, they may help you avoid pitfalls and disputes.

This icon speaks for itself. It highlights useful points of law.

Where to Go from Here

Any contact with the law can be quite intimidating. The more information you have about your rights, the less likely you are to get into trouble in the first place. I'm not suggesting you read this whole book from cover to cover in one sitting. Use it to check up on your rights before you do something, such as buying a car or moving in with your partner.

Above all, though, remember that this book has room for only very basic information, and you should always get legal advice about your own particular individual circumstance.

Part I
Living with the
Legal System

In this part . . .

I explain the role played by the UK Parliament, the Government, local government, and Europe in making the rules. After the laws are passed and come into force, the courts ultimately have the responsibility to enforce them. But the law writers aren't always very clear about exactly what they intended, and sometimes you can interpret the wording in more than one way. You may be involved in a dispute with someone who doesn't agree with your interpretation of a law. If you both consult solicitors, they may not be able to agree. Eventually two barristers may end up presenting two very different arguments to a judge who has to make the decision, which then becomes part of the law and clarifies its meaning.

This part looks at the role of everyone involved in the law and at the rights those laws give you in some of the most basic areas of human life in the UK, such as living and working, renting or buying a home, and getting medical treatment and an education for your children. I also explain what you should do if you have to take a case to court and what the powers of the police are if they think you've broken the law.

Chapter 1

Unravelling the Legal Web

*T*he legal system in the UK is complex. The Government draws up laws, while Parliament passes them. Because the UK is part of the European Union, the UK Government must put into practice laws drawn up in Europe. If UK laws and European laws conflict, European law wins.

The judges in courts have the difficult job of making sense of all the laws and working out exactly what the legislation says and means. Their decisions are important when it comes to clarifying legislation. In addition, there are local laws in different parts of the country (you probably won't hear about them until you've broken them), as well as old laws still in existence that everyone forgot about years ago.

This chapter helps make the whole legal process a little bit more comprehensible and less intimidating. The law is what your rights are based on, and if you want to be sure you understand your rights, you need to understand the system.

Untangling the Legal System

The legal system is multilayered. Laws come from two different sources – the UK and Europe. But no piece of legislation is clear-cut, and each law can often be interpreted in more than one way. That's why the courts play a role in helping citizens understand what the legislation was meant to mean. This section gives you an idea of how UK laws come into force.

Legal differences throughout the UK

England and Wales share a *legal system* – the same court structure and the same laws. However, since the establishment of the Welsh Assembly, Wales does have limited powers to make some of its own laws, which is why some law or policy differences may exist. For example, prescription charges for medicines are different in Wales.

Northern Ireland also has an Assembly, but due to political disagreements, it's often suspended, and so government reverts to Westminster. As a result, Northern Ireland and England have some differences between laws – for example, in Northern Ireland, you have to be married for two years before you can apply for divorce, whereas in the rest of the UK it's only one year, and the High Court in Northern Ireland deals with divorce instead of the country court. (For more information on the Northern Ireland system, visit www.direct.gov.uk.)

Scotland has its own parliament, consisting of Scottish MPs who can pass legislation for Scotland. The education system is different in Scotland, and University students there don't have to pay fees. In addition, the rules on paying for long-term care for elderly people, and the house buying and legal systems are substantially different. (You can find more information on the Scottish legal system at www.scotland.gov.uk.)

Constitution, Acts of Parliaments, and common law

The UK has no constitution in the sense that no one document sets out the powers of the Government. The Parliament Acts of 1911 and 1949 set out the powers of the Houses of Commons and Lords. The *House of Commons* is the chamber of Parliament where elected MPs sit and debate; the *House of Lords* is where the Peers influence the law-making process and is the highest court in the UK. The European Communities Act makes the UK part of the European Community – the European Union of 25 member countries – with all the legal implication that entails.

The Government uses its powers to draw up legislation. At the beginning of each parliamentary year, the Queen gives a speech in which she outlines the laws the Government wants to make or change during that year. Parliament then debates each bill drawn up.

Parliament includes members of the House of Commons and the House of Lords. MPs in the Commons debate each bill at several readings and ask for amendments before the bill is presented in its final form for voting on whether it should become law. If Parliament passes the bill, it then goes to the House of Lords for approval. If the MPs vote to pass a piece of legislation but the Lords reject it, it goes back to the House of Commons for MPs to look at it again, but ultimately, the Lords can't stop the Commons from passing a bill. Eventually, the legislation is either rejected because too many MPs vote against it, or it's passed and becomes law.

At the time of writing, the Government has drafted an *Animal Welfare Bill,* which, amongst other things, if passed, raises the age at which a child can buy a pet from 12 to 16 and makes it illegal to dock dogs' tails. If the legislation becomes law, it will become the *Animal Welfare Act* and be dated with the year it passed. It will then be an *Act of Parliament.*

The Queen has to approve each *Act of Parliament* – it's given *Royal Assent* – and then it becomes law. The Government, which came up with the proposals in the first place, then has to put the law into use. The Government is different from Parliament. The elected MPs who are appointed by the Prime Minister to act as cabinet ministers, their government departments (such as the Department of Health), local authorities such as the members of a City Council, and civil servants are the Government. Not only does the Government have to make the laws and put them into practice, it also has to abide by them.

Acts of Parliament also give government ministers the power to make changes through what's called *secondary legislation* or *statutory instruments,* which are usually used to make minor changes and go through a much less rigorous process before becoming law.

The problem with most pieces of legislation is that you can interpret the many clauses in multiple ways. That's where the courts come into the equation. *Judges* interpret the law, and their decisions build up into a body of case law, known as *common law.* Judges are independent of Parliament. They can't decide that legislation passed by Parliament is unlawful, although they can, in some cases, overrule statutory instruments. Judges, however, can decide that the Government has broken its own laws and can preside over cases taken against the Government.

As an example, take the law on discrimination. If someone makes a claim against someone else, for discrimination on the grounds of disability, *solicitors*, appointed to act for each side, try to reach a settlement. Each solicitor is arguing that his client is in the right. If a settlement isn't reached and the case goes to court, each side has a *barrister,* or an *advocate* in Scotland, representing them. Each barrister prepares an argument that supports her client, and the judge then decides who is right and who is wrong. In certain types of cases, the decision then influences the outcome of other similar cases. That's common law.

The lower courts are bound by decisions made in higher courts. These decisions set *precedents*. The House of Lords is the highest court in the land, and all the lower courts must adhere to its decisions. The House of Lords is also the highest court of appeal for all the UK, except Scotland, where it is the highest court of appeal for civil cases only.

Because of the role the courts play in interpreting legislation, the law changes and matures as time passes. Each time they decide a case, the courts are clarifying the laws. For that reason, predicting an outcome of a particular case may be difficult. Any previous court case on a similar matter may be a factor.

Outside influences

Because the UK is a member of the European Union, European law has become more important. If UK law says one thing and European law says another, European law takes priority. For example, the *Working Time Regulations under the European Working Time Directive* sets out the rules about how long an employee can be expected to work during the average working week (see Chapter 9). When the Directive first came into effect, the UK was allowed to opt out of implementing the rules for a while for certain workers. It has now had to fall into line with the other European Union countries.

Businesses in the UK often complain about the red tape imposed on them by Europe, but the *UK Members of the European Parliament* (MEPs) have the chance to debate new legislation before it becomes law. It's up to the UK Government to interpret that legislation and put it into practice.

The European Commission comes up with the new laws. The European Parliament consists of all the MEPs and advises on those proposals. The Council of Ministers represents all the governments of the 25 member countries and has the final say on what becomes law. The European Courts of Justice interpret the law in the same way that UK judges interpret UK laws.

Europe can pass a range of different laws. *Regulations* have to be followed to the letter by all member countries. *Directives* have to be achieved, but it's up to each country how they're implemented. The decisions of the Courts of Justice affect how the law is put into practice.

Bylaws

Bylaws are laws made by local authorities, and they apply to certain limited geographical areas. Bylaws usually cover issues that are of concern to local people and about which no laws already exist. If you check with your local authority, you may find that it has laws about riding horses in the local parks or restricting the hours that children can work. Before bylaws come into force, the Secretary of State, on behalf of the Government, must pass them.

Understanding How the Courts Work

The job of the courts and all the people who work in them is to make sense of the law and to penalise people for breaking it. The four sorts of courts are civil courts, criminal courts, tribunals, other courts, such as the Coroner's Court and the European Court of Human Rights.

The system is far from easy to understand, partly because some courts can deal with both criminal and civil matters. Sometimes you can choose which court you'd like to hear your case or the different Acts of Parliament you can use to make a claim.

If you're about to get involved with the court system in any capacity, take advice. You may not need to enlist the help of a solicitor, but do talk to your nearest Citizens Advice Bureau or Law Centre for free advice and assistance. (You can find their details in the phone book.) These organisations may be able to supply all the information you need, but if they can't, they can point you in the right direction. If you do need to employ a legal professional, these groups can provide referrals as well.

The criminal courts

If the police charge you with committing a criminal offence in England and Wales, the *Crown Prosecution Service* (CPS), a Government department, decides whether you should be prosecuted. (In Scotland, the Crown Office and the Procurator Fiscal play the role of the CPS.)

The police often complain that they do all the legwork on a case, and then the CPS decides not to prosecute. When that happens, it's usually because the CPS feels that it doesn't have enough evidence to obtain a conviction. In some cases, the police themselves carry out prosecutions, and in the case of tax fraud, Her Majesty's Revenue and Customs will prosecute.

If the CPS gives the go ahead to prosecute you, it prepares a case against you and presents it in court.

All criminal cases start in the Magistrates' Court. The less serious or summary offences, such as shoplifting or illegal parking, start and finish there. More serious offences, such as burglary or assault, can be tried in the Magistrates' Court or sent to a higher court – the Crown Court – to be tried by a jury. The Magistrates will decide whether a case goes to the Crown Court, and they may send it there if they feel that a jury trial would be more appropriate or that they can't hand out a severe enough punishment. The Crown Court tries by jury all the most serious offences, such as manslaughter and murder, rape, and arson.

The Crown Court also deals with appeals against decisions made in the Magistrates' Court. The Court of Appeal Criminal Division deals with Appeals against Crown Court decisions. The House of Lords sits at the top of the tree and is the last resort for an appeal.

In Scotland, the Lord Advocate brings all the prosecutions, and the Advocate Depute prosecutes. The least serious summary cases, such as drunkenness charges and petty theft, are dealt with in *District Courts,* located in each local authority area. *Sheriffs Courts* deal with more serious offences. If they feel they can't hand out tough enough penalties, they can hand the case on to the High Court to be heard in front of a jury. The High Court also deals with the most serious cases – the *Solemn* cases. The High Court is the highest court of appeal for criminal cases in Scotland.

Northern Ireland has the same system of Magistrates' and Crown Courts as England and Wales. The main difference in criminal law in Northern Ireland is in the handling of cases relating to terrorism.

The civil courts

If you want to take a case against someone – to claim compensation for poor building work or for personal injury, for example – it's considered a *civil case.* Individuals, companies, and public organisations can take civil cases, which are usually heard by a circuit or a district judge without a jury. Most cases are dealt with by the County Courts, but some cases are handled by Magistrates in the Magistrates' Courts. The more complex cases go to the High Court.

The operations of the civil courts are as follows:

✔ **Magistrates' Courts** deal with arrears of council tax, income tax, and VAT, which are not criminal offences. The *Family Proceedings Courts,* which are part of the Magistrates Courts, deal with family matters, such as maintenance payments, adoptions, and care proceedings and orders to get a spouse out of the family home (see Chapter 6).

- ✔ **County Courts** deal with the majority of civil cases, such as disputes between landlord and tenant (see Chapter 3), faulty goods and services (see Chapters 13 and 14), personal injuries, domestic violence (see Chapter 6), debt (see Chapter 15), discrimination, and some employment cases (see Chapter 9). If the county court has divorce jurisdiction, it can deal with undefended divorce cases (see Chapter 6). If you want to claim a sum of money from someone and it's under £5,000, you can use the *Small Claims Track* at the County Court (see 'Making a small claim' later in this chapter). Sheriffs Courts in Scotland are roughly the equivalent of County Courts and deal with both civil and criminal matters.

- ✔ **High Courts** have three divisions. *The Family Division* deals with family issues, such as defended divorces (see Chapter 6), adoption, and domestic violence. The *Queen's Bench Division* deals with large claims for compensation, libel, and slander. The *Chancery Division* deals with wills, trusts, bankruptcy, and winding up companies.

Some cases, such as domestic violence, can be dealt with by more than one court. The Magistrates' Court can give an order to get a spouse out of the family home, but the County and High courts also deal with domestic violence. You do need to take legal advice about which court to start a case in and under which laws you should take your case.

The *Court of Appeal Civil Division* deals with appeals against decisions made in civil cases in the High Court, County Court, and Employment Appeal Tribunals. (See the upcoming section 'Using a Tribunal to Get Justice.') The House of Lords handles appeals from the Court of Appeal and sometimes from the High Court.

The system in Scotland is very different. The Sheriff's court can deal with civil as well as criminal cases. The *Court of Session* is the equivalent of the High Court in the rest of the UK. Its *Outer House* hears the less complicated cases, while the *Inner House* deals with the more complex cases and appeals from Outer House cases. The House of Lords appeals from the Court of Session.

In Northern Ireland, the system is very similar to that in England and Wales. The County Courts are presided over by County Court judges or recorders and deal with the vast majority of civil cases. They also deal with appeals from the Magistrates' Courts. The High Court handles all divorces.

Tribunals

Tribunals are panels of specialists in particular areas of law who can make decisions on some disputes. For example, *employment tribunals* (see Chapter 9) handle most disputes between employees and their employers. Tribunals are less formal than courts, and the people making the decisions can talk directly to both parties in the dispute.

Tribunals also handle land disputes – for example, disagreements about the value of land that's being bought under compulsory purchase orders. *Social Security Appeal Tribunals* deal with claims by people that they've been unfairly refused welfare benefits. The *Immigration Appeals Tribunals* handle immigration cases.

The rest

As well as the Criminal courts, the Civil courts, and the tribunals, many other courts sit in the UK or in Europe and have a role to play in the UK's judicial system:

- ✓ **Coroners' Courts:** Coroners deal with the circumstances surrounding a sudden death. They investigate deaths in prison, for example, deaths where the cause is unknown, and violent deaths, such as murder. Coroners can decide to hold an inquest into how someone died, and the coroner may even call a jury to decide on the cause of death. In Scotland, the Crown Office and the Procurator Fiscal play the role of the Coroners' Court. Strangely, the Coroners' Court also deals with buried treasure. If you find a treasure trove, the Coroner is the person who decides who it belongs to!

- ✓ **The Privy Council:** This court handles appeals for decisions made in civil and criminal cases in courts in the Isle of Man, the Channel Islands, the Colonies, and some independent Commonwealth countries.

- ✓ **The European Court of Human Rights:** This court applies to cases where human rights have been violated.

- ✓ **The Court of First Instance:** If you're in dispute about a decision made by a European Union institution and the decision affects you directly, this court hears your case. It also deals with competition law.

- ✓ **The European Court of Justice:** The Court of Justice has the final say. It makes sure European Union Law is adhered to by the member states, and it can overrule all other courts, including the House of Lords.

Knowing Who's Who: The Lawyers

All sorts of different legal titles pop up as you explore the legal system. The list of different people who may ultimately be involved in any case is long, and their different roles can be bewildering.

Dealing with young people

The *Youth Court* deals with young people between the ages of 10 to 17 who have committed criminal offences. Children under 10 aren't old enough to be charged with criminal offences. The Youth Court is part of the Magistrates' Court. The young person can be sent in to the Crown Court for trial if the offence is very serious.

The County or High Court handles matters concerning children during a divorce. If a local authority is taking a child into care, it usually applies to the Family Proceedings Court, which is part of the Magistrates' Court (see Chapter 7).

In Scotland, *Children's Hearings* deal with young offenders who are under 16, as well as cases that relate to care and protection. The Procurator Fiscal can decide whether the case is serious enough to go to the criminal court. A Children's Hearing panel can order a child be taken into care or foster care, take part in a particular programme, have regular contact with a social worker, and appoint a representative to attend the hearing with the child to protect his rights.

Magistrates

Magistrates hear criminal and some civil and family cases in Magistrates' Courts. The official name for a Magistrate is a Justice of the Peace. In Scotland, Sheriffs, Magistrates, and Justices of the Peace can hear summary criminal cases. In Northern Ireland, some Justices of the Peace aren't Magistrates and don't have the power to hear legal cases.

The majority of Magistrates aren't qualified lawyers; they're lay people who have been appointed by the Secretary of State for Constitutional Affairs and the Lord Chancellor. Local Advisory Committees are made up of Magistrates and local people who advise on the appointments. Most Magistrates are between the ages of 27 and 65, and they must retire at 70.

You won't be appointed if you aren't of good character and personal standing or if you're bankrupt, a member of the armed forces or police, a traffic warden, or closely related to someone who is already a Magistrate.

Lay Magistrates are unpaid. Because they aren't legally qualified, Lay Magistrates sit in panels of three and have a qualified court clerk in attendance to advise them on various aspects of the law and procedure.

Stipendiary Magistrates are paid and are legally qualified, usually as solicitors. They can try cases alone and have the same powers as two lay magistrates.

Solicitors

A solicitor is likely to be the first legal professional you encounter if you intend to take a legal case through the civil courts, get a divorce, buy or sell a property, check out your rights if you're involved in some sort of legal dispute, or you're charged with a criminal offence. You can get legal advice from other sources – for example, an accountant can advise you on tax law, and Citizens Advice Bureaux or Law Centres have staff that can give you all sorts of information about your legal rights. Trade unions and other organisations, such as money advice or housing advice centres, can also help. You may have a suitable mediation service in your area that can help you resolve your dispute without the help of a solicitor. Or you may have an Ombudsman's scheme, such as the ones mentioned in the upcoming section 'Using Alternatives to the Courts.' You may even be able to present your own case in court. Explore all the options before appointing a solicitor to act for you.

Solicitors can advise you on your rights and the possible outcomes of your case, as well as help you prepare a case. They can represent you and try to reach a settlement without the case reaching court.

You should only hire the services of a solicitor who has experience in the area of law you're involved in. You can get details from the CAB, Law Centre, or the Law Society. (See the end of this chapter for contact details.)

If you're at a police station, a duty solicitor is available to advise you. Take that advice. If you're at a Magistrates' court, similar arrangements for legal advice are available; ask the court staff.

Solicitors can sometimes bamboozle you with their legal jargon. If you can, take someone else with you to an appointment with your solicitor. It may be easier for someone who's not as close to the issue as you are to take notes and ask pertinent questions. If the solicitor says anything you don't understand, make sure that you ask for explanation.

If you have complaints about your solicitor or the size of the bill, or if you can't afford their services, you can complain or obtain financial help. (See the section 'Claiming Help with Legal Costs,' later in this chapter, for more information.)

Barristers

Solicitors try to sort out your legal problems themselves, but if your case has to go to court, you're likely to need a barrister to represent you. You may be able to represent yourself if the case is uncomplicated, such as a small claim in the County Court (see the upcoming section 'Taking a Case through the Civil Courts') or a tribunal hearing, but if you're charged with a criminal offence or you need someone to argue your case in a civil court, it will usually be a barrister who is appointed. In most cases, solicitors don't have the right to act as your advocate in court.

In Scotland, the person who does the same job as the Barrister is called an Advocate.

QCs

Queen's Counsel (QCs) are senior barristers appointed by the Lord Chancellor as counsel to the Queen. They don't have any extra duties in court, but they're more experienced than normal barristers and solicitors, so their fees are likely to be higher.

Judges

A judge is a highly trained legal professional who is appointed to hear cases in a court of law. Different types of judge hear and try both civil and criminal cases. The *Law Lords* are the most senior judges and make decisions on appeals to the House of Lords. The *Lord Chancellor* is the most senior of the lot.

Court of Appeal judges come next in the pecking order and preside over Court of Appeal hearings. *High Court judges* hear civil cases in the High Court and try serious criminal cases in the Crown Court. *Masters* and *Registrars* deal with most of the ordinary cases in the High Court.

Circuit judges hear County Court civil cases and try less serious criminal cases. *Recorders* are part-time barristers and solicitors with at least ten years experience who deal with Crown and County Court cases. *District judges* deal with smaller County Court hearings and family matters and are usually solicitors.

Depending on the court she's presiding over, the judge may be joined by another judge or a jury (see next section) or sit on her own. A judge is there to apply the law, and in some cases, the outcome of the trial may set legal precedents that must be followed by other legal professionals.

In Scotland, the Sheriffs' Courts are the workhorses of the legal system and the judges are called *sheriffs*. They can hear and try a wide range of civil and criminal cases. The most senior judges are called Sheriff *Principals*.

Jury

A judge with a *jury* hears some cases. In Scotland, 15 people sit on a jury, while in the rest of the UK, that number is 12.

If your name is on the electoral register, you may be selected for jury service. You don't need to have any legal training. If you're selected, you may be excused only in exceptional circumstances, but you may be able to have your jury duty deferred until a later date.

Your work commitments won't get you off the hook. You'll be expected to sit on a jury for ten working days and may be involved in more than one case in that time.

You can claim some expenses while you're on the jury – for travelling, childcare costs, some financial losses, and a subsistence allowance to keep you alive for those ten days. You can get more information on jury duty from the Jury Central Summoning Bureau (0845 3555567 or www.juror.cjsonline.org).

Dealing with Crime

As far as the law is concerned, a crime is a crime whether it's a parking offence or a murder; the only difference is in the punishment of the offender. However, an underlying principle implies that it's better that a few guilty people get off than one innocent person be punished for something he didn't do. The following guidelines help uphold that principle:

- ✔ If you're charged with an offence, you're presumed innocent until proven guilty.
- ✔ The prosecution has to prove 'beyond all reasonable doubt' that you committed the offence. If reasonable doubt exists, you go free.
- ✔ You don't have to 'help the police with their enquiries' or give them a statement, and you can remain silent. If you don't cooperate, it can't be held against you at the trial unless the circumstances are exceptional.
- ✔ Any previous convictions aren't revealed to the jury during a trial unless they're relevant to that trial – for example, someone on trial for child sex offences may have previous child sex offences revealed.
- ✔ *Hearsay* – something heard from someone else – isn't accepted as evidence – witnesses have to report what they saw and heard for themselves.
- ✔ The press and media can't speculate on cases that are going through the courts. They can report only the facts.

You can end up in court because you're sent a summons to appear, or you can be arrested and charged. The more serious the impact the case could have on your life, the more important it is to get legal advice. If you may lose your driving licence, for example, and you make your living as a driver, you really should get legal advice straight away. If you may be sent to prison or are likely to lose your job, you need all the help you can get.

Police powers

The police can stop you in the street and ask you to accompany them to the station. You can refuse. You don't have to help them with their enquiries, but most people do.

However, the police can make you go with them if they arrest you. In addition, the police can stop and search you if they have reasonable grounds to believe that you're carrying certain items, such as knives or other weapons that can be used to commit an offence.

The police can arrest you with a warrant signed by a Magistrate, but they have wide powers of arrest in serious cases so they often don't need warrants. They can arrest you without a warrant if you have committed an *arrestable offence,* are in the act of committing an arrestable offence, or are suspected of committing an arrestable offence. An arrestable offence is one that can result in a prison sentence of five years or more – such as arson, burglary, death by reckless driving, manslaughter, murder, or rape.

The police can also arrest you without a warrant in all sorts of circumstances relating to breaches of the peace and drunkenness. If you're arrested, the police have powers to search you. You do have to be told that you're being arrested and why. If you're held at a police station, you have to be allowed to see a solicitor. You also have the right to have someone told that you've been arrested, and you can look at the codes of practice the police have to follow. The custody officer has to give you a written notice of those rights and should also caution you that 'you do not have to say anything, but it may harm your defence if you do not mention when questioned something which you later rely on in court. Anything you do say may be given in evidence.'

You can't be made to answer police questions, and they can't use force to get the answers out of you. You can't be forced to give a statement.

A solicitor is on duty 24 hours a day to help anyone who is detained at a police station. Before you decide whether to answer a question or give a statement, make sure that you see that solicitor for advice. However, in serious cases, the police can delay your interview with a solicitor if they think it will interfere with the evidence, alert other suspects, or make recovering stolen property more difficult.

You have to be charged or released within 24 hours of your arrest. In serious cases, you can be held for up to 36 hours, and the police can ask Magistrates for an extension up to 96 hours. The police have a wide range of powers to take fingerprints, photographs, and DNA samples. Records of fingerprints and photographs don't have to be destroyed if you're acquitted and can placed in a database to be used in crime investigations.

If you're arrested and charged, you can be kept in custody or allowed out on bail. In legal jargon, you're *remanded in custody* or *remanded on bail*. The police can grant you bail, or, if they refuse, you can apply to a Magistrate for bail. You shouldn't be refused bail unnecessarily. If the Magistrate does refuse, you have to be given the reasons in writing, and you go to prison as a *remand prisoner*. The time spent in prison on remand counts toward any eventual prison sentence the court passes.

Crime and punishment

Whether you're summoned or arrested and charged, your case starts in the Magistrates' Court – unless you're in Scotland, in which case the court system is different. (See the section 'Understanding How the Courts Work,' earlier in this chapter.) Some cases – the least serious, or *summary offences* – can be tried only in the Magistrates' Court. Other, more serious offences – known as *triable either way offences* – can be tried in either the Crown Court or the Magistrates' Court. The most serious cases – *indictable offences* – are transferred to the Crown Court.

If the offence can be tried only in the Magistrates' Court, the prosecutor – usually the Crown Prosecution Service – must inform the Magistrates and ask for a summons to be issued within six months of the offence being committed. If the Magistrates aren't informed within six months, you usually can't be prosecuted, but as with every rule, there are exceptions, particularly in the case of motoring offences.

If an offence can be tried in either the Magistrates' Court or the Crown court, you may be charged with an offence you committed years ago.

After it has been decided which court will try the case, you receive a hearing date and are eventually found guilty and sentenced, or acquitted. You may be able to plead guilty by post if the offence is a summary one, such as a minor motoring offence, that doesn't carry a maximum sentence of more than three months in prison. You can't plead 'not guilty' by post – you have to appear in court.

Private individuals can also bring prosecutions in the criminal courts. For example some shop owners prosecute shoplifting cases themselves rather than resorting to the Crown Prosecution Service.

If you're thinking of prosecuting someone for a criminal offence, take legal advice. You may end up paying all the legal costs and facing a claim for compensation if the case goes against you.

If you're found guilty, the court sentences you. Penalties range from suspended sentences and *community service orders* (where you do community work for a prescribed number of hours) to large fines and periods in prison or both. Maximum sentences also exist for each offence, and a solicitor can tell you what sentence you may be facing.

Criminal records

If you're convicted of a crime, you'll have a criminal record until the sentence becomes *spent* under the terms of the Rehabilitation of Offenders Act 1974. After the sentence is spent, you're considered rehabilitated, and you no longer have to reveal the conviction on forms. The length of time it takes for a sentence to become spent depends on the sentence itself. The time starts ticking as soon as you're convicted.

To give you a few examples (for adult offenders who are 18 and over):

- ✔ If you're sentenced to prison for more than 30 months, the sentence will never be spent. It's the length of the original sentence that counts and not the time you spend in prison.

- ✔ If you go to prison for between 6 months and 30 months, it will take ten years before the sentence is spent.

- ✔ If you get a community service order, the sentence is spent in five years.

- ✔ If you're given an *absolute discharge* (you may be guilty of the offence, but the court feels it wouldn't be fair to punish you), it takes six months before the slate is wiped clean again.

Committing another offence while you're waiting for the first sentence to be spent may extend the time it takes for you to be rehabilitated. After the sentence is spent and you've been rehabilitated, it will be as if you had not been charged and convicted. In most circumstances, you won't have to reveal that you have a spent conviction. However, exceptions abound.

Members of certain professions always have to reveal spent convictions: doctors, dentists, lawyers, accountants, teachers, probation officers, prison officers, vets, traffic wardens, and those working with children and vulnerable adults. Discuss your own particular case with your solicitor.

The Rehabilitation of Offenders Act 1974 doesn't apply outside the UK, so you always have to reveal details when applying for jobs or visas in foreign countries.

Prisoners' rights

If you're sent to prison, your rights – and any restrictions of those rights – are covered by the *Prison Act 1952* and *Prison Rules 1999*. You have the right to access your solicitor, food, clothes, exercise, at least two visits a month, to send and receive at least one letter a week, and to a fair hearing if a disciplinary problem occurs. If work is available, you have to work up to ten hours a day unless you're excused on medical grounds. The Prison Medical Service provides medical and dental treatment.

When you go to prison, you're categorised as an A,B,C, or D prisoner. Category A prisoners are the highest risk and have extra security restrictions. Category D prisoners are the least risk. Categories can be reviewed and changed.

You don't have the right to choose the prison you go to, but you may be able to apply for a transfer if your location poses your family big problems – for example, your parents can't travel to visit you because of age or disability.

Checking criminal records

The Criminal Records Bureau (CRB) keeps a database of all convictions, cautions, and warnings, spent and unspent. Employers taking on employees and volunteers to work with children and vulnerable adults must check criminal records with the CRB. A standard disclosure from CRB reveals to the employer the applicant's spent and unspent convictions and any police cautions or reprimands. If no criminal record exists, the Bureau will say so.

If the job means regular contact with children and being in sole charge of them, an enhanced disclosure provides the same details as the standard disclosure, but also adds any information from local police records, such as allegations made to the police by other people even if those weren't followed up. The disclosures appear if someone is banned from working with children.

You can be segregated from the other prisoners if you request it for your "own protection or if the prison authorities think it's advisable because you're causing bad behaviour and poor discipline. You can't be segregated for more than three days without the authority of the Board of Visitors or the Secretary of State.

Women prisoners may be allowed to keep their babies with them up to 9- or 18-months-old, depending on which prison they're in. That limit may be stretched in some circumstances. Women prisoners don't have to wear prison uniform.

Remand prisoners who haven't been convicted have more rights than convicted prisoners. They don't have to work unless they want to; they're allowed to wear their own clothes and are allowed as many visits as they like on at least three days a week and are allowed a weekend visit at least once every two weeks. They can also send and receive as many letters as they like. They can also use the Prison Medical Service or be treated by their own doctor or dentist.

Young people in young offender's institutions are subject to similar rules to adults. If they're under 17, they are given at least 15 hours of education or training each week.

Victims of crime

The victims of crime have long complained that the law is on the side of the perpetrators and that their views aren't considered. Things are changing, and the courts do now have a responsibility under the Human Rights Act 1998 to make sure that the rights of the victims of crime are balanced with the rights of defendants. If you've been the victim of a crime and you report it to the police, you should receive a leaflet that explains your rights. In addition, your local Victim Support Scheme offers support and advice and can help you through the emotional and practical aspects of crime. You can contact them direct if you haven't yet decided to report a crime. Call 0845 3030900 for details on your local branch.

If you're a witness in court, you should be sent a leaflet that explains the court process. In addition, Victim Support provides a witness service in all Crown Courts to help you through the process.

You will have no say in the sentence that is handed down to the accused, but if the accused is convicted and appeals against that conviction, you have the right to be informed. If the offence was a serious sexual or violent assault, probation services also have to tell you when the defendant is released. If you're being subjected to intimidation, you must tell the police. The Criminal Justice and Public Order Act 1994 makes intimidation an offense, and several other acts, including the Family Law Act 1996, give you additional protection from harassment.

The Criminal Injuries Compensation Scheme

If you're injured as a result of a crime, in theory, you can sue the person who injured you for compensation, but he probably wouldn't be able to pay. The Criminal Injuries Compensation Act 1995 set up the Criminal Injuries Compensation Scheme. The scheme has more than 400 different classes of injury and pays out small amounts (at least compared to the compensation payments people can claim in the civil courts) to victims.

The minimum award under the scheme is £1,000. If you don't qualify for at least £1,000, you get nothing. Tariffs exist on each class of injury. A sprained wrist that disables you for more than 13 weeks is worth £2,500, a loss of an ear £11,000, and permanent and extreme brain damage is awarded £250,000 (but compensation for loss of earnings and special expenses can bring a total award up to a maximum of £500,000).

Any award you get from the scheme may be reduced if you didn't report the crime to the police straight away, you didn't cooperate with the police, you have a previous criminal conviction yourself even though it's completely unrelated to the incident you're claiming for, or you're judged to have contributed in some way to your own injury.

You must normally claim within two years of the incident. You claim from the Criminal Injuries Compensation Authority at Tay House, 300 Bath Street, Glasgow G2 4LN – 0800 3583601, www.cica.gov.uk.

Taking a Case through the Civil Courts

Civil cases are cases brought by someone who wants a judge to decide that another person is in the wrong. Many civil cases are accompanied by a claim for a sum of money in compensation for that wrong. For example, you may have bought faulty goods and are unable to get the retailer to return your money. Or you may have been injured as a result of an accident and want compensation. The earlier section 'Understanding How the Courts Work' describes how the civil court system works – civil cases go through the County or High Courts or their equivalents in Scotland.

Taking a case to court can be time consuming and expensive. Small claim cases are easier to deal with than the more complex cases, but you do have to think your decision through before proceeding.

Make sure that you really have a claim in the first instance. If you've bought faulty goods from a retailer, you do have a claim, but if you've bought it from a private individual, you usually aren't able to claim. Make sure that you can find the person you want to claim from and that he is able to pay you if you do prove that you're owed money and awarded compensation. In addition, different time limits apply to different types of cases, so check that you aren't too late to sue.

You may be able to take your own case to court if you're claiming for less than £5,000, but if you decide you need the help of a solicitor, it can prove expensive. Talk the case over with the Citizens Advice Bureau or Law Centre before you decide to go ahead. If you need the help of a solicitor, these organisations can give you details of suitable ones. Bear in mind that a mediation service may be available to resolve your particular dispute through a trade association or an Ombudsman's scheme. (See the section 'Using alternatives to the courts,' later in this chapter).

Making a small claim

If you're claiming less than £15,000, your case must be started in the County Court. If you're claiming less than £5,000 from a person or a company (£1,000 or less for personal injury), you can usually use the Small Claims Track of the County Court. It's a quick and informal way of settling a dispute perhaps with a builder over work not done and for which you want your money back. You don't have to use a solicitor, and the costs are kept to a minimum. However, even if you're using the Small Claims Track and the case is fairly straightforward, get advice from the Citizens Advice Bureau or Law Centre before you apply to the court. If the case is more complicated, even though the claim is less than £5,000, the judge may transfer it to another track.

You start your claim by filling in the claim form. Copies of the claim are sent to the defendant, who has a limited time in which to reply. If no reply comes, you can ask the court to go ahead and pass judgment in the defendant's absence. If the defendant does reply, he or she may accept your claim and make you an offer to pay in a lump sum or in instalments. You can accept and go back to the court for an enforcement order if the defendant doesn't stick to the agreement. If the defendant doesn't accept, a date is allocated for the hearing.

After the judge has heard all the evidence and that of any witnesses or experts, she decides whether you have a claim and how much you should be paid. If the defendant doesn't pay, you can then apply to the court for some type of enforcement order (see Chapter 15).

You have to pay the court fees, which are dependent on how much you're claiming and the expenses of any witnesses and experts. If the defendant is an individual who defends your claim for a fixed amount of money, he may be able to have the case transferred to his own local County Court, in which case you incur travel costs. However, if you win, the judge may order the defendant to pay all or part of your costs.

Claiming larger compensation

If you're claiming compensation for more than £5,000 or more than £1,000 in a personal injury case or the case isn't quite straightforward, you may have to use a different track of the County Court or claim in the High Court. The kinds of cases that are dealt with in the High Court are often high-profile claims against city finance firms for sex discrimination or harassment or serious personal injury through an accident. In these kinds of cases, the claimant isn't asking for a set amount of money, but has gone to court with an idea of how much she might settle for and is asking the judge not only to decide whether she has a valid legal claim but also to decide how much compensation should be paid.

If you're involved in a case of this sort, you must take good legal advice from solicitors and barristers who are experienced in the relevant areas of law.

Claiming for personal injury

If the injury is the result of a crime, take a look at the earlier section on criminal injuries compensation. If you know who caused your personal injury, you can make a claim through the civil courts. You will need the advice of a solicitor experienced at dealing with personal injury claims.

Strict time limits exist, and solicitors usually take on these kinds of cases on conditional fee agreements – where you pay the legal fees from any compensation you're awarded. If you lose, you don't have to pay the fees for your own solicitor, but you may have to pay the costs run up by the other side. You should take out insurance against that eventuality. These cases are sometimes called *no-win no-fee agreements,* but as you can see, that description isn't accurate, given that you may have the other side's costs to pay.

Claims assessors offer to get compensation in personal injury cases. Claims assessors usually offer to deal with your case on a no-win no-fee basis, but they expect you to pay them a percentage of any award they get for you. If you do decide to use a risk assessor, make sure that you find one who is experienced in your kind of case. If not a solicitor, he won't be able to take your claim through the courts, but will rely on reaching a settlement with the other side without taking legal action. Many claims for compensation are settled out of court before the case is ever heard, or at some point in the process, when it becomes apparent to the defendant that they're going to have to pay up.

Be wary of refusing a proposed settlement figure. You may be awarded less by the judge. Always discuss the implications of any offer with your solicitor.

Using a tribunal to get justice

Tribunals are less formal than courts and can resolve all sorts of issues. *Tribunals* are usually a panel of three people with experience relevant to the types of cases they're dealing with. The idea is that you bring your own case to tribunal and do without the services of a solicitor. Ideally, tribunals should be informal and much less intimidating than the formal courts. However, in practice, that scenario isn't always the case.

The percentage of cases won by people who have no representation is low. You have a better chance of winning your case if you have someone at the tribunal with you. Talk to your local Citizens Advice Bureau or Law Centre before you start tribunal proceedings.

As with any claim through any part of the court system, what you write on your initial claim form is important. You must adhere to strict time limits to make particular claims.

Using Alternatives to the Courts

Using the courts and the legal system to resolve a dispute should always be the last resort. If you can't come to an acceptable agreement with the other side in the dispute, look at other options such as the following before you take court action:

- ✔ **Ombudsmen:** Ombudsmen's schemes can help you resolve some disputes without the need to get involved in court action, and usually their services are free. Many ombudsmen's schemes exist, including the following:

- **Health Service Ombudsman** deals with complaints about GPs, dentists, opticians, nurses, and NHS Trusts.

- **Local Government Ombudsman** deals with complaints about local councils.

- **Pensions Ombudsman** deals with occupational and private pension schemes.

- **Financial Services Ombudsman** deals with complaints about banks, building societies, general insurance companies, and many other financial services.

- **Estate Agents Ombudsman** deals with complaints about estate agents.

- **Legal Services Ombudsman** deals with complaints against solicitors, barristers, and legal executives.

You must take all available steps to resolve your dispute with the organisation concerned before the Ombudsman's office will take it on. Some schemes offer mediation to help the two sides reach an agreement. In most cases, mediation precludes you from going to court. Check with the Citizens Advice Bureau whether a scheme covers your dispute and how to contact the relevant Ombudsman. Some schemes cover only England and Wales.

✔ **Mediation:** If no Ombudsman scheme can help with your particular issue, you may be able to use a private mediation scheme. If the person or company you have a dispute with is a member of a trade association, that association may offer mediation services to resolve disputes. (Chapter 6 has information on family mediation, and Citizens Advice Bureaux can advise you on any private services in your area.) Mediators help you and the other side in the dispute to reach an agreement that you can both accept and stick to without the need to go to court.

Mediation can be much less expensive than paying for a solicitor and court costs.

Claiming Help with Legal Costs

The *Legal Aid Fund* was set up to help people who otherwise wouldn't be able to afford the costs of taking a legal action or making a claim get access to justice. Only certain cases qualify for legal aid – for example, you can't get legal aid to help you if you're in debt or making a claim at an employment tribunal or claiming under £5,000 in the County Court. In some cases, you may qualify for help to pay for initial advice and assistance, but not for the case itself.

Strict guidelines also limit the amount of income and savings you can have and still qualify. In many cases where you're granted legal aid, the money must be reimbursed out of any settlement you get, or at a later date when you sell assets.

If you approach a solicitor about any legal matter, you should check out your eligibility for legal aid straight away.

If you don't qualify for financial help and can't afford to take a case, talk to the advice agencies about the help they can give you and think about mediation (see preceding section) as an alternative way to resolve a case without going to court. The organisations listed at the end of this chapter may be able to help.

Complaining about Professional Negligence

Just because you're dealing with the law, courts, police, and legal professions doesn't mean that those people are above the law or that they always follow the law or treat you fairly. If the government, local authorities, police, solicitors, or barristers break the law, they will be treated as anyone else. The government can be taken to court, for example, if it breaks the law, as can a local authority, the health service, or your next-door neighbour.

If you're unfairly treated by any of these people or organisations, you can complain and make a claim against those who've violated your rights. Sometimes you may be reluctant to press a complaint against the police or a lawyer because you're likely to feel intimidated or that you're bound to lose. However, you can go through accepted procedures because you aren't the first to complain, and the different organisations concerned recognise that unfair treatment does happen. You may find that you need the help of one member of the legal profession to make a claim against another. They won't all be happy to take you on as a client but persist. If you're in the right, you can find someone willing to help.

If you think you've been unfairly treated in any way by the police or legal professions, talk to your Citizens Advice Bureau or Law Centre about the right way to make a complaint.

Getting help and advice

Some organisations can help whatever the circumstances. The **Citizens Advice Bureau** is a good place to start. It may be able to help you resolve your problem, but if not, it can point you in the direction of someone who can. Look in your phone book for the details of the nearest bureau or find it online at www.advice guide.org.uk.

You may also have a **Law Centre** in your area. Look in the phone book or contact the **Law Centres Federation** at 0207-387-8570 or at www.lawcentres.org.uk for details. You can reach the **Scottish Association of Law Centres** at 0141-440-2503 or www.gov anlc.com/salc. **Law Centres Northern Ireland** on 02890-244-401 or www.law centreni.org.

In some areas of the UK, the mediation services are quite good. Ask your nearest Citizens Advice Bureau if a service in your area handles disputes. Try **Mediation UK** on (0117-904-6661 or www.mediationuk.org.uk.)

You can find more information on the courts at www.hmcourts-service.gov.uk, and the **BBC** has a Web site that can help you make sense of the whole legal system at www.bbc.co.uk/crime/law/jargon buster, which also has links to laws in Scotland and Northern Ireland.

The **Law Society** can give you lists of solicitors. Call 0870-606-6565 in England and Wales, 0845-113-0018 in Scotland, and 02890-231-614 in Northern Ireland. If you want to complain about a solicitor or a bill, talk to the Law Society on 0845-608-6565 or have a look at the Web site www.lawsociety.org.uk.

Other useful contacts include The **Association of Personal Injury Lawyers** (0115-958-0585 or www.apil.com); **Victim Support** (0845-303-0900 or www.victimsupport.org.uk); The **Independent Police Complaints Commission** (08453-002-002 or www.ipcc.gov.uk), The **Miscarriage of Justice Organisation** (0121-789-8443); and the **Prisoners' Advice Service** (0207-253-3323).

Chapter 2

Living as a Citizen

....

In This Chapter

▶ Understanding what it means to be a citizen of the UK

▶ Knowing the rights of citizenship

▶ Putting your rights into practice

▶ Making UK law work for you

....

A citizen is a member of a political community. The UK – the United Kingdom of Great Britain and Northern Ireland – is a political community. The word *citizen* originally referred to a member of a particular city, but has since come to mean a member of a state. UK or British citizens have British nationality. British citizens are people who have the right to live in the UK, have rights under UK law and the protection of the state, and who have the right to take part in the UK's political process.

Having British nationality is more or less the same as being a British citizen or having British citizenship, and the terms are used interchangeably, but legally you can have British nationality without the full rights of citizenship. If you're in prison, for example, you don't lose your British nationality, but you do lose your right to vote.

Citizenship is also about your responsibility to respect the laws and the rights of other people who are also citizens. Citizenship is now on the national curriculum, and pupils are expected to learn how to be good citizens. People applying for UK citizenship are expected to take an English language test and take part in a ceremony where they swear an oath of allegiance.

Under the Nationality, Immigration, and Asylum Act 2002, your British nationality can be taken away if you do something that is 'seriously prejudicial to the vital interests of the UK'. The law is extremely complicated, and you should take legal advice from a solicitor experienced in citizenship and nationality cases if you have come to the UK hoping to remain here.

Citizenship and You: It's Not a Birth Right Anymore

You can be born a British citizen, or you can be granted the right to British citizenship.

People born in the UK before the first of January 1983 were automatically entitled to British citizenship or nationality just because they were born here. No other qualification was needed. The laws have been tightened up since that time.

When a child is born, he usually takes the nationality of the father or of the place where he was born. If your father was a British citizen and you were born in another country, you can choose which country you become a citizen of or which nationality you have. In some cases, you can have dual nationality if both countries allow dual nationality. The UK does; the United States doesn't.

If a baby is born abroad and has a British mother and a French father, for example, the parents can apply for the baby to have UK nationality, and it's up to the Secretary of State to decide. If the parents weren't married at the time of the birth, a baby born in the UK can have British nationality if the mother is a British citizen or is settled in the UK, but it is no longer automatically a British citizen by virtue of being born in the UK. A baby whose parents aren't married and who is born outside the UK is entitled to British nationality only if her mother is a British citizen, but that may not be the case if the mother was born abroad.

As you can see, working out citizenship if a baby is born here with foreign parents, or abroad with a British parent, can be difficult. It's even more difficult for people wanting to come to the UK and obtain UK citizenship.

Coming to Live in the UK

Thousands of people come to the UK every year hoping to remain here. Some are allowed to come into the country for a short time and then expected to leave again. Some apply for the right to live and work here. Some apply to become UK citizens, and some are asylum seekers who may have no rights to citizenship but can apply to stay indefinitely on the grounds that it will be dangerous for them to return to their own countries. None of these people have the same rights as UK citizens until they're granted citizenship. Some may never be granted citizenship, but may be allowed to stay with some restrictions. Others are eventually sent home.

You can come into the UK and stay here, without any restrictions, if you're a UK citizen. People born in the UK before January 1983 are UK citizens. Anyone else is not automatically entitled to UK citizenship. Some people from the former British colonies were allowed to retain full rights to British citizenship, but working out who is entitled can be difficult.

There have been many stories of people coming to the UK and marrying UK citizens so that they themselves become UK citizens. However, you don't automatically acquire a new British nationality through marriage. You have to apply to become a UK citizen. The marriage itself is not enough. You may be allowed to remain in the country – granted residency, but that's not the same as having full citizenship rights.

A UK national marrying a foreign national doesn't lose her right to British nationality and may be entitled to dual nationality – of the UK and of the spouse's country – if both countries allow dual nationality.

Being domiciled in the UK

You're *domiciled* in the UK if it's where you have your permanent home or it's the home you plan to return to after a period abroad. A baby's domicile is where the parents have their domicile, or the father's domicile if two different countries are involved. When the child grows up, she can change domicile by moving abroad. A spouse who comes to live in the UK with a husband or wife, or a partner coming to the UK following a civil partnership, doesn't have to become domiciled, here but usually will because the couple is intending to live here together. Being domiciled in the UK is not the same as being a resident or having nationality or citizenship.

Residing in the UK

You can be resident in the UK, but have your permanent home in another country. You may be resident here while you're doing a job, but your domicile remains the country you intend to go back to. If you're resident in the UK, you may have restrictions on how long you can stay and you can only work here, while resident, if you have the correct work permits (see the section 'The right to work,' later in this chapter) or are free to work here because you're a citizen of a country that is a member of the European Union. Someone who is working here can apply to remain indefinitely after four years.

If you have permission to be in the UK for a particular length of time, you may be able to apply to stay longer, but if you stay without applying, you're committing a criminal offence.

Getting permission to come into the UK

The Immigration Laws set out the rules about who can and can't come into the UK, how long they can stay, and what they can do while they're here. The rules are complicated and strictly applied, and I can't cover them in this book because each individual's circumstances will be different.

If people come to the UK without the automatic right to be here and then stay here, they will need permission to come into the country. People may come in as visitors, students, spouses, refugees, and asylum seekers or even to work. Different rules apply to each type.

Visitors from some countries may be allowed to visit as and when they like, but they usually need to show that they intend to go home again when their visit is over. Other visitors need to get visas in their own countries before they come to the UK and will be refused entry unless they have those visas. The visa allows them to stay for a specified time, and at the end of that time, they must leave. The maximum time anyone is allowed to stay on any one visit is six months. Visitors who stay beyond the date of their visa may be prosecuted and deported.

Visitors on a visa who want to stay longer – to study, for example – usually have to leave, go home, and reapply to return as students. Students need to show that they're coming here to study full time. They are usually allowed to stay for a year and will have to apply for an extension if the course lasts longer. If they want to get married while they're in the UK, they have to convince immigration officials that they did originally come to the country as a student.

A spouse coming to the UK, to join a husband or wife who is entitled to stay in the UK, is allowed to come into the country for two years. The spouse has to show that the marriage is a genuine and permanent one and not just a way of being allowed to stay in the UK. If the couple is still together at the end of two years, the foreign spouse is granted the right to stay indefinitely. This right also applies to partners in a civil partnership.

Most people who come to the UK have to show that they can support themselves financially. The rules for refugees and asylum seekers are different. (See the upcoming section 'Seeking asylum.')

If you know anyone who isn't a British citizen and wants to come to the UK for any reason, advise them to check with the British Embassy in their own country about the rules they will need to comply with. If you know anyone already in the country who wants to stay longer than they have permission to stay or who wants to work or to apply for citizenship, make sure that they take advice either from a Citizens Advice Bureau or Law Centre – you can find details in the phone book – or an adviser who is registered with the Office of Immigration Services Commissioner and displays the OISC logo. (See the following section 'Seeking asylum'.)

Seeking asylum

Refugees and asylum seekers don't need to prove that they're entitled to come into the UK under the immigration rules. They can come into the country and then try to prove to the immigration authorities that they should be allowed to stay.

Refugees are people who are without a home because they've had to leave their own home because of conflict or natural disaster. Many of the world's estimated 30 million refugees are still inside their own country, but some have moved to other countries, such as the UK, to look for refuge.

The *1951 Geneva Convention* says that a refugee is 'A person who is outside his or her own country of nationality or habitual residence; has a well-founded fear of persecution because of his or her race, religion, nationality, membership in a particular social group or political opinion; and is unable or unwilling to avail himself or herself of the protection of that country, or to return there, for fear of persecution.'

When people have to leave their own country and come to the UK to *seek asylum,* they're allowed to come into the country. Most asylum seekers want to stay until it's safe to go home, but some may want to stay permanently. Once they're in the UK, they must apply for refugee status – which means that they have to convince the immigration authorities that they are a refugee as defined by the Geneva Convention.

If they're granted refugee status, they're allowed to stay indefinitely or for a set period of time. If the application is refused, they may be deported back to the place they came from. International law on refugees says that they shouldn't be sent back to a country where they're at risk of being persecuted and tortured, and the UK has a legal obligation to accept a certain number of asylum seekers.

Asylum seekers have the right to temporary accommodation, food, and a small amount of financial support from the state, as long as they can prove that they're destitute. A single asylum seeker, aged 25 or older, is entitled to £40.22 per week, which is less than a UK citizen who claims the basic state benefit Income Support (see Chapter 11). *The UK Immigration and Asylum Act 2002* says that asylum seekers who don't apply to stay in the UK 'as soon as reasonably practicable' after they arrive aren't eligible for any support, even if they're destitute.

Asylum seekers aren't allowed to work to support themselves and their families while their claim is being decided. Anyone arriving here under these circumstances should get advice straight away from a Citizens Advice Bureau or Law Centre or an adviser who is registered with the Office of Immigration Services Commissioner and displays the OISC logo. You can contact the OISC at 0845-000-0046 or www.oisc.org.uk.

Other useful organisations are **The Immigration Advisory Service** (0207-967-1200, www.iasuk.org); **The Refugee Legal Centre** (0207-780-3220, www.refugee-legal-centre.org.uk); **The Refugee Council** (England 0207-820-3085, www.refugeecouncil.org.uk; Wales 02920-489-800; and Scotland 0800-085-6087, www.scottishrefugeecouncil.org.uk); and **The Northern Ireland Council for Ethnic Minorities** (02890-238-645 www.nicem.org.uk).

In addition, **The Immigration Law Practitioners' Association** (0207-251-8383 www.ilpa.org.uk) should be able to give you details of solicitors specialising in immigration law.

Applying for Citizenship

If you're planning to apply for citizenship, or *naturalisation* as it's also called, take advice. Unless you can apply for citizenship on the basis of ancestry, you will probably have to apply on the basis of having been in the UK for five years, or for three years as the spouse or registered civil partner (see Chapter 6) of a UK citizen.

If you aren't married to a British citizen, to apply for citizenship you must meet the following requirements:

✔ Be aged 18 or older and of sound mind.

✔ Be of good character.

✔ Be able to speak English, Welsh, or Scottish Gaelic (This requirement does have exemptions, such as if you're elderly or have a mental health problem.)

✔ Intend to live in the UK or abroad working for a UK Government organisation, or be employed by an international organisation of which the UK is a member, or be employed by a company or association established in the United Kingdom.

✔ Have lived in the UK for at least five years before the date your application reaches the Home Office.

✔ Have not been outside the UK for more than 450 days in total (about 15 months) during that time.

✔ Have not been outside the UK for more than 90 days in the last 12 months of that 5 years.

✔ Have held permanent residence or indefinite leave to remain in the UK during the last 12 months of the five-year period.

✔ Have not been living in the UK in breach of the UK immigration rules at any time during the five years.

If you apply for citizenship after three years in the UK, as a spouse of a UK Citizen (or the partner of a UK citizen if you've registered a civil partnership), the requirements are very similar to the preceding ones (except, of course, that you have lived in the UK for only three years before your application date). During that time, you must not have been outside the UK for more than 270 days.

In addition to the preceding requirements, you also have to pass the Life in the UK test before you can apply for citizenship. The test is a series of 24 questions based on Chapters 2, 3, and 4 of *Life in the United Kingdom: A Journey to Citizenship,* which you can buy from bookshops. The book covers UK history, Government and laws, religious and ethnic diversity, the role of women, language courses, information on the test, and where you can get help and information.

If your language skills aren't up to the required standard, you may have to take language and citizenship classes. Under the Nationality Immigration Act 2002, anyone applying for UK citizenship has to demonstrate that he has a knowledge of English, Welsh, or Scottish Gaelic and of life in the UK through the test.

The UK has 90 test centres, and you will need to take documents that have a photograph to verify your identity. You also pay a £34 fee to take the 45-minute test. If you want more information, call the Life in the UK Test Helpline on 0800-015-4245 or go to the Home Office Web site at www.ind.homeoffice.gov.uk.

If you pass the test, you receive a pass notification letter, which you must attach to your citizenship application form and send both to the Home Office. If you fail the test, you can sit it again.

About 90,000 people successfully apply each year to become British citizens, and they each have to take part in a Citizenship Ceremony where they swear an oath of allegiance to the Queen and promise to respect the UK's rights and freedoms. Ceremonies are held in towns and cities around the UK.

Taking Part in the UK's Democratic Process

Being a British citizen gives you the right to vote in UK general and local government elections and by-elections after you reach the age of 18. Others are also allowed to vote in these elections:

- ✔ Citizens of Ireland who live in the UK

- ✔ British nationals who are overseas (but not allowed to vote in local government elections)

- ✔ British Overseas Territory citizens

- ✔ Commonwealth citizens

- ✔ European Union citizens living in the UK (allowed to vote in local government elections only)

UK elections aren't the only ones in the democratic process. As part of the European Union, UK citizens have the right to vote in elections for the European Parliament.

If you happen to be a UK citizen living in another EU country, you can vote in European elections either in the UK or in the country you're living in, but not both.

However, if you're a British citizen or fall into one of the other preceding categories, you may not be allowed to exercise your right to vote in certain circumstances – for example, you're a convicted prisoner or have a severe mental health problem and don't understand the voting procedure. You also have to be on the electoral register on the day the election is held, or you aren't able to vote. (See the next section for information on getting on the electoral register.)

Although the right to vote is a democratic right, it isn't compulsory.

Getting onto the electoral register

Every year, the local authority updates and amends its *electoral register* – the list of people who live within its political boundaries and who are eligible to vote. You're usually sent a form so that you can provide details of all the people in your household who are eligible to vote, including anyone who turns 18 in the 12 months after the register is published. If you don't fill in the form with the information asked for or give false information, you can be prosecuted and fined.

The new register is published on the first of December each year, and copies appear in the local council offices, libraries, and main post offices for the public to inspect. You can have your name added to the register at any time throughout the year – because you move to a new house, for example.

The electoral register comes in a full version and a short version. The full version gives all the details of everyone entitled to vote in each constituency, and that's the one available for you to look at, as well as different political parties and some government agencies. Credit Reference Agencies (see Chapter 15) can also access it. All sorts of organisations, including some commercial companies, can purchase the short version, and you have the right not to have your name included.

If you live abroad and want to carry on voting, you can apply to be registered each year in the constituency where you last had the right to vote. If you're homeless, you can register to vote using the address of a place you spend a lot of your time, such as a hostel or drop-in centre. People who are in psychiatric hospitals can register by giving their usual address outside the hospital.

People who have homes in more than one constituency may be able to register in both constituencies, but can only vote in one. If your second home is a holiday home and you don't spend much time in it, you may be refused the right to register in that constituency. If you're a student, you can register at home and in the place where you're at college or university.

Voting

When an election is called, you're sent a voting or polling card, which details where you should go to vote and the polling station's hours. If you don't want to go to the polling station, or can't go, you may be able to vote by post or vote by *proxy* (appoint someone else to vote for you).

If you want to apply for a postal vote, you can get a form from the electoral registration office at your local council or from www.postalvotes.co.uk. You must get your application in at least six working days prior to Election Day. Your voting or ballot paper will be sent to you, and you have to sign a form in the presence of a witness to confirm that you're the person registered to vote by post.

If you want to appoint someone else to vote on your behalf, that person must be someone who is eligible to vote in their own right. The application process

is similar to that for postal votes, but you have to convince the electoral registration officer that you can't be expected to vote in person on polling day.
Your application may be turned down.

People with disabilities can apply for postal and proxy votes, but if you have
a visual impairment and you want to vote in person, the polling station has to
provide a large print version of the ballot paper for you. If you have a physical disability or can't read, you may be allowed to take someone with you to
help you, but that person must be eligible to vote themselves. If you don't
have anyone to go with you, you can ask the presiding officer of the polling
station for help. For more information, go to `www.direct.gov.uk` or contact your local authority.

The Government is trying out online voting at some elections, and it may be
an option for all voters in the future.

Protecting Your Human Rights

UK citizens have all the rights and protection of the UK law.

You have some basic rights simply because you are a human being living in
the UK. These rights, which affect matters of life and death and your everyday life, have been incorporated into UK law through the Human Rights
Act 1998:

- ✔ The right to life

- ✔ The right not to be tortured or treated in an inhumane or degrading way

- ✔ The right not to be held a slave or forced to work

- ✔ The right to liberty and security

- ✔ The right to a fair trial (see Chapter 1)

- ✔ The right not to be punished without going through the legal process

- ✔ The right to respect for private and family life

- ✔ Freedom of thought, conscience, and religion

- ✔ Freedom of expression (see the upcoming section 'Freedom of speech')

- ✔ Freedom of peaceful assembly and association (see the upcoming section 'The right to demonstrate')

- ✔ The right to marry and to build a family (see Chapter 6)

✔ The right not to be discriminated against

✔ The right to protect your property

✔ The right to education (see the upcoming section 'The Right to an Education')

✔ The right to free elections (see the previous section 'Taking part in the UK's Democratic Process')

✔ The right not to be condemned to death or executed

Human rights influence how the police deal with suspects, how the courts conduct trials, and how prisoners are treated.

The Human Rights Act 1998 came into force in October 2000. Basically, this Act is the UK version of the European Convention on Human Rights, which the UK originally signed up to in 1950. However, until the Act was incorporated into UK law, you had to physically take any legal action using the protection of the Act to The European Court of Human Rights in Strasbourg, which was a long and expensive process. Now you can take a case under the Act in the UK Courts and tribunals.

The Act covers all public bodies, such as the police, courts, or local councils. If these entities violate your human rights under the Act, you can take a case against them.

The Human Rights Act gives absolute, limited, and qualified rights. You have an absolute right to life and not to be tortured or treated and punished in an inhumane and degrading way. You have the right to a fair trail, not to be detained unlawfully and to marry – but these rights are limited by the requirements set out in the Act. You have the *qualified right* to freedom of expression. Qualified rights have to strike a balance between your rights and everyone else's rights. Other qualified rights include the right to a private and family life, the right to freedom of religion, the right to freedom of assembly, and the right to freedom from discrimination (see Chapter 9).

Discrimination is most likely to happen at work. However, keep in mind that some types of discrimination that are unlawful at work are not unlawful in other situations. The law is complicated. You should get advice if you think you're being discriminated against.

If you think your human rights have been breached through discrimination or in some other way, talk to your nearest Citizens Advice Bureau or Law Centre. (You can find their details in the phone book.) Try to resolve the problem without going to court. If that's not possible, you can take legal action under the Human Rights Act in a court or tribunal. (See Chapter 1 for information on how the legal system works.)

The right to demonstrate

The Human Rights Act gives you the right to peaceful assembly and association. This right isn't an absolute right and can be restricted, and it only applies to lawful demonstrations. All the relevant old law that existed before the Human Rights Act came into force in 2000 is being reinterpreted to allow for these rights. The Public Order Act 1986, for example, allows the police to ban a demonstration if it's concerned that it can't take any other step to prevent a serious public disorder. That decision may be challenged under the Human Rights Act.

However, the Human Rights Act doesn't apply to unlawful demonstrations, and these are ones that break the law – say, by obstructing the highway. As a demonstrator, you may be committing an offence if you obstruct or assault a police officer in the execution of his duty, cause an affray by threatening violence against someone, use violence, riot along with at least 11 other people, or you use insulting words or behaviour.

Freedom of speech

There was no right to freedom of speech in the UK until the Human Rights Act was implemented. Parliament has always been free to restrict freedom of expression, and any rights have come through common law (see Chapter 1).

The Human Rights Act now incorporates freedom of expression into UK laws, but it's not an absolute right. Your rights to say whatever you want are balanced against the rights of other people's rights to not be attacked, abused, harassed, or discriminated against or have their reputation unfairly damaged. The courts work out where that balance lies. Ultimately, the rights under the Human Rights Act may be little different from the rights already held under common law.

The right to have your personal data protected

The Data Protection Act protects your *personal data,* such as your medical records (see Chapter 5), your credit reference files (see Chapter 15), or your employment file (see Chapter 9).

Data held about you has to be accurate, up to date, and secure. It also shouldn't be kept any longer than necessary. Only relevant people should be given access to it without your consent – in other words, for example, your boss needs to ensure that your work records aren't in an unlocked filing cabinet where your colleagues can get their hands on them and your council tax department shouldn't pass on your name and address to a company selling double glazing.

Of course, some exceptions exist. If the Police National Computer contains an entry about you, it can be passed on to a prospective employer who is hiring you to work with children or vulnerable adults and who is checking through the Criminal Records Bureau (see Chapter 1).

You have the right to see information held about you by any organisation, although you may be charged for a copy. You should put your request in writing to the person you think holds the information. For more information, go to the Web site of the Information Commissioner at www.information commissioner.gov.uk.

The right to have access to information

The Freedom of Information Act is very new, and current cases are clarifying its meaning. Basically, this Act gives you the right to ask for information from public bodies. You have the right to be told if that body has the information you want and to have access to it. You don't have to say why you want it, and you're not restricted on what you can do with it once you have it.

For example, you may want information from your child's school about playing fields that are being sold. You should put your request in writing or e-mail. If there are good reasons for keeping the information confidential, you may be refused. You may be refused information if it would reveal someone else's personal details. If you are refused, you can ask for an internal review. If you're still refused, you can ask the Information Commissioner to review the decision. For more information on the Act, go to the Information Commissioner's Web site at www.informationcommissioner.gov.uk.

The Act doesn't cover private bodies, such as individuals and private businesses.

The right to work

British citizens, Commonwealth citizens who have the right to live in the UK, European Economic Area (EEA) nationals, and all their family members can work here without restrictions on the length of time or the work they do.

People who come into the UK under the Highly Skilled Migrant Programme or under the *Working Holidaymaker Scheme,* which allows Commonwealth citizens aged 17 to 30 to stay in the UK for two years, can work without work permits. Some students from outside the EEA over the age of 16 can work here, too, for up to 20 hours a week during term time and full-time during holidays.

If you want to work in the UK and don't fall into one of those categories, you usually need a work permit. If you apply for a job, the employer will check that you have permission to work and do that kind of work before offering you the job. It's a criminal offence to employ anyone 16 or over who doesn't have that permission.

An employer may be able to get you a work permit from Work Permits (UK), which is part of the Home Office. Work Permits has to be convinced that no suitable and available person settled in the UK or EEA can take the job. If you're thinking about applying for a job and know that you may need a work permit, you can get all the information and application forms you need from the Work Permits (UK) Enquiry Line on 08705-210-224 or at the Home Office Web site at www.homeoffice.gov.uk.

The right to a home

Local authorities must provide homeless people with somewhere to live if they're eligible for help, are in priority need, and haven't intentionally made themselves homeless. In theory, that arrangement sounds as if everyone should have a home, but in practice, the council may not have the capacity to provide homes for any but those in the greatest need – usually families with children. A single person is not likely to qualify for help unless pregnant or vulnerable, perhaps because of disability or age.

Under the Housing Act of 1996, local councils have to provide people who qualify with accommodation for a minimum of two years. When councils allocate council-owned property, it must give homeless people higher priority than those who already have somewhere to live.

People can be classified as homeless even though they have a roof over their heads – if they are living somewhere but there's no room for the family to live with them, or when they can't go on living there because of overcrowding or domestic violence, for example.

If you're homeless or living temporarily with friends or relatives but can't go on living there and you think you may qualify for help from your local authority, talk to the nearest Citizens Advice Bureau. The law is complicated, and the CAB will know how the local authority system works.

If you're on a low income or welfare benefits, you may be entitled to Housing Benefit and Council Tax Benefit to allow you to pay rent and council tax for a rented home (see Chapter 11).

If you're an asylum seeker, you're entitled to temporary accommodation while your application to stay in the UK is processed. You must apply as soon as you arrive in the UK for help. (See the section 'Seeking Asylum,' earlier in this chapter.)

The right to medical treatment

If you usually live in the UK – even if you aren't a UK citizen – you have the right to register with a doctor. The GP of your choice can refuse to add you to his list. The list may already be full. You can get a list of GPs from NHS Direct (0845-4647 or at www.nhsdirect.nhs.uk). If you don't already have a medical card – which babies are given at birth if they're born in the UK – you will be sent one. After you've registered, you're entitled to any treatments that you need that are available on the National Health Service (NHS).

You have the right not to be examined or given any treatment or an operation without your consent unless your life is in danger and you can't consent, or you have a notifiable disease. For more information about how the NHS works, see Chapter 5.

The right to an education

Any child living in the UK is entitled to free education from the state. If you're a parent, you must make sure that your children are educated between the ages of 5 and 16. You may choose to educate your children at home or to send them to a school that isn't a free state school, but you have to make sure that they're educated. If they're educated in a school you must make sure that they attend regularly and abide by the school rules. For more information on the education system, see Chapter 5.

Out and About

British citizens can come into and go out of the UK as they please, unless, for example, they've been convicted of a crime and are on bail, in which case they can't leave the country. Children shouldn't be taken out of the UK without the consent of both parents. How long you can remain outside the UK depends on the country you're visiting. Nothing in UK law says that you must come back within a particular period of time.

Getting a passport

If you're entitled to British citizenship, you can have a British passport. If you're living in the UK but are not a British citizen, you don't have the right to a British passport.

Your passport allows you to travel to other countries and to come back into the UK. It allows you to identify yourself as a British citizen. When you present your passport to immigration officials in other countries, they know what your rights are. You may need more than a passport to enter a foreign country; you may need visas or certificates to prove that you've had particular vaccinations as well.

All children born after the 5 October 1998, need a passport. If your child was born before that date and you added that child's details to your passport, they can go on travelling with you until they're 16. However, if the passport expires in the meantime or has to be amended – perhaps because you've changed your name – your children will have to apply for their own passports.

The guidelines that come with the application form set out rules about the type of photograph you need on your passport and the documents you need to present when you apply in order to prove your identity. You can get an application form from main post offices. You can get more information from the UK Passport Service (0870-521-0410 or www.ukpa.gov.uk).

In certain circumstances, organisations in the UK need proof of your identity. A bank may ask for ID when you're opening an account, and you can use a passport for that purpose. Many internal flight operators ask for photo ID, too, and if you don't have a UK driving licence with a photograph, you should carry your passport.

Going abroad

Most countries have similar restrictions to the UK and let you stay only for a limited time, depending on your reason for being there. You may also need visas and other documentation, such as medical or vaccination certificates, to get into many other countries. If you're intending to work in another country, you may need its equivalent of a work permit. You may also need translations of your passport and other documents, such as your birth certificate, in the language of the country you're going to.

Before you go, check with the Foreign Office to see what your rights are and what preparations you need to make. (For travel information, call 0845-850-2829; for information on visas, call 0207-008-8438; or visit the Web site at www.fco.gov.uk.) You need a valid passport to travel out of the UK, but you should check that this passport is still valid by the time you return. Some countries, such as South Africa, won't let you in unless your passport will still be valid for a particular period of time after you leave. Check before you go.

You won't lose your British citizenship, no matter how long you stay away, unless you decide to choose the nationality of another country that doesn't allow dual nationality. You can live in France, for example, and apply for French nationality as well as British nationality, but if you want to become a United States citizen, you will have to give up your British citizenship.

Emigrating

Emigrating is leaving the UK for good and going to live as a citizen of another country. Just as the UK has strict immigration laws about who can and can't live in the UK and who can apply for UK citizenship, so, too, do other countries. Some, such as New Zealand, accept only people under a certain age. Others allow people to live and work there only if they bring skills that are in short supply or if they have family members already living there.

Getting permission to emigrate to another country can take years during which you need to go through all sorts of vetting procedures and applications forms. The Foreign Office can advise you, and you can also pay private companies to do all the necessary paperwork for you.

If you do intend to make your home outside the UK but you would like to be sure that any children born abroad are entitled to UK citizenship, should they decide to come back, you should check the situation before you go.

The laws in the country you want to live in are different from those of the UK, so you should get as much information as possible before you apply so that you're sure you're making the right move.

If you want to take your children to live abroad but you are no longer with their other parent, you should have the permission of that parent. If they refuses, you or the other parent can apply to the court for a decision about where the children live (see Chapter 7).

Chapter 3

Keeping a Roof Over Your Head

• •

• •

*A*ccording to the last census, more than two-thirds of the almost 24.5 million households in the UK have been bought by the people living in them. More people in the UK own homes than the people of most other European Union countries. That means that less than a third of the population live in rented accommodation – rented from private landlords or from the public sector (the local authorities or housing associations).

This chapter looks at the ins and out of buying and selling property. I cover how owner-occupied property can be divided if the owners split up, and I look at the rights and responsibilities of people renting their homes.

Renting

If you're renting a property or part of a property, you're a *tenant*. Whoever owns the property – the local authority or council, a housing association, or a private owner – is the *landlord*. The *tenancy agreement* – the contract under which a landlord gives a tenant exclusive use of a property or part of a property to live in – sets out the terms and conditions under which you agree to rent the property. This agreement covers information such as how long you've agreed to rent the property:

▸ A *fixed-term tenancy* has a set term, such as six months, or two years.

▸ A *periodic tenancy* says that the agreement is renewable every year or two years. It does not have a set term, and you can move out at any time, as long as you give the period of notice set out in the agreement.

When you sign a tenancy agreement, you also have the protection of the law. Local authority tenants are usually *secure tenants,* which gives them protection against eviction. (See the section 'Avoiding eviction,' later in this chapter.) Agreements between tenants and housing associations or private landlords, signed after 15 January 1989, fall under the Housing Act 1988. If the landlord and tenant have a dispute, and the subject of the dispute is covered under the provisions of the act, a court will be able to decide who is right as far as the law is concerned. The Housing Act 1988 covers, for example, the circumstances under which tenants can be evicted. (See the section 'Avoiding eviction,' later in this chapter.)

Business premises are different and aren't covered by the same laws.

You can rent a bedsit with its own kitchen and bathroom facilities, or shared facilities, in a private house, or you can rent a whole house to yourself; in both cases, you are a tenant. However, if you're sharing a whole house with a group of people and you have no right to exclusive use of any part of it, or if the landlord lives on the premises, you may have a *licence* rather than a tenancy, and your rights will be different.

No matter who you're renting property from, you need to check your rights before you sign. Private tenants and landlords who aren't used to operating in the private sector are well-advised to let and rent property through reputable property letting agents.

Local authority property

Local authorities or *councils* have long been the main providers of *social housing.* They have a duty to provide decent homes for rent to people who can't afford to rent from private owners at a commercial rent. Local authorities have waiting lists for their properties. People who meet their criteria go on the list and where they are slotted into the list depends on how urgently they need a home.

In recent years, many councils have sold off large proportions of their social housing stock to housing associations that own and manage that stock. The local authorities fulfil their obligation to provide decent rented housing through their links with the housing associations and by overseeing the planning and building of new social housing. In Northern Ireland, the social housing stock is owned and managed by the Housing Executive, which is a government department.

In some areas of the country, people are forced into the private rented sector because of a shortage of social housing. Some – mainly single people who are not usually a priority for social housing – are homeless and living with friends and family, in overcrowded conditions or in temporary accommodation, such as rooms in bed-and-breakfast hotels or hostels. A small number – often the most vulnerable – don't have those options open to them for various reasons, such as mental health problems or relationship breakdown, and end up living on the streets.

You can be on some local authority waiting lists for years before being given the keys to your new home. Most councils don't have enough homes to offer one immediately to everyone who asks. Your council may accept you on its list, but most lists don't operate on a simple first-come, first-served basis. Most authorities work on a points system, and when people apply, they're assessed and give a certain number of points. Those people in greatest need are usually slotted onto the list ahead of people who have been waiting but whose need is less urgent. Factors taken into consideration include

- ✔ The applicant's age and state of health
- ✔ How many people are sharing the current accommodation
- ✔ Whether family members are living apart because of their housing situation
- ✔ What facilities, such as a shared cooker or lack of a bathroom, are in their current accommodation
- ✔ Sleeping arrangements, such as boys and girls having to share
- ✔ How long they have been in the area and on the waiting list

A family with children will have more points than a single person; someone with a disability will have more points than someone who doesn't have a disability; and someone who already has a home will have fewer points than someone who is living with friends or relatives in overcrowded conditions. Each local authority may award different numbers of points for each factor. If you're applying to go on a waiting list, ask for details of how the council in question makes its selection of tenants.

If you're offered a council property, you pay a reasonable rent as assessed by the council. If the rent is to go up, you must be given four weeks' notice of the increases. If you're on a low income, you may qualify for help to pay your rent from *housing benefit* and to pay your council tax through *council tax benefit.* Departments at the local authority offices deal with both of these benefits (see Chapter 11).

Local authority tenants are usually *secure tenants,* which means that you can't be evicted unless a court is convinced that the council has all the right grounds on which to evict you and that it's reasonable to evict you. (See the section 'Avoiding eviction,' later in this chapter.) Some councils offer you a tenancy on an introductory basis. The first year is a trial period, and if the council decides you aren't a suitable tenant, it can evict you without proving to the court that it has grounds to do so. If you do turn out to be suitable, at the end of the year, your tenancy automatically becomes a secure tenancy.

Not all local authority tenants are secure tenants. If you're given short-term temporary accommodation, are a student or a council employee, or the property is part of a commercial or agricultural property, you aren't usually a secure tenant. Check your tenancy agreement terms carefully and, if necessary, get legal advice from your nearest CAB. (You can find contact information in the phone book or at www.adviceguide.org.uk.)

If you accept a council tenancy, the council is your landlord, and you have to accept its terms and conditions. These terms vary between councils, so read them carefully. Some councils expect you to sign a tenancy agreement, and others simply give you a rent book with the main terms and conditions in it. You have to be given a rent book if you pay your rent weekly. If you pay other than weekly – for example, every month or every fortnight – the law doesn't say that you have the right to have included information about your responsibilities for the upkeep of the property and the repairs and improvements the landlord will carry out. (See the section 'Getting repairs done,' later in this chapter.)

If you want to make improvements to your home at your own expense, you must get the council's permission, and the council can't up your rent because of those improvements. You can usually take in a lodger to live with your family and share meals with you, but if you *sublet* part of the property to someone – for example, you let two rooms to them, and they don't live as part of your family – you need the council's permission.

If you move from your home and let all of the property to someone else, your tenant doesn't have a secure tenancy. In addition, you are no longer a secure tenant, and the council can to evict both you and your tenant.

Housing association property

Housing associations or *registered social landlords* are now the biggest providers of social housing in many parts of the UK. These companies or charities build new homes or take over existing property or stock from local authorities. Most housing associations are registered with the Housing Corporation or Housing for Wales, which are government agencies, from which they get grants to build or repair properties and then let them out. The law about the types of tenancies tenants will have, and how the rent is controlled, depends on the type of housing association and the date of the tenancy. The Housing Corporation also regulates the work and operation of housing associations.

If you apply to your local authority for housing, you may be referred to various local housing associations. Many local authorities have transferred their entire housing stock, or a big part of it, to housing associations. Local CABs also have lists of housing associations with property to let.

If you're offered a home by a housing association, you're likely to become an *assured tenant.* If the lease is for a short time, you will probably be an *assured shorthold tenant* under the terms of the Housing Act 1988. An assured tenancy gives you protection against eviction but no control over rents. You can stay put, even if the landlord wants you out, until a court is convinced that the landlord has grounds to have you evicted and grants an eviction order. An assured shorthold tenancy gives some control over the rent charged, but no protection against eviction. These are the same kinds of tenancies you are offered by private landlords. (See the section 'Private property,' later in this chapter.) If you were a local authority tenant and your home was transferred to a housing association, your tenancy is an *assured tenancy.*

Under an assured tenancy, there is no rent control. You have to pay the rent set by the housing association and any increases it decides on, but the idea is that the homes should be affordable for people on low incomes or unemployed. You have a *tenant's guarantee,* which sets out how the association's properties are managed and maintained and your rights to take in lodgers, for example.

If you were living as a tenant in a housing association property before 15 January 1989, the Rent Act provides some control over rent increases. This Act also applies to tenants of private landlords (see the upcoming section 'Private property'), and you have the same protection from eviction as council tenants. (For more information, see the section 'Avoiding eviction,' later in this chapter.)

Housing associations that aren't registered with the Housing Corporation or Housing For Wales don't get grants and are independent. Tenants have assured tenancies, but they don't have a tenant's guarantee. An independent association may operate *shared ownership schemes* where you can buy a proportion of your home and rent the rest. As you can afford to buy more of the property, you do so and pay less in rent. Registered housing associations aren't allowed to operate these schemes.

Be sure you know what type of association you're renting from. Talk to the nearest CAB about your tenancy agreement before signing.

Private property

The law gets rather complicated when it comes to renting a property from a private landlord. Private agreements between landlord and tenant are usually assured or assured shorthold tenancies.

Tenancy agreements signed before 15 January 1989, fall under the Rent Act 1977. Agreements signed after 15 January 1989, come under the Housing Act 1988. Tenancy agreements signed after 28 February 1997, also come under the Housing Act 1988, but with new rules about assured shorthold tenancies.

Here's what the preceding Acts mean:

- ✔ If your tenancy was signed before 15 January 1989, the Rent Act 1977 protects against eviction and restricts what the landlord can charge.

- ✔ If your tenancy was signed after 15 January 1989, the Housing Act 1988 gives the landlord the choice of offering you an assured tenancy or an assured shorthold tenancy. The tenant can ask the independent Rent Assessment Committee to set a reasonable rent for the property. The landlord can get possession of the property at the end of the agreed period of time by giving you at least two month's notice; if you refuse to move, a court will agree that you should be evicted without any grounds or reasons. Most tenancy agreements after 15 January 1989, were ordinary assured tenancies unless the tenant was given notice that it was to be an assured shorthold tenancy.

- ✔ If your tenancy was signed on or after 28 February 1997, it's probably an assured shorthold unless the agreement specifically says that it's an assured tenancy. That's the complete reversal of the situation up until 28 February 1997.

Assured shorthold tenancies are very popular with most landlords because getting their properties back at the end of an agreed letting period is a lot easier than it is if the tenancy is assured.

An assured shorthold isn't an assured shorthold simply because the landlord says it is. It has to meet the conditions set out in the Housing Act 1988.

If you're a tenant and facing eviction, but you don't want to leave, talk to your nearest CAB or a Law Centre if one is in your area. Law Centres usually have people who specialise in housing law. Look in the phone book or contact The Law Centres Federation (0207-387-8570 or at www.lawcentres.org.uk); The Scottish Association of Law Centres (0141-440-2503 or www.govanlc.com/salc); or Law Centres Northern Ireland (02890-244-401 or www.law centreni.org).

In some situations, a tenancy won't be an assured or assured shorthold one, and you may not have the protection of the Housing Act. If the tenancy was signed before 15 January 1989, the Rent Act applies, and you may have a *protected* or *statutory* tenancy. These old tenancies give tenants different protection under the Rent Act of 1977. The tenancy agreements won't be assured or assured shorthold if:

- ✔ The annual rents are very high or very low.
- ✔ The property is let to students or for holidays.
- ✔ The landlord lives on the premises.

The law is complicated and becomes more so when it comes to renting a room in someone else's home or sharing with a group of people. Your position depends on whether you have your own room, your own facilities (such as kitchen and bathroom), or shared facilities and whether the landlord lives on the premises.

If you're renting a property from a private landlord or privately letting out property, go through a reputable letting agent who knows the law, can guide you through the process, vet prospective tenants, do all the paper work, collect the rent, and help sort out any disputes.

Getting repairs done

Disputes between landlords and tenants often arise over who is to carry out repairs. The tenancy agreement normally spells out who is responsible for the repairs, and the law is the same whether the landlord is a private owner, a housing association, or a local authority.

Part of the problem is that there isn't a clear definition of what is a repair. Repairs are not the same as home improvements, such as extensions or adding double glazing, even though they improve your living conditions. A total renovation doesn't come within the terms of a tenancy agreement. The replacement of something that is broken, such as a light switch, or something that has worn out, such as the wiring, is normally considered a repair. However, if life is being made difficult by condensation in winter because of lack of ventilation, you may find that the landlord doesn't accept that it's his problem to sort it out.

The Landlord and Tenant Act 1985 says that landlords have a duty to repair and maintain the property if it's let for seven years or less. It also covers situations where the property has been let to the same tenant for longer than seven years if it was a tenancy that was renewed periodically – say, every two years. If the tenancy agreement tries to put the responsibility for repairs onto the tenant in these cases, that clause won't be valid.

The landlord has to repair and maintain only the structure of the building, the plumbing, and the electrics. That's not likely to mean that the landlord has to redecorate or install appliances that weren't there when the property was first let out. For example, if no washing machine was there when you moved in, you can't make the landlord supply one later. If the tenancy was signed on or after 15 January 1989, the landlord has to keep up the communal parts of the building too, if he owns the whole building.

You won't get your repairs done by the landlord if you refuse to let him into the property. Landlords can come into tenants' property if they need to carry out essential repairs, but they have to give you at least 24-hours notice in writing and visit at a reasonable time of day. If the repairs aren't essential, you can refuse to have them done unless you've signed a tenancy agreement that says you'll allow access for repairs.

If you're an assured shorthold tenant, the landlord can easily get you evicted, so you may have little choice but to agree to the repairs or move.

If the tenancy agreement is for longer than seven years or the repairs in question aren't covered by the Landlord and Tenant Act, most landlords place the responsibility on the tenant. Read any tenancy agreement carefully so that you know where you stand before you sign.

If you do get involved in a dispute that you can't resolve, take legal advice before starting any court action. The CAB or Law Centre can help. You may be able to do repairs yourself and claim the money back from the landlord; enlist the help of the local authority that has powers to force landlords to carry out repairs in some circumstances; or get a court order.

If the landlord knows that repairs are needed and doesn't do them and someone is injured, the injured person may be able to claim compensation (see Chapter 1). Contact your CAB or Law Centre for advice.

Your responsibilities

The tenancy agreement usually spells out your responsibilities. You're usually expected to keep the property in a reasonably good decorative state. The agreement may even set out how often the inside has to be painted. A clause is likely to allow the landlord access to carry out essential repairs. You should be given reasonable notice if the landlord is intending to come into the property. Visiting more than is necessary or reasonable may amount to harassment.

When you take the tenancy of a private property, you usually make a deposit, which is money held by the landlord as a guarantee that you'll leave the place in a reasonable condition when you move. If you don't, the landlord deducts money from the deposit to pay for cleaning or redecorating, and you're given back what's left. If the property is furnished, you have to check and sign an inventory of all the items in the property when you move in. The inventory is rechecked when you're giving up the tenancy, and your deposit is docked for any missing items.

Replace broken or missing items as you go along so that you don't lose your deposit or need a lot of money to buy replacements all at once.

Deposits can be a big bone of contention between landlords and tenants, with landlords holding back more than tenants expect from the deposit. Tenants often complain that landlords claim that carpets need cleaning when they don't. The Association of Residential Letting Agents (ARLA) runs a scheme that helps settle deposit disputes between landlords and tenants using agents registered with the association, and the government is considering the introduction of a new nationwide scheme. You can find more information on that and various aspects of letting and renting property on the ARLA Web site at www.arla.co.uk.

Avoiding eviction

The last resort for any landlord who has a problem tenant is to evict that tenant. Whoever the landlord and whatever the circumstances, a tenant can be evicted only with a court order.

Private landlords who have let their properties on assured shorthold tenancies need only apply to the court for an order, and they will get it. With most other types of tenancies, the court will want proof that there are grounds on which to evict the tenant under the relevant law and that it's reasonable to evict that tenant.

If you're a secure tenant renting a home from your local authority, the grounds the council may use to try to persuade the court that you should be evicted include the following:

- ✔ Breaking your tenancy agreement in some way, such as having a bad record for not paying the rent
- ✔ Causing a serious nuisance to your neighbours and other people in the area – you're the 'neighbour from hell'!
- ✔ Damaging the property or furniture provided by the council
- ✔ Lying in order to get the tenancy of the property

The court needs to be convinced that it's reasonable to evict you before it will grant the local authority an eviction order. You're not likely to be evicted if you got into arrears with your rent once and you've paid the money you owe, or if you've caused your neighbours to call the council because of one noisy row with your partner. In some cases, the court will grant an eviction order against you but expect the council to provide you with alternative accommodation. This is likely where:

- ✔ You're living in overcrowded conditions, or the property you have is bigger than you need.

- ✔ The property has to be demolished or renovated.

- ✔ The property is suitable for a disabled person or someone with special needs, no one with a disability or special needs is living with you, and the council needs it for a person with a disability or special needs.

If you're renting your home from a housing association, the grounds for eviction are similar. If you're renting from a private landlord, the courts have to grant eviction orders in certain situations, regardless of whether it's reasonable to evict you or of any hardship it may cause you.

If you've had letters from the landlord threatening to evict you or ordering you to leave by a certain date, get advice straight away from the nearest CAB or Law Centre in the first instance.

Don't wait until you have to appear in court before taking advice and don't simply ignore the threat until it's too late. If you don't go to any court hearings, you may find that the court has granted an eviction order, and bailiffs are turning up to take your belongings out of the property and change the locks.

The landlord must have a court order to evict you. Throwing you out without a court order is a criminal offence under the Protection from Eviction Act 1977. The landlord can be fined and sent to prison, and you may be awarded compensation. If the landlord tries to get you to leave by changing the locks, turning off the gas or electricity, or threatening you with eviction, it may qualify as harassment, and you can apply for a court injunction to stop it. Take advice straight away.

Transferring a tenancy

If the person who is the tenant of a property leaves that property or dies, the family members still living there don't always have the right to take over the tenancy and stay. If you're left in a property and your name isn't on the tenancy agreement, take advice straight away from your nearest CAB or Law Centre.

If a couple both have their names on a tenancy agreement and one leaves, the other is still a tenant and can stay on. If only one name is on the tenancy and that person moves out, leaving a spouse or partner, the council has to accept the rent from the person still living in the property, but it may not agree to transfer the tenancy to that person. The end result of that situation is that the person living in the property without a tenancy does not have protection by law and may be evicted.

If a divorce, judicial separation, or dissolution of civil partnership occurs (see Chapter 6), a court can order that a tenancy is transferred from one partner to the other. That's likely to happen if children are living in the council property with the partner who didn't originally sign the tenancy agreement.

If two people are living together – *cohabiting* (see Chapter 6) – and the partner who is the tenant leaves, the other partner has no right to stay on in the property. Other members of the tenant's family usually have no rights to stay on if the tenant is no longer living in the property unless the council agrees to give them a tenancy in their own right.

The rules are similar if the property is rented from a housing association.

If the property is rented from a private landlord, the rules are different and quite complicated. The tenancy usually belongs to the tenant, and so, in theory, he can sell it, give it away, or assign it to someone else, as well as sublet the property. But most private landlords put a clause in the tenancy agreement to stop that from happening without their permission. If you think your landlord has been unreasonable in refusing permission, you may have a case against him under the Landlord and Tenant Act 1988, which says that a landlord can't withhold consent unreasonably. Take advice.

If you're renting from a private landlord or have a fixed-term tenancy and you die, it passes to your nearest and dearest in the same way as any other property you own. If you've made a will, the tenancy passes to the person named in your will. If you haven't made a will, the tenancy passes to the person who gets your estate under the rules of intestacy. For more information about wills and intestacy, see Chapter 8.

If you have a periodic tenancy, the tenancy passes to your spouse or partner regardless of what you've said in your will, as long as she has been living in the home before your death. However, that inheritance can happen only once. If you inherited the tenancy in that way, when you die it doesn't pass automatically to your partner or spouse, but passes to whoever is named in your will or under the rules on intestacy, the same as a fixed-term tenancy. If you want to make sure that your spouse or partner is protected, take advice.

Tenancies signed before 15 January 1989, are secured or protected tenancies covered by the Rent Act, and the rules are slightly different. Take advice if you want to assign your tenancy to someone else or if you're concerned about your partner's situation if you die.

The right to buy

Most council and housing association tenants can acquire the right to buy their properties. Tenants of some housing associations, such as charities, live in properties that weren't built with public money, and so don't have the right to buy. Under the Housing Act 1985, you have the right to buy if you've been living in your home for at least two years. You will then be able to buy your home at the amount that it would make if it was put up for sale, minus a discount, depending on how long you've lived there. The discount is 32 per cent after two years as a tenant, up to a maximum of 60 per cent for houses and 70 percent for flats. However, a maximum amount of discount in money terms is between £16,000 and £38,000, depending on where you live, and that amount changes from time to time.

If you sell the home again within three years of buying it, some or all of the discount has to be paid back.

Private tenants have no right to buy.

Buying Property

The price of property is a hugely popular topic of discussion when you get people together – coming second only to the weather! With the average property price now at around £200,000, it's hardly surprising that it's become something of an obsession. If you have a dozen people in a room, someone's sure to be in the selling, buying, moving cycle, with a story to tell.

Buying freehold

Most of the houses for sale, outside central London and some areas of other big cities, are *freehold:* You can buy the property, sell it, live in it, or give it away as you please for ever – unless you die without making a will and have no relatives, in which case it goes to the Crown (see Chapter 8).

Even though your property is freehold, *restrictive covenants* in the *deeds* – or ownership documents – may stop you from doing certain things. For example, you may not be allowed to build fences or walls around your garden or keep a boat or caravan outside your property if a covenant in the deeds says so. In addition, a right of way across your property may mean that you have to let certain people walk across your land (see Chapter 4). When you're buying a property, these details are the kind that of you need to check carefully.

Buying leasehold

The other main type of property that you may see advertised for sale in estate agents' windows is *leasehold*. Flats are usually leasehold, which means you buy the lease for a fixed period of time, such as 75 years, 100 years, or 999 years, and you have the right to live in the property. However, someone else owns the freehold and is the landlord. At the end of the lease, the landlord has the right to take back the property. It's like renting, but you pay all of your rent at the beginning when you buy the lease. You can sell the remainder of the lease to someone else at any time and keep any profit. You can let a sublease to someone else for some of the time you own the lease.

On top of the amount you pay to buy the lease, *service charges* are payable to the freeholder. These charges cover repairs and maintenance of the building and may also cover your share of the building's insurance. Service charges can be high – figures of £5,000 a year aren't unheard of for some London flats. You may get a 24-hour concierge service for that money, but the service charge may make a difference in whether you can afford to buy. In addition, you may also pay a ground rent for the piece of land that the property sits on.

Landlords often put all sorts of restrictions in leases as to what you can and can't do without their permission. When you're buying a property, you need to check all the details of the freehold or leasehold and all the additional charges you have to pay.

Leasehold properties are generally a bit cheaper than their freehold equivalents, but they can have problems. Some leases for sale aren't very long. If they have less than 50 years left to run, you may find it difficult to get a buyer or to find a lender who will offer you a mortgage to buy one.

The landlord is normally the person who is responsible for the maintenance and repairs of the building. A managing agent or management company usually does the work. However, you may find that the work doesn't get done or isn't satisfactory. Under the Landlord and Tenant Act 1985, your landlord has to give you a summary of what your services charges are used to pay for if you ask. Under new rules due to come into effect in 2006, you have to be given those annual summaries automatically. If you don't receive the information, you can withhold payment until you do get it.

Commonhold

Under the Commonhold and Leasehold Reform Act 2002, new developments of flats or empty blocks will be *commonhold,* and commonhold will eventually replace leasehold. Commonhold means that each flat owner owns the freehold of their own flat, and the *commonhold associ-ation,* of which all flat owners are members, owns the freehold of the common parts, such as the stairs, walls, and roof.

The commonhold association is a private com-pany registered at Companies' House. (See Chapter 10 for more information on setting up companies.) It's responsible for the repairs and maintenance, and the flat owners who are its members pay their service charges to the com-pany. In an existing block of leasehold flats, the landlord can volunteer to convert to common-hold, and it can go ahead if all the leaseholders and all their lenders agree.

If the repairs aren't being done in your block, and you think you can manage the building better yourself, you and the other leaseholders may be able to take over the *right to manage.* You can set up your own management com-pany or appoint new managing agents. You may be able to take even more control of your property and buy the freehold from the landlord. Under the Landlord and Tenant Act 1987, if the landlord wants to sell his freehold, the leaseholders may have to be given the opportunity to buy before anyone else is approached. Under the Leasehold Reform, Housing and Urban Development Act 1993, the leaseholders can get together and may be able to buy the free-hold whether the landlord likes it or not. You can't buy the freehold of your individual flat; you all have to get together and buy the freehold of the whole block. The other alternative under the Act is the right to buy a new lease, extending your current lease by 90 years.

If you want to pursue any of those options, talk to a solicitor who specialises in housing law. The nearest Law Centre may have a specialist, or you can obtain help from the government-backed Residential Property Tribunal Service (RPTS), which can help with property disputes and polices the way leaseholders are treated. RPTS can decide, for example, whether service charges are fair and whether the repair and maintenance work is of a reason-able standard. You can contact the RPTS on 0845-600-3178 or go to its Web site at www.rpts.gov.uk.

Getting a mortgage

Most people aren't lucky enough to have the cash to buy their home without borrowing at least some of the money. Banks and building societies lend money to buy property. If you take out a loan, or *mortgage,* from one of these lenders, the loan is *secured* against the property, which means that if you don't keep up your payments on the loan, the lender can ask a court for an order to allow them to repossess the property, evict you, and sell it so that it can get their money back.

Like everything else, you need to shop around to find the right mortgage for you, and the many choices can be bewildering. You can get a specific type of mortgage if you're a first-time buyer or you're buying a place to let out. You may qualify for a discount for an initial period of time after the start of the loan. Interest may be charged at *standard variable rate,* which means it goes up or down as the Bank of England increases or reduces the base rates of interest, or you may be able to borrow at a *fixed rate* of interest for the first few years of the loan. You can agree to repay some of the capital sum you borrow, as well as interest each month through a *repayment mortgage,* or you can choose an *interest-only mortgage* where the amount you pay to your lender each month covers only the interest, but you also usually save monthly into some other kind of investment plan, which matures and pays off the capital you borrowed at the end of the mortgage term.

You also have the question of what happens if you pay off your mortgage before the agreed term is up. For example, if you arrange to borrow £120,000 and pay it off over 25 years, the lender may charge you a sum of money as a penalty if you pay it off earlier. Usually, the agreement says that if you move house and pay off your original mortgage within a certain time of taking it out – say, five years – you have to pay the penalty. Check the terms and conditions before you opt for a particular loan.

Take the advice of a range of independent financial advisers or use a mortgage broker to find the best loan for you. The Association of Independent Financial Advisers is on 0207-628-1287 or www.unbiased.co.uk.

Try your own bank or building society if you need a loan because it already has all your details and may be more willing to loan you money. Then compare its offer with what you can find elsewhere. Don't just go for the big, high street names. Many smaller building societies may come up with better deals.

Buying property by yourself

If you buy your property by yourself, you're the sole owner. You have the right to sell the property, transfer ownership, and decide who lives in it. You can let it out to a tenant and charge rent in a private arrangement (see the earlier section 'Private property'), although if you have a mortgage, the lender will have to agree and may change some mortgage terms, such as charging you a higher rate of interest.

If you invite someone else to live with you in the property, they have no claim over a share of the property unless you give them a share or unless they can convince a court that they actually own a share because they have put enough money into the structure and fabric of the building. If you start living with someone and they come to live in your home, you should take legal advice. If you intend to give your partner a share of your property, put the details in writing.

If you don't want your partner to be able to claim a share of the property, don't allow them to spend money on repairing the roof, installing central heating, or making any other substantial improvement. If you have children together and later split up, a court may order you to leave your home and allow your partner and children to live there until the children leave school (see Chapter 6).

If you get married or register a civil partnership and your partner moves into your home, she may eventually be able to claim a share or even all of the property. The courts have powers to transfer ownership of property between spouses and partners in a civil partnership. (See the section 'Splitting the Property,' later in this chapter, and Chapter 6.) Talk to your nearest CAB or Law Centre if you need advice.

Buying property with others

Many people who buy property buy with someone else – a spouse, a partner, or a friend. As property prices rise, it's becoming more common for friends to buy together as a way to get a step on the property ladder. If more than four people want to buy together, it all gets a bit complicated, and you need the advice of an experienced solicitor.

If you're buying with a spouse, partner, or friend, you can both own the property as joint tenants or as tenants in common:

✔ **Joint tenants:** Husbands and wives, partners who have registered a civil partnership, and many people who live together decide to own their property as *joint tenants*. Both owners own half of the property unless they split up and decide to divide it differently or a court orders that some of one person's share is transferred to the other person. If one tenant dies, the other automatically becomes the owner of the whole home. If you don't want that transfer to happen, you need to buy the property as tenants in common. You can buy as joint tenants and then change to tenants in common later if your circumstances change.

> ✔ **Tenants in common:** When friends buy property together, they usually buy as *tenants in common*. Each can own a different share. If one person puts up half of the money and two others put up a quarter each, then one owns half and the others each own a quarter. If one of the tenants dies, their share goes to whoever is named in their will as the beneficiary. That person may be the other tenant or tenants, but it may be someone else entirely. One tenant can also sell his share of the property to whoever he chooses.

When you're referring to buying, *tenant* doesn't mean someone who is renting a property. It's a legal term used to describe how you own the land.

Understanding the buying process

After you've decided to buy a property, on your own or with a partner or friend, the next step is to decide where you want to live and how much you're prepared to spend. Armed with those decisions, you can then start house hunting. Estate agents are the obvious people to turn to, but don't forget that properties may be sold at auction, too, so keep an eye on your local press. Most estate agents use the Internet, as well as their shop windows and for sale boards, to advertise properties.

Making an offer

When you find a property you want to buy, in Scotland you register your interest in the property with the estate agent. You find a lender willing to lend you the money you need and have a survey done before you make an offer.

Anywhere else in the UK, after you've found a home you want to buy, you make an offer of the amount you're prepared to pay, *subject to survey,* which means you'll pay the offered amount provided a survey carried out by a surveyor doesn't throw up any unexpected repairs that will cost thousands of pounds to put right. If the seller accepts your offer, you go ahead and get your survey done and arrange your mortgage. If the seller doesn't accept your offer, you're free to offer again as many times as you like. (For information on using surveyors, see Chapter 14.)

Surveying your purchase

Lenders won't lend unless they're happy that you have enough income to be able to afford the payments on the loan and that the property you're buying is worth at least the amount that you want to borrow. Lenders usually expect you to have enough savings to pay a deposit of around 10 percent. (For more on mortgages, see Chapters 15.) Shop around for the best mortgage deal. (See the section 'Getting a mortgage,' earlier in this chapter.)

Lenders appoint surveyors to carry out the most basic surveys, which are *valuation reports*. These reports do little more than give the lender information about the value of the property and point out any major repairs that may be needed. The lender may offer to lend you the money, but hold back part of the money until those repairs have been made.

If you want to know more about the property for your own peace of mind, you will want a *home buyer's report* or, if the place is fairly old, a full *structural survey*.

The fee for the valuation report is added onto the loan, and you pay it back as part of your mortgage. If you want a more comprehensive report, you have to pay for it yourself. (The full structural survey is the most expensive.) The fees vary depending on the amount of work the surveyor has to do.

The Royal Institution of Chartered Surveyors (0870-333-1600 or www.rics.org.uk) can give you details of surveyors in your area and has a dispute resolution scheme if you have a problem with a surveyor.

Exchanging contracts

In Scotland, it's only after you've had the survey done that you put in your offer. The seller in Scotland decides – depending on how many people have registered an interest in the property and how many potential buyers have had surveys carried out – on a date by which all offers must be submitted. On that date, your bid, along with any others, goes to the seller, who decides who to sell to. Usually, sellers choose the highest bidder, but they can opt to sell to someone else if they prefer. If the sellers accept your bid, you have a contract, and the house is yours. Your solicitor goes ahead with drawing up the necessary contracts to transfer the home to you and get the money from your lender.

In the rest of the UK, by the time the survey is done, your offer has already been accepted, so you instruct your solicitor or licensed conveyancer to do all the necessary paperwork to complete the purchase. A *licensed conveyancer* is someone who is licensed to do all this paperwork, but, unlike a solicitor, doesn't do any other legal work. If you need to find someone reliable to do the job, ask for recommendations from friends and family or contact the Law Society (0870 606-6575 or www.lawsociety.org.uk) or the Council for Licensed Conveyancers (01245-349-599 or www.conveyancer.org.uk).

When the paperwork is ready, you and the seller exchange contracts. At that point, you have to pay a deposit, which is usually 10 per cent of the price you've agreed to pay. The sale is completed at an agreed period of time – usually a month – later. Apart from Scotland, the property isn't yours until the purchase is completed, and sellers can change their minds – perhaps because someone else comes up with a better offer and gazumps you. If the sellers change their mind after the contracts are exchanged, they have to pay back your deposit. If you've lost out financially as a result, talk to your solicitor about the possibility of making a claim for compensation. If you change your mind or can't complete the purchase after the contracts have been exchanged, you'll lose the deposit.

The advantage of the system in Scotland is that once your offer has been accepted, the house is yours, and the seller can't decide to sell it to someone else for a higher price. However, you can have surveys carried out on several properties before you make an offer that a seller will accept, which can add up to several thousands of pounds.

Doing the searches

During the buying process, the solicitor who is acting for the buyer will do what is called the *searches*. This term literally means searching for information about the property that may affect your desire to buy – such as whether there's planning permission for building work on any of the land around the property, or whether there's anything you should know about the land the place is built on, such as it's on an old landfill site.

The solicitor may ask for information on drainage and water supplies, the amounts of all the different service charges and ground rent, and the behaviour of neighbours. The solicitor gets the searches done by asking the local council, the seller's solicitor, and the freeholder (if the property is a leasehold property) for the information. The more sources checked, the longer the process may take. After the solicitor is happy that all bases are covered and you have all the relevant information, he will agrees with the sellers' solicitor on a date for the contracts to be exchanged.

Adding on the stamp duty and other expenses

The buyer's solicitor also works out how much stamp duty has to be paid. *Stamp duty* is a sum of money you have to pay to the Government if the property you're buying is worth more than the threshold amount – which may change each year in the budget. If you buy a property worth less than £125,000, you don't pay stamp duty. If you pay more than £125,000, you pay stamp duty to the Government at 1 per cent of the total value of property. Stamp duty is charged at 3 per cent on properties worth between £250,000 and £500,000 and 4 per cent on those worth £501,000 and over.

Buying property is an expensive business. When you're working out how much your home will cost you, add the mortgage arrangement fees, stamp duty, fees for searches, solicitors, and surveyors charges to the purchase price. You can cut down the bill by doing the solicitor's job yourself, but it is time consuming, and unless you've done it before, you may miss something vital. If you do opt for DIY conveyancing, check that it's okay with your lender. Plenty of books and information on the Internet can help, but remember, if something goes wrong, you carry the can.

Your lender will insist that you have insurance to cover the building from the moment you become the owner. This insurance covers you in case the property is damaged by flood or fires, for example (see Chapter 18). You don't have to buy any policy that the lender offers you. If you have dependents, you may want to buy life insurance so that the policy pays out enough to pay off the mortgage if you die (see Chapter 18). As soon as you become a property owner, you should make a will, or the property may pass to someone you don't want it to (see Chapter 8).

Splitting the Property

A question that often arises when a relationship breaks down is what happens to the property owned by the couple. The property in question is usually the family home. What happens to that property and how it's divided depends on various factors. If the home is owned by one of the partners or by both as joint tenants or as tenants in common (see the earlier section 'Buying property with others'), they can decide to split it in any way they like provided that they can agree. The couple may agree that it should become the property of one of them or that it should be sold and the proceeds of the sale divided in any proportion they like.

If the couple can't agree on how a property should be divided, they can get help. *Mediation* services are the cheapest option (see Chapter 6) and may be able to help the couple come to their own agreement. If mediation fails, solicitors can advise each party on the possible outcome and may then be able negotiate a settlement. If the solicitors can't come up with a plan that the couple agrees to, the courts can make a decision.

Mediators and solicitors bear in mind the factors that the courts take into consideration and are also aware of past court decisions made in similar cases. Taking legal action can be very costly and will reduce the amount of assets a couple has to divide between them.

The courts, if asked, consider

✔ Whether a couple is married or living together

✔ If they're married, whether they're separating or divorcing

- ✔ How long the relationship lasted
- ✔ Whether one or both members of the couple owned the property
- ✔ How much one or the other contributed to the structure and fabric of the building, such as paying for the new roof or the central heating
- ✔ Whether any children are involved and their needs
- ✔ What other assets the couple has

The courts have powers to transfer property between husband and wife or between partners who have registered a civil partnership. They have fewer powers to transfer property from the ownership of one partner to the other if the couple isn't married or if a married couple is separating rather than divorcing. Outcomes can vary, from transferring the whole property from the owner to the spouse who previously didn't own any proportion of it, to allowing the partner with the children to stay in the property until the children leave full-time education and then selling the home and splitting the proceeds. (Chapters 6 and 7 provide more information on property division at the end of a relationship.)

If you're living in a property with your partner and you're separating or divorcing, you should try to resolve the division of the property between you without getting embroiled in costly legal proceedings. However, you should also take legal advice about the possible outcome of the split. Your CAB or Law Centre can help with free advice and point you in the direction of a specialist lawyer if necessary.

Parting Ways with a Property

Dream home or not, eventually your circumstances may change, and you'll want to move on. Estate agents act for sellers of property by advertising their properties in their shop windows, over the Internet, and in the relevant press. You should shop around for an agent who offers the range of services you want because their services differ (see Chapter 14).

You don't have to use an estate agent to sell your property. A growing number of sellers are doing without agents and advertising their own properties in the press and on the Internet.

After you've put your property up for sale, all you can do is sit back and hope to have a stream of would-be buyers lining up to have a look. You can ask the estate agent to show people around, or you can choose to be there as people inspect, and are rude about, your beloved home.

Remember capital gains tax

You don't have to pay tax on the proceeds of the sale of your only or main residence, and for most people, the family home is just that – their only residence. However, if you have more than one property and you sell the one that isn't your main residence, you normally have to pay *capital gains tax* at 40 per cent on any profit you make over £8,800 after inflation and your annual exemption are considered. The calculation is quite complicated. If you're lucky enough to have a second property to sell, talk to an accountant about the best time to sell in order to keep the tax bill as low as possible.

The estate agent has to let you know about every offer that is made unless you've asked them not to let you know about offers you simply won't consider. You don't have to accept the first offer you get. You may decide to wait for a higher one, or you may decide that you don't want to sell to particular buyers, and you'll wait for someone else to bid.

When you accept an offer, you can take your property off the market so that you're no longer showing prospective buyers around, and most buyers will want you to do so. On the other hand, you may worry that your buyers may change their minds and thus leave the property on the market just in case. It's a difficult decision to make. Some sellers keep their properties on the market and hope to get a better offer, in which case they accept it and let the first buyer down. That's called *gazumping*.

The buyer normally makes you an offer subject to survey. (See the section 'Surveying your purchase,' earlier in this chapter.) If the survey shows all is well and the buyer's lender is happy, your solicitor and the buyer's solicitor will do all the necessary paperwork and contracts will be exchanged. At that point, you get a deposit from the buyer. The sale is completed an agreed period of time later.

In most cases, sales go through quite smoothly, but if you're selling your current home and buying a new one at the same time, you'll probably want to complete both transactions at the same time so that you can move all your belongings from one home directly to the other. Your buyer may be in the same situation, and the person from whom you're buying your next property may also be buying somewhere else. You'll be in a chain.

Difficulties arise if one person in the chain encounters a problem and has to pull out. The whole chain can break, leaving you with one of two situations: with your current place sold and nowhere to go or with the keys to your new home but no buyer for your current home. You may find that you have to rent somewhere to live and start house hunting all over again or have to borrow a *bridging loan* from your lender so that you can pay for both properties at once. No wonder psychiatrists say that moving house is the most stressful experience after bereavement and divorce!

Seller's information packs

The government intends to change the law on selling property. Sellers will have to provide buyers with a pack of information, to be known as *home information packs,* about the property that is up for sale. This pack should include things such as the costs of heating and lighting; information that would previously have been collected by the solicitors on fixtures and fittings, utility supplies, and service charges; and a basic survey. The aim is to speed up the buying and selling process and cut down on the opportunities for gazumping. The seller will have to pay to have all the information gathered before putting the property up for sale. There's no date as yet for the introduction of the pack, but it should be launched sometime in 2006 or 2007.

Transferring ownership

When you sell a property, ownership is transferred from you to the new owner, and in England and Wales, it's registered with the Land Registry. You may have a deed – a paper document – showing that your property is owned by you and details of past owners and the prices paid. Usually, the lender keeps the deed until you pay off your mortgage, or your solicitor has it in safe keeping and gives you a copy. Most properties bought and sold in England and Wales after 1998 are registered with the Land Registry instead. You can also register your property, even if you're not buying or selling. For more information, visit the Web site at www.landreg.gov.uk or contact your local office by phone. You can find the numbers on the Web site or in the phone book.

Selling a property isn't the only situation in which ownership may be passed from one person to another. When it comes to dividing property, if a couple applies for a judicial separation, divorce, or dissolution of a civil partnership, the courts can order property to be transferred between the partners. If you make a will, your property is transferred to whomever your will names as your beneficiary. If you die without a will, it may go to one of your relatives according to the rules of intestacy (see Chapter 8).

At any other time, you may decide to transfer your property to another person, such as a spouse or partner, child, or other relative or friend. If you're the sole owner of a property, you can sell it or give it away as you like. If you own it as joint tenants, you can sell or transfer it only with their consent. If you own part of a property as a tenant in common with someone else, you can transfer your share to anyone else you please. A solicitor draws up all the documents needed, and in England and Wales, the new owner is registered with the Land Registry.

Squatting

Squatters are people who gain access to an empty property and live there without the owner's consent and without paying rent. Despite the unconventional living arrangements, squatters have rights. If you've been living in a property for at least 12 years without the owner's permission, you become the owner of that property. Even though the place is registered to another owner, if you can prove that you've been living there for 12 years, the register will be changed to show you as the owner.

However, the *Land Registration Act 2002* says that after ten years of living in a property without the owner's permission, the squatter can apply to be registered as the owner, but if the registered owner objects, the squatter is very unlikely to have the application granted. The registered owner then has two more years in which to get the squatter out.

If you have squatters living on your property, you can use the courts to get them evicted as long as they haven't been there for at least 12 years.

Chapter 4

Dealing with Neighbours

. . . .

In This Chapter

▶ Staying on the good side of the neighbours

▶ Knowing your rights when it comes to all those neighbourly niggles

▶ Avoiding disagreements blowing out of proportion and ending up in court

▶ Keeping your home shipshape

▶ Ensuring that your neighbours and visitors are covered for every risk

. . . .

*W*hen you buy a property, you have certain rights over it and the area around it. But those rights are limited by the rights of other people. Your neighbours have rights over their property and sometimes will disagree with you about whose rights take precedence. The argument may be over something as simple as parking or tree roots.

Wherever you live – in the middle of town with neighbours on each side, above and below, or out in the countryside where your neighbours are further away – the community around you has rights, too. For example, if you want to build on your land or extend your property, the planning laws may restrict your rights. Other people may have rights to walk over your property because it has a *right of way* over it. The people around you have rights to stop you from causing a *nuisance* by, say, having noisy parties or dumping rubbish that attracts rats. Just because you've made it on to the property ladder doesn't mean that you can do exactly as you please. The people around you have rights too.

Where there are people, it's a racing certainty that disagreements will pop up. If you have a party, someone will complain about the noise. If you put out your rubbish, you're sure to put it in the wrong place. Your dog may well be guilty of digging up the next-door neighbour's rose bushes, even though he's been in the house all day. The possibilities for rows are endless. In this chapter, I cover the main causes of dispute, the law relating to them, and the organisations and departments that can help you resolve them without ending up in front of a judge.

Being a Good Neighbour

'Neighbours from hell' are beloved of newspaper reporters and television producers, but it's not so amusing to find yourself living beside one. And on the other side of the fence, your neighbour may be thinking that you're the one who falls into that category.

Whenever possible, try to avoid disputes with your neighbours. Fault usually occurs on both sides, and things can get a whole lot worse when fingers start pointing out legal rights. Live and let live, or you may find that your street isn't big enough for both of you.

Being a good neighbour isn't just about not upsetting your neighbours with your anti-social behaviour – it's about not picking fights with them about minor indiscretions that annoy you. If a neighbourhood dispute ends up in court, the law expects that you have been reasonable.

Keeping the noise down

Unless you live in a grand detached mansion in the middle of the country-side, noise can be a big bugbear. Many people live in homes with paper-thin walls and no escape. Increasingly, it's a 24-hour society; your neighbours may be at home trying to sleep during the day because they work at night, or they may come home from work at 3 a.m. and need time to unwind. Your noise can upset them, and their noise can upset you.

It's not just your immediate neighbours who may make your lives a misery with noise. Burglar alarms, car alarms, stereos, and so on all add to the cacophony of noise pollution. Local councils have the powers to deal with noise if it constitutes a *nuisance*.

Something is a *nuisance* in the legal sense if it causes damage to, or substan-tially interferes with the enjoyment of, land. The land, in this case, is your property. Noise, smells, thousands of outside Christmas lights illuminated at night, and anything else that substantially interferes with your enjoyment of your property may be considered a nuisance. And if you substantially inter-fere with your neighbours' enjoyment of their properties, you may be the one who's the nuisance.

Most neighbourly noise doesn't fall into the nuisance category. You have the right to enjoy your home, and that means going about your daily business without being nagged at for making a normal noise. Your neighbour has the same right. Be reasonable. You can't complain about loos flushing and the noise of the vacuum cleaner during the day. You make the same noises yourself, after all.

Think about the noise you make. Your neighbours have the same right to enjoy their homes as you do.

If the noises of ordinary living bother you, think about having cavity wall insulation installed or splurging on sound-proofing. The trend toward replacing carpets with wooden flooring or tiles can be difficult to live with – especially in flats. You can't dictate that your neighbours have carpets, but you can try talking to them about walking around after a particular time at night in slippers instead of hobnail boots.

However, loud music every night may constitute a nuisance because it substantially interferes with your enjoyment of your property. As always, try discussing the problem with your neighbours before you call in backup. If the problem doesn't resolve itself, you and two neighbours can write to the person causing the problem, saying that you regard the noise as a nuisance and giving them 14 days in which to stop causing that nuisance. If the noise goes on beyond the 14 days, the offender can be prosecuted. Alternatively, you can ask the Environmental Health Department at your local council to investigate. The government's Web site at `www.direct.gov.uk` has information on the services you can expect from Environmental Health departments and an A to Z listing of all the UK local authorities.

If the neighbouring factory uses noisy machinery or vibrations from it are damaging your property, it may be a nuisance.

Officers can measure the noise level and give their judgment on whether something qualifies as a noise nuisance. If Environmental Health officers decide that it is a nuisance, they will try to resolve the problem by talking to your neighbours about it. If that approach doesn't work, they can serve notices on them to stop the nuisance and ultimately take away whatever is making the noise, prosecute them, or issue an *injunction,* which is a court order to make them stop.

When it comes to street noise, the local authority officers can break into a car to stop a car alarm if they have to. No law allows them to do the same with a burglar alarm on a property, but some local authorities in London can use force to enter a building if the alarm has been ringing for more than an hour. However, they still need a warrant and a police officer in tow.

Noisy children playing in the street don't fall into the category of nuisance. If you're trying to sleep during the day, you'll have to appeal to their better nature or buy earplugs.

Under the Road Traffic Act 1974, it's illegal to blow your horn while the car is stationary, and if the car is moving, you can't sound the horn between 11.30 p.m. and 7 a.m. on most streets unless there's a danger to another moving vehicle. For more on the law and the car, see Chapter 16.

Smelling of roses

Smells can constitute a nuisance in the same way as noise. (See the preceding section.) If you're living next to a glue factory where animal bones are being boiled down, the smell can be fairly pungent, but is it a nuisance? If the smell causes damage to or interferes with your enjoyment of your property, it may be a nuisance. Strong animal smells or heavy black sooty smoke may be a nuisance. But someone keeping pigs in the countryside in Suffolk is a lot less likely to be a nuisance than someone keeping their Vietnamese pot-bellied relations in Chelsea. You have to be reasonable.

Your neighbours' compost heap may smell a bit in hot weather, but it's only temporary and so not likely to be a nuisance. If they start using it to dump their entire household rubbish and it attracts rats, that's a different matter.

If you have a problem about smells that can't be resolved with your neighbours, talk to your Environmental Health Department at your local council.

Respecting boundaries

You and your neighbours may be separated by a whole range of different boundaries – fences, walls, party walls, hedges – you may share no boundaries at all. No law says that you have to have a fence or other barrier between you and your neighbour or around your property unless a clause in your property deeds says that you must have one. In some new property developments, the deeds may contain a restrictive covenant that says you can't take down the walls that have been built or hedges that have been planted between properties. On the other hand, a clause may say that it's all to remain open plan, and you must not build a wall or plant a hedge.

Even if you don't see a boundary between properties, a boundary exists. If you have a dispute with your neighbour about where the boundary between you lies, look at the deeds for the properties. The measurements should be there to clearly indicate who owns what. Bear in mind that the boundary may have moved over the years because previous neighbours agreed to change it or because one neighbour encroached on the land of the other and got away with it.

If you do have a visible boundary between your properties, the most common dispute is over who owns it and who is responsible for keeping it in good repair. Sometimes the row ensues because one neighbour removes a barrier, such as a fence, while the other person wants it to stay in place. Again, you need to look at the legal documents to decide who owns a particular barrier. You may find that you own the fence that runs along the right boundary of your property, and your neighbour owns the left boundary. You may own all the barriers jointly with your neighbours. If you own a boundary fence or railing, you can do what you please with it. If you own it jointly with your neighbour, you have to come to agreements. If the legal documents don't clear up the ownership dispute, it's generally accepted that a fence belongs to the land on the side that the fence posts or vertical support are on.

Whatever the dispute, come to an agreement. Boundary disputes can go on for years and result in lengthy and expensive court battles. You only have to read the papers to see how neighbours can come to blows and ruin their lives over the garden fence. Do anything other than get the lawyers involved.

Mending fences

After you know who owns the fence, hedge, railing, or any other barrier, you know who is responsible for keeping it in good repair. If you own it, you can do what you like with it as long as it's safe. You can take it down if you want, but think about whether its removal may endanger someone. If you have dogs, for example, they may get into the neighbour's garden and hurt the neighbour's grandchildren; if that happened, you may be taken to court for compensation, and the dogs can be destroyed. Even if no children live next door, do you want to start a dispute with your neighbour over your dogs digging up the lawn to bury their bones?

You don't have to keep your fence maintained or repaired unless it says so in your deeds, but if it falls over into your neighbour's property and injures someone or causes damage, again, you may be sued – yet another source of neighbourly dissent! If you own the barrier, you can attach things to it, such as climbing plants, but your neighbour can't do the same without your permission. (I can hear another row!)

If your boundary has no barrier, you can build one with your neighbour's agreement. You may agree to share the expense and ownership. If you share ownership, you pay for repairs jointly, and you can both attach things to your respective side.

If you have a property that is next to the street, think about putting up a barrier of some sort if the public could be any danger – from dogs, for example. You may simply want to stop your animals from roaming, but without a wall or gate, they may also run across the road and cause an accident.

If you do have a wall, railing, fence, or other barrier along the street, keep it in good repair so that it doesn't injure a passer-by. Even hedges can cause injury if they aren't kept trimmed back off the street. A person with a visual impairment may not realise sharp branches are at face level. Someone forced into the street to avoid a hedge may be injured by a car.

If something is dangerous about your property – maybe it's a building site – think about putting up a barrier, even temporarily, to keep people out of danger. However, don't put up a barbed wire fence or a wall with glass along the top because it may cause an injury.

Hedging your bets

I'm sure your hedge looks wonderful from where you're standing, but have you ever wondered what it looks like from your neighbour's garden? It may be cutting out the light from their garden or even their kitchen. Stories of Leylandi hedges that are out of control and are 60 feet or more are common-place. People have actually been murdered over them. Now there's even a law to deal with high hedges!

If your neighbour's high hedge is bothering you, and you can't settle the matter between you, you can ask the local authority for help if:

- ✔ The hedge is made up of or mainly made up of two or more evergreen or semi-evergreen trees or shrubs.
- ✔ It is more than 2 metres high.
- ✔ The hedge cuts out light or makes access difficult.
- ✔ Because of its height, the hedge adversely affects your enjoyment of your home or garden.

The local authority can charge you a fee for dealing with the complaint. If it decides your enjoyment of your home or garden is being affected, it can issue a formal notice outlining what needs to be done – for example reducing the height of the hedge or replacing it. Your neighbours' opinions will be taken into consideration too.

If your neighbour's high hedge bothers you and you've tried talking to them about it without results, don't be tempted to cut it yourself. The row will only escalate. Appeal to the local authority. For more information on the laws and potential solutions if you're involved in a dispute, go to www.hedgeline.org.

Lighting up your life

You own the airspace above your property, but you don't have an automatic right to the light that comes onto your property or to the view from it. That means you can't usually stop your neighbours from planting a high hedge or building an extension that will cut out your light.

You can acquire a *Right to Light* over a period of 20 years. If you've lived in your home for 20 years and enjoyed all that light coming in for 20 years, you can object to someone doing something that seriously reduces the light coming in. The Right to Light applies only to your home and not to your garden – although a greenhouse may be an exception. If someone does plan to build something that will reduce your light, get legal advice. You may be able to take out a court injunction in the civil courts to stop them from going ahead.

If you get back from holiday to discover that a shed or extension has been built in your absence, take legal advice before you take action. Your neighbour may be well within his rights.

Getting to those problem roots and branches

Sometimes the bottom of the hedge causes the problems. If your neighbours' roots have spread into your garden, you can remove them.

If a tree's roots are spreading, check that it isn't covered by a *preservation order,* which is an order that stops anyone, even the owner, from cutting it down, uprooting it, topping it, or damaging it. All trees in designated conservation areas are automatically preserved, and you can't start cutting bits off them. Talk to your local council to find out whether a preservation order pertains to a particular tree. The government Web site at www.odpm.gov.uk has more information on how the orders work.

Because you must remove the roots by the least damaging method, you may need some specialised help with this one. If you have to go on to your neighbour's property, you'll have to give reasonable notice. Tree and hedge roots can cause a lot of damage, growing into drains and uprooting paving stones – even growing into the foundations of the house and damaging walls and boundary walls. If neighbours' roots damage your property, you can claim compensation if the tree owner knew, or should have known, about the danger.

Look out for your own roots. What are they doing to your neighbours' property? If you know one of your trees is dead or dying and may well fall on the next stormy night, you need to make it safe. If it blows over into your neighbour's property and causes structural damage or even injury to someone, you may be landed with an enormous compensation bill because you've been negligent.

If you don't take action to deal with a dangerous tree, your neighbour can enlist the help of the local authority, which can order you to make the tree safe or do so itself and get the costs back from you. If your tree roots are growing under your neighbours' house and causing the walls of the house to gradually sink and crack, your neighbours can sue.

Branches are yet another bone of contention between neighbours. If your tree's branches hang over into your neighbours' garden, they can ask you to remove them. If you don't, they have the right to trim the branches back to the boundary line. They can't reduce the tree in height or trim it further than the boundary. The branches and any fruit on them belong to you, and so you should get them back, but that provision may mean that they'll be unceremoniously dumped over the wall onto your property. It's much better to go round and trim the branches as requested.

If the branches of the tree hanging into the neighbours' garden are dangerous or poisonous and cause damage or injury, that's another compensation claim coming up.

Keeping animals

If you have pets, you have to keep them under control, but that doesn't mean that you have to put up fences or build walls to keep them in. If you don't have fences or walls and you can stop your dogs from roaming into the road (causing accidents) or into neighbours' gardens (destroying lawns), they're under control. If you can't control them by keeping them indoors, having them on a lead, or training them, you probably need a fence. Otherwise, you may face a compensation claim for damage to property or injury.

Cats aren't treated the same way as dogs. You aren't expected to control them, fortunately. They're a law unto themselves. But don't get upset when yours finds a second home with a kindly neighbour who feeds her and enjoys her company. And don't be surprised if your neighbours hate her and chase her for using their garden as a toilet.

When it comes to farm animals, you need fences that are well maintained and in good repair. If an animal escapes from a field because the fences are in a neglected state and an accident ensues, you can be sued for compensation. If your fences are in good condition and an animal escapes – perhaps because he's been frightened by something – it will be very hard for someone injured as a result to prove you were negligent. If your horse has been nicknamed the Great Escaper because she's well-known for jumping out of fields, you'll need to take steps to stop her. If you don't and someone is injured in an accident, you can be blamed.

Dealing with pests

What is and isn't a pest is probably something you have your own views about. You may include children in the list – but I couldn't possibly comment! All things small and furry, or with wings and a sting, can be pests if they're where you don't really want them to be and pose a health risk or a threat. Wasp's nests in neighbours' hedges or rats on a nearby building site can make unpleasant neighbours. Contact the Environmental Health Department at your local council.

Dumping rubbish

Rubbish comes in all shapes and sizes – from the sweet wrapper to the broken-down fridge and even unwanted cars. Penalties exist for those who are guilty of *fly-tipping* – dumping anything unwanted onto land that doesn't have a licence to accept waste. People fly-tip to avoid paying for their old sofas or washing machines to be hauled away or dumped legally in waste sites.

If you're found guilty of fly-tipping, you can be fined up to £20,000 and sent to prison for two years – or even up to five years if the material you illegally dumped was hazardous. You can also have the vehicle you used confiscated.

If you dump your old car illegally at the end of its life, you can be fined £2,500 and go to jail for three months. If you simply abandon it on a street, the local authority can remove it and charge you for its disposal. If you have big items to get rid of, contact your local council's waste-collection service or take them yourself to the local tip. All the council department details are in your phone book.

Rights-of-way

A person who goes onto another person's land without permission is trespassing. But footpaths and rights-of-way across land give other people the right to be there, and the landowner has no right to stop them. An individual may have a right-of-way across your land to get to their own property by arrangement with a previous owner. It can be acquired by using the right-of-way or footpath for 20 years without permission. As long as they stick to the footpath, they aren't trespassing.

The public may also have a right-of-way. A public right-of-way can come about by the public using it without permission for 20 years. If members of the general public are using your land but no public right-of-way exists and you don't want one to be created, you can put up notices to that effect and block it off one day a year just to make the point.

Check that the right-of-way doesn't already exist. You may end up in a very public dispute with lots of your neighbours.

Parking

Parking is one of the biggest causes of neighbour disputes. You come home after a long day, and you can't park outside your house because your neighbour is in 'your' space, and you see red. Unfortunately, you have no right to park outside your house on a public road. Local parking restrictions may give you the right to a particular space – for example, in a housing development where parking spaces have been allocated to each property. However, you do have the right to get into your drive to park there. If someone is illegally parked and blocking your access to your drive, the local authority and the police have the powers to remove the vehicles.

Putting aside the differences

Remaining a good neighbour can be difficult if you feel you're constantly under attack. Petty little disagreements can spiral out of all proportion to the point where everyone involved views everyone else with deep loathing but has forgotten what the original difference of opinion was about.

Just as you have rights to enjoy your property, so, too, do the neighbours. Discuss your party plans. If possible, schedule them when the neighbours are away. If that's not possible, invite your neighbours to join you and your friends. Make sure that you turn off the music at midnight. Think about how you'd feel if you were kept awake all night by a party next door when you had to get up for work at 6 a.m.

Make concessions. Come to agreements and stick to them. Discuss the issues and work out a mutually satisfactory solution. Don't just go ahead and do something that you know will upset the neighbours just because you can. You'll have to deal with the consequences later. If solicitors get involved in neighbour disputes, the solicitors come out of the confrontation richer, and either you or your neighbour can end up having to move.

If a problem develops, approach your neighbour first. If the property is let out, contact the landlord, which may be a private landlord, the local authority, or a housing association. The Environmental Health Department or the police are the usual next ports of call.

As soon as someone else gets involved, the level of the dispute is likely to rise dramatically. Relationships may never be restored. The very last resort is to take legal action.

In some areas of the UK, the mediation services are quite good. Ask your nearest Citizens Advice Bureau whether a service in your area handles neighbour disputes. Try Mediation UK – 0117-904-6661 – www.mediationuk.org.uk.

Being a Good Home Owner

As if you don't have enough to think about keeping the neighbours happy (see preceding section), you have the house itself to worry about and the people who come and go. Only after you've bought it and moved in can you begin to see all the defects and work out what needs to be done to make the house the way you want it. If you want to make major changes, you need to find the money, acquire any necessary planning permission, and get the consent of anyone else who may have to be consulted – such as your neighbours. Now you see why it's so important not to get on the wrong side of them!

Improving your home

If you want to carry out home improvements, you probably have to use savings or borrow more from a mortgage lender. The days of big grants from the local authority are past.

You may be able to get help through a disabled facilities grant if the improvements are intended to adapt the property for the needs of a person with a disability. To apply for the grant, contact your local authority.

Acquiring planning permission

The next step is to think about whether you need planning permission. Planning permission is needed for any *development,* which covers a multitude of sins. It's needed if you want to build an extension or if you want to convert a flat into an office and so change the property's use. Talk to the council planning department right at the start. It can tell you whether you have to apply for planning permission. The planning department can go through the applications process with you and tell you what documents and plans you need to produce. After you've made the application, the local authority advertises that you've applied and what you plan to do so that neighbours have a chance to lodge their objections.

You don't need planning permission for aerials and satellite dishes, fences and walls, internal alterations, or certain-sized loft conversions, for example, but you do need it for some extensions depending on their size and location, conservatories (they're extensions), and change of use.

Gaining other permissions

In some cases, you may need the permission of your neighbours, as well as planning permission, because of particular covenants attached to the property. Check your deeds. They may say, for example, that you can't build any extensions on your property without the permission of your next-door neighbour on the right. This limitation goes back to an agreement made between neighbours when the properties were originally built. The logic may have become lost in the mists of time, but the covenant still stands. If your neighbour doesn't give permission, get legal advice.

Your mortgage documents usually say that you must get your lender's permission before doing any alterations or building work or changing the property's use. It's usually just a case of rubber-stamping your plans but if you don't obtain permission, the lender can go to court for possession of your property and receive an order to sell it so that the lender can get its money back.

Check that your building work won't be interfering with a neighbour's Right to Light – see the 'Lighting up your life' section, earlier in this chapter.

You must let your insurers know what you're up to. The work may increase the risk that a claim may be made on the policy. Your insurers may charge you a little extra or set conditions on how the work is completed, but if you don't tell them and have to make a claim, they may not pay out or may pay a reduced amount.

Defying the rules

Don't be tempted to go ahead without the necessary planning permission from the local authority. You can be served with an *enforcement notice* that says that you must take your extension down and return the property to its original state. It's an expensive option. If you don't comply with an enforcement notice, you can be prosecuted. If you've had building work done, the council has four years in which to serve you an enforcement notice. If you've just changed the property's use but no building work occurred, the council has ten years in which to catch up with you.

If your property is a *listed building,* it has certain restrictions – depending on the type of listing the building has been given – on what you can and can't do to it. To make any changes you probably need listed-building consent, as well as planning permission. In conservation areas, the rules are very strict, so planning permission is usually needed, and every tree is automatically protected.

Thinking about party walls

If your property is in a row of houses or semi-detached, you can't take down a *party wall* – a wall between two properties. Your neighbour has the right of support of that wall. If you live in a flat, don't forget to check that the wall you want to take down isn't a *load-bearing wall,* which supports the flat above you. You may bring down a whole ton of bricks – quite literally – on your head.

Keeping your home in good repair

Sometimes you need access to your neighbour's property to carry out repairs on your own property. If the wall of your house is right up against the boundary line between you and next door, you can't paint it unless you can put your ladder in neighbour's garden. You can't trespass, so you must get permission. If your neighbour doesn't give you permission, as often happens after there's been a row about noise or fences, the *Access to Neighbouring Land Act 1992* can help you out.

Under the act, you can apply to the court for an order to allow you to go onto your neighbour's land to carry out repairs or improvements, if it's reasonably necessary. You have to pay any costs and expenses your neighbour has.

Given how long it takes to go through the courts and the costs involved, you want to avoid the process, if at all possible. Get back on speaking terms before you need to do your next round of repairs.

If you start piling up rubbish in your garden and it smells or attracts rats, your neighbour can complain to the local authority about the nuisance. The noise of the building work may constitute a nuisance, too, if it goes on at night, involves a lot of hammering or drilling, and cause fumes and dust. Your neighbours can apply for an injunction to restrict the work to certain hours (such as between 7 a.m. and 8 p.m.) when it causes fewer disturbances.

Keeping visitors safe

While improvements or repairs are going on, a lot of people are probably coming and going. In the ordinary run of things, most people have visitors to their homes – friends and family, as well as the post person or the plumber. You have an obligation to make sure that people are safe while on your premises and that they don't get injured because you've been negligent. People have successfully claimed compensation because a path has been cleared of snow but is still slippery or they've fallen off a rickety chair and injured themselves.

If you're negligent – you know ice is on the path but you haven't warned people or you know that the chair is on its last legs but you still let your visitor sit in it – you can be sued for compensation.

Getting Insurance

One of the first things your solicitor will tell you to do, or your mortgage lender will expect you to do, before you accept the keys to your new home is to arrange insurance. No law says that you have to have home insurance policies. Legally, the only insurance you must have is car insurance (see Chapter 16). But you do need to have the building itself insured, or your lender won't lend you money. If you want real peace of mind, you need to insure the contents, too. Make sure that one of your policies covers you for injuries to other people. Chapter 18 explains more about insurance policies, including home buildings and home contents policies.

You need to do your homework to ensure that you're fully insured.

The Association of British Insurers has a lot of information on insurance for homeowners available in leaflet form or at www.abi.org.uk. Most of the big insurance companies that provide this type of insurance are members.

Chapter 5

Using Public Services

. . . .

In This Chapter

▶ Knowing what services your taxes cover

▶ Getting treatment on the National Health Service

▶ Educating your children through the state system

▶ Knowing what the town hall staff does with your money

. . . .

*P*ublic services are those that you pay for through your taxes and which are provided by government departments or at the local government level. The two major services that are rarely out of the headlines are the National Health Service and the state education system. Police and emergencies services also come into the category of public services, and at a local level, your council taxes – or rates in Northern Ireland – pay for day-to-day services, such as rubbish collection and street lighting.

Despite being public, some services are carried out by private companies. Some hospital cleaning services, for example, are no longer carried out by hospital staff but by cleaners brought in from private firms. Private firms now run some state schools and hospitals, or the private and public sectors run them as joint ventures. Some services that used to be public, such as the train service, have been sold off to private companies,. Increasingly, the lines between public and private are blurred.

Because you've already paid for public services through your taxes, you have the right to those services free at the point of delivery. You have the right, for example, to free treatment on the NHS and to a free education from the state for your children. However, a growing debate surrounds just how much your taxes can be expected to cover. This chapter takes a look at the services you use and what you can expect from them. (The services you have to pay for, such as those of lawyers or estate agents, are covered in Chapter 14.)

Calling the Emergency Services

In emergency situations, the first thing to do is to dial 999 or 112, the new European emergency service number that you can call no matter where you are in the European Union. The emergency services do what it says on the tin – they deal with emergencies.

Don't dial 999 because the batteries in your television remote control have died, as someone did recently, or because the turkey is stuck in the oven, as happens most Christmases. Those situations may be emergencies to you, but the fire brigade shouldn't be expected to deal them. The ambulance service isn't there to take you home when you've had too much to drink on a night out. By dialling 999 when it's not a genuine emergency, you may be blocking a phone call from someone who is in danger.

If you do have an emergency, think whether you can deal with it more quickly yourself – for example, by driving an injured person directly to an accident and emergency department (see the section 'Going to Accident and Emergency,' later in this chapter) at a local hospital or by calling NHS Direct, the national health service 24-hour helpline, on 0845 4647 for advice – rather than calling 999.

Otherwise, go ahead and dial. The person who answers the call will ask for all your details and which service you need. Sometimes – such as when a car accident has occurred – you may need police, ambulance, and fire brigade. Keep calm and help the operator with as many details as possible so that she can get the service you need to you as quickly as possible.

The police should be called if a crime has been committed (refer to Chapter 1) or if a road accident needs to be reported (see Chapter 16). However, these events don't always mean it's an emergency. If you arrive home to find a burglar in your home, it's an emergency; if your home has been ransacked and the thief has already fled, call your local police station instead. If someone is seriously injured in a road accident, call emergency services; if everyone involved is okay, then, if you can contact the police on another number, you don't need to dial 999.

Apart from the ambulance, fire, and police services, you can get help from the Lifeboat Service or the Mountain Rescue service by calling 999 or 112. Rescue operations for people in trouble at sea are coordinated by the Maritime and Coastguard Agency. Lifeboats rescue on average 21 people a day. For more information on the Royal National Lifeboat Institution, call the head office on 0845-122-6999 or go to www.rnli.org.uk. The Maritime and Coastguard Agency also helps people in danger on the coastal cliffs. People who are in danger in the mountains in the UK are rescued by the Mountain

Rescue services (`www.mountain.rescue.org.uk`). The people who come to your aid are volunteers, and the police coordinate rescue plans.

In most cases, the services are free, but you may incur some charges – for example, a driver at an accident scene may be sent a bill for emergency medical treatment even though he didn't cause the accident (See Chapter 16). You may also be sent a bill if you're found to have been wasting emergency services time.

Using the NHS

The National Health Service (NHS) was launched in 1948 to give free health care based on need, not on ability to pay. In Northern Ireland, the NHS is called the Health and Personal Social Services, and in Scotland, it's called NHS Scotland. Of course, there's no such a thing as a free lunch, and the NHS is paid for by the government from the taxes it collects – so you do, in reality, pay for the service. However, the service is free to all at the point of delivery – that is, it's free at the doctor's surgery and at the hospital.

Not every treatment is free. Charges were introduced for prescriptions in 1952, and over the years, taxpayers have had to pay for eye tests and dental check-ups. Because of a shortage of dentists offering NHS dental treatment in some areas, more people are having to pay for treatment from private dentists.

The NHS gives you at least one course of in vitro fertilisation (IVF) treatment free if you are aged 23 to 39 and have a specific medical problem, such as blocked fallopian tubes, or you have been trying to conceive for three years without any luck. You usually have to pay for more if that first attempt isn't successful. If you don't fit the NHS criteria, you have to pay for all your treatment.

As technology advances and more and better drugs become available, the NHS faces many more demands. As a result, many hospitals are in debt and closing wards to keep costs down. In the future, it's possible that some costly drugs and treatments won't be offered on the NHS because they can't be funded out of the ordinary taxes you pay, or the tax increases required to pay for it all would be too high. In the meantime, despite all the complaints, the NHS is one of the best health services in the world. For more information about the services you can get, call 0845-4647 or go to the NHS Direct Web site at `www.nhsdirect.nhs.uk`.

The NHS has a patients' charter that lists your rights:

✔ To register with a general practitioner (GP) while living in the UK, even if you're from overseas

✔ To have a health check annually if you're 75 or over or if you register with a GP and haven't seen one for three years

✔ To change your GP when you want

✔ To be given information on all your GP's services and the local health services available

✔ To be referred to a consultant, or for a second opinion, with your GP's agreement

✔ To be treated no more than two years after being put on a waiting list (for most treatments) and to have any treatment explained along with the alternatives and the risks

✔ To say no to taking part in student training or medical research that's going on at the time of your treatment

✔ To have access to your health records

✔ To have the right to complaint and have those complaints dealt with quickly and in writing

Seeing the GP

If you live in the UK, you have the right to register with a GP. You can get a list of GPs from NHS Direct (0845- 4647 or www.nhsdirect.nhs.uk). You may not be accepted by the first GP you approach because GPs can turn you down, if their practice is full, for example. If you're living somewhere for less than three months, or you're ill while on holiday in a different part of the UK, you can register with a local GP on a temporary basis. In an emergency, if you need treatment, any GP has to provide it even if you aren't registered with them. You can change your GP for any reason just by registering with another practice.

When babies are born in the UK, they receive medical cards with their national health number on them. Take your card with you when you register with a GP. If you don't have a card, you can still register, and you'll be sent one. After you've registered, you're entitled to any treatments that you need that are available on the NHS. Your national health number allows NHS staff, wherever they're working, to get information about your treatment if they need it.

After you've registered with a GP, you can get treatment from that practice, although you may not always see your particular doctor. Check what the arrangements are for making appointments and for getting help when the surgery is closed. You should have a number to call and a doctor available after hours, even though he may not normally work in that surgery. If you ask the doctor to visit you at home, the GP decides whether the visit is necessary. Check out local doctors' practices to see what facilities they offer. Some may offer alternative treatments, as well as conventional medicines, or special clinics, for example.

NHS Direct can advise you about the health problems you're experiencing. The service can also advise you if you're ill after hours, if you're not sure whether you need to see a GP, if you haven't managed to register with a GP, if you're away from home, or if you can't get an appointment with your GP straight away. Experienced nurses are on the lines 24-hours a day.

Your GP can remove you from his list without giving you a reason. The health authority or primary care organisation for your area will tell you that you have been removed from the list. Patients who are violent or who threaten practice staff with violence are likely to be struck off the list and the police informed.

Understanding confidentiality

In 1997, the Caldicott Report identified weaknesses in the way parts of the NHS handled patient information. The NHS now has a Confidentiality Code of Practice. The code says that although in some situations, health professionals are required by law to divulge information about you, they generally can't give information that may identify you to anyone who is not involved in your healthcare unless you agree.

It may not always be obvious to you that in order to give you the best possible treatment, your information has to be disclosed to other NHS departments or to bodies outside the NHS. If that's the case, NHS staff has to make every effort to explain to you that your information needs to be disclosed to other people and why it's necessary. In some situations, your information may be very important and of benefit to society – for example, through medical research or student training. If your healthcare isn't directly affected by the use of your information,

you must be told and you have the right to say no.

You also have the right to refuse to allow confidential information that identifies you to be passed on. Sometimes, however, that refusal may result in you not getting the best possible healthcare or being offered certain treatments. Make sure that you understand the full consequences of your refusal before you say no.

Young people have the right to confidential treatment from their health practitioners. A court recently decided that parents don't have the right to be told by doctors if their daughter is having an abortion unless the young person agrees. A young person will be given treatment without their parents' consent if the doctor is happy that he or she can fully understand what the treatment involves. However, a doctor who is unwilling to accept a young person's request for confidentiality can refuse to discuss the matter.

You only have the right under the Patients' Charter (see the preceding section) to be referred to a consultant or to have a second opinion with your GP's agreement. If your GP refuses, you can change your GP.

Being referred to a specialist

You can ask your GP to refer you to a specialist, but GPs don't have to agree if they don't think it's necessary. However, you do have the right to see someone who is qualified and competent to treat you. If your GP does agree or wants you to see a specialist, you can't insist that you see any particular person. If you know that you really don't want to be treated by a particular individual, however, you have the right to refuse.

If you ask to be referred to a specialist and your GP refuses, you may want a second opinion. You can change your GP if your request is refused, and a new GP may agree that you should have a referral.

Going to accident and emergency

Some, but not all, hospitals have accident and emergency departments (A&E), which deal with patients who have been in accidents or emergencies. When you move to a new area, locate the nearest hospital with an A&E department because other hospitals aren't able to accept or treat people in those situations. This department is usually at the main hospital for your area, and road signs point you to it.

If someone is seriously injured or ill, you can call an ambulance by dialling 999 or drive them to the hospital yourself. Don't expect the A&E department to treat minor bruises and cuts; it has much more serious cases to deal with. When you arrive, you're assessed, and if your case isn't urgent, you're sent to another part of the NHS, such as your GP.

Some people treat A&E departments as GP surgeries because they don't want to wait for a GP's appointment. That isn't what these departments are there for. If you're worried that you need treatment but it isn't an emergency, call NHS Direct on 0845-4647 for advice.

Even if your case is urgent and Accident and Emergency can treat it, you may have to wait while more serious cases are dealt with.

Going to hospital

If you need treatment in hospital, you either get it because you have to go to an accident and emergency department (see preceding section), or you're referred by your GP or a special clinic you're attending. You may have to wait for an appointment to see a consultant, and if he decides that you need hospital treatment, such as an operation, you may go on another waiting list until that treatment is available.

Where you are on the waiting list depends on how serious your problem is and how many other people are more urgently in need of treatment, amongst other things. You may move up the list if your condition gets worse. Under the Patients' Charter (see the earlier section 'Using the NHS'), you should not have to wait more than two years for an operation after you've gone on the waiting list. In that time, you need to let your GP know if your health deteriorates.

You may be sent to a different hospital to get your operation done quicker. If you have a date for an operation and it's cancelled, you should receive a new date within four weeks.

While you're in hospital, your treatment is free, but you have to pay for such items as phone calls, television, food that's not on the regular menu, and a bed in a private room. Despite promises by the Government, mixed sex wards still exist in some hospitals. You don't have the right to insist on being in a single sex ward, but you do have to be told if you'll be in a mixed ward.

If your child has to stay in hospital, you may be allowed to visit at any time and to stay with them overnight. Hospitals should let patients spend as much time as possible with their children, but that accommodation depends on the facilities available.

If you get welfare benefits or tax credits, you may be entitled to less money while in hospital. You or your family may be entitled to help with the costs of travelling to and from the hospital for treatment or to visit a sick relative. An adviser from your nearest CAB can help you – see Chapter 11 for more details.

You shouldn't be sent home from hospital until an assessment of your follow-up care occurs and someone is available to give you that care. You and your family should be allowed to have a say in the arrangements. If you aren't going home to be cared for by family and friends, arrangements may need to be made for you to have care in your home, such as help to get out of bed, dress, and bath. An alternative may be to go into a care home until you're ready to go back to your own home.

Consenting to treatment

If you need treatment or an operation, you must give your consent, which usually means signing a consent form. You should be given all the information you need to come to a decision, and if you give consent for one form of treatment, you haven't given consent for other types of treatment.

Although you can refuse any treatment and the doctors can't go against your wishes, some circumstances don't require your consent:

✔ If you can't consent because you're unconscious and your life is in danger, doctors can do what they have to do without your consent.

✔ If you're sectioned under the Mental Health Act (see the upcoming section 'Handling mental health problems'), in some cases, treatment can go ahead without your consent.

✔ If you have a disease that has to be notified to the health authority – such as meningitis, rabies, scarlet fever, or hepatitis – doctors don't need your consent to treat you.

Young people aged 16 and 17 can give consent for their own treatment, and children younger than 16 can give consent as long as the doctor thinks they are capable of fully understanding what's involved and the consequences. Parents or the courts must give consent for younger children and those who can't give their own consent because they're disabled, for example. But if you refuse treatment that the doctor thinks a child must have, the doctor must go ahead and treat the child, which may mean applying to a court for consent if there's time to go through that procedure.

If you don't give your consent with regard to a child, you may be seen to be unreasonably refusing treatment or failing to provide medical help and prosecuted for neglect – see Chapter 7.

Naming a next of kin

When you go into hospital, you're asked to give details of your next of kin. Strictly speaking, that person is legally your closest relative – your spouse if you're married or in a civil partnership, a parent, brother, or sister if you're not married. However, for most purposes, including giving consent for treatment, you can give details of a partner as the next of kin, and it's accepted.

If you're too ill to give your consent, treatment will go ahead. However, in some situations, people don't want to be treated if they fall ill – if they already have a terminal illness, for example, and want to be allowed to die without being revived the next time they fall into a coma. The only way you may have a say in that circumstance is by making a *living will* – or *advance directive* or *advance statement* – setting out your wishes not to be treated. You can give instruction about when you would like medical treatment to be withdrawn and the kind of treatment you'll accept, such as painkillers, which may shorten your life. For more information on living wills, see Chapter 8.

Handling mental health problems

People who have mental illnesses can go into hospital voluntarily – which is what happens in the vast majority of cases where people agree to hospital treatment. They can discharge themselves at any time, even though doctors advise against it.

Under the Mental Health Act 1983, a person can be detained in hospital if she meets the following criteria:

- She's suffering from a mental illness of a nature or degree that warrants detention in hospital.

- The detention is in the interests of the health and safety of that person or for the protection of others.

People who refuse hospital treatment can be admitted compulsorily – or *sectioned* – under the Mental Health Act. A patient's nearest relative or a social worker can apply to have the patient sectioned. A nearest relative is the one who comes first on the list of spouse, child, parent, brother or sister, grandparent, grandchild, uncle or aunt, or nephew or niece.

A social worker provides an assessment of the patient, which two doctors need to agree with. All the health professionals involved in the process have to be approved under the Mental Health Act. The treatment and the length of hospital stay depend on the type of illness. The Mental Health Act sets out circumstances in which patients can be treated without their consent and when the opinion of a second doctor is required. It also sets out details of when a patient can be discharged.

Mental Health Review Tribunals decide when a patient should be discharged if they have been compulsorily detained. Independent of courts, these panels are usually made up of a lawyer, a psychiatrist, and a lay person. Their job is to make sure that the patient meets all the criteria for discharge set down by the Mental Health Act.

A new Mental Health Bill was first published in June 2002 and is still being revised and amended. When that bill eventually becomes law, it may change some of the rules on detention and treatment of people with mental health problems, the role of the nearest relative, and the criteria used to decide whether someone can be discharged The Human Rights Act 1998 (see Chapter 2) has also affected the Mental Health Act 1983, and so mental health law is changing as the courts hear more cases. In Scotland, the Mental Health (Care and Treatment) (Scotland) Act 2003 became law in October 2005.

Because of all these changes, the law is extremely complicated. If you need information on your rights or the rights of a relative or friend with mental health problems, contact the mental health charity Mind (0845-766-0163 or www.mind.org.uk).

Receiving private treatment

All the health services available on the NHS, and many more, such as Botox and cosmetic surgery, are available from private practices, clinics, and hospitals. You can arrange to have any treatment that you need done privately as long as you can afford to pay or have an insurance policy that will cover the cost. Increasingly, people are being forced to depend on the private sector for their dental treatment as more dentists turn their back on the NHS and offer treatment on a private basis only.

If you want to buy private medical insurance, talk to an insurance broker about the best policy for your needs. You can find an insurance broker through the British Insurance Brokers' Association (0870 9501790 or www.biba.org.uk).

The providers of private medical care aren't as well regulated as the NHS. Health authorities inspect such clinics and hospitals only twice a year. Private care homes fall into this category, too. That lack of regulation can make it more difficult to get a complaint dealt with.

Complaining about your treatment

If you have a complaint about any health service you are provided by the NHS, you must first complain to that person. You must complain within six months of the problem arising. You should be given an explanation, and an apology may be forthcoming.

If you want to talk to someone who isn't directly involved with your case, ask to talk to the person who manages complaints at the hospital or the surgery.

That person should investigate your complaint and give you a written reply. If that step doesn't resolve the problem, you have 28 days after receiving that letter to ask for an independent review panel to look into the matter.

If a review panel is set up, it must investigate again and report back to you within 12 weeks. If you still aren't happy with the outcome, you can write to the Health Service Ombudsman or Northern Ireland Ombudsman. The Ombudsman may resolve the issue, but can't award you compensation. (See the upcoming section 'Claiming Clinical Negligence.') You can contact the Ombudsman for England on 0845- 015-4033; for Wales on 02920-394-621; and for Northern Ireland on 0800-343-424. You can also visit the Web site at www.ombudsman.org.uk and the NHS in Scotland at www.show.scot.nhs.uk.

The Independent Complaints Advocacy Service is run by CAB and can help with your complaints about the NHS. You can find details of your nearest CAB in the phone book and more information at www.adviceguide.org.uk.

If you think the person you're complaining about acted unprofessionally or unethically, you can also complain to the relevant professional body. Doctors are members of the General Medical Council (0845-357-3456 or www.gmc-uk.org). Dentists belong to the General Dental Council (0207- 887-3800 or www.gdc-uk.org). Nurses, midwives, and health visitors belong to the Nursing and Midwifery Council (0207-637-7181 or www.nmc-uk.org).

Dealing with medical accidents

Accidents do happen, even when you're being treated by the very people who are there to undo the medical problems caused by accidents. A *medical accident* is when you're injured because something goes wrong with your medical treatment.

The first thing to do is to make sure that you get the necessary treatment to put things right if possible. Then you can think about what you want to happen. Most people in these situations say that they want an apology and steps to be taken to ensure that the same thing can't happen again to someone else. You may also want compensation. Sometimes a healthcare provider will admit a mistake and offer you compensation. If you accept, you aren't able to take legal action later. However, in most cases, you will have to go to court to prove a claim of clinical negligence (see the upcoming section 'Claiming clinical negligence') before you get any compensation.

Ask your doctor or the person who was involved in your treatment for an explanation as to what went wrong. They have to give you that explanation and an apology, if that's appropriate. If you don't get an explanation and an apology, you have to follow the complaints procedure outlined in the earlier section 'Complaining about your Treatment'. If you aren't satisfied with the outcome or appear to be getting nowhere fast, the charity Action against Medical Accidents can help (0845-123-2352 or www.avma.org.uk).

If you think that the person against whom you're complaining was unprofessional or poses a danger to other patients, you should also complain to his professional organisation. (See the section 'Complaining about your treatment,' earlier in this chapter.)

Claiming clinical negligence

If you've been the victim of a medical accident, you may be satisfied that it was an accident, and with an apology and an assurance that it won't happen again. However, if you think that someone involved was negligent and you want to make a claim for financial compensation, you should take legal advice. You may be able to claim if you've been injured physically or emotionally. If your claim is refused, you may have to take legal action in court.

Think carefully about going to court. You may have no choice if you need to pay for care or equipment or you've lost a lot of money by not being able to work, but the case will be stressful and expensive and there's no guarantee you'll win.

If you do take legal action, you have to make your claim within three years of the event that caused your injury. Children can put off claiming until the age of 21, or a parent or other close friend or relative can take a claim before that time on their behalf.

You can't claim compensation just because someone did something wrong. You have to prove that by doing something wrong, they caused you injury. You have to prove that the care you had was below the standard expected from a reasonably competent person giving that kind of care, and that you've suffered a physical or psychological injury as a direct result of that negligence.

You can claim compensation for the injury, such as amounts for pain and suffering and ongoing treatment, and for losses, such as loss of earnings. You may also be able to claim for the costs of adapting your home to your needs, nursing care, psychological injury, and loss of amenity, which is an amount to make up for not being able to do your usual activities, such as hobbies. You may also make a claim if someone has died as a result of clinical negligence.

These cases are complicated, and you need good legal advice and ongoing support. The organisation Action against Medical Accidents (0845- 1232352 or www.avma.org.uk) is the best place to start.

Using the Education System

The education system in England and Wales is a little different than the systems in Northern Ireland and Scotland. Children sit different exams in Scotland and may go to university a year earlier than children educated in the rest of the UK. Scottish universities have different courses to fit in with the schools system. However, the idea is basically the same. All children in the UK have to be educated from age five to 16.

Children can be educated at home or at school, and you can choose from a whole range of schools – from state-funded schools to private ones for which the parents pay all the fees. Children must start school by the beginning of the first term after their fifth birthday. Some education authorities accept children earlier, and all four-year-olds are entitled to a nursery or school place. They have to stay at school until they're 16. Students can leave on the last Friday of June if they've reached 16 or will be 16 before the start of the next school year.

Stating the case: The state system

The *Further and Higher Education Act 1992* says that all young people have the right to a full-time state education until the age of 19 and to further education for those who want it.

In theory, a state education is free for all children. In practice, many schools are struggling to make ends meet and will ask parents for contributions for all sorts of equipment and sometimes even for books. Parents also have to fund extras, such as school trips, if they want their children to take part.

State schools all teach the national curriculum, which is set down by the Department for Education and Skills, but schools do vary quite a bit in terms of facilities, buildings, and success rates at exams. The Government has a system of inspections, which are carried out by Ofsted inspectors, to check on the standards of teaching and management of schools. League tables, published every year, show how well pupils do in exams. Parents have access to those league tables, which may influence their decisions about where they'd like their children to go to school.

Finding a school

If you have parental responsibility, you have the right to express a preference about which school your child should go to. Expressing a preference isn't the same as choosing the school, and many children don't get into the school they and their parents would prefer. Many parents complain that, especially if you live in most big cities, that this amounts to having no choice at all.

The Local Education Authorities fund most primary and secondary schools. They have a duty to provide suitable schools. Your area may have a range of schools, such as grammar, religious, or private schools, city technology colleges, or city academies. Many schools give priority to children living in the area or to those who already have another family member at the school.

When you're choosing a school, you'll probably want to look at all available choices. Schools have to make their exam results public. For some parents, how successful the school is at getting pupils through exams influences their choice. The size of the classes may be another important factor for parents. Five-, six-, and seven-year-olds must be in classes of no more than 30 children, but classes for older children have no maximum class sizes.

If you don't get your child into the school you prefer, you can appeal to the Local Education Authority. This process can be long and drawn-out, so your child will have to be given an education elsewhere until the appeal is dealt with. If you want to appeal, the authority can give you details of how to go about it. You can find more information on choosing a school at www.direct.gov.uk, which also has links to information for Scotland and Northern Ireland.

Under the Education Act 1981, children with special educational needs should go to the same schools as their peers, if at all possible. The Local Education Authority has to make a formal assessment of the child's needs and give the parents a statement of those needs, along with what support the authority will provide. The parents can appeal against the outcome of the assessment. The government's Web site at www.direct.gov.uk has all the information.

Attending school

Once your children are in a school, you're responsible for making sure that they go each day. You'll be committing an offence if your child doesn't attend regularly – even if you didn't know about the absences. There will be days when illness or some other unavoidable disaster strikes, and they can also have days off if they're celebrating their own religion's major festivals. But if the regular absences occur for no good reason, you may be prosecuted, fined, and sent to prison for a month, or your child may be referred to a child guidance clinic or even, in extreme cases, taken into care.

You may want to take your children on holiday during term time. You can take them up to ten school days in any one school year, but you have to ask the permission of the head before you do. Most schools will always want you to avoid the time before and during exams and SAT tests.

Being excluded

The school governors make the rules, and the head teacher enforces them. The rules can cover what to wear to school, what not to wear, hair, jewellery, and makeup, but they can't force someone not to wear something that their religion dictates they must wear, such as a turban. They have to be reasonable.

If your children persistently refuse to follow the school rules, such as wearing a uniform, the school can refuse to allow them in. In that event, you can be held responsible and failing in your duty to see that your children are educated.

Under the Education Act 2002, the head teacher can exclude a child from school for up to 45 days in a school year for serious breaches of the school's behaviour policy. If allowing the child to stay in school would seriously harm his welfare and the welfare of other pupils – in extreme cases, such as committing violence or dealing drugs – the head teacher can exclude a child permanently. The school governors have to meet if a child is excluded for more than 15 days in any one term – unless the parents of a child excluded for a short period of time request a meeting with the pupil discipline panel. The governors have to make sure that they're satisfied that the head teacher has not overstepped the mark. If they disagree with the head teacher, they can overrule his or her decision, and the child has to be allowed back to school. If a pupil is permanently excluded, the Local Education Authority has to provide a place at another school, or home or individual tuition. Contact the Advisory Centre for Education for advice on 0207 749822.

Teaching the kids at home

You can educate your children at home rather than send them to school, but if the Local Education Authority thinks that you aren't complying with the law, you'll have 14 days to prove them wrong.

If the Local Education Authority still doesn't accept that your child is receiving a full-time education or one that's up to the right standard, it can apply for an education supervision order, meaning that you have to send the child to a school of the authority's choice. If you ignore the order, you can be taken to court.

If you do decide to educate your children at home, you should contact the Local Education Authority. The Internet also offers a wealth of information about home education. You can also try Education Otherwise, which is a charity that provides support. The helpline number is 0870- 730-0074, and the Web site address is www.education-otherwise.org.

Educating Rita – privately

Independent – or private – schools rely for all or most of their funding on fees paid by parents rather than funding from the government. The fees run into thousands of pounds per term, and a private education can cost you £12,000 a year. Having said that, about a third of all private school pupils do get some help with their fees, mainly from the schools they go to, through scholarships and bursaries.

Investment schemes are also available to help parents save up for future school fees. An independent financial advisor can help. Take the advice of three advisors before you decide how best to invest. You can contact independent financial advisers through the Association of Independent Financial Advisers (0207-628-1287 or www.unbiased.co.uk).

Independent schools have full control over their admissions and curriculum. The National Curriculum is taught in state schools. Private or independent schools and children taught at home don't have to follow it, although many do. The schools do have to meet certain standards and are inspected by the Independent Schools Inspectorate or regional inspectorates in Wales, Scotland, and Northern Ireland every six years.

If you're considering a private education for your children, you want to know how well children do at the school in terms of GCSE and A-level passes; what facilities the school provides; and how much the fees are. The Independent Schools Council (0207-766-7070 or www.isc.co.uk) has a list of the independent UK schools that belong to the council, as well as information on fees. The council gives advice and information to parents through its regional offices.

As with medical treatment, the private education sector isn't as highly regulated as the state sector. Schools are required to have complaint procedures, but if you can't resolve any dispute with the school, you have to take legal action under contract law – you have to prove that the school has broken the terms of the contract you have with it.

Taking education to a higher level

Children can leave school once they're of school-leaving age, but they can stay in the education system for as long as they like. The Local Education Authority has no obligation to provide education for students over 16, so if your children do want to stay on, they may have to change schools. They may prefer to move to a further education college and take a more vocational course, which prepares them for a particular job rather than do A-levels (A-levels are called Highers in Scotland).

The teacher who is in charge of career advice at their school should be able to talk to you and your children about the choices available, or try the Connexions service at www.connexions.gov.uk. Sixteen to 18-year-olds still at Local Education Authority-funded schools or colleges aren't charged fees. Students over 16 on other college courses may be able to get financial help from Local Education Authorities.

You may be able to get an Education Maintenance Allowance (EMA). You can get these if you're over 16 and going to college or school sixth form or staying on in a special school. This weekly payment ranges from £10, £20 or £30 and depends on your household income. The allowance is intended to help with day-to-day costs, such as travel, books, and equipment for your course. You also receive bonuses if you stay on the course and make good progress.

At the age of 18 (some children may be ready to move to higher education sooner), pupils who want to go to college or university will have a choice of diploma or certificate, university degree courses, or professional qualification study. Many students take a gap year while they decide what to do next. Connexions can help with choices, or the Universities and Colleges Admissions Service (UCAS) can help with applying to university – 0870-112-2211 or www.ucas.ac.uk.

University students, apart from those in Scotland, have to pay tuition fees. If your income is low, you may receive some financial help toward the fees. A system of loans also helps pay for living costs. The loans have to be paid back once the student goes to work and is earning enough; the employer deducts the payments from the borrower's wages. For more information about financial help for students and about all aspects of education, go to the Department for Education and Skills Web site at www.dfes.gov.uk.

Using Local Authority Services

Apart from the public services that are paid for from general taxation, local authorities – or councils – use the money from *council tax* (or *rates* in Northern Ireland) to provide local services. Depending on where you are in the UK, you may have a regional council, such as a county council, a district, and a parish council. Each one takes a share of the local government responsibilities.

Money collected through council tax or rates pays for a long list of facilities, including rubbish collections, recycling, and street lighting. Local authorities work closely with the various police forces to cut crime and provide community policing. They are responsible for social work departments and childcare, school and education services, museums and art galleries, bus services, social housing and sports facilities, traffic regulation and planning, and building regulations. Local authorities also provide Trading Standards Departments and Environmental Health Departments. Throughout this book, you come across services provided by local authorities and more information on how they work.

If you want to know what your own local authorities provide and how your council taxes or rates are being spent, you can request that information from your local council. You can discover more information about local authority responsibilities at www.local.gov.uk, and you can find your local government department listed in your phone book.

If you have any problems with the services provided by your local authority, talk to your nearest Citizens Advice Bureau. The CAB may be able to help you resolve the problem. If, for example, you've had an accident as a result of tripping over a paving stone, you may be able to claim against the council responsible for compensation if you can prove it was negligent and failed to do necessary repairs. The CAB may be able to help you settle the matter or can point you toward an experienced solicitor, if necessary.

You must go through the local authority's complaints procedure. If your complaint still isn't resolved, you can then ask the Local Government Ombudsman (0845-602-1983 or www.lgo.org.uk) to investigate.

If you're on a low income or claiming welfare benefits, you may be entitled to financial help to pay your council tax or rates (see Chapter 11).

Part II
Keeping on the Right Side of Family and Friends

"Darryl, I want to break off our engagement but I'm keeping the ring."

In this part . . .

In this part, I cover how the law affects relationships and the family. The courts don't interfere in family life unless they're asked to do so, but laws do exist on who can marry and what rights marriages and civil partnerships give the people involved. For example, a popular myth is that cohabitees who live together without a marriage or civil partnership certificate have almost as many rights as those who do exchange their vows, but that's just not the case. You can find information in the following chapters about how the legal status of your partnership affects your rights over children, property, assets, and even any pension funds and about what happens when a relationship breaks down.

Chapter 7 deals with children, both from the point of view of their parents and their upbringing, and from the point of view of the children and when they acquire various rights for themselves.

In any kind of relationship, you need to think ahead and plan so that any property, savings, or assets you have go to the people you want to benefit when you're no longer around, so Chapter 8 looks at the importance of wills and financial planning.

Chapter 6

Managing Relationships

• •

In This Chapter

▶ Knowing your rights if you're living together

▶ Understanding the responsibilities that come with the wedding ring

▶ Pairing up in a civil partnership

▶ Breaking up

▶ Agreeing on how to divide your worldly goods

• •

*T*hese days, many people opt to live together rather than getting married – taking the view that a marriage certificate is just a piece of paper and makes no difference. However, that's not the case. That little piece of paper makes a big difference to the rights each partner has and to their responsibilities toward one another. Registering a civil partnership, too, changes the legal nature of a couple's relationship.

Couples who do decide to tie the knot often live together for a while first. That means that the legal status of their relationship goes through different phases. Yet most couples make those life-changing decisions without any legal advice. Unromantic as it may seem, you should read a book on the legalities of marriage or spend half and hour with a solicitor and an accountant in addition to deciding where and how to plan your big day or which house to buy. Ironically, probably the most important knowledge to arm yourself with is what your rights are if the relationship breaks down.

This chapter outlines your legal rights and responsibilities when living together, marrying, entering into a civil partnership, and splitting up. This area of law is very complex, particularly when it comes to divorce and the dissolution of partnerships. Decisions made by the courts on how to divide up possessions depend entirely on that couple's circumstances – so if you do find yourself in that situation, you need good legal advice from a specialist solicitor.

Living Together

In the past, financial incentives lured couples to get married. They could claim the married couple's allowance, for example, which gave them more untaxed income. But that incentive has gone. It may not be for this reason, but more couples are choosing not to marry. About seven out of ten first partnerships are cohabitations, and they last on average two years, according to One Plus One, the research organisation (www.oneplusone.org.uk).

If couples decide to live together rather than marrying, they don't have the same legal rights as married couples. While the relationship is working well, this difference doesn't matter much. However, when it comes to splitting up or one partner dying, it can make a big difference. The law assumes that if the partners wanted each other to have the legal protection that marriage would give them, then they would have married or entered into a civil partnership.

How cohabitation changes things

When two people live together, it may change everything, and yet change nothing. One doesn't automatically own a share in the property if it's in the other's name, for example. The father doesn't automatically have rights over the children if his name isn't on the birth certificate, or he doesn't have a court order giving him parental rights (see Chapter 7). One won't automatically inherit anything if the other dies.

It's not very romantic to think about legal and financial issues at the height of a great passion, but nearly two-thirds of people think that they have rights they just don't have. You can live together for 60 years in the UK, apart from Scotland, and it makes no difference to your legal rights. Marriage or civil partnership, on the other hand, does change things by giving those partners legal rights over property, children, and other assets.

When you move into a house or flat owned by someone else, you have no rights over that property. If the relationship falls apart and someone has to move out, it will be you unless children are involved. If you ask the court to intervene, the judge may decide that you should go on living in the family home if the children are to stay with you even though your partner owns it outright. The courts are reluctant to issue these kinds of occupation orders, but if they do, the order is likely to say that you can stay in the family home while the children are in full-time education. What the court is unlikely to do, unless you have put a lot of money into mortgage repayments or the structure and fabric of the building – such as paying for a new roof or central heatin is transfer ownership of the home or part of it to you. Just paying the bills and keeping house don't count.

If you both buy the home together and own it jointly, you'll own it 50/50, and the court won't usually give either of you a bigger share. Again, one of you may stay put in the home with the children until they leave education.

The courts take a different approach to married couples and same-sex couples in civil partnerships. (See the section 'Being part of a same sex couple,' later in this chapter.) If you're living together and not married or in a civil partnership, you don't have a legal obligation to keep one another, so if you split up, you can't claim maintenance for yourself. You may, however, be able to claim child support for children (see Chapter 7). If you don't make a will, your partner won't inherit anything on your death; everything you own will go to your family. If your cohabitee does inherit through your will, she will have to pay inheritance tax; married partners do not.

For all of these reasons, you need legal advice so that you know where you stand before you move in with someone. You can draw up a trust deed setting out who owns what proportion of the home and what's to happen if you split up. Making a will and deciding what legal rights and responsibilities each partner has regarding the children is important. Check out the Web site www.oneplusone.org.uk or contact your nearest Citizens Advice Bureau for more information and for the details of solicitors who specialise in family law. You can find the CAB details in the phone book.

Common law marriages

The Marriage Act of 1753 basically put an end to common law marriages. The law in Scotland is slightly different to the rest of the UK, but elsewhere, only legal marriages conducted in church or in buildings registered for civil marriages and overseen by registrars give the partners the legal status of a married couple. You may choose to have the type of ceremony that would once have sufficed as a marriage 'in the eyes of God', such as jumping over the broom, plighting your troth, and handfasting, with the exchange of rings, but it won't stand up in the eyes of the law.

In Scotland, couples who have been living together may be treated as if they are 'married by habitation and repute' or by 'custom and repute.' If the courts are asked to make decisions about the division of property or assets, judges will treat them the same as if they had married.

Being part of a same-sex couple

If you're living together as a same-sex couple, you're in the same position as a heterosexual couple living together. (See the earlier section 'How cohabitation changes things.') However, since December 2005, you can register a *civil partnership,* which gives you very similar rights to those of a marriage.

Tying the Knot

Despite the number of people living together, marriage is still popular in the UK, with nearly nine out of ten people questioned saying that they'd like to marry at some point. Not all of those people will be marrying for the first time! Experience doesn't seem to be putting people off, and statistics show that people who marry are five times more likely to stay together than those who cohabit. So there must be something to be said for marriage!

Knowing who can and who can't get married

Young people in Scotland can get married at 16 whether their parents give consent or not. In the rest of the UK, you can marry at 16 only with the consent of both parents; if that consent isn't forthcoming, you must wait until you're 18, apply for a court order, or elope to Scotland. That's why Gretna Green is seen as such a romantic place – it's the first stop over the border into Scotland where 16- and 17-year-olds from England and Wales can legally marry without their parents knowing. After the couple is married, the marriage is legal, even though they didn't get the necessary consent.

Before 1929, believe it or not, boys could marry at 14 and girls at 12. Now, if people marry before they are 16, they're breaking the law, and the marriage will be null and void.

You also have to be *free to marry* – that is, not already married to someone else. If you do marry while still legally married, the second marriage is bigamous and void. You must also both be entering into the marriage of your own free will. If you're forced into it (and that doesn't mean you did it because you wanted to please your mum) by real fear and under real duress, the marriage won't be valid. This situation may be the case in some arranged marriages. If you didn't know what you were doing – because some had spiked your drink, for example, or as in the recent case of a 101-year-old woman who asked at the register office, 'Why am I here' – the marriage is invalid.

You don't have the legal right to marry anyone you want. A man can't marry his mother, daughter, grandmother, granddaughter, sister, aunt, or niece, and a woman can't marry her male equivalents. Cousins can marry, but complications arise when a mother or father-in-law wants to marry a son or daughter-in-law; or people want to marry step or adopted relations. If you want to marry a close relation, you need to take legal advice.

Homosexual couples can register civil partnerships, which gives them similar rights to the rights married couples have. Ceremonies occur in register offices or other buildings licensed for civil partnerships, and a few church ministers will do blessings. You're treated the same as a married couple for inheritance and capital gains tax. If the partnership breaks down, it can be dissolved after one year. One difference between civil partnership and marriage is that if you marry a Lord, you won't become a Lady!

Following the rules of engagement

There are no rules of engagement. You don't have to get engaged, and if you do and then break it off, you can't be forced to go through with the marriage. Before 1970, if you promised to marry and then changed your mind, you could be sued for breach of contract; that's no longer the case today.

If your fiancé breaks off the engagement, you can't do anything about it. If you've already spent a lot of money arranging the wedding, apart from the loss of pride and the emotional upset, you may have a large hole in your finances, but you can't get that money back.

A bigger problem may be deciding what happens to a house or any other possessions you bought together. You'll probably have to sell the house, unless one of you can buy out the other person's share, and then split the rest 50/50. (Don't take that literally as a friend did and chop everything in two with an axe.) Anything that clearly belonged to one of you when you got together still belongs to that person.

If you can't agree on how to divide jointly bought possessions, you can ask the court to decide, but that option is expensive. Try mediation first. For more information on mediation, see the section 'Separating informally,' later in this chapter.

However, if you were given engagement presents, you need to return them to the people who gave them. That's because the law sees it that they were given on the understanding that you would get married. The chances are that no one will want their presents back. Engagement presents aren't usually big gifts. If they don't want them back, you should keep the ones given by your family and friends, and your ex should keep the ones from his family and friends.

Usually when you give someone a gift, it's a gift, and they're entitled to keep it even if you change your mind and want it back. But if you have given each other engagement presents, as with presents from family and friends, the giver is entitled to have them back – because they were given on the understanding that a marriage was to occur. You'll probably feel like throwing them at your former betrothed anyway, but even if he was the one to call the whole thing off, he's entitled to get the presents back – apart from the engagement ring!

You can keep the ring unless it was given to you with (again the legal term is 'on' rather than 'with') the understanding that because it was a family heirloom, for example, it was to be returned if things went wrong.

Planning religious ceremonies

If you decide on a wedding in the parish church, the vicar will be licensed to carry it out. If it's to be in a Catholic church, synagogue, or other religious meeting house, a Superintendent Registrar needs to issue a certificate, and a registrar may need to supervise the signing of the register. Some vicars and priests marry a couple only if one of them belongs to the church or lives in the area, and they may insist that you attend services. If one of you has already been married, you need divorce or death certificates to prove that you're free to marry. Some vicars refuse to marry couples if one or both have divorced, and as a divorcee, you won't be allowed to remarry in the Catholic church.

Talk to the vicar, priest, or minister and contact your local register office for all the information you need. You need to pay fees for the marriage certificate, the church, and to the registrar if one has to attend.

Two witnesses must sign the register for the marriage to be valid. These can be friends and family or people you stop in the street.

Opting for civil ceremonies

Civil ceremonies take place in the register office or in other buildings approved for weddings, such as upmarket hotels. If the ceremony isn't in a church, a registrar conducts it, and the content is completely non-religious. Some couples marry in a civil ceremony because they aren't allowed to marry in their church – for example, because one or the other is divorced – and then have a blessing in the church. The fees depend on where the ceremony's located. You need to produce documents to prove your identity and that you're free to marry. Divorce or death certificates are needed if one of you has been married before.

Posting the banns

The *banns* are read out when a marriage is to take place in the parish church. The banns give the details of the two people who are to marry. That means that the names of the couple are read out on three consecutive Sundays, and then the wedding has to take place within three months.

The phrase is often also used inaccurately to describe the three weeks notice that has to be given to the registrars if the wedding is to take place somewhere other than a parish church, such as a hotel, register office, or chapel.

In some situations, you can get special licences to be married the next day or anywhere at any time. Usually, these cases occur when one of the couple has just been posted abroad or is in hospital and too ill to leave.

Understanding the Legal Responsibilities of Marriage

Some people take the view that a marriage certificate is just a piece of paper and that living together is the same thing. On a daily basis, that viewpoint may appear to be the case, but marriage does change your legal relationship to each other. You have legal responsibilities and rights toward each other after you've exchanged vows and rings.

You become liable to *keep* each other – which means to look after each other's welfare as well as keeping each other financially. You have a duty to live together, and it's implied that you will have a reasonable amount of sex with each other. What is a reasonable amount of sex has stimulated quite a lot of debate for couples down the ages! If you don't live together, have sex, or keep each other, one of you may have grounds for divorce. (See the section 'Divorcing and being free to remarry', later in this chapter.)

If the married couple never *consummates* the marriage – they never have penetrative sex – it may be possible to have the marriage annulled. But there's no sexual implication in a civil partnership – two friends of the same sex, who don't intend to be in a sexual relationship, can register a civil partnership.

Your nationality isn't affected by marriage. If you were born in the UK and have British nationality, you keep that citizenship even if your spouse has foreign nationality. You may be entitled to dual nationality, depending on the laws of the other country (refer to Chapter 2). Spouses can't be made to give evidence against each other in criminal court cases because they have the right to tell each other things in confidence that they wouldn't tell other people, and the courts respect that right. The courts won't get involved in a marriage that's working, but they can become involved if it's breaking down and end the marriage or make decisions about how property and assets should be divided (see the later section Dividing the Assets') and on the arrangements for the children (see Chapter 7).

Both marriages and civil partnerships give the partners the right to inherit from the other's estate (see Chapter 8), which they don't have if they're living together. They're each entitled to the single person's tax allowance so that each can earn the same amount before they become liable for tax on the rest of their income. Husbands and wives aren't liable for each other's individual debts, but if they borrow jointly, they're both liable for the whole of the debts, and both are liable for the household bills.

If you're married and want to give your spouse a gift of something valuable that you own, such as a painting, you can, but make sure that a document proves the transfer. If you go bankrupt at a later date, your spouse may lose the painting if you can't prove that you no longer own it. Talk to an accountant about capital gains tax and the advantages of transferring assets between spouses.

Any wills made before the marriage ceremony are invalid unless they were made specifically setting out what was to happen after the marriage took place. Make a new will as soon as possible after the marriage. Otherwise, your possessions may be divided up in a way you wouldn't have wanted.

Drawing up prenuptial agreements

Prenuptial agreements, or marriage contracts, are a good way of setting out exactly what each partner can expect from the marriage, but they're not the most romantic of concepts, as they're often used mainly to set out what will happen if you separate or divorce. Very rich people trying to protect their wealth from grasping ex-partners are the main users of such agreements.

However, prenuptial agreements aren't legally enforceable. A court can make a different set of decisions if one partner chooses to ignore the agreement, but will take the contents of the agreement into consideration.

You can cover just about anything in a prenuptial agreement, such as who receives the family home and who pays the other how much in a settlement. You can also put in the agreement things such as your decisions about having children.

The longer the marriage goes on, the more likely it is that the original agreement may no longer be appropriate. Your circumstances will change, so you may want to update your prenuptial agreement with other marriage agreements from time to time.

Getting married abroad

If you get married abroad, the UK recognises the marriage as legal and valid as long as you complied with all the laws relating to marriage of the country in which the wedding took place and as long as you were both capable of marrying according to the rules of your countries of domicile. Your country of domicile is the one in which you permanently live or the one you intend to go back to live in permanently after a period abroad (see Chapter 2). If your domicile is the UK, you have to comply with all the rules explained in the section 'Knowing who can and can't get married,' earlier in this chapter.

Changing names

You can use whatever surname you like. Marrying doesn't mean that a wife has to take the surname of her husband, and increasingly women keep their own. Some use their own surname at work and use their husband's name for everything else, such as social contacts and bank accounts.

A husband can take his wife's surname. Or the couple may decide to use both, with or without a hyphen. People living together may decide to use the same surname. The partners in a same-sex relationship can do the same. Changing your name is simply a matter of using the new name you've chosen and letting anyone who needs to know, know. You can't change your name on your birth certificate, however.

Some places want proof of a name change, such as the bank or the tax office. If you're changing your name because you're getting married, your marriage certificate is usually enough proof. If you're not changing your name as the result of marriage, some organisations you do business with will accept a note signed by a JP, solicitor, doctor, or some other respected pillar of the community, saying that the new name is the name you're usually known by. Others may want more formal documentation.

You can make a sworn statement, drawn up by a solicitor, called a *statutory declaration*. You will have to pay for this service, so shop around. The most recognised document for a change of name is a *deed poll*. People often say they've changed their name by deed poll when what they've done is change their name and then had a deed poll drawn up by a solicitor as proof of the name change. It has to be signed, witnessed, and stamped by another solicitor and can be registered with the Supreme Court or just kept as permanent proof of the change of name.

If you want to change a child's name, see Chapter 7.

Splitting Up Is Hard to Do: Separations and Annulments

Breaking up is hard to do, according to the song, and that's very true unless couples can agree on who should have what and come to their own amicable arrangements about the children, the home, and any other assets.

Leaving because of domestic violence

Sometimes the cause of a separation is domestic violence. Sometimes a separation leads to domestic violence. The police are becoming more willing to act in these cases, and anyone, in any kind of relationship – whether living together or married, in a heterosexual or same-sex relationship – is protected by law.

Various legal options are open to someone who is being subjected to domestic violence. Two acts offer protection: the *Protection from Harassment Act 1997* and the *Family Law Act 1996*. Under these two acts, the courts can issue a variety of orders to stop harassment, assault, and threatening behaviour, and you may be able to get *nonmolestation* or *occupation orders* – injunctions – to keep the violent partner away from you, the children, and the family home. If these orders come with *power of arrest* attached, the police have greater powers to intervene.

The Family Proceedings Panel at the Magistrates' Court, the High Court, and the County Court can all get involved in domestic violence cases, and the procedures are different and can

be long drawn out. You need good legal advice as to which court and which orders best apply in your particular case. The Citizens Advice Bureau can give you details of solicitors with experience of domestic violence cases. You can find CAB details in the phone book.

Deciding to leave the family home with or without the children is a big step. If you're facing violence, you may have no choice. Once you've left the family home, it may be harder to return and get the violent partner to leave. It may also be harder to claim your share of the property and other assets. If you can, take legal advice before you leave home. If you have to leave, get advice as soon as possible afterward.

Many organisations can help. If you have access to the Internet, you can find a long list of organisations by typing 'domestic violence' into a search engine. Two of these are Refuge (0808-200-0247 or www.refuge.org.uk), which runs a national helpline and has refuges around the country, and Mankind (0870-794-4124 www.mankind.org.uk), which helps male victims.

The courts should be asked to make decisions only as a last resort. Hiring solicitors and taking legal action can turn out to be a long, drawn-out, and costly business. However, you should seek legal advice about your situation if you're splitting from your partner or spouse. Knowing your legal rights may help you reach an agreement. You can take advice without contracting the solicitor to act for you.

Separating informally

If you aren't married or in a civil partnership, you can separate as informally as you got together. Neither partner can claim maintenance from the other as they were never under a legal obligation to keep each other financially.

If you have children and property, you may find it difficult to agree about what should happen. You can ask solicitors to act for you or go to court for decisions, but if you can't come to an agreement, try mediation before you bring in the big guns. Ask the Citizens Advice Bureau for details of mediation services in your area. You can find their details in the phone book. Or contact National Family Mediation at 01392-271-610 or www.nfm.u-net.com; the Family Mediation Association at 0808-200-0033 or www.fmassoc.co.uk; or the UK College of Family Mediators at 0117-904-7223 or www.ukcfm.co.uk. Services are throughout the UK, although they seem to be thinner on the ground in Scotland and Northern Ireland, so the waiting lists in those areas may be fairly long. Mediators are there to help you to reach an agreement without resorting to the courts.

If you think that the relationship may be able to be put back on track, you can try *Relate*. It's for people living together, as well as married couples, and offers a range of services, including mediation. You can make an appointment through 0845-130-4016 or find your nearest branch at www.relate.co.uk.

If you ask the courts to make decisions about property, they will look at who owned the property when you started to live together and whether you had the intent to share it. The courts have fewer powers to transfer ownership of property, or a share in a property, between cohabitees than they do if the partners are married or in a civil partnership. If cases involving children, the welfare of those children is high on the court's list of priorities, and the partner who has the children living with them may be allowed to stay in the family home until they leave school, even if he doesn't own a share in the property. The rights of each partner over the children depend on whether both have parental responsibilities. For more information, see Chapter 7.

Married couples can separate, too, on the same kind of informal basis and simply live separately without any intervention from the courts, as long as both partners agree. Nothing says that you have to make the separation formal, draw up any kind of legal agreement between you, or divorce. Many couples simply stay married until one meets someone else they want to marry, and the divorce can be a quick, straightforward, do-it-yourself set of papers, which I explain in the upcoming section 'Divorcing and being free to remarry.'

However, most splits aren't quite so stress free, and even when divorce isn't on the cards, many couples want a more formal arrangement. At any stage in the separation of a married couple, the courts have powers to sort out your financial affairs if you can't agree.

Until a married couple divorces, the marriage is annulled, or a civil partnership is dissolved, the partners can't get married again.

Sometimes when a marriage or any other kind of partnership is in trouble, a bit of time apart can give both people the space to decide what they want to do next. You may decide you were better together and give it another go. Even if you do decide to separate formally or divorce, the time spent apart can take the heat out of the situation and help you agree on a settlement.

Legally separating

If you don't put anything in writing about what's to happen to the children or who is to have what share of the property and assets, you may later disagree about who said what. You can draw up an agreement between you and put it in writing, but if it isn't drawn up with the help of legal advice, a court may later pay little attention to it. Judges take the view that if you agree to something, having had the legal implications fully explained by a solicitor, the agreement should stand, but if you do the same thing without being fully aware of your rights, it shouldn't.

If you draw up a formal deed of separation with the help of solicitors, the courts are much less likely to alter the terms of the agreement. Be careful about making any formal agreement. You must have good legal advice. If the agreement is well thought out and the future implications considered, you're less likely to argue, but you shouldn't be bullied into accepting something, just for the sake of speed, that you may regret later.

You can include in the deed arrangements for the children, the division of assets, and any maintenance. The court still has the power to alter the terms of the agreement. You may find out at a later date that your partner is worth much more money that you were led to believe. In that case, you can ask the court to change the level of maintenance you agreed to.

Another alternative to divorce is *judicial separation*. Some couples who want to avoid divorce, usually for religious reasons, go for this legal alternative. They get a legal document that leaves them free of the obligation to live together. They can apply within the first year of marriage (unlike divorce), and they must have grounds for divorce, such as adultery or unreasonable behaviour. (See the upcoming section 'Divorcing and being free to remarry.') However, they aren't free to remarry. If you take this option, you can apply for a divorce at a later date.

Annulling a marriage

If a marriage isn't valid (rather than broken down) in the first place, it can be *annulled*. If it's annulled, it's as if the marriage never took place. For that reason, people who wouldn't be able to remarry in church if they were divorced may try to have the marriage annulled. You can apply for an annulment at any time after you marry. You don't have to wait a year as you do for divorce.

The marriage may not be valid if any of the following reasons apply:

- ✔ One person is too young.
- ✔ The relationship is too close (for example, you've married your aunt).
- ✔ One partner is already married.
- ✔ Some of the marriage formalities, such as completing the marriage certificate weren't carried out properly.

In such cases, the marriage is *void*. If the marriage isn't consummated, or if one partner didn't consent to the marriage perhaps because of mental health problems or was forced to marry, the marriage is *voidable*. It is also voidable if the woman was pregnant with another man's child without telling her new husband, or one partner had a sexually transmitted disease at the time without the other knowing.

Divorcing and Being Free to Remarry

You can start divorce proceedings, or dissolution in the case of a civil partnership, after you've been married for a year (or two years in Northern Ireland). If the relationship falls apart before that time is up, you can separate, but you'll have to wait to file for divorce – unless the marriage can be annulled (see preceding section).

After this time is up, you have to prove that the marriage has *irretrievably broken down* – the only ground for divorce. By irretrievably broken down, the law means that there's no hope that the marriage can be saved. If the court decides that hope exists, the divorce isn't granted, although that doesn't often happen. In order to prove that the marriage has irretrievably broken down, one of the following five facts must be present:

✔ **Adultery:** If one partner has committed adultery **and** the other finds it intolerable to continue to live together, a court will accept that the marriage has irretrievably broken down because of adultery. The adultery itself isn't enough. One partner has to find it intolerable to live with the other who committed adultery. You can go on living in the same home for up to six months in an attempt to work things out, but if you stay longer, the court will say there isn't proof that the marriage has irretrievably broken down. Adultery doesn't apply to civil partnerships.

✔ **Unreasonable behaviour:** This behaviour is difficult to define. Excessive demands for sex may be unreasonable behaviour, but so can the refusal to have sex. Violence is unreasonable behaviour, but so, too, is a series of small verbal insults that eventually become too much. One partner has to find it intolerable to live with the other's unreasonable behaviour, and what is seen as intolerable for one person to live with may not be seen as intolerable for another.

✔ **Desertion:** If one partner leaves the other against his wishes and without any reason, such as unreasonable behaviour, after two years of living apart, the deserted spouse can apply, or *petition*, for a divorce.

✔ **Separation for two years:** There are two rules about separation. If a couple agrees to separate, one or the other can petition for divorce after two years if they both agree.

✔ **Separation for five years:** If one spouse doesn't agree to a divorce after two years of separation, the person who wants the divorce can petition again after five years without the other's agreement.

If any of these five facts is used to prove that a marriage has irretrievably broken, the couple is allowed to have had a six-month period of living together as a time for trying to get the relationship back on track. If the couple lives together for longer than six months, the divorce won't be granted. If you get back together again for more than six months during five years of separation, the five years will have to start building up again from the date of the second separation.

Gone are the days of gathering photographs and eyewitness accounts from private detectives to prove adultery. Usually one partner admits to adultery, and the third person involved doesn't have to be named. It does mean, though, that some couples are using this approach as a way around separating and waiting for two years.

Unreasonable behaviour is an emotive fact to use on a divorce petition because it can stir up some very hostile reactions in partners who don't believe their behaviour was unreasonable and feel as if all the blame for the failure of the marriage is being left at their door. Even if unreasonable behaviour has occurred, some couples prefer to wait until they've been separated for two years rather than add fuel to their hostility. It can make it harder to reach agreements about children and property if one partner feels unfairly blamed by the other. You can usually prove unreasonable behaviour by describing five or six incidents on the divorce petition and keeping a diary of events.

Marriages are recognised in the UK as long as they comply with the rules of the country you married in and as long as you would have been allowed to marry in the UK. So if you usually live in the UK, you should be able to get your divorce here. If your marriage certificate is in a foreign language, you will need a translation. Otherwise, the same rules apply.

Doing it yourself

If a divorce is straightforward and *undefended* – you both agree to the divorce – you can do it all yourself without any need for solicitors to act for you. If the divorce is *defended* – one partner wants the divorce, but the other doesn't and tries to stop it happening, see the upcoming section 'Defending a divorce petition'.

The most straightforward case is where the partners split up, divide up their property, and wait for two years. They then agree which one should complete the forms to start the ball rolling and then split the costs of the divorce between them. Even when children are involved, if the partners agree on all aspects of the children's future and it's working well, they don't need solicitors. The divorce is an undefended divorce and dealt with by the county court (or the high court in Northern Ireland).

You can get the necessary forms from the court, along with a booklet explaining undefended divorce and what the procedure is. You need to explain why the marriage has irretrievably broken down, and if you have children, you'll have to describe on the forms the arrangements you've made for them. After the court has your *petition,* it sends copies to your former partner, the *defendant,* for his response. If he isn't defending the divorce, the court looks at the petition and grants the *decree nisi* without a court hearing. You receive a copy of the decree nisi through the post. At this stage, you still aren't divorced. You have to apply to the court six weeks and one day after the nisi arrives for your *decree absolute*. After the decree absolute is granted, you're divorced and free to remarry.

If you're dissolving a civil partnership, the first order you're granted is a *conditional order for dissolution,* followed six weeks later by the *final order for dissolution.*

Everything can go through the court process without a court hearing, but the court may want to discuss the arrangements for the children and order a hearing. The children may be asked to go to that hearing if they're old enough. Only when the court is happy with the arrangements for the children will it grant the decree absolute or final order for dissolution.

You may get some help to pay for initial advice and assistance from a solicitor if you need it. The court fees are £300, and you pay £40 for the decree absolute. If you're on a low income, you may be exempt from the fees.

Dealing with a more complicated divorce

If your circumstances are more complicated, you may not be able to sort them out without outside help, and that's when the costs can pile up. An undefended divorce itself costs around £340. When people talk about a divorce being expensive, it's the solicitor's bills and the amount they've had to hand over to their former partner that adds up. The more you spend on solicitors, the less you have to divide, so try to come to an agreement if at all possible. However, it makes sense to have an appointment with a specialist solicitor so that you know what your rights are and the kinds of decisions the court might make in your case about children and property.

If you can't agree on the division of property and other assets and on the arrangements for the children, try mediation. *Mediation* is a process aimed at helping you reach an agreement, which can then be drawn up in the form of a legal document. (See the section 'Separating legally,' earlier in the chapter, for more details.) Mediation is much cheaper than hiring solicitors, and, in fact, many mediators are trained solicitors. If your income and savings are fairly low, you may even be entitled to free mediation.

If mediation fails, you'll probably have little choice but to each hire a solicitor. At that point, the two solicitors are duty bound to advise their clients on their rights and to get the best possible settlement. They'll try to come to a settlement agreeable to both divorcing partners, but if not, the courts will be asked to decide on who the children should live with, what contact the other parent should have with them, and how the family home and other assets should be divided up. The divorce itself goes through the legal process at the same time that all the other, or *ancillary matters,* are being sorted out. The ancillary matters are the children, the property and any other assets, maintenance, and child support. These matters can all be dealt with while the divorce goes through. Even if you can't agree over the ancillary matters, you can still have an undefended divorce. If the one thing that you agree on is that you both want a divorce, it will be undefended.

The court has the power to intervene to make sure that a financial settlement is reached, that property is divided fairly, and that the children's welfare has been put first. After the decree nisi is granted, a judge won't grant the final decree absolute until he is happy with the arrangements for the children. The divorce may be granted, and you may be free to remarry, but the financial wrangling may go on for years afterward. Either partner can go back to ask for a variation of the orders if circumstances change.

With all the solicitor and court time involved, it's easy to see why divorces can cost hundreds of thousands of pounds. But the divorce itself isn't the costly bit. You may be able to get financial help through the legal aid system to go to court over the ancillary matters, but usually, if you get a settlement of money or property, you have to pay back that legal aid. The court can order it to be paid back at a later date – after the children have left school and the family home is sold, for example. If that's the case, interest is added on to the amount you owe.

Defending a divorce petition

In most cases, there's little point in defending a divorce, and the divorce can go ahead undefended, even though you're arguing about everything else. You may disagree about the children, property, assets, and maintenance, but that's not the same as defending the divorce. You can defend a divorce only if you don't want to be divorced and you have a good reason.

You may defend a divorce on the grounds that the facts in the petition aren't true; that the marriage hasn't irretrievably broken down; that you have lived together for more than the six months the court accepts as time to patch things up; or that you'd suffer grave financial hardship even though you've already lived apart for five years. You can also ask the court not to grant the decree absolute because you aren't happy with the financial arrangements made for you.

You're really only delaying the inevitable. If your partner wants to divorce you, she will get the divorce eventually. All you will do by defending it is to make your point and run up bigger legal bills. You may, however, qualify for financial help to defend your divorce if you qualify.

Divorcing if you're Jewish

If you're Jewish and want to remarry someone else who is Jewish and in your faith, you will need a Jewish divorce, called a *Get,* as well as your civil divorce. The Get needs the consent of both partners. Under The Divorce (Religious Marriages) Act 2002, the decree nisi can be granted, but the decree absolute won't be unless a Get has been granted. This law is aimed at stopping one partner from agreeing to a civil divorce but not obtaining a Get in order to stop the other partner from remarrying another Jew.

Think about the divorce and the rest of the issues as separate – hard to do, I know. The divorce can go ahead undefended and be straightforward, but you can still battle it out on all the other fronts.

A defended divorce itself, without hearings to settle matters about children and money, can cost you around £4,000. If you each pay that amount of money, you have much less in the pot to divide between you. Add to that another £5,000 or more to settle disputes over the children and the finances, and the family savings can disappear rapidly.

Dividing the assets

Your *assets* consist of all the homes, accounts, savings, valuables, shares, and so on that you may have accumulated between you. If you can reach an agreement as to how your assets should be divided, you don't have to go to court. When a marriage ends, the courts – if asked by the couple to intervene – have a free hand in dividing up the assets between the two partners. No set rules set out what each spouse will get, and each case is looked at individually. A solicitor can advise you on what he thinks the outcome will be, given decisions made in recent similar cases. The same applies to the dissolution of civil partnerships.

Couples who are living together often keep their assets separate and set up a joint account into which they put their contributions toward the household bills. Because they have no legal obligation to keep each other, they can leave and take their own assets with them. It's then a matter of deciding who owns what and, if items were bought together, who should have those possessions. If you have children, many of the possessions may be left in the home with the children for their benefit.

Married couples and couples in civil partnerships will probably face tougher decisions about who should have what, as they're likely to have tied their finances together more closely. They may share joint accounts and investments, as well as valuables and pensions. How these items are divided depends on whether the couple has decided to divorce or just to separate. It also depends, to a large extent, on whether there are children to be supported and on how much each partner earns or is capable of earning.

Married partners have a legal responsibility to keep each other, so the lower earning partner may be entitled to maintenance payments from the higher earner. Take legal advice from a solicitor who specialises in this kind of case. The Citizens Advice Bureau can give you a list – you can find its details in the phone book.

If the courts become involved in making decisions about how assets are to be divided, they examine all the details of the marriage: how long it lasted; what the financial situation of each partner was before they married; what each partner earned and contributed during the marriage; what each partner is capable of earning in future; and any savings and pensions. Every little detail is considered. Some spouses are keen to reach a settlement without the court's help so that they don't have to reveal the full extent of their wealth. If you think your spouse may be hiding a few hundred thousand pounds from you, you may lose out by not taking legal advice.

Some couples want, above all else, to come to a final settlement that allows them to be free of each other financially – a *clean break*. The court has to look at whether that's possible. It may give the lower earning partner a bigger share of the assets as long as there is no claim for maintenance. A clean break isn't possible if there are children; both parents are liable for the children until they're at least 16, and usually beyond, while they're in full-time education.

Going to court is expensive, and anything you pay to solicitors and in court costs means less in the pot to be divided between the two warring partners.

Dividing the property

When it comes to deciding what should happen to the family home, the big question is what's best for the children. The court has the power to transfer ownership of bricks and mortar between divorcing partners in whatever way it thinks best. For more information on property division, refer to Chapter 3.

If the couple isn't married, the court has more limited powers to transfer property between the two of you.

Paying child support

If children are involved, you need to think about child support payments (see Chapter 7). The higher earning partner may have the children living with them and pay for the children's upbringing. If not, the lower earning parent is entitled to claim payments from the higher earner on behalf of the children. If the higher earner refuses to pay, the courts and the Child Support Agency can calculate the amount and collect the payments. If a father refuses to pay and disputes that he is the father, the Child Support Agency may require a DNA test (see Chapter 7).

Paying maintenance

Every spouse has the right to be maintained by his spouse. Even if the couple stops living together or the marriage ends in divorce, the spouse with the lower income may have the right to maintenance from the other. If the maintenance can be agreed between the two of you, you don't need to go to court.

If you do decide to apply to the court for a maintenance order, which court you apply to will depend on whether you're getting divorced. If you're getting divorced, then you can apply to the County Court with divorce jurisdiction. If you're separating but not divorcing, you can apply to the Family Proceedings Court. (Refer to Chapter 1, which explains how the court system works.)

What was a reasonable income for one household is very rarely going to be enough to support two. Unless you're mega-rich, a separation or divorce is going to mean a drop in your standard of living.

The amount of child support the higher earning partner has to pay is usually worked out first, and then it's decided what's left, if any, for the lower earning spouse. The court also looks at what other possible sources of income the lower-income partner may have – such as welfare benefits (see Chapter 11) – and whether this partner can go back to work. The person who has to pay maintenance won't be left with less to live on than he would get in welfare benefits from the state. If there is a second family, their needs will be taken into consideration, too.

If the ex-spouse who is getting maintenance remarries, the maintenance stops.

Dividing the pension

Sometimes the single most valuable asset the family has is the pension. If you're taking legal advice about the possibility of divorce, don't forget to mention the pension. The courts can order pensions to be shared or split. The pension holder gets to keep a part of the pension fund, and the partner who isn't a pension holder gets a share to put into a separate pension of her own. The figure that's used to make the calculation is the *cash equivalent transfer value*. Basically, that's the amount of money you would get if you decided to take your money out of your current pension fund and put it into a different fund. The court decides on how much of that amount the pension holder should keep and how much should be given to the other spouse.

Chapter 7

Having Children

The days of 2 parents and 2.4 children are long past. The birth rate in the UK has dropped to around 1.68 children per family, which is not enough children to keep the population from falling. There are many arguments about whether that's a good or bad thing.

It's not just the birth rate that's changed in recent years. The family unit has, too. Children increasingly live with just one parent; two parents who are married; couples made up of one parent and that parent's new partner or spouse; and same-sex couples. They may also live with someone like a grandparent who has a residence order that gives them rights and responsibilities toward the child, or with adoptive or foster parents.

The law has had to keep up by changing the rights of the various adults involved in a child's life so that they can have parental rights and responsibility over children who may not be their own. Parents with parental rights and responsibilities toward their children have an equal say in how they're brought up until the age of 18. This chapter explains those parental rights and responsibilities, as well as the rights of the children.

Creating the Family Unit

Whatever the set-up in the home, someone has to take legal responsibility for a child until he becomes legally responsible at the age of 18. Knowing who has parental responsibility is important because that person has the right to make decisions about how the child is brought up, such as choosing a school and religion, disciplining, and deciding on the child's name. The child usually takes the nationality of the father or of the place of birth, but the rules are complicated (refer to Chapter 2).

Single parents

Single parents (mostly women) and their children make up a large proportion of the family units in the UK. Some parents are single because a relationship broke down before or after the child was born; some because they've chosen to bring up children on their own; and some because their partners have deserted them or died.

When a woman has a child and isn't married to the father, even if they're living together, she can refuse to have the father's name put on the birth certificate. If that's the case, he can have parental responsibility over the child only if she gives him responsibility or if he gets a court order. If a woman isn't living with the father of her child when that child is born, she's unlikely to give him parental responsibility, and a court is unlikely to agree if he applies, unless he can pass the threefold test of attachment, commitment, and motive. If the mother, or the court, refuses the father parental responsibilities, the single mother has the right to make all the decisions about the child.

If the mother is living with the father at the time of the birth and does give the father parental responsibility, she can't later change her mind. Even if they split up and she becomes a single parent, he still has those rights and responsibilities unless a court takes them away. He has an equal say in how the child is brought up until the child reaches 18.

A single parent, therefore, may have sole parental responsibility or may share parental responsibility with a former partner.

A man who has parental responsibility goes on having that responsibility until the child is 18. If the mother leaves him literally holding the baby because she walks out and leaves the child behind or she dies, the father becomes a single parent with parental responsibility for his child. The mother keeps her rights, too, unless a court takes them away.

Single people can also adopt children. When you adopt, you're given full parental responsibility; the birth parents lose all rights. To be considered single, you must be unmarried or permanently living apart from your spouse.

Living together

If the parents of a child aren't married at the time of the birth but they are living together, only the mother has automatic legal rights and responsibilities

When you don't want to be a parent

If you're pregnant and don't want the baby, you may be able to have an abortion. Doctors can carry out abortion during the first 24 weeks for your pregnancy if going on with the pregnancy would risk your life or your or your other children's physical or mental health; or there's a risk the baby may be born with a serious abnormality. To do so, you need the consent of two doctors, and you may have to pay for the abortion to be done at a fee-paying clinic. The Internet contains a lot of information about abortion, but you should talk to your doctor first about where to go for further advice.

If you're told you're a dad and you don't believe it, you can resolve the issue by taking a DNA test. You have to pay for a test at a private clinic, which will need a sample of DNA from you and the baby. (The sample is obtained by rubbing a swab on the inside of the cheek.) Of course, the baby's mother must give her consent.

In addition, a court may order you to have a DNA test if you're disputing your paternity, or the Child Support Agency may want a test if the mother has named you as the father. (For more details on child support, see the section 'Paying Child Support', later in this chapter.)

Anyone thinking of abortion or paternity testing may want some counselling before taking the decision. Talk to your GP.

If you want to avoid the possibility of becoming a parent, you can have a vasectomy or be sterilised. However, the operation is not 100 per cent guaranteed, and you do have a very small chance that you may be left holding the baby.

The Department of Health has a code of practice that clinics have to sign up to. You can get more information on DNA testing and abortion and a list of approved clinics from NHS Direct at www.nhsdirect.nhs.uk or call 0845-4647.

for that child. If the father wants an equal say in how the child is brought up, he has to acquire parental responsibility by getting the mother's consent or a court order.

Since December 2003, if both parents register the birth together, the father automatically acquires parental responsibility. Alternatively, both parents can sign a parental responsibility agreement at a local court and lodge it with the Principal Registry of the Family Division at 1st Avenue House, 42–49 High Holborn, London WC1V 6NP –0207-947-6000, www.hmcourts-service.gov.uk. If the mother doesn't agree to share parental responsibilities, the only way the father can acquire them – even though they're living together – is to apply to the court for a Parental Responsibility Order under the Children Act 1989.

Parents who are living together won't necessarily both have parental responsibility over their children, and people who are living together won't necessarily both be parents. It's unlikely to do a relationship much good in the long run to refuse the father of your children, with whom you live, parental rights and responsibility for his children, and he may well get them anyway through the court. However, if you're in any doubt about his suitability to have rights and responsibilities over a child, think very carefully before taking the step of refusing them.

Unmarried couples can adopt. If you're granted an adoption order, you both have parental rights and responsibilities over your adopted child, and the birth parents lose their rights.

Married parents

If parents are married at the time of a child's birth, they both automatically have parental rights and responsibilities over the child – unless a court later takes them away from one or both. They both have equal say in how the child is brought up until the age of 18. Either parent can register the birth or make decisions for the child, such as how the child is educated or what medical treatment he should receive.

One parent may lose rights and responsibilities in a divorce situation, although it's unlikely. Both may lose their rights if a child is taken into care, or a court grants an adoption order to someone else.

Dealing with Different Stork Arrival Methods

In days gone by, the stork either delivered, or it didn't. If it didn't, the only realistic alternative was adoption or fostering. Now, with many couples settling down later and having children only after they've established their careers and bought a home, more couples are having *in vitro fertilisation* (IVF) treatment in order to conceive. Although the medical advances have been enormous and women can conceive in their 50s and even 60s using IVF, the procedure still has a very low success rate and is extremely expensive. When IVF fails, some would-be parents turn to surrogate mothers to have the baby for them, although this situation is still rare.

The adoption option

Adoption may be an option if you haven't conceived or given birth to a living child. Relatively few babies are available for adoption, but many older children are waiting for homes.

You may even have a child who is related to you and living with you who you'd like to adopt. Contact your local authority social services or social work department for advice and information about adoption. Otherwise, contact the adoption agencies. Social workers can give you a list of agencies, or you contact the British Agencies for Adoption and Fostering at www.baaf.org.uk or 0207-593-2060. The agencies can tell you whether you can be considered as adoptive parents.

Since the Adoption and Children Act 2002, more people can apply to adopt, including:

✔ Couples who are married and both over 21.

✔ A parent and a step-parent

✔ A single person who is at least 21 and unmarried, or married but permanently living apart from her spouse

✔ Unmarried couples, including same-sex couples

The various adoption agencies have other criteria they use to decide whether you should be approved as an adoptive parent. For example, many people complain of being told they're too old.

The Adoption and Children Act 2002 set up a register of all children waiting to be adopted and of all the families approved to become adoptive parents. A baby or child can be put up for adoption by the birth parents through an adoption agency. Social workers at the local authority can get a court order allowing them to put a child in their care up for adoption.

If you want to adopt a child who is related to you and living with you, you can apply to the court for an adoption order after three months. If an agency places a child with you, after 12 months you can apply to the courts. The courts usually want the consent of the birth parents, but can proceed without it. The courts can then

✔ Reject your application.

✔ Make an interim order lasting up to two years, during which time the child lives with you, and you can reapply for an adoption order.

✔ Make an adoption order giving you full parental rights over the child.

You have more chance of finding a child to adopt if you're willing to take an older child or siblings. Most people want babies and single children.

If you want to adopt a child from abroad, you must go through the same checks and balances as you do in the UK, or it's a criminal offence. Local authorities have to provide adoption services between the UK and other countries.

People over 18 who were adopted as a child can get the details of their birth parents from the original birth register. The Children Act 1989 set up an adoption Contact Register so that both adopted people and their relatives can have their name put on it in the hope of tracing relatives or being traced. It's kept at the General Register Office, PO Box 2, Southport, PR8 2JD – 0870-243-7788.

Under the Adoption and Children Act 2002, birth relatives can ask an intermediary service to contact an adopted adult and find out whether she would welcome contact with the birth family. For more information, visit the General Register Office Web site at www.gro.gov.uk.

Step-parenting

Your future children may come to you as part of a package when you meet your new partner. As a step-parent, you don't have any legal parental rights over a child unless all the parents involved give consent, or you apply and get a court order giving you parental responsibility.

You can apply to adopt the children of your new husband or wife. The two of you have to adopt them jointly. The courts aren't usually keen on this arrangement because it means taking all rights away from the other natural parent who no longer lives with the children. If they're still active in their children's lives, a court is unlikely to grant your application.

A more acceptable alternative is to apply, jointly with your partner, for a residence order instead. (For more details, see the section 'Absent Parents,' later in this chapter.) The other parent of your new spouse's children is unlikely to want to lose their rights. By obtaining a residence order saying that the children should live with you, you receive parental responsibility without taking it away from the other parent.

If you have the consent of both parents of your new spouse's children or your spouse is happy for you to adopt his children and the other parent has died, for example, you can both apply to adopt them as a couple. Contact social workers at your local authority.

Conceiving through IVF

Around one in seven couples is infertile – they have been trying for a baby for 12 months without success. For some of them, IVF is the answer to their prayers. Others try and spend thousands of pounds on the procedure, only to be disappointed. The rest decide that as nature hasn't granted their wishes, it's just not going to happen.

Changing a stepchild's name

A child or young person can change his own name once he reaches the age of 16. Before that time, the parents can change the child's name. The most likely reason for wanting to change a child's name is that the mother is remarrying, plans to change her name, and wants everyone in the new family to have the same name. However, many fathers object to their children having another man's name.

Under the Children Act 1989, if one parent – for the sake of simplicity, say the mother – has a residence order allowing the child to go on living with her after a split, she can change the child's name only if the father, who has parental responsibility, agrees. If agreement isn't forthcoming, the mother needs to apply to the court. If no residence order is in place, she can go ahead and change the child's name, and the father has to apply to the court to stop it.

You don't need to go through a legal procedure to change a name. You just start using the child's new name and let everyone else know the change. However, you can't change the name on the birth certificate, and you may, at some stage, need proof of the name change. Chapter 6 explains the various documents you can have drawn up to provide that proof.

Around 6,000 babies are born each year through IVF. The law is fairly complicated. The NHS gives you at least one course of IVF treatment for free if you're a woman age 23 to 39 and have a specific medical problem, such as blocked fallopian tubes, or you've been trying to conceive for three years without any luck. (The man's age doesn't matter.) You usually have to pay for more treatments if the first attempt isn't successful. For more information, visit the NHS Direct Web site at www.nhsdirect.nhs.uk or call 0845-4647. If you don't fit the NHS criteria, you have to pay for all your treatment. Keep in mind that the procedure has a very low success rate of just 15 percent.

If you're married and your husband consents, he is treated by law as the baby's father, even if the sperm came from a donor. If you're unmarried, but the treatment was given to you both together, even if he's not the genetic father, your partner will still legally be the dad. However, those rules only apply if the treatment was carried out under the rules of the Human Fertilisation and Embryology Act 1990 by the NHS or a licensed clinic. If a private clinic isn't licensed, a court may decide that the child is fatherless. If the woman uses a self-help method, the donor will legally be the father. However, some cases aren't clear-cut and may have to be decided by the courts if paternity becomes an issue between the partners.

Because of a 2003 court decision, if a couple has an embryo frozen, it can't be used later unless both partners involved give their consent.

Surrogacy

If you've tried all options and failed to have a child, you may consider finding a *surrogate mother* – a woman who will agree to have a child for you and hand it over to you when it's born. This kind of arrangement is usually made between members of the same family. The arrangement is legal as long as you don't pay for the child. You can pay all the costs related to the pregnancy and the birth. The law can allow the woman to change her mind about handing over the baby in some circumstances.

Within six months of the birth, you can apply to the court for an order to be treated as the baby's parents, or you can adopt the child or apply for a residence order so that you legally have the parental rights and responsibilities for that child. Take legal advice before becoming involved in a surrogacy arrangement. The voluntary organisation Childlessness Overcome Through Surrogacy (COTS), operating since 1988, can help with advice and information, and you can contact it on 0844-414-0181 or at www.surrogacy.org.uk.

Dealing with the Blessed Event

However children arrive, it's always a blessed event – and usually a blessed relief for the woman who has been carrying the baby for the past nine months. Now the hard work is really beginning. When you become new parents, your feelings are mixed. Sometimes you just want to be left alone to get on with it in your little family unit, and at other times, you feel isolated and at a loss to know where to turn.

Even if you don't have grandparents, friends, and the extended family to help you, you do have health professionals, such as your health visitor, to contact. Parentline Plus is a charity that offers support to any parent bringing up a child – from 0 to 18. You can call any time on 0808-800-2222. If you take a look at the Web site www.parentlineplus.org.uk, you can see that no topic is too big or too small to help you with.

Registering the birth

The birth of your newly arrived bundle of joy must be registered within six weeks with the local Registrar for Births, Marriages, and Deaths. All the details of the sex, place of birth, names, and the names of both parents (if they're married) will be put in the register.

If the parents aren't married, then the father's details are only added if the mother agrees or he has a court order to prove he's the father. If the unmarried parents both register the birth, the father automatically has parental rights and responsibilities over the child. (See the section 'Creating the Family Unit,' earlier in this chapter, for more details.)

When parents are married, or unmarried but living together, the child is usually given the father's surname. When a single mother registers a birth, the child usually has her surname. You don't need to stick to that convention, though. You can use either surname or a combination of both.

If the father isn't named at the time the birth is registered, his name can be added later. If a mistake has occurred in the details, or you want to change the child's name, you can do so within 12 months. The register can't be altered after that time, however, unless a child is adopted or in very exceptional circumstances. If a child's name is changed later, it isn't changed on the birth certificate. For more information on changing a child's name, see the section on step-parenting, earlier in this chapter.

After the birth is registered, you receive a copy of the birth certificate. A short version, which you receive for free, doesn't show the details, while the long version, which you can purchase, has all the details. If you need replacements, you can go back to the register office where the birth was registered or apply to the General Register Office by post. (For details, see the earlier section 'The adoption option.')

When a child is adopted, the register is updated. A new certificate replaces the original birth certificate, and the short version doesn't show the details of the birth parents or that the child was adopted.

Taking time off work

Mothers and fathers, and the parents of adopted children, are entitled to time off work at the time of the event and during the first five years of the child's life – some with pay and some unpaid.

Some mothers are entitled to up to 52 weeks of maternity leave depending on how long they've worked for their employer. The first 26 weeks of *ordinary maternity leave* is paid. At present, some women also qualify for another 26 weeks of nonpaid *additional maternity leave*. The Government plans to extend that to nine months of paid leave and eventually to have the whole 52 weeks paid if the mother is entitled to it. Plans also allow mums to share some of the maternity leave with the dads.

At the moment dads get just two weeks paid paternity leave unless their employers are more generous. All parents have the right to take off up to 13 weeks of unpaid leave in the first five years of each child's life to spend more time with their children. Parents can also request flexible working, such as a different schedule, and employers must consider their request. For more information, see Chapter 9.

Claiming child benefit

You're entitled to claim child benefit for a child under 16, or under 19 and still in full time non-advanced education, if that child is living with you or you pay for the child's maintenance. The Government pays *Child Benefit* for each child at the rate of £17.45 for the eldest child and £11.70 for younger children. Only one lot of benefit is payable per child, and sometimes disputes occur about who claims it if a couple have split up but share parental responsibilities.

You will probably get a welcome pack from the hospital when your baby is born, and this pack may contain a child benefit claim form. Fill it in and post it off quickly so that you don't miss out on any benefit you're entitled to. If you don't get a form from the hospital, call 0845-302-1444 (or 0845-603-2000 if you're in Northern Ireland), and it will be sent to you. For more information, visit Her Majesty's Revenue and Customs Web site at www.hmrc.gov.uk.

You may be able to apply for other benefits as well when the baby arrives or a child comes to live with you. Refer to Chapter 11 for details.

Bringing Up Children

The individuals with parental responsibility for a child are the ones who make the decisions about how that child is brought up. They're legally responsible for the child until she reaches the age of 18. Not all parents have parental responsibility, and not all those with parental responsibility are parents. You may have sole parental responsibility, or you may share it with your partner or a former partner.

Not only do you have responsibility for the child and the right to decide how she's brought up, but the child has rights, too, and acquires different rights at different ages.

Living up to your responsibilities

The Children Act 1989 says that having *parental responsibility* means having all rights, powers, responsibilities, and authority that by law a parent has in relation to a child and his property. What it means is that you must, amongst other things:

- Register the child's birth and name her
- Keep the child is safe from harm
- Ensure that the child gets medical treatment when it's needed
- Ensure that the child gets an education from the age of 5 to 16
- Choose the child's school, religion, and residence
- Appoint a guardian to look after the child if you die (see Chapter 8)

If you don't live up to your responsibilities, social workers from your local authority can take your child into care. (See the upcoming section 'Being taken into care.') That event only happens if a child has been treated cruelly or violently, is at risk of abuse, or has been neglected. If a child is taken into care, he may eventually be put up for adoption, even though you don't give your consent, and your parental rights and responsibility will be taken from you and given to the adopters. (See the section 'The adoption option,' earlier in this chapter.)

Keeping them out of harm's way

Children can come to all sorts of harm, and it's easy to see danger lurking around every corner and become overprotective. Children have to learn through experience, so it's about getting the balance right between protecting and mollycoddling. The place where children spend most of their time is home, and it's the place where they can be most at risk, too. You have to make sure that home is a safe place for children to be. You may need to place gates at the top and bottom of the stairs, for example, or covers on the electrical sockets or keep sharp objects out of reach.

If you injure your child, he – or rather, another adult on behalf of the child – can sue you for compensation. If a court decides you caused the accident through your negligence, the child will be awarded damages. If the accident is a road accident, the child can claim from your insurance company as long as you're insured (see Chapter 18).

Children and the Internet

With stories of children being lured into meeting strangers through the Internet or being groomed by paedophiles, you may be thinking of cutting your Internet connection. The advantages of the Net, though, still outweigh the disadvantages when it comes to education and learning for children, so it's up to parents to monitor what their children are up to on the World Wide Web and to establish strict rules about its use. You can install software filters that make accessing certain sites impossible, but make sure that they don't use your login details to get around that safety net.

It's also your job to protect your children from other people they may meet. That means only leaving them with people who are old enough and behave responsibly enough to take care of them until they can safely be left on their own. There's no set age at which you can leave a child at home alone, but you can't leave a child under 12 alone in a room with an unprotected heater or an open fire. There's no set age at which you can let them go out on the streets by themselves. All you can do is to teach them about the possible risks and how to avoid them and assess when those lessons have been well enough absorbed.

Anyone working with children is legally obliged to take care of them as a careful parent would. If they don't and the child is injured in some way, they can be sued for damages. Schools, for example, are responsible for the safety and welfare of their pupils. If equipment in the playground isn't safe or an accident occurs on a school trip, the school may be liable.

If a dog attacks a child, the dog must be put down, and you may be able to claim compensation for the injuries from its owner. Fireworks can't be sold to anyone under 16, and special regulations regulate the flammability of children's nightclothes. Young people over 16 can go into a bar, but can't drink until they're 18. Tobacco can't be sold to children under 16, although many shopkeepers don't seem to have heard of that law.

Dealing with cruelty and violence

To smack or not to smack is still the big debate. Parents still have the right to use reasonable chastisement. If you're prosecuted for being violent to the child when you smacked him, the court looks at whether a reasonable parent would have smacked. If you use violence and leave a mark, teachers, or other people the child comes into contact with, may call social services, and you may have your child taken away from you.

The law may change. The European Court of Human Rights has said that physical discipline violates a child's human rights.

You can be charged with a range of criminal offences if you're cruel or violent to your children, deliberately injure them, or they're injured because of negligence. Not only can you be prosecuted or have the child taken into care, but in some cases, the child can sue you for damages.

It's often neighbours or relatives who alert social workers to child abuse. If you're worried that someone else's child is being badly treated, you can talk to social workers or to the National Society for the Prevention of Cruelty to Children (NSPCC) on 0808-800-5000. The agency will handle the problem without revealing who called.

Under the Children and Young Persons Act 1933, you can be charged with cruelty to a child under 16. Cruelty covers deliberate assault, ill treatment, neglect or abandonment, and general threats and abuse that damage the child physically or mentally. If you're prosecuted, you may face a prison sentence or a fine. However, it's more likely that the child will be taken away from you by social workers.

If a mother's husband is violent to her child, she can divorce him on the grounds of unreasonable behaviour or get an injunction to force him to stop hurting the child or to stay away from him (see Chapter 6).

Being liable when they misbehave

If your little angel gets up to mischief and injures someone, you may be made to pay. If the person who was injured felt that you had been negligent in some way, and that negligence had led to the child's behaviour, this person may make a successful claim against you in court. If you allowed a young child to fire an air rifle, for example, when the child was too young to appreciate the damage it could do and to control it properly, and someone was injured as a result, you can be sued for negligence, and the injured person may be awarded damages. Even if you told your child never to use the gun unsupervised, but he got hold of it without your knowledge, because you hadn't locked it away, you may be guilty of negligence.

People won't usually sue children, because they're unlikely to have any money. If they did sue a child, the court would have to decide if the child had been negligent, which would depend largely on whether he was thought to be old enough to understand the dangers.

Children can't be convicted of criminal offences before the age of ten. From then on, if they make life miserable for other people because of their behaviour, they can be given an *anti-social behaviour order* (ASBO) in the Magistrates' Court. The order will have details of what they must not do. Once they reach ten, if they're found guilty of a crime, they will be punished.

If children under ten are anti-social or commit crimes, they can be taken into care or placed under the supervision of a social worker. For example, a child curfew scheme may ban a child under ten from public places between 9 p.m. and 6 a.m. unless they're with an adult.

Educating Rita

Various Education Acts govern the education system in England and Wales. Scotland and Northern Ireland have slightly different systems. However, the basic rules are the same.

You must make sure that your children get an education from the ages of 5 to 16. If they attend school, they must start by the beginning of the first term after their fifth birthday. Some education authorities will accept them earlier, and all four-year-olds are entitled to a nursery or school place. They have to stay in school until they're 16. They can leave on the last Friday of June if they've reached 16 or will reach it before the start of the next school year.

You can educate your children at home rather than send them to school, but if the Local Education Authority thinks that you aren't complying with the law, you'll have 14 days to prove it wrong. If it still doesn't accept that your child is being given a full-time education or that the education is not up to the right standard, the Local Education Authority can apply for an *education supervision order,* meaning that you have to send the child to a school of the authority's choice. If you ignore that order, the authority can take you to court.

If you do decide to educate your children at home, you should contact your Local Education Authority. You can find details in the phone book. You should also take advantage of the wealth of information about home education available on the Internet. Try Education Otherwise, which is a charity providing support. The helpline number is 0870-730-0074, and the Web site address is www.education-otherwise.org.

You can send your children to all sorts of different schools. See Chapter 5 about using public services, including the education system).

Bringing them up in a religion

You don't have to bring your children up in a religion. Schools have to start the day with a morning assembly that has religious content but is non-denominational. They also have to teach religious education. However, many schools ignore the rules, and you have the legal right to take your children out of both the assembly and the religious instruction classes. In addition, children are allowed time off school to celebrate major festivals for their own particular religion.

No legal requirement forces you to have your children christened in a religious ceremony. That's your choice. Your only legal obligation is to name the child and put the name on the birth register. (See the section 'Registering the birth,' earlier in this chapter.)

Dealing with illness

The child's welfare is the most important thing when it comes to medical treatment, and your wishes take second place. If you don't take your children to the doctor when they need treatment, you can be guilty of neglect and prosecuted, or the children may be taken into care.

While a child is under 16, he can give his own consent to medical treatment if the doctor is happy that he understands what's involved. Otherwise, you're asked for consent. If you object to your child having a particular treatment, a doctor can call social workers who can apply for a court order to overrule your objections.

If your child is under 18 and refuses medical treatment, you or the doctor can take steps to get a court order overruling that refusal.

Under 16 and 16- to 18-year-olds in full-time education are entitled to free prescriptions, dental treatment, eye tests, and vouchers for glasses. In Wales, young people under 25 get free prescriptions.

Social workers have a duty to safeguard and promote the welfare of children in their area who are in need, so if you have a child who is ill or has a disability, you should contact social workers at your local authority for help. Depending on the severity of the situation, you and your child may be eligible for a range of services, from advice and counselling, to home help and day care. Your local authority has to keep a register of children with disabilities in its area and provide services to help them lead as normal lives as possible.

Teaching about sex and contraception

Some parents feel that teaching children about sex and contraception is their job, while other feels it's up to the schools. School governors for primary schools must think about offering sex education to pupils and at what age. If they do provide classes, a written document should outline what will be taught, and you can ask to see a copy.

State secondary schools have to provide sex education classes, which must include lessons on HIV, AIDS, and other sexually transmitted diseases.

You can take your children out of all or part of these classes, but you can't take them out of science classes that cover reproduction.

Being taken into care

Local authorities are under an obligation to provide services for children in need in their area. Some services, such as advice and counselling or home help, must be appropriate for children living with their families. They also have to provide family centres where absent parents and their children can meet, as well as day care for children in need who are under five and not yet at school and for those who are school age but need a place to go after school and during school holidays.

Under the Children Act 1989, all children have the right to basic standards of care, nurture, and upbringing. If your care doesn't meet those standards, the local authority can step in. Social workers aren't simply going to whisk your children away and put them in care. They will do all they can to keep the children at home – although tragically, sometimes that turns out to be the wrong decision. Only after they've exhausted all the possibilities of children staying with their own families can they make arrangements for them to live elsewhere. If social workers go down that route, they must involve the parents in the decisions and make sure that the parents and children can keep in contact. Parents keep their parental responsibilities and share them with social workers. Anyone with parental responsibility can take a child away from accommodation arranged by the local authority at any time.

Getting a care order

If social workers feel that arranging for a child to live away from his family isn't likely to be enough of a safeguard, they may decide to take steps to take that child into care. Local authorities have to have grounds for taking children into care, which is not the same as arranging accommodation for them outside the family home. They can take steps to protect a child if:

- ✔ The child is likely to suffer significant harm if she doesn't remain in their current accommodation (it may be accommodation arranged by social workers or a hospital where the child is receiving treatment)
- ✔ Social workers or the National Society for the Prevention of Cruelty to Children (NSPCC) aren't being allowed access to the child

Significant harm usually means neglect or physical, sexual, or emotional abuse. Local authorities or the NSPCC may apply for an *Emergency Protection Order,* which means that they can intervene to protect the child. The parents can challenge the order after 72 hours.

If the local authority knows that a child is the subject of an Emergency Protection Order or is in police protection, or if they have reasonable grounds to suspect that a child is suffering, or is likely to suffer significant harm, it will investigate and may then have grounds to take all the necessary steps to take a child into care.

After the investigation is complete, the local authority will have a case conference and decide whether to apply to the Family Proceedings Court for a Care Order under the Children Act. The court appoints an adult called a *litigation friend* to help the child in court. After hearing all the evidence, the litigation friend decides whether to grant a care order, which can last until the child is 18. Parents and children will be consulted about the child's living arrangements. If the local authority won't allow parents and children to see each other, they can apply for a *contact order,* which allows them to stay in touch. The contact order sets out how frequent the contact can be and how it should be made – by letter or visit, for example.

Local authorities arrange accommodation in a residential home or with foster parents, and a child may be put up for adoption in some circumstances. (See the section on adoption, earlier in this chapter.) When the child leaves care between the ages of 16 and 21, social workers must provide advice and assistance to ease the child's way in the big bad world.

Minding Their Rights

If you have parental responsibility for a child, you have rights to decide how the child is to be brought up. But children have rights, too, and acquire different rights as they get older. The list is much too long to include them all, so here are the main ones:

- ✔ When they're born, children have the right to a have a bank or building society account and premium bonds; they need their own passport to travel abroad, and they can be put up for adoption.

- ✔ At 19 weeks, they can be adopted.

- ✔ At the age of five, children must be given full-time education, can drink alcohol at home (get a lock on that drinks cupboard!), and have to pay the full fare on trains.

- ✔ At seven, they can take money out of their National Savings Account or one with the TSB bank if they have them.

- ✔ At ten, they can open a current account and be convicted of a crime if they knew it was wrong.

- ✔ At 12, they can buy a pet, although the government proposes to change this age to 16 in its new Animal Welfare Bill. They can also sign their own passport.

- ✔ At 14, they can work for up to 12 hours in a school week – up to 2 and a half hours on a school day and not more than 2 hours on a Sunday, and go into a bar with an adult but not drink or buy alcohol.

- ✔ At 15, they can be sent to a young offenders' institution.

- ✔ At 16, lots of changes occur, including the right to get married with the consent of parents (no consent needed in Scotland), the right to have sex if both parties consent, join the Armed Forces with the consent of parents, buy cigarettes, fireworks, premium bonds, drive a moped or tractor, change their name, and drink beer or cider in the part of a pub set aside for meals. They can also apply for their own passport and buy a lottery ticket.

- ✔ At 17, young people can give blood, drive, fly a plane, go into a betting shop but not bet, and go to prison. They can buy or hire a shotgun or airgun and ammunition.

- ✔ At 18, children officially become adults and can do everything adults can do apart from stand in a political election, apply for a liquor licence, and drive a bus or a lorry. You can't do those until you're 21.

No laws govern when you can have parts of your body pierced, but reputable establishments are likely to want young children to be accompanied by an adult and to have their parents consent. Legally, you can't have a tattoo until you're 18, although some places ignore that rule.

Children can own money and possessions, but they can't own land and houses until they're 18. If they're left property, it remains in a trust for them until they're at least 18. Chapter 8 explains the law on wills and inheritance.

Babysitting

Adults usually assume that there is a legal age at which people can babysit, but there isn't. You can leave your child with anyone you think is old enough and responsible enough. You may want an older or more responsible person to look after a young baby than someone you'd be happy to have look after an 8-year-old. However, if someone 16 or over leaves someone under 12 in a room with an unprotected heater or an open fire, and the child is injured as a result, the older person can be prosecuted. That rule seems to indicate that the law sees someone of 16 as old enough to know better, and 16 is also the age some children's organisations recommend for as the minimum for babysitters.

Leaving home

Young people can leave home at 18, but in reality, little will be done about bringing them back if they leave home at 16. Social services and the police are unlikely to get involved beyond making sure that they're capable of looking after themselves, if they find them. The courts are highly unlikely to intervene and order them to go home.

Providing for Children When You Split Up

Breaking up is hard to do, especially when children are involved. The court will put the needs of the children first if it's asked to intervene because the couple can't agree what should happen. For more information on how the courts deal with decisions involving the future of any children, see Chapter 6. Usually the agreement reached is that children should live with one parent and see the other and or stay with the other part of the time. The parents go on sharing parental responsibility, and the parent who is best able to support the children financially pays an agreed sum of money to the other. You may have to make payments through the Child Support Agency. (See the section 'Paying child support,' later in this chapter.)

The parent with whom the children live often keeps the family home. The home may become the property of that parent, or they may just live in it until the children reach age 18, or leave full-time education. At that time, the home is sold, and the proceeds split in whatever proportions have been agreed. If the family home is worth enough, another option is to sell it and buy two smaller, less expensive places.

Agreeing on all the details between yourselves usually leads to a more amicable split, which is better for your children. You may no longer be each other's spouse or partner, but you'll always be the children's parents. At times, you'll want to meet or talk about the children. If you do come to an agreement and apply for a divorce, the court will want to know what arrangements you've made for the children, and if the judge isn't happy, you may be called to a court hearing.

If you can't agree and solicitors get involved on both sides, the split can become bitter, and the costs will rocket. Try mediation first if it's available in your area. Your local Citizens Advice Bureau can give you details. You can find its number in the phone book.

Absent parents

The majority of absent parents are fathers, and many resent the term *absent parents* because they're still very much involved with their children and still there for them. Many also make the point that they don't wish to be absent, but they've been dumped! *Nonresident parents* is a better phrase.

Nonresident parents who have parental responsibilities usually keep those parental responsibilities unless a court takes them away, perhaps because of violence. However, fathers who weren't married to their children's mother may never have been given parental responsibilities and may have no rights over the children if they leave – unless they go to court to be given rights.

The court will only make orders to do with the children if it feels it is in the children's best interests. It expects you to come to an agreement with your ex-partner. If you can come to an agreement yourselves, you're much more likely to stick to it. By the time the court becomes involved, the split is likely to have become very bitter. The court will usually make residence and contact orders:

✔ **Residence orders:** When parents split up, the parent with whom the children live may apply for a *residence order*. Sometimes the courts will grant a joint residence order or grant each parent a residence order, and the children will spend a specified time with each parent. The court will ask an older child which parent he prefers to live with.

Expressing an opinion can be difficult for a child to do because of fear of hurting one parent. Agree to the arrangements between yourselves if at all possible and make sure that the children are as happy as they can be with what you've come up with. If the court does make an order, you can go back to have the order changed if circumstances change.

> ✔ **Contact orders:** A nonresident parent will usually be given access to the children. You should agree between yourselves how frequent contact should be and for how long and where. If you can't agree, you can apply to the court for a *contact order,* which sets out how often the child will have contact with that parent, whether contact means visits, phone calls and letters, how long the contact lasts (and sometimes where the contact should take place), and the arrangements for picking the children up and taking them home again.

In exceptional circumstances, a nonresident parent may not be granted a contact order or may only be allowed to see the children under supervision. You can go back to court to get the terms of the order changed if it isn't working as it should, but you shouldn't simply ignore the order.

Other people, such as grandparents and family friends, can also apply for contact orders.

Paying child support

Child support is another big issue when parents split up and one that causes a great deal of rancour. If you can agree on a financial settlement, you may have very little to argue about if neither of you earns very much. If you have joint residence and the children will spend half of the week with each of you and you both earn the same, then each will simply split the costs. Unfortunately, it rarely works like that.

The person with whom the children live the majority of the time will have the bigger care costs and often will have the lower income, especially if the children are young and need a parent at home most or some of the time or need childcare. If you can't agree on an amount, the Child Support Agency (CSA) will become involved in calculating how much child support should be paid and by whom and will collect the money. If one parent simply leaves the other in the lurch, the CSA can track them down and collect money if there's any to collect. The CSA is usually chasing nonresident fathers, but mothers who are higher earners have to pay child support to fathers who earn less and have the children living with them.

If the parent who has the children is claiming income support or job seeker's allowance (see Chapter 11), she normally has to go through the CSA to claim money for the children. Otherwise, the agency doesn't need to be involved unless you can't agree.

New rules about the way child support is calculated came into force in March 2003. For the sake of this explanation, assume that the father will be paying child support to the mother for the children. The system is more complicated than this explanation, but basically the father pays 15 per cent of his income if he has one child; 20 per cent if he has two; and 25 per cent if he has three. He pays no more than 25 per cent, and if he is a high earner, only £104,000 a year of his earnings will be taken into account. If his income is less than £200 a week, he'll pay reduced rates, and if it is less than £100 or he is on benefits, he'll pay a flat rate of £5 a week.

The amount of child support the father pays is also reduced if the children stay overnight with him during the week. The mother can also ask for a lump sum or periodical payments. If the father denies he is the father, the CSA can ask for a DNA test. (See the sidebar 'When you don't want to be a parent,' earlier in this chapter). If he refuses, the CSA is likely to assume that he really is the father.

If you're the higher earner and you go on to have a second family, you're still expected to pay child support for the children of your first family, although it may be reduced because of the needs of the second family.

Taking the children abroad

If you want to take your children abroad, you should get the consent of the other parent who has parental rights first. It's a criminal offence to take a child out of the country without the consent of both parents or of the court. If you have a residence order in your favour, you can take the children away for up to four-week holiday. If the other parent objects, you can get a court order. If no residence order exists and you can't agree between you, you should apply for a court order.

If you have the children and you want to emigrate, it has big implications for the children and the nonresident parent. The court will go through a list of issues about the welfare of the children. If older children object, your application to take them abroad may be refused, but usually the applications are granted, even if it makes it very difficult for the other parent to see the children.

If you suspect the other parent is planning to abduct your children, take legal advice straight away. It can be very difficult to get abducted children returned to the UK despite an international convention where countries that have signed up will enforce each other's court orders. A solicitor can take steps with the police to try to stop the parent and children leaving the UK through ports and airports. Ask your local Citizens Advice Bureau for the best solicitor to contact. The details are in the phone book.

Chapter 8

Passing On

● ●

● ●

*Y*our own demise probably isn't something you spend too much time thinking about. Or perhaps I should rephrase that. Your own demise is something you don't spend enough time thinking about. Being prepared has big advantages, and your loved ones will reap the benefits. If you don't plan, the only person who will be laughing is the tax inspector.

If you were to die tomorrow, what would happen? Does any one person know what assets you own, such as savings accounts and life insurance policies, where all your bank accounts are held, and who you owe money to? Someone has to sort out the mess you leave behind, so you need to get it in order and make it easy for someone else to clear up after you.

No matter how little you have to leave, most people have some property, money, or personal treasures that they'd like to give to family and friends. If you don't plan, people can get the wrong things, or, in the worst-case scenario, Her Majesty's Government may be the main beneficiary.

Deciding Whether You Need a Will

Not everyone needs to make a will. If you don't have anything to leave – perhaps you live by yourself in rented accommodation and have no savings, or your income comes from state pension with a few additional benefits to help pay the rent and council tax bills – then you probably don't need to make a will. But most people have a few assets that they'd like to share with loved ones. The assets may be nothing more than a couple of china ornaments or inexpensive pieces of jewellery, but if you want to be sure that your wishes are carried out and your belongings are divided up the way you want, then don't leave things to chance: make a will.

People mistakenly assume that they don't need to make a will because they have a spouse or a civil partner, and that everything will go to that spouse anyway. That's not necessarily the case. If you have children and no will, your spouse automatically gets a part of your estate, and the children receive the rest. You may create a situation where your beloved spouse or civil partner has to sell the family home in order to give your children their inheritance – all because you didn't make a will.

If you're living with someone, unless you make provision for that unmarried partner in your will, that person will not automatically get anything and would have to go to court to stake a claim.

As well as setting out who is to get what, your will puts someone, known as an *executor,* in charge of carrying out your wishes, and you can say how you want your funeral to be handled. If you have children, you can make provision for them and name the people you want to take care of them if they're left without parents.

As soon as you have anything at all worth leaving to someone, consider making a will. Along with the will, include a list of all your bank accounts, insurance policies, and any other important documents, including information about anything you owe. This paperwork saves a lot of hard work and heartache for the person who has to sort it out later.

If you die without a will, you die *intestate.* Intestate means that your assets will be divided up according to the laws of intestacy rather than your wishes. If you have no relatives, your friends won't get a look in, and the Crown (the Government) will take everything after your debts are cleared and your funeral paid for. You'll be spinning in your grave.

Adding Up the Value of Your Estate

Your estate is how much you're worth minus whatever you owe. Most people have little idea of what they're really worth until they start to do the sums. They usually come up with a bit more worth than they realised.

Write it all down: your home, other property, savings and investments, shares and pensions, any money that would come from a work pension if you die in service, and insurance policies that pay out on your death.

Then take a look around your home. You may have some good jewellery, a car, or paintings – perhaps not worth much in money terms, but worth something to your loved ones – or a nice rug and a case of increasingly valuable wine. What about your high-tech computer equipment and state-of-the-art TV and music centre? Even your clothes are probably worth a fair bit when you consider it. You may have some vintage stuff or an expensive coat worth earmarking for a friend or relative.

The person who sorts out your affairs after you've gone has to value your estate and tell HM Revenue and Customs how much you're worth. There's no place to hide from the tax collector.

Not everything on your list forms part of your estate. Most couples own their home jointly as joint tenants, in which case the surviving spouse or partner automatically inherits your part of the property, even if you don't say so in your will. The same goes for any other assets, such as shares and savings accounts that you own jointly. Probably most of the contents of your home were bought jointly, too, and so automatically belong to the surviving partner on your death.

If, however, you own your home as tenants in common (see Chapter 3), you own a specified part of it, and your partner owns a specified part. If you own half and your partner owns half, you can leave your half in your will to anyone you like – as can your partner. The next thing to do after you make your list is to check what on that list you own outright as sole owner and what is owned jointly with someone else.

Even if you do hold property or assets jointly, it does no harm and makes things clear if you include them in the will and state that the intention is that they should belong to your partner after your death.

Complete your perusal of your estate by making a list of what you owe and to whom. Your debts don't die with you. People who are owed money by you will be paid from your estate before your *beneficiaries* – the people you name in your will who are to receive legacies – can claim their share. If you don't have enough left over to give your beneficiaries what you've requested they be given, they will get less than you intended.

The value of your estate changes over time. Do a quick reassessment of your worth once a year.

Factoring In Inheritance Tax

Sometimes you'll hear people talking about death duties or capital transfer tax. They're old names for the past regimes the tax office used to take a share of your estate on your death. These days, it's called *Inheritance Tax* (IHT). After you've worked out exactly how much in your estate you're free to leave to whoever you please, you have to reduce it by the amount of IHT to be paid.

If your estate is worth more than £285,000, your beneficiaries may need to pay IHT. With average house prices escalating over the past few years, more estates are becoming subject to IHT. Anything you leave to your spouse doesn't attract IHT. That means your spouse's estate gets bigger, and that means more IHT to pay when your spouse dies. If the whole lot is passed on from your spouse to your children, they can face a big bill.

If a portion of your estate is subject to IHT, HM Revenue and Customs takes 40 per cent. The person dealing with your estate has to pay over some or all of that IHT to HM Revenue and Customs before it's all sorted out, and so may end up borrowing that money.

If you think you're worth more than £285,000 or approaching that figure, think about leaving an account specifically for paying the IHT and do some inheritance planning. Good inheritance tax lawyers can be worth their weight in gold. They can advise you on all the steps you can take, legally, to reduce the amount of IHT that has to be paid. Check with your nearest tax office or at www.hmrc.gov.uk for more information.

After you know how much you're worth and what you have to leave, you can decide who you want it to go to – up to a point.

You can't omit certain people from your will. If you exclude your closest family and dependents, they can ask the courts to change your will. The Provision for Family and Dependents Act 1975 says that you must, wherever possible, leave your dependents with enough to live on. Dependents are likely to be your spouse and children, but you may have an ex-spouse who hasn't remarried or another family member who has been kept by you. They can dispute your will if you leave them out.

So, too, can someone who isn't your child, but has been treated as such, or someone you lived with for two years or more before your death. The court decides whether the person left out of the will has a valid claim and, if so, how much they should get. Spouses and children are seen as having a more valid claim than ex-spouses.

Under Scottish law, your surviving spouse and children can claim legal rights to your estate. Your spouse is legally entitled to half of your movable assets, such as cash, cars, and jewellery, if you have no children, and a third of your movable assets if you have children. If the amount you leave your spouse is less than his legal right, your spouse can dispute your will.

Deciding who gets what

Look after your immediate family first. Think about where they're at in their lives when you're working out how much to leave them. If your spouse already jointly owns your home with you, it automatically becomes hers when you die. If your spouse already has enough investments and savings, pensions, and so on to live on, you can consider leaving more to other people. If your children are well established in their careers and have their own homes and assets, you may decide that they don't need much from your will, but that you'll leave something to the grandchildren or the cats' and dogs' home.

You may have a list of friends you'd like to leave amounts of money or more personal possessions to. Decide who gets what and make a list. Describe items you're leaving very clearly so that there's no dispute over which picture you meant to leave to Mary-Jane or which crystal vase you've left to your nephew. And make sure that it's very clear from your list which nephew you mean so that no one can dispute your wishes.

You can always change your list after you create it. The vase may get broken, or you may sell the picture. If so, you can go back and change what the beneficiaries are to get. When it comes to writing your will, you can attach your list to it and refer to the attached list in the will.

Taking care of your spouse

Talk to your other half about your will and what you intend to do with your estate. If you die, it will be deeply distressing for your spouse, so you should make sure that he knows what's in your will so that he doesn't have to worry about selling the home if it's not necessary.

When people build a home together, sometimes one buys some of the contents; sometimes the other does. But if one were to leave some of those contents to other people – maybe a painting to a friend – it can leave a big gap not only on the wall. The missing painting can be a constant reminder of a missing partner. Talk it over if you want to leave personal possessions to someone outside the family home.

If you have a mortgage on your home, think about taking out a life insurance policy that pays out enough on your death to clear the mortgage. That way, your spouse won't have to struggle to meet the mortgage payments if she has no other money to clear the debt.

You may decide to leave everything you own to your spouse, especially if your spouse is still quite young and the children are young. You can leave a lump sum of money, your saving accounts, and any death-in-service benefits from your work pension to your spouse. Alternatively you can leave your spouse a *life interest* in some of your assets. A life interest generates an income for your spouse for as long as she survives you, and then the assets pass on to someone else – your children perhaps.

Whatever you leave outright to your spouse is hers to dispose of as she wishes. Your spouse can marry again and leave everything you've left to a new spouse without passing on a share to your children. If you don't like that idea, plan ahead and take advice before making your will.

If you don't provide adequately for your spouse, she can go to court to dispute your will. You can't cut your spouse out unless she's independently wealthy and has agreed not to be a beneficiary of your will.

Change your will if your circumstances change. If you split up from your spouse and no longer want her to inherit, change your will. It's only when you divorce that any gifts you've left are automatically cancelled.

Taking care of the children

If you die, you want to know that your children are as well provided for as possible. Your surviving spouse automatically has sole guardianship over the children. If you can, you'll probably want to provide for the day-to-day costs of bringing up the children and for the extras that they'll need as they get older. Think about school books and trips, university if they do well, buying their first home, and getting married. While the children are young, most people simply leave everything to their surviving spouses who will have the expense of the children's upbringing.

Knowing that your children are provided for

If you can afford it and you want your children to have a private education, for example, you can leave the surviving parent a sum of money to be used specifically for private schooling.

Your offspring can't inherit until they're at least 18, so if you do make a specific gift to each of your children in your will, it will be held in *trust* until 18 or any later age you've specified. Trust means that the person in charge of sorting out your will has to look after the money or set up a trust with trustees to manage the money until it's passed on to your child. Trusts are complicated. Get advice before going down that route.

If you want to leave money to be used by your child for a specific purpose, you can make it *conditional* so that it's used to pay for university fees or a wedding. But if the conditions are too restrictive, a court can set them aside.

Your children may not want to go to university, but to train to be electricians. Are you really saying that they can't have the money unless they go to university? Be careful about setting conditions.

If you're worried that your surviving spouse will remarry and leave everything you have left them to the new spouse, cutting out your children, think about leaving gifts for your children in your own will, through trusts or by giving your spouse a life interest in some of your assets, which then pass to your children on your spouse's death.

Appointing guardians

If you're a parent – one of a couple or a lone parent – you need to consider what would happen to your children if they were left without parents. Who would bring them up? You can appoint *guardians* to do the job. Your close relatives – your parents or brothers or sisters – may be willing and suitable to look after your children. If they're willing to be guardians, name them in your will. You can name more than one set of guardians.

Think it through. You probably don't want to leave your children to the mercy of a sister who is a drug addict, for example. Your own parents may simply be too old to take on responsibility for a whole new family. You can appoint different guardians for each of your children, but would you really want them to be split up and grow up apart? Do your children like the proposed guardians and their own children? Will they bring them up in the way you'd like them to be brought up?

Talk to the guardians you have in mind. Write a letter to go with your will about how you'd like the children to be brought up and leave the guardians money in your will to make sure that they can afford to follow your wishes as far as possible. Once they're 18, your offspring are adults, and their guardians no longer have a legal responsibility toward them.

Putting It All Down on Paper

After you know what you want to do with your estate, you need to get it all down on paper. It has to be in writing to be valid unless you're on active military service. You can make your own will. If your will is very straightforward – for example, you're leaving all your property, assets, and personal possessions to your spouse – you can simply buy a will form from the stationers and follow the instructions.

Finding the right person to make your will

If you want help with your will, see advisers at your nearest CAB for a referral. Solicitors generally charge from £50 upward. The more complicated the will, the more time it takes, and the more it costs. Some advisers offer you a special deal when they're handling your property purchase. Just because they're good at house buying doesn't mean that they're great at wills, though.

The Law Society (0870-606-6565 in England and Wales; 0845-113-0018 in Scotland; and 02890-231-614 in Northern Ireland) can also give you a list of solicitors. If you look on the Internet or even on your high street, you can find firms to write your will for you, but you can't tell how good these people are. They may be solicitors who have been struck off. Don't go ahead until you've checked them out or had a recommendation.

If you do DIY your will, follow these guidelines:

- ✔ **Make your handwriting as legible as possible and write it all with the same pen.** If you write in different inks, the person sorting it all out for you (your executor) may assume that part of it was added by someone else in a different ink and ignore your instructions. Think about typing your will so that it's easier to read.

- ✔ **Get someone to check the grammar.** You can give a sentence an unintended meaning by putting a comma in the wrong place. Be very clear – don't use words like *around* or *about* or *approximately*.

- ✔ **Make your wishes absolutely clear.** Describe what you're leaving in such a way that no one can be in any doubt as to exactly what you mean and make sure that you put in enough detail about your beneficiaries so your executors will have no trouble in finding the right person.

If your wishes aren't absolutely straightforward, get help. (See the sidebar 'Finding the right person to make your will.') Solicitors make far more money out of disentangling badly made wills than they do from writing them in the first place. Solicitors have a bad name for charging through the nose for a few minutes of their time, but it's relatively inexpensive to have a will made and you have the peace of mind that's all the 'i's' are dotted and the 't's' crossed. Besides, you can do all the legwork yourself.

You will need all the information you've already gathered about your estate and how you want to leave it. Some things should go in your will. Others can be on separate paper attached to your will. Put all the details of the major bequests to your family in your will. Small gifts to other friends and relatives can be put in a letter attached to the will. The will should refer to the attached letter. You can also attach a list of all your assets and details of where to find all your various accounts, policies, and investments, along with details of your solicitor and accountant.

Appointing executors

One vital piece of information that must be in your will is the name or names of the people you're appointing as your *executors*. Executors, or *executor-nominates* in Scotland, are the people who make your wishes come true. They gather up all your assets, pay your debts and taxes, and divide up what's left according to what's written in your will.

You don't have to appoint an executor if you're leaving everything you own to one person who is over 18. That beneficiary effectively acts as the executor and does all the work themselves.

Think carefully about who to appoint. You want someone wise and trustworthy who will do the work quickly and efficiently and not disappear with the dosh. He needs to have the time to sort everything out for you and be willing to take on the job. The person you appoint can also benefit from your will.

You can appoint solicitors, accountants, or bank managers, but they all charge professional fees for doing the job, and as their fees come out of your estate, it leaves less to be shared between your loved ones.

Don't appoint someone without talking to them about it first. It's safer to appoint someone who is younger than you; otherwise, he may have died before the services are required. An executor or executors can pay for the services of a solicitor – out of your estate – if they come across a situation they can't resolve. Executors can claim any expenses they run up from your estate.

Put all the details of your executors in the will – names and addresses. You don't have to include addresses, but those kinds of details leave less room for confusion.

It's a good idea to appoint more than one executor in case, when the time comes, one of them can't or doesn't want to do the job. But if you appoint too many executors, delays in administering the estate can push up the costs. Go for three at the most.

Making sure that the will is legal

A will has to be written by someone who is over 18 and of *sound mind*. If someone doesn't have the mental capacity to understand fully what they're doing, the will isn't valid. If you go to a solicitor to have your will made, that solicitor has to make the judgment that you're of sound mind or refuse your request. If you make your own will, a court can later decide that you weren't of sound mind when you drew it up. If that's the case, the rules of intestacy kick in. (See the section on intestacy, later in this chapter.) People who have certain mental illnesses can make wills – for example, if you have a depressive illness or schizophrenia, which is being medically treated, you still have the right to make a will. Your GP can advise you on this situation.

If you can't read or write, it doesn't stop you making a will. You can dictate your wishes to a solicitor and make a cross on the document instead of a signature.

In the opening paragraph of your will, you state that you're of sound mind; this is your last will and testament and that you revoke all previous wills and *codicils* (later additions to a will). You must put your name, address, and date the will is being made. After you write down all the details of your wishes – who gets what, who your executors, and who any trustees are – your will needs to be signed by you in the presence of two witnesses who also sign the document before it will be valid. Your witnesses must see you sign the will and see each other sign it. They don't, however, have to be there when you write it, and they don't have to know what's in it.

In Scotland, you need the signature of only one witness who doesn't need to see you sign the document. You just have to show the witness your signature.

Number the pages of your will and sign each at the bottom – as close to the end of the content of that page as possible. These precautions just safeguard you against pages going missing or someone else adding something between the end of the writing and your signature.

The people who act as witnesses cannot be beneficiaries of the will or spouses of the beneficiary, or they won't be allowed to inherit.

Don't make the mistake of making your will and leaving it unsigned in your solicitor's office. If something happens to you before it's signed, the will isn't valid. Any previous will stands, and if no previous will exists, your estate will be divided up according to the rules of intestacy. Your wishes won't get a look in.

Changing a Will

You should regard your will as a living document to be reread and reviewed every time your circumstances change. You may be spurred on to make a will when you buy your first home. You need to rethink it if you later get married or live with a partner. If you have children, you'll need to update it again, and when they grow up and leave home, you'll probably want to change it again.

All changes to your will need to be signed and witnessed in the same way as your original will (see preceding section), and if you use a solicitor, it's an expensive business. Make sure that you really do need to make changes.

When you get married, your will is automatically revoked unless you live in Scotland. If you die before you make a new one, you'll be treated as if you had died without a will. If you're going to try white-water rafting on honeymoon, you'd better make the new will before you go. You can make a will *in expectation of marriage* – saying that you leave your property and assets to your intended and get around this hitch.

If you get divorced, your ex-spouse automatically gets cut out of the will, whether you intend him to or not, unless you live in Scotland. Everything else in the will stands. If you don't want your former spouse cut out because you're still the best of friends, change your will immediately. If your former spouse was named as your executor, he can't carry out that role after the divorce.

If you and your ex-spouse own a home together as joint tenants and you die, that home automatically becomes the property of your ex-spouse unless you change the terms of ownership or sell and split the proceeds.

In Scotland, once you have children, your old will automatically becomes void. You have to make a new will mentioning the bairns, or you'll be treated as not having a will if you die.

You can change a will in two ways. You either make a new one *revoking* (cancelling) all previous wills and *codicils* (changes to your will), or you add a codicil to your will. A codicil is a separate document drawn up after the original will, which adds to or alters your will. It has the same legal standing as the original will.

Destroying a will

If you do write a new will revoking all previous wills, you should destroy all previous wills and all copies of them. Burn them – it's the only sure way to make sure that no legible text remains. But don't forget that if you do destroy a will and don't get around to making another one before you die, you'll be treated as if you'd never made a will. If someone else destroys your will without your permission, it will still be valid, but it may be somewhat difficult to prove what was in it unless copies exist.

If you have a lot of changes or the change is a major one, make a new will. If the change is minor, you can add a codicil, which is signed and witnessed in the same way as your original will (see preceding section). You can also appoint a guardian by adding a codicil. The more complicated the will, the bigger the case for making a new will. Added codicils can simply add to the complications.

Keeping the Documents Safe

After you make your will, you need to keep it somewhere safe and where the right people know where it is. If your solicitor has drawn up the will for you, he'll probably offer to store it for you. If he's one of your executors, that's not a bad idea. Check out any charges.

For a fee, you can also keep your will in the bank in a safety deposit box or in the bank's safe. Take a few copies so that you don't keep having to go to the bank if you want to review your will, especially because the bank may charge you for each time you get it out of the safe.

A fireproof safe at home is as good a place as any to keep a will. Wherever you store your will, keep important documents with it, such as any letters or lists of bequests you refer to in your will, and make sure that any codicils are attached. Give a copy of everything to your executors and make sure that they know where the will is kept. They'll need the original when the time comes.

Keep a list with your will of all your savings and bank accounts, investments, shares, premium bonds, and insurance policies – basically, a list of anything your executors may need to track down in the event of your death. It makes it easier all round.

Suffering the Consequences of Not Making a Will

If you die without a will, you die intestate, and it's not you who faces the consequences of your inaction, but your loved ones. The law of intestacy is quite strict and makes the decisions as to who in your family circle should inherit and what proportion of your estate. If you look at the rules, you may find them to your liking and decide to carry on without a will because the law of intestacy will divide things up in a way that suits you just fine.

If you and your spouse own your home together as joint tenants, your spouse automatically becomes the owner of the home on your death. If you're the sole owner, your home goes into the pot to be divided up according to the intestacy rules.

Dividing up the spoils under intestacy rules

Your spouse gets the first chunk of your estate. If you don't have any children or other surviving relatives, your surviving spouse gets everything, minus anything you owe and the costs of administering your estate.

 The rules of intestacy apply to spouses and civil partners but not to unmarried partners. They get nothing unless you've made a will and specifically left them something or unless you owned a home together as joint tenants, in which case the home becomes the property of your partner.

If you have children, your surviving spouse or civil partner gets all your personal items, the first £125,000 of your estate, and a life interest in half of the rest. The remainder is divided equally between your children. If you leave £285,000, your spouse gets £125,000 plus £80,000, which is invested to produce an income – keeping the capital intact. The children get the remaining £80,000 between them. When your surviving spouse eventually dies, the children inherit the £80,000 your spouse had the life interest in.

The rules are a bit different in Scotland where the spouse has prior rights to your estate and gets (currently) the first £130,000 of the value of a house or shop. If the family home is worth more, the spouse is usually allowed to go on living there. The spouse is also entitled to the £22,000 worth of furnishing and household goods and the first £35,000 worth of moveable assets, such as cash and savings in banks accounts. The spouse may get more of the movable assets depending on which other relatives are alive.

 Many homes are worth more than £125,000 these days. Say that your home is worth £285,000, and you were the sole owner of it so it forms part of your estate instead of automatically becoming the property of your surviving spouse. If you leave no other savings, your spouse will be entitled to £125,000 worth of the property, plus a life interest in £80,000 worth of it. But the only way to find the money to give your children their £80,000 share may be to sell the home. Do you really want your spouse to have to do that?

If you have no children but your parents are still alive, your spouse gets all your personal belongings, the first £200,000 of your estate, and half the rest.

The remainder goes to your parents. If your parents are dead, their share goes to your brothers and sisters, or on down the line to half-brothers and half-sisters, grandparents, uncles and aunts, or finally, if none of those are alive, the Government.

Your grandchildren inherit only if their own parents – your children – have died before you. If that's the case, the share of your deceased child passes on to be split amongst their offspring. If you want your grandchildren to benefit, you have to make a will.

If you don't have a surviving spouse or children, the people in the preceding list inherit your estate in almost the same order, but with nieces and nephews and half-nieces and nephews thrown into the mix. All sorts of relatives who you wouldn't want to have a penny may be in line. If that's the case, make a will.

Unmarried partners can end up with nothing, no matter how long you've lived with them, if you don't make provision for them – either by putting all your assets in joint ownership or making a will. If your partner has been dependent on you, she can ask the court to rule that she should have something from your estate, but what a terrible position to put a loved one in.

The Government's Civil Partnership Bill, which came about in December 2005, means that same-sex partners who have gone through a civil ceremony will inherit under the intestacy rules, but it will be a long time before all the wrinkles of these new rules are ironed out in court. Don't leave it to chance. Make a will.

Deciding who sorts out your estate

When you make a will, you decide who you want to be your executor and carry out your wishes. If you die intestate, someone has to take on the responsibility of sorting out the muddle. One of your close relatives will no doubt volunteer. This relative will have to apply to the Probate office for *letters of administration* to allow her to do much the same job the executor would do if you did leave a will – to gather up your estate, pay your debts and taxes, and distribute what's left – according to the rules of intestacy. That person will be the *administrator* (*executor-dative* in Scotland). The letters of administration are the official documents that give the administrator the right to go ahead and sort out your estate.

If no one volunteers to be your administrator, the courts step in. The Probate office is very helpful about all of the ins and outs of dealing with estates. Your nearest CAB can help you and point you in the direction of your nearest probate office. You can find more information on the HM Customs and Excise Web site at www.hmrc.gov.uk or from the Probate and IHT helpline – 0845-302-0900.

Giving Your Assets Away Before You Die

You can take steps throughout your life to reduce the amount of inheritance tax (IHT) paid on your estate when you die. Here are a few ideas:

- Any gifts that you give to your spouse during your lifetime or after your death are IHT free.

- You can give away money out of your income as long as it doesn't eat into capital or savings and the gifts are free of IHT.

- You can make small gifts regularly to other people. You can give away as many lots of £250 or less as you like in each year as long as you give them to different people.

- You can give your sister or anyone else up to £3,000 a year – but just one of those gifts each year and not to someone who also got a small gift.

- You can give up to £5,000 for your child's wedding.

- You can give up to £2,500 for a grandchild's wedding.

- You can give up to £1,000 for the wedding for other family members of friends.

You can give away larger amounts, but they remain as part of your estate for seven years. If you die within seven years of giving someone £20,000, for example, IHT may be payable on it at your death. The amount of IHT due reduces over the 7 years.

Certain properties, too, can be inherited free of IHT or at a reduced rate of IHT. Business assets and agricultural property and woodland are exempt from IHT. Think about putting money into these kinds of properties so that you can leave them to your nearest and dearest knowing that they'll be exempt for IHT. But be careful. You can take steps to avoid paying IHT by getting the laws to work for you. It's a small step over the boundary into tax evasion. Evasion amounts to the illegal spiriting away of parts of your estate so that the tax collector can't get hold of it, but it may land you – or more likely, your estate – with big fines.

If you want to do some tax planning, give away money during your lifetime – quite legally, and reduce the IHT liability of your estate while keeping it all above board, see a good tax lawyer or accountant. Try the Institute of Chartered Accountants at www.icaew.co.uk or the Association of Chartered Accountants at www.acca.co.uk.

Planning the Practicalities

Apart from the big questions about how to divide up your estate when you're gone and how you can reduce the amount of IHT on your estate, you need to consider more down-to-earth issues, too. What kind of a funeral would you want if you were going to be there to see it yourself, and when would you prefer to stop receiving medical treatment?

While you're thinking about the future, consider these issues, too. They're quite often the ones that perplex the nearest and dearest most because they may not know how you feel – especially when you're well, and death still seems an improbability.

Living wills

Think about an entirely different kind of will. *Living wills* are documents that set out your wishes relating to ongoing medical treatment if you become too ill to communicate your wishes to doctors and family. You can set out the circumstances in which you'd like medical treatment to be withdrawn so that you can drift away – an *advance directive*. You can also set out the kind of treatment you'd accept, such as painkillers that may shorten your life, in an *advance statement*.

If you don't want to be kept alive by medical science, then discuss it with your nearest and dearest. Living wills are becoming more popular and doctors must take them into account when deciding on future treatment. If you go into hospital or a nursing home and you haven't made clear the circumstances in which you'd no longer want to be treated, doctors must do their best to keep you alive. The courts have decided that you can refuse medical treatment in advance only if you were fully aware of the implications and had thought about the situation that you later find yourself in. Don't leave it too late.

For more information on living wills, try the British Medical Association (www.bma.org.uk); the Law Society (www.lawsociety.org.uk); or the charity Age Concern (Age Concern England 0208-765-7200, www.ace.org.uk; Age Concern Wales 02920-431-555, www.accymru.org.uk; Age Concern Scotland 0845-833-0200 or free phone 0800-009-966, www.ageconcern scotland.org.uk; or Age Concern Northern Ireland 02890-245-729, www. ageconcernni.org). If you do decide to draw up a living will, keep it with your ordinary will and make sure that people know where to find it. Talk it over with your doctor and next of kin so that they all know your wishes and appoint someone, a *medical proxy,* who can make decisions about your medical care on your behalf and relay the wishes you've expressed in your living will to the hospital doctors. Name that person in your living will but talk it all over with them first. That person has a say only in your medical treatment and not in any other aspect of your demise unless you've given them some other powers.

Assisted dying and euthanasia

Euthanasia and assisted dying are both illegal. *Euthanasia* is the painless killing of someone who has an incurable disease or illness. *Assisted dying* is where the patient, assisted by someone else, takes his own life using lethal drugs. An ongoing debate surrounds whether either should be legalised, but the issue is a long way from resolution.

If you say in a living will that you want to be helped to die, doctors will ignore your wishes. They, or anyone else who helps you kill yourself or who kills you painlessly, or even takes you abroad to be helped in countries where it's legal, face prosecution.

Planning for going into care

Many people can no longer stay at home by themselves, and not wishing to live with other family members – or not having family members who want them to move in – they have little choice but to go into care.

If you have the money to pay for care in a private care home, the choice is yours. If you're less well off and dependent on state help to pay part of your care costs (see Chapter 11), you may have less of a choice about the care home that you go to.

One way of planning ahead is to take out an insurance policy that covers care costs in your own home or in a care home. Just like any other insurance policies, policies vary in what they cover, so you need to shop around to find the best policy at the best price to meet your needs.

The Association of British Insurers produces a leaflet on long-term care policies, available at www.abi.org.uk. The Association of Independent Financial Advisers (0207-628-1287 or www.unbiased.co.uk) can give you a list of advisers who specialise in these kinds of policies.

Planning for financial help

As you get older, the day may come when you can't manage your own finances. You can create a *power of attorney,* which gives someone else the right to deal with your property and financial affairs.

The rules are a different in Scotland, but you can designate an *ordinary power of attorney* where that person can act for you for a set period of time – perhaps while you're in hospital or abroad. This power becomes invalid if you become mentally incapable of managing your affairs.

An *enduring power of attorney* is drawn up in case you become incapable of managing your affairs and kicks in only if that happens – due to a serious or degenerative illness perhaps. The person to whom you've given enduring power of attorney has to apply to the *Court of Protection* for permission to go ahead and manage your finances. If you haven't appointed someone in advance, a relative can apply to the court in the event you become incapable, and the court can appoint a *receiver* to manage things for you – usually a member of your family.

In Scotland, a *general power of attorney* and *a continuing power of attorney* are similar to an ordinary power of attorney and an enduring power of attorney, and you can also appoint a *welfare power of attorney* to look after your welfare and care arrangements or to operate your bank accounts and sign cheques. A solicitor can help you draw up the necessary documents and talk you through the legal ramifications.

Planning your funeral

Your funeral is your last big party – you may as well have a say in how it's to be organised. You can draw up a list of your wishes for the funeral and attach it to your will or, even better, put it in a letter to your loved ones in advance. You can set aside a sum of money in your will to pay for it all – the ceremony, the burial or cremation, and the party afterwards.

Set out the basics, such as whether you want to be cremated or buried, whether you want a religious or non-religious ceremony or an environmentally friendly funeral with a cardboard coffin and horse-drawn carriage. You don't have to have an official at the funeral – you can have the ceremony in your own front garden – but the cremation has to take place in a crematorium. You can be buried in a churchyard, local authority burial ground, or on private land. Anyone living within the parish has the right to be buried in the parish churchyard. The UK has only three sites where you can be buried at sea. There are green burial sites – usually woodland sites – but in most, you can't have headstones.

If you decide to be cremated, you can also set out what you'd like done with your ashes. You may want them taken up in a balloon aircraft and scattered over the Kalahari Desert. You can take ashes out of the UK, but you need to check that you can take them into the country of your choice.

Don't forget to specify if you want your body to be donated to medical research. Carry a donor card and let your close family know if you want your organs to be used for transplants. Neither may be possible when it comes time, but make your wishes known all the same.

You can have the cost of the funeral taken out of your estate. You can even pay for it all in advance through a prepaid funeral plan. You basically agree with the funeral director what kind of departure you want, with all the details down to the coffin handles, and pay for it up front. The funeral director invests the money, and the interest on it covers any increases in cost between paying and calling on his services. Plans can cost thousands and usually start at around the £2,000 mark. The charity Age Concern can give you information on prepaid funeral plans.

It's all very well paying in advance because you're certain to need the service, but if you don't tell your family what you've done, they could well go out and arrange and pay for another funeral unnecessarily. Find out what happens to your money if the funeral director you choose goes bankrupt. You need to know that you're protected.

If you have no money in your estate for the funeral and the person who arranges it is on means-tested state benefits, he may be able to get help with the funeral costs. If no one is there to arrange the funeral, the local authority or health authority arranges it and tries to recover the costs from your estate.

Receiving Death Benefits

If your husband or wife or civil partner dies, you may be able to claim some help, depending on your age, whether you have dependent children, and whether the spouse who died had paid the right National Insurance contributions. From December 2005, this assistance also applies to people who have registered civil partnerships (see Chapter 6).

If your spouse has paid National Insurance contributions, you may be entitled to a lump sum bereavement payment of £2,000. If you're under pension age and have children, you may get the Widowed Parent's Allowance. If you're 45 or over but under pension age, you may get a Bereavement Allowance for up to a year after your spouse's death. Both the allowances can be stopped if you remarry or start living with someone. Your nearest CAB can help you.

Part III
Making Enough to Live On – Legally!

"We're both looking forward to a nice quiet
retirement and Eric's says he's going to learn
a musical instrument"

In this part . . .

In this part, I look at a subject that people are still reticent to talk about – money! If you're like most people, you earn your income by working for an employer. The law has changed many times over the past few years, and today you have the right to be paid a minimum wage and to have at least 20 days holiday a year. Mums-to-be and new parents are entitled to leave and to ask for flexible working hours. Chapter 9 goes into the details of your rights at work, while Chapter 10 looks at the delights of working for yourself and the ins and outs of running a business.

Of course, not everyone can work, and Chapter 11 goes into the rights you may have to claim welfare benefits for you and your family, from the state, if you're out of work or unable to work because of sickness. Chapter 12 is devoted to saving for retirement through pensions. As pension schemes become less generous and everyone faces the prospect of working longer, it's more important than ever to understand the way the state system operates and why you're risking a poor old age if you don't start planning for retirement as early in your career as possible.

Chapter 9

Working for an Employer

In This Chapter

▶ Knowing your rights at work

▶ Acquiring those rights

▶ Knowing what to do if your boss refuses your rights

▶ Being responsible toward your boss and colleagues

*O*ver the past few years, the law has given employees increasing rights. Some rights, such as the right to not be discriminated against, you have from the minute you decide to apply for a job. Other rights, such as the right to be paid at least the minimum wage, begin as soon as you start a job. Then you acquire other rights the longer you work for the same employer, such as the right to claim unfair dismissal after a year or the right to a redundancy payment after two years.

Many employers deny employees their rights – often because they don't know the law or because they're poor employers who think that they can get away with treating their staff badly. If you're refused holiday you're entitled to, paid less than the minimum wage or the amount stated in your contract, your boss changes the terms of your contract without your agreement, you're dismissed unfairly without going through the correct procedures, or you're refused any of the other rights outlined in this chapter, you may be able to claim compensation at an employment tribunal.

Being a Knowledgeable Employee

Employers sometimes try to get away without giving employees their rights. Sometimes employees miss out because they're scared of speaking up in case they lose their jobs. Sometimes they miss out because they simply don't know their rights in the first place. I can't cover every aspect of employment law and your rights as an employee in detail in this one chapter, so I'm aiming to give you enough information to alert you to when you should ask for help.

If you're a member of a union, your union representative can help. However, many workplaces – especially small businesses – don't recognise a union.

If you don't have a union to turn to, the CAB can help and will have leaflets on various aspects of employment rights. It also has a Web site you can visit at www.adviceguide.org.uk. You can find details of your nearest CAB in the phone book. You may also have a Law Centre in your area. Look in the phone book or contact The Law Centres Federation (020-7387-8570 or www.lawcentres.org.uk) for details.

If you're an employee (not self-employed), you're employed full time or part time, and you've been employed for the relevant qualifying period, your employment rights include the following:

- ✔ To be paid at least the National Minimum Wage
- ✔ To work no more than the maximum weekly working hours (with breaks)
- ✔ To get equal pay for equal work
- ✔ To have at least four weeks paid holiday
- ✔ To be protected from discrimination
- ✔ To work in a safe and healthy environment
- ✔ To be given notice that your employment is ending (after one month)
- ✔ To have a written Statement of Employment Particulars (within the first 8 weeks)
- ✔ To be paid statutory sick pay and statutory maternity, paternity, and adoption pay
- ✔ To have maternity, paternity, and adoption leave
- ✔ To take parental leave and time off for family emergencies
- ✔ To request flexible working arrangements
- ✔ To have protection from unfair dismissal (after one year)
- ✔ To receive written reasons for dismissal
- ✔ To receive redundancy pay (after two years)

These rights are covered by law, but the law sets out the minimum that your employer is expected to do. Employers can do better than the law expects by giving you more rights in your contract. Employers can't give you fewer rights than the law says. If they do, you can take a claim against them. If your employer does offer you greater rights through your contract, then those rights are what the law says the employer has to deliver. If your company doesn't live up to the promises made, you can make a claim against it for breach of contract.

In most cases, the law is fairly clear about your rights because they're enshrined in legislation passed by Parliament. But some areas of employment law are governed by common law. *Common law* is the body of law that builds up as cases are heard in courts and tribunals. As judges and tribunal members make their decisions, the law changes and evolves.

If you think you've been unfairly treated, the decision the tribunal or court makes will depend on the legislation and on the decisions that have been made in previous cases like yours.

Knowing Your Rights During the Hiring Process

As soon as you start looking for a job, the law protects you. The law says employers must not discriminate against any would-be applicant in a job advertisement. They can't put anything in an ad that would rule you out from applying on the grounds of race, sex, religious or other beliefs, or sexual orientation. After October 2006, the same law applies to age – young or old.

Nothing in job ads can state that, for example, Asian or African people or wheelchair users shouldn't apply. Ads can't say that the employer is looking for a man, which would be *direct discrimination,* unless the nature of the job is such that it can only be done by a man – for example, an attendant for a male toilet.

But ads shouldn't indirectly discriminate either. If one says that the job requires good English, that ad can rule out people for whom English isn't their first language. If good English isn't an important skill for that particular job, then the employer is guilty of *indirect discrimination.* There's more on discrimination in the section 'Dealing with Issues at Work', later in this chapter.

You have the right not to be discriminated against the whole way through the application and selection process. Application forms should only ask questions related to your skills and qualifications, and the same goes for interviews. As a woman, you shouldn't be asked whether you intend to get married and have children when a man wouldn't be asked the same question. If you have a disability, you shouldn't be told that you can't be interviewed or employed because the premises aren't accessible for you. The employer is expected to make reasonable adjustments to make it possible for you to do the job if you have all the necessary skills and qualifications, your disability doesn't prevent you from doing the job, and you are the best candidate.

Employers who make decisions to turn you down for a job on the grounds that you are, for example, gay, Jewish, black, have a hearing impairment, or are a woman of child-bearing age are breaking the law, and you can take a case against them for discrimination.

You also have the right not to be refused a job because you belong to a union or don't belong to any union or particular union and don't want to join.

Another right you have as a job applicant is to have all the information you give the employer used only for the purpose of going through the job selection procedure. *The Data Protection Act* says that the employer has to keep any information he holds on you safe and secure so that other people not involved in the process can't get to it. The employer also shouldn't pass it on to anyone else unless you agree.

Potential employers have the right to make some checks on you before offering you a job. They can verify that you have the qualifications you say you have, are entitled to work in the UK, and references and check to see whether you have a criminal record that would stop you working with children or vulnerable adults. They can also ask you to undertake a health check. If they make you a job offer, conditional on the checks being satisfactory, they can withdraw the offer if the checks aren't satisfactory, and you can't do anything about it. If, however, an employer withdraws a job offer because of poor references and you've lost out as a result, you should take advice.

Accepting the contract

Employers usually decide which applicant they want to employ and phone up with a job offer. From the minute that offer is made and accepted by you, a contract exists, even if the offer isn't in writing. A good employer will follow up the phone call with a letter setting out the main terms and conditions, such as pay, holiday entitlement, hours, place of work, job title, and starting date. You are then entitled to a *Written Statement of Employment Particulars* within eight weeks of starting your job. That statement should have all the previous details, plus:

- ✔ Your job description
- ✔ Details, or where to find details, of disciplinary and grievance procedures
- ✔ Information about the pension scheme
- ✔ Information on what happens if you're sick
- ✔ Information on how much notice either side has to give the other if the employment contract is ending

✔ The procedure that occurs if staff have to be made redundant

✔ The retirement age in the firm

✔ Any work that will have to be done outside the UK

✔ Any collective bargains that have been agreed to with a recognised union about something like pay or holidays

✔ The length of the contract, if the job isn't permanent

Not all the details have to be in the written statement – the employer may point you to where you can find the details written down, such as in a staff handbook or in a computer document. Of course, the written statement or the firm's handbook can have all sorts of other details, such as the health and safety policy, the smoking policy, the dress code, and guidance for sending and receiving private e-mails, using the Internet, and making private phone calls.

The terms discussed by you and your employer or written down are *express terms* of the contract. But other terms may not be written down and may not have been mentioned but still form part of the contract by implication. The employer is entitled to expect you to do a good job and to obey instructions. You're entitled to be paid and to be given work to do so that you can be paid. There has to be trust and confidence between you. It's implied in your contract that you won't do anything to damage your employer's business, such as working for competitors, and that you'll keep information about the business confidential. You have the right to expect that your boss will take care of you by giving you a safe and healthy place to work.

In addition, other terms and conditions may be implied in your contract simply because they have become custom and practice in the workplace – everyone may go home early on Friday simply because over a period of time, they've got into the habit of going home early on Friday, and the employer has never stopped the practice.

The terms and conditions in your contract, either expressed or implied, are what your employer has to deliver. If an employer changes any of those terms and conditions without your agreement, the employer will be in breach of contract, and you may be able to make a claim against the company.

Your employer shouldn't make deductions from your pay that you haven't already agreed to, or the deduction is unlawful. Your boss can't change your working hours without your agreement or give you fewer holidays than it says in the contract. And don't forget the laws that protect you, such as the Health and Safety at Work Act, The Equal Pay Act 1970 or the Working Time Regulations under the European Working Time Directive.

Knowing your responsibilities as an employee

After you've accepted a job, you also have responsibilities as an employee. Some things may not be written down or even discussed between you, but they're still part of your contract. Your employer has to pay you for the job, but you have a responsibility to carry out that job to the best of your abilities, competently and safely.

Your employer has to be able to trust you and be able to have confidence in you. If you do something to undermine that trust and confidence, such as stealing from your employer or passing on confidential information that would damage the business, your employer may be able to regard the contract between you as being at an end. Similarly, you have to be faithful to your company and not do work for somebody else or for yourself that would be in conflict with your company, compete with the business, or damage it in any way. (So selling the clothes your boss sells in his shop for half the price on a market stall is out!)

You have a duty to obey your employer's instructions as long as they're reasonable and lawful. They're considered reasonable as long as they're part of your job description, and you're capable of carrying them out.

Not only do you have responsibilities to your employer, but you have responsibilities to your fellow workers, too. You must not do anything that may result in them being injured because you're lax about Health and Safety, for example.

Getting the idea

While you're at work, you're there to work for your employer, not for yourself. It follows therefore that any ideas and inventions that you come up with in the course of your job belong to your employer, not to you. After all, you're being paid to come up with those ideas and inventions.

However, it can be hard to prove that a great idea came to you in your own time away from work. If you're in the kind of job that depends on ideas and inventions, talk the whole issue of ownership over with your boss so that you know exactly where you stand and can avoid future disputes. Many employers put clauses in the contract to make it clear when an idea belongs to the company, and when it's yours.

Working Hard for the Money

You have a responsibility to work for your money; to do the job to the best of your abilities; to use the skills your employer has hired you for; and to work competently and safely. Your employer should be able to trust that if you say you're off sick, you're genuinely ill and not just malingering. In return, your employer should pay you the salary agreed as part of your contract.

Getting a fair day's pay

The main legislation that covers pay is the *National Minimum Wage* legislation. Under this law, employees are entitled to be paid at least the minimum wage unless they're workers living as part of a family or school children. The hourly rate differs depending on what age you are:

✔ The adult rate for anyone 22 and over is £5.05 an hour and will go up to £5.35 in October 2006.

✔ The development rate for 18- to 21-years-olds is £4.25 an hour (£4.45 from October 2006). If you're 22 and over and getting accredited training during the first six months in a job, this rate also applies to you, You need a written agreement, and you have to attend at least 26 days training in those six months.

✔ The younger workers' rate of £3 an hour is paid to 16- and 17-year-olds who have reached the minimum school-leaving age. It will increase to £3.30 from October 2006. Apprentices under 18 and those under the age of 26 who are in the first year of their apprenticeship are exempt.

If you aren't paid at least the minimum wage, you can make a claim against your employer in the civil courts or an employment tribunal. If your employer sacks you for claiming your right to the minimum wage, the dismissal is automatically unfair, and you can claim that at an employment tribunal, too.

Under the National Minimum Wage, on top of your hourly pay, you're entitled to tips given to you directly by customers, allowances, expenses and travel costs while travelling on the job, extra wages from overtime and shift work, and benefits in kind, such as the use of the company car, fuels, or meals. Bonuses and commissions, incentive payments, and performance-related pay can count toward your minimum wage. If you live in accommodation provided by your employer, £4.15 a day of the value of that accommodation counts toward the minimum wage.

Out of your wages, the employer has to deduct income tax and national insurance. (See the section 'Paying Tax and National Insurance,' later in this chapter.) You may also have other deductions, such as contributions to your company's pension scheme if it provides one (see 'Paying into a Pension,' later in this chapter), deductions for repayment of your student loan if you're earning enough (go to the HMRC Web site at www.hmrc.gov.uk for information), or union subscriptions if you're a union member. Your boss should let you know about any deductions to be made from your pay and get your agreement. With deductions that are regular and the same every month, your employer can give you an annual notice of what the deductions will be.

Your employer doesn't need your permission to make other deductions, such as those the law says have to be made. If a court orders that you must repay a debt or make payments to the Child Support Agency for child support through an attachment of earnings order, the employer has to comply. If you work in the retail trade and a shortfall occurs in the till or in stock, the company can take the money back from your wages, but they must get your agreement or have a clause in your contract that says that should the situation arise, that's what they'll do. If you've been overpaid, then your employer can usually reclaim that money from you through your wages. You may be able to argue that you couldn't have been expected to know that you'd been overpaid, and that because of the extra money, you had put yourself in such a financial position that having to repay the money would cause you hardship. If you do find yourself in that position, get advice from the CAB.

If your company usually pays you on the 15th of the month, they'll be in breach of contract if they pay you a few days late. But you can't do much about it if you have no quantifiable loss.

Another important piece of legislation relating to pay is the *Equal Pay Act 1970.* It was brought in to ensure that women and men are paid the same for *like work.* The rules are fairly complicated, and if you think that you're being paid less than a male or female colleague who does basically the same job and you want advice, talk to the Equal Opportunities Commission (0845-601-5901 or www.eoc.org.uk).

Bear in mind, of course, that employers are within their rights to increase people's pay over time or to pay better qualified people more, so some people doing similar jobs are being paid more because they're better qualified.

If you work part time, the Part-Time Workers Regulations also protect you. You must not be treated less favourably than full-time workers just because you work fewer hours. That law means that you're entitled to the same hourly rate of pay and have the same rights to holiday and overtime pay and all the other rights in your contract as someone doing the same job on a full-time basis.

Putting in the hours

The rules about the number of hours most employees work come from the European Working Time Directive. Apart from junior doctors who won't come fully under the directive until 2009 and employees who decide their own hours or whose working time isn't measured, such as managers, most other workers are protected.

Here are the directive's guidelines:

- ✔ You should work a maximum of 48 hours in an average working week.

- ✔ You should be allowed a break of at least 20 minutes if you're working more than 6 hours a day.

- ✔ You should have 11 consecutive hours off in every 24 hours.

- ✔ You should have 24 continuous hours off in every 7 days.

- ✔ If you're working at night, you should work, on average, a maximum of 8 hours in every 24 hours.

The 48-hour maximum is an average rather than a definite limit. The Working Time Directive suggests that the average is worked out over the last 17 weeks you've worked, but that period's not set in stone and can be changed as long as the period over which the hours are averaged out isn't shorter than 4 months.

At the moment, a group of workers can opt out of the 48-hour maximum, but you can't be forced to opt out by your employer, and you can take a claim against him if he treats you less favourably than other employees because you refuse to opt out. If you have opted out, you can give notice of up to three months that you want to opt back in. The UK may be forced to drop the opt-out by the EU.

The continuous 24 hours that you have to have off in every seven days doesn't have to be the same day each week. You can have Sunday off one week; work Monday to Saturday; work Sunday to Friday; and then have the Saturday off at the end of the second week.

Working hours include overtime, time spent travelling to see clients or having working lunches, training and time when you're on call at work. They don't include time travelling to and from work and home, breaks while at work, or training away from work. The situation regarding being on call at home is still far from clear and is being considered by the European Commission.

Be careful about taking work home. You may end up putting in hours that your boss won't count as working hours. If you do take work home, discuss it with him and come to an agreement about what time will count and what won't. Otherwise, it may be up to a tribunal to decide if you disagree.

Taking breaks

In most jobs, you're entitled to breaks. The European Working Time Directive says that you must be allowed one break of 20 minutes if your working day is more than six hours long. Your employer may allow more frequent and longer breaks – most people are allowed a lunch hour. If you work constantly at a computer screen, you have to be allowed a 10-minute break every hour – away from the screen, but not away from work – for health and safety reasons. Your boss doesn't have to make you take your breaks, but he has to make it possible, and impossible, for you to take them.

Taking Time Off

You may want to take time off during the working year for all sorts of reasons. Your employer should make it clear from the beginning what the company policy is on holidays. The law covers your rights to paid holidays, but your employer may be more generous than the law requires. Laws cover how much you have to be paid if you're off sick, having a baby, adopting, or spending time with young children, as well as how much time off you're allowed. You also have to be allowed time off with pay to do your public duty, and at other times, the employer has to let you take off but doesn't have to pay you.

Taking holidays

Most employees are entitled to at least four weeks paid holiday a year. Your employer may be more generous than that. If you do get just the minimum four weeks leave and you work 5 days a week, you're entitled to 20 days off. If you work 3 days a week, you're entitled to 12 days off with pay.

Bank holidays can be counted toward your total holiday entitlement, or you may be given your four weeks plus the bank holidays. Whether or not bank holidays are included, you don't have to be given the actual day of the bank holiday off if your employer is usually operating on that day. You may be given another day instead. If you do work on the bank holiday, you aren't entitled to be paid any more than a normal day's pay for it unless that's been agreed in your contract.

When you want to take some of your annual leave, you have to give your employer notice. If you want two weeks off, you have to give at least four weeks notice. If your boss can't allow you to take that particular time off, he has to give you notice of at least the length of time off you've requested, so in this case, he has to give you two week's notice that the answer to your request is no.

Employers can dictate that you have to take holiday at particular times when their workplaces are closed, such as Christmas, or that you can't take holiday at particularly busy times. If you want to take time off for certain religious festivals and are refused, take advice. Your employer may be guilty of discrimination on the grounds of religion.

Your boss has to make it possible for you to take all your leave, but he doesn't have to make you take it. If you don't take all your leave within your holiday year (defined in your contract – usually beginning of January to end of December or beginning of April to end of March), your employer doesn't have to let you carry the unused days over into the next holiday year or pay you for them. If you don't use it, you could lose it! You should make sure that you find out what company policy is.

Taking time off sick

If you're off sick, you're likely to be entitled to statutory sick pay (SSP). Your employer is entitled not to pay you for the first three days off (the waiting days); he has to pay you from the fourth day.

SSP is paid for a maximum of 28 weeks at a rate of £70.05. If you're still unable to work after that time, you have to apply for Incapacity Benefit from the state welfare benefit system through your Benefits Agency Office or Job Centre Plus. Your employer may be more generous when it comes to sick pay and pay contractual sick pay on top of your SSP. Contractual sick pay usually amounts to your usual wages for a period of time without any waiting days. If your contract says that you're entitled to contractual sick pay, your employer has to pay you that higher amount.

Taking time off for babies

Nearly 750,000 babies are born each year in the UK, so you aren't alone if you take time off to have a baby or bring up children. In the past, some employers have simply sacked women who got pregnant, treated them unfairly and hoped they'd leave, or made their jobs mysteriously disappear while they were on maternity leave and refused to take them back. The law has changed in this area probably more than any other area of employment law, and employers can no longer act in this way without risking the wrath of employment tribunals. Check out exactly what your entitlement is when you find out you're pregnant and check what it says in your employment contract.

The law doesn't allow women to be unfairly treated or dismissed because they're pregnant or having a baby. You're entitled to:

✔ Paid time off for antenatal care

✔ Protection against unfair treatment or dismissal

✔ Protection of your terms and conditions whilst on maternity leave

✔ Maternity pay

✔ Maternity leave if you've been employed long enough

✔ The right to return to work

From day one in your job, you're entitled to reasonable time off to go to antenatal appointments that your doctor or midwife has recommended and to be paid your normal hourly rate while you're off. If your employer refuses, you can take a claim against the company to an employment tribunal. (See the upcoming section 'Taking a Case Against Your Boss.')

If you're sick before the birth, the period of illness should be treated the same as any other period of illness, with normal sick leave and sick pay rules applying. If you're sick within four weeks of the expected week of childbirth, but before the date you intended to start your maternity leave and the illness is related to your pregnancy, your maternity leave automatically starts.

There are two types of maternity leave:

✔ **Ordinary maternity leave:** You're entitled to this 26-week leave regardless of how long you've worked for your employer.

✔ **Additional maternity leave:** You're entitled to an extra 26 weeks as long as you have worked for your employer for at least 26 weeks at the beginning of the 15th week before the expected week of confinement.

You can qualify for one or both periods of leave, but you have to tell your employer by the start of the 15th week before the expected week of the birth when you intend to start your leave. You can change your mind about that date, but you have to give 28 days notice. Your employer will probably want a certificate MAT B1 from your doctor or midwife verifying the week the birth is expected. Your maternity leave can't start any earlier than the 11th week before the week in which the baby is due.

After the baby is born, you can't go back to work any sooner than 14 days after the birth. If you take your full leave entitlement, you don't have to do anything other than turn up on the day you're due back to work, but if you intend to go back early, you have to give your employer 28 days notice. If you don't give the correct notice, your company can delay the date of your return and take disciplinary action against you, but it can't make you give up your maternity rights. If you're sick at the end of your maternity leave, the normal rules about sickness apply.

While you're off on 26 weeks ordinary maternity leave, you're entitled to all the benefits set out in your contract. Your holiday entitlement still builds up. You have the same rights if you're made redundant, but you can't be made redundant rather than someone else because you're on maternity leave. You're entitled to pension contributions from your employer, as well as private medical insurance, permanent health insurance, use of the company car, and any other benefits that appear in your contract. You have similar rights if you're adopting a child, and most fathers have the right to up to two weeks paternity leave.

You may also be entitled to some maternity pay for the time you're off. You must be paid Statutory Maternity Pay (SMP) if you've worked for your employer for 26 weeks by the 15th week before the expected week of birth and have earned enough to pay National Insurance Contributions. The £84.00 SMP currently lasts for 26 weeks. (The Government is planning to extend maternity pay to cover up to 52 weeks off.) For the first 6 weeks, SMP is 90 per cent of your normal wages. For the next 20 weeks, it's either the £108.85 set by the Government or 90 per cent of your salary – whichever is the lower amount. Of course, your employer can be more generous than that, and if your contract says the company will pay you more, then it has to do so.

When you return to work, you're entitled to go back to the same job on the same terms and conditions as when you started your maternity leave. You don't have a legal right to work part-time or to work some of the time at home, but if you ask your company for those changes, it has to consider them. If the company rejects your request without a good business reason, you may be able to make a claim against it for sex discrimination on the grounds that, because women usually have the primary childcare responsibilities, refusing to let you work fewer hours or from home has more impact on your life than a man's. You can also request flexible working. (See the upcoming section 'Taking time off for family reasons.')

This whole area of employment law is complicated, and you should make sure that you get all the information you can right from the start of your pregnancy. *Pregnancy For Dummies* by Jarvis, Stone, Eddleman, and Duenwald (Wiley) has all the information and advice you'll need, and your local CAB can help. Find it in your phone book or on the Internet at www.adviceguide.co.uk.

Taking time off for public duties

The law says that you have to be given time off with pay if you're a trade union official carrying out certain trade union duties, including duties as a health and safety representative. You must also be given time off if you're a company pension fund trustee. On top of that, employees are entitled to reasonable time off – unpaid – to carry out various public duties. If you're lucky, your employer may be more generous and pay you for time off to act as a magistrate or local councillor.

The problem is that the law isn't clear on how much time off is reasonable and which public duties should count. Some employers draw the line at being a magistrate or councillor, while others give time off to do voluntary, charity, or community work.

As far as jury service is concerned, you don't have a legal right to time off, but if your company refuses to allow you to go, it may fall foul of the law for contempt of court. Not only that, but it's automatically unfair to dismiss you for taking time off for jury duty, so you would be able to make a claim against the company at an employment tribunal.

Taking time off for family reasons

Most parents have the right to time off to spend with their children. Each parent can take up to a total of 13 weeks parental leave for each child for the first 5 years of that child's life – unpaid. You still work for the company while you're off, and you have to be allowed to come back to the same job if you take four weeks or less off at any one time. If you take longer and it's not reasonably practicable for you to return to the same job, you have to be offered a similar one with the same or better status and terms and conditions.

You also have the right to ask for flexible working conditions, such as working different hours, working longer one day and less the next, or doing some of your work from home. Your boss doesn't have to say yes, but if he refuses, he has to have a good business reason for saying no. A refusal may amount to indirect sex discrimination. You can make complaints over a refusal to agree to flexible working and indirect discrimination to an employment tribunal.

If someone close to you dies you have no legal right to time off but if the dead person was a dependent – someone who lives in your household as part of the family – usually a relative such as a spouse, child, parent or other relative, the Government expects your employer to give you a reasonable amount of time off. The closer the relative the more time you're likely to need to make all the necessary arrangements and to recover enough to be able to get back to work.

If a dependent is ill, you should be given enough time off to help them, arrange care, or deal with unexpected emergencies. There's no limit to what's reasonable or to the number of times an employee can take time off, and if your employer says no, you can complain to an employment tribunal. However, you have a responsibility to be reasonable, too, and not exploit the situation.

Paying Tax, National Insurance, and Other Deductions

Your employer has to deduct income tax and national insurance from your pay and hand it over to the Government, whether you like it or not. Your wage slip may have other deductions, too. Under the Employment Rights Act 1996, you're entitled to know in advance about most deductions that will be made from your gross pay and why. Your contract should explain them, and if it doesn't, you should be asked for your written consent before they're deducted. But tax and national insurance are among those excluded from that rule because they have to be made by the employer under law.

Your *net pay* is what you're left with after all the deductions have been made. You normally have to pay tax on:

- ✔ Wages
- ✔ Overtime and shift pay
- ✔ Tips
- ✔ Bonuses and commissions
- ✔ Statutory sick pay, maternity pay, paternity pay, and adoption pay
- ✔ Lump sums, such as pay in lieu of notice or ex-gratia payments
- ✔ Some cash expenses allowances

You can earn up to £5,035 a year (up to your 65th birthday) before you start paying tax, and the rest is taxed at different rates, depending on how much you earn. On top of that tax, you have to pay National Insurance contributions, which go into the fund that eventually pays your state pension, and most other benefits, such as Job Seeker's Allowance, that you may have to claim during your working life (see Chapter 11). Your employer should give you a form P60 each year showing how much tax and national insurance has been deducted.

If you leave your job, you should get a P45, which shows this information. You'll need to give your P45 to your new employer so that he can see what you've already paid during the tax year up until you started your new job.

If you have any problems with tax and national insurance, your local tax office can give you all the information you need, or visit the Web site www.hmrc.gov.uk.

Paying into a pension

Your employer must offer you an occupational pension; pay a contribution worth the equivalent of 3 per cent of your salary into your personal pension; or offer you access to a stakeholder pension if your place of work has five or more employees. (For more information on pensions, see Chapter 12.)

You don't have to join a scheme that your employer offers you, but if you do, most employers will expect you to make contributions from your wages – which will be deducted before you get your pay packet. Many employers will make contributions to your pension, although the law doesn't say that they have to contribute. If your employer does, it's usually well worth your while joining the scheme.

Without an additional pension of some sort, you'll be left to depend on the state pension for your income in retirement unless you have an inheritance, some property you can sell to generate income, or some savings. If you don't have a pension that you can join at work, you can make your own provision through a personal plan or a stakeholder scheme (see Chapter 12).

Claiming Welfare Benefits and Working

The fact that you're employed and working doesn't mean that you aren't entitled to any welfare benefits from the state. Some of the benefits you're entitled to depend on your income and are means-tested. Others depend on the national insurance contributions you've paid in the past, but aren't means-tested. Chapter 11 covers welfare benefits.

The benefit system is complicated because of the range of benefits and the many different offices that deal with them. If you do think your wages are low enough or you're employed but not getting any wages because you're off sick, talk to your nearest Citizens Advice Bureau. An advisor there can go through all the figures with you and tell you how to claim.

Dealing with Issues at Work

No matter how well run the workplace, it will have issues to be dealt with from time to time. If your company has played its cards right, everything you ever needed to know about your workplace and how it should run is spelled out in your contract and in the company handbook. If you do have a problem, find out what your rights are before you approach your boss so that you're more likely to be able to avoid disputes. I can't cover every eventuality in one chapter. so I've just picked a few of the problems that can arise. Your nearest

CAB or Law Centre can give you much more advice and take your individual circumstances into account.

Health and safety

Your employer has a duty to look after your health, safety, and welfare at work, which means providing a safe place to work where hazards have been identified and removed, if possible. If your company can't remove the hazards, it needs to reduce any risk they pose to you and your work colleagues. When the risks have been reduced as far as possible but still exist, your employer must provide protective equipment. Your boss also has to ensure that you work safely and don't endanger your colleagues, and that they don't endanger you. That may mean that the employer has to check that people have the right qualifications for the jobs they're doing or to make sure that they're fully trained and that training is up to date.

Obviously, working in a manufacturing plant is more hazardous than working in an office. But sometimes it's the less obvious hazards that do the most harm. The most common accidents are slips and trips, and the most common cause of illness these days is stress.

A wide range of regulations cover every aspect of workplace health and safety, from noise, temperature, lighting, and use of computers to lifting, dangerous chemicals, lorries, forklift trucks, and heavy machinery.

If you're injured at work or become ill and you think that your employer may have been negligent in some way, you can take out a personal injury claim through the civil courts. Unlike in the case of employment tribunals, no limits exist on the amounts that can be awarded to you in compensation. However, the last thing you want is to be unable to work or lead your life because of accident or ill health, so you should take your own welfare seriously. If your employer has put up warning signs at danger points in the workplace, don't ignore them. If you're provided with protective equipment, make sure that you use it and use it properly, including reporting when it needs to be repaired or renewed. Make sure that you report any potential hazards to the appropriate people in your workplace, and if you do feel that you're suffering from stress or that you may be getting repetitive strain injury, for example, talk to your line manager.

Discrimination

You have the right not to be discriminated against on the grounds of race, sex, religious or other beliefs, sexual orientation, or disability at any stage of your dealings with an employer. The same applies to age discrimination after October 2006.

You don't have to be working for an employer to be discriminated against. If you can prove to an employment tribunal you've been discriminated against in the selection or interviewing process (see the earlier section 'Knowing your rights during the hiring process') – perhaps not given a job you were fully qualified and capable of doing because you use a wheelchair – you can be awarded compensation. You also have the right not to be discriminated against after you've left – perhaps through your references. And, of course, you shouldn't be discriminated against while you're working for an employer. The discrimination may not come from the boss himself, but from one of the other employees. Your employer is still responsible because he allows it to happen in the workplace.

Your employer should have an Equal Opportunities Policy in place so that everyone in your workplace understands that discrimination of any sort, against anyone working there, is not tolerated. If you feel you've been discriminated against and take a case against your employer, that policy is the first thing the tribunal will want to see.

If you make a complaint about being discriminated against and you're treated less favourably than other employees because you've complained, it may be *victimisation*. For example, if you're black and claiming discrimination after a less qualified white person is promoted over your head and you're dismissed or demoted, it's likely to be victimisation, and a tribunal is likely to view that as a form of discrimination.

Harassment is anything that violates your dignity or creates an intimidating, hostile, degrading, humiliating, or offensive working environment for you. That includes sexist or racist jokes, language, or graffiti, or being picked on or ostracised by other employees or managers because of ethnic origins, colour, or sex. The same goes for disability, beliefs, and sexual orientation.

Your employer has a duty to protect you, and the company's Equal Opportunities Policy should make it clear that harassment isn't tolerated. If you're subjected to harassment, you can take a case against your company for discrimination and claim that it didn't provide a safe and healthy working environment. Alternately, you can claim that you had no choice but to quit because of your employer's actions – a *constructive dismissal*. (See the upcoming section 'Dismissal.')

Being Fired

Being fired is probably not something you want to contemplate, and the law does protect you from employers who simply decide your face no longer fits. Many dismissals are automatically unfair and don't require you to have worked for the employer for at least one year. However, after your employer has employed you for a year, extra protection means that you can't be unfairly dismissed, and if you are, you can take a case against your employer at an employment tribunal for compensation, which I explain in the upcoming section 'Taking a Case Against Your Boss.' Your employer can fire you for misconduct; on the grounds that you aren't capable of doing the job; or because the company's facing a downturn in business and needs to cut jobs and your job is redundant. But your employer has to have a fair reason for firing you, and has to follow all the right procedures, or the dismissal is considered unfair.

If you're guilty of *gross misconduct* – something as serious as hitting a colleague or fraud – you can be fired because the relationship between the two of you has broken down. In theory, in those kinds of circumstances, you can be fired without notice, but even then the employer is taking a big risk if he doesn't fully investigate the situation and give you an opportunity to explain yourself.

If you're fired because you've complained about a situation at work or you've been forced to leave work because of something your employer has or hasn't done, it may count as unfair dismissal, too. If you're at risk of losing your job, talk to your union representative or go to your local CAB for advice.

Going through the disciplinary procedures

Every employer has to have a written disciplinary procedure, and you should have details of it in your Written Statement of Employment Particulars, or the statement should point you to where you can read the policy. The policy has to meet minimum standards, but your employer can go further and make the procedures even more flexible.

Before the company can dismiss you, it has to follow those disciplinary procedures, and before it starts a disciplinary action, the company has to investigate the situation fully and be certain that the dispute can't be resolved informally. Your boss should tell you why the company's investigating and what he thinks can be done to resolve the matter informally, such as giving you extra training or counselling and giving you time in which to improve.

If your company decides that it has no choice but to start disciplinary action – either because your misdemeanour is too serious to be resolved informally or because the informal approach has been tried and didn't work – it has to tell you that they're starting formal proceedings. The company has to hold meetings with you to discuss the matter and allow you to put your side of the story and present any evidence and witnesses. You have the right to be accompanied at those meetings by a union representative or work colleague. Your boss has to tell you what the decision is after each meeting and give you opportunities to improve. He can set deadlines for improvement, and you have the right to appeal during the process, in which case the employer has to hold further appeal meetings. Ultimately and eventually, if no resolution or improvement occurs, the employer can dismiss you.

If you feel your employer has been unfair in the decision to dismiss you, you can take a case for unfair dismissal to an employment tribunal. If your employer failed to follow the correct procedures, the dismissal is automatically unfair.

The aim of the Dispute Resolution Regulations is to make employers think carefully and be absolutely sure that nothing can be done to keep you in your job before deciding on dismissal. The procedure gives several opportunities to discuss the problems and look for ways to keep employees rather than sack them. There is also the option along the way to bring in people to mediate a resolution. If you feel your dismissal has been unfair, go to the CAB or Law Centre for advice.

Making a complaint

Your employer has to have a grievance procedure in place, which sets out how you can go about making a complaint about some aspect of your working conditions. Amongst the most common reasons for employees to complain are bullying, harassment, and discrimination by other members of staff or by their immediate line managers. Your complaints have to be fully and fairly investigated.

Sometimes employees have cause for complaint, but are too worried about losing their jobs to speak up, or perhaps the problem is with their immediate boss. Sometimes an employer starts a disciplinary procedure against an employee, and the reason that employee hasn't been doing the job properly is because of a problem in the workplace. If that happens to you, you should consider starting a grievance procedure. Make sure that you read your employer's grievance procedure carefully and follow it and get help from your union or CAB.

Many complaints that you can bring to an employment tribunal require you to enter into a grievance against your employer and wait 28 days before complaining to the tribunal. If you don't, the tribunal may refuse to allow your claim to go ahead, and any compensation you're eventually awarded can be reduced by as much as half. It's very important to take advice before you take action.

Dismissal

If the end result is that your employer fires you, the dismissal is fair only if it was for a good reason and the dispute resolution procedures were followed correctly. If the employer had a fair reason to sack you, but didn't follow all the correct procedures, your dismissal is automatically unfair, and an employment tribunal can award you increased compensation. In most cases, the dispute resolution procedures require you to appeal against your dismissal before you make any complaint to an employment tribunal. If you don't, any compensation you're eventually awarded can be reduced by half. Take advice.

Your employer must not sack you for asking for something that is your right in law, such as pay of at least the National Minimum Wage or at least four weeks paid holiday a year. You also have the right to be given written reasons for your dismissal. If you suspect you've been unfairly treated, get advice.

Don't be tempted to make a claim against your employer if you know in your heart that your treatment has been fair (a *vexations case*), just because you want to get back at the company or your boss. Tribunals are set up to spot such cases and throw them out before they get to a full tribunal hearing.

Sometimes an employee can leave a job, but still be seen as being dismissed. If your employer's behaviour left you with no choice but to go – for example, your boss didn't give you any work, and the relationship between you had broken down, or he allowed you to be bullied despite your complaints – it may be seen as a dismissal. If the boss's behaviour, or that of colleagues, has pushed you into resigning, you may have a case to claim *constructive unfair dismissal*. Take advice from your union, CAB, or Law Centre.

When your job comes to an end because you leave, you must give your employer at least a week's notice – or longer, if you've agreed to that in your contract. If the company wants you to leave, it must give you notice. The law says the following:

- ✔ If you've worked for an employer from one month up to two years you should receive one week's notice.

- ✔ If you've been employed for two years, you receive at least two weeks notice; three years, three weeks; and so on up to a maximum of 12 weeks notice for people who've been employed by their employer for 12 years or more.

- ✔ If your contract says you're entitled to longer notice, then the employer must give you the notice in your contract.

If your company doesn't want you to go on working until the end of your notice period, it must pay you for that time. If you don't get paid that money, you should be able to take a claim against the company for *wrongful dismissal*. You shouldn't be any worse off if you aren't allowed to work your notice period than you would have been if you'd still been at work. If you would normally have the use of a company car, for example, you should still be able to use it or be compensated for not having it. Get advice.

Redundancy

When you're made redundant, you're dismissed because your employer's need for employees to do a particular kind of work is reduced or no longer exists. The employer may be moving to another location or ceasing to trade. To be genuinely redundant, jobs must go, but it doesn't have to be your job that disappears. In certain circumstances, your employer can make you redundant and move someone else in the business to do your job, which is called *bumping*. However, your employer can't just make you redundant one day and take someone else on to do your job the next – that's an unfair dismissal. Your employer may have to cut jobs if a downturn in business occurs or if the demand declines for the type of work you do.

Sometimes it's clear that a particular employee's skills are no longer needed so that person should go, but sometimes ten people are employed to do similar jobs, and only seven are needed. When your boss is deciding who should be made redundant, he should select people on an objective and fair basis and be careful not to select people just because he doesn't like them, or because of their race or sex, for example. (See the discrimination section, earlier in this chapter.) If an employee is off on maternity leave when jobs are being made redundant, she should be offered any suitable alternative job available.

Before deciding to make people redundant, your company may decide to take temporary measures, such as laying people off for a few weeks or putting them on short-time working. The company can only do that if it's allowed in your contract. If it isn't, your employer is in breach of contract. If you're laid off or put on short-time working, you may be able to claim a redundancy payment, even if the employer doesn't dismiss you. Get advice.

Most people who have worked for their employer for two years or more are entitled to a redundancy payment, if they're made redundant. The law says that any employment before the age of 18 doesn't count. Someone employed by the same employer for two years at the age of 20 is entitled to one week's pay as a statutory redundancy payment up to a maximum of £290 a week. The amount of statutory redundancy pay you're entitled to increases with age and length of employment, so someone employed for 20 years at the age of 61 is entitled to the maximum amount – 30 weeks pay at a maximum of £290 a week.

If you're 65, you aren't entitled to a redundancy payment at the moment. From the age of 64, you lose 1/12 of your redundancy entitlement for every month you're over 64. The Government may change those rules when the new Age Discrimination laws come into force in October 2006.

If you're being made redundant and want to see how much the law says you're entitled to as well as more information about being made redundant, look an the Department of Trade and Industry (DTI) Web site at www.dti.gov.uk.

Of course, your employer may have set out more generous terms for employees being made redundant, and if your contract says you'll get a bigger redundancy payment, that's what your employer must give you.

If you're made redundant, you're entitled to the same notice periods explained in the earlier section on dismissal. If you aren't allowed to work out your notice, you should be paid money in lieu. When you leave, you should be given any outstanding pay, notice pay, holiday pay, and your redundancy payment.

Sometimes employers have to make redundancies because their business is in financial trouble, so it follows that sometimes they don't have all the money needed to pay everyone what they're owed. If that's the case, a receiver or administrator appointed to handle the company's affairs can help you claim from the state, or you can contact a Redundancy Payment Office to claim at least some of the money you're owed. You can find details on the DTI Web site at www.dti.gov.uk.

Employers sometimes make their employees redundant when they're selling their business to another owner. The new owner may want to make some or all of the existing workforce redundant. In these situations, the dismissals are automatically unfair because the dismissals are the result of the business transfer. You may be protected under the Transfer of Undertakings (Protection of Employment) Regulations. The law is particularly complicated, and you should take advice.

Taking a Case Against Your Boss

You may want to take a case against your employer for many reasons. Unfair dismissal is just one of them, but it's one of the most common. Others include:

- ✔ Not getting equal pay
- ✔ Not being paid at least the national minimum wage
- ✔ Breaches of contract
- ✔ Discrimination
- ✔ Wrongful dismissal
- ✔ Not being given written reasons for dismissal
- ✔ Dismissal for requesting statutory rights or taking industrial action
- ✔ Unfair selection for redundancy
- ✔ Long hours or lack of holiday pay
- ✔ Unfair treatment as a part-time worker
- ✔ Not being given maternity, paternity, adoption, and parental leave or leave for family emergencies

✔ Requests for flexible working haven't been considered

✔ Not being given Written Statement of Particulars of Employment

✔ Not being allowed to bring a union representative or colleague to disciplinary or grievance hearings in the workplace

✔ Being refused time off for trade union activities or as a pension fund trustee

✔ Being sacked or victimized for *whistle blowing* – reporting illegal or potentially fraudulent practices in the workplace.

An employment tribunal handles most claims against an employer. A panel of three people usually make tribunal decisions. The tribunal chairperson will be an experienced lawyer.

The tribunals were set up to allow employees and employers to represent themselves, but over time they've become very legalistic, and employers usually pay for representation by a solicitor. That makes it all the more difficult for an employee to win a case without representation. If you belong to a union, talk to the union official before starting your claim. If you don't belong to a union, your local CAB can help you. Many have advisers who specialise in employment tribunal cases.

Get advice right at the start so that you comply with the appeal and grievance procedures and don't leave any vital information out when you fill in the forms to start the process. In most cases, you need to start your claim within three months of the event that led to it.

You start the claim process by filling in form ET1. A copy of this form is sent to the employer for a response within 28 days. When the tribunal gets the reply, it sends a copy to you and to the Advisory, Conciliation, and Arbitration Service (ACAS), which will offer to conciliate between you and your employer. Before the tribunal hearing, you and your employer can agree to a settlement, or you can withdraw your claim.

If the case is fairly straightforward, you may be given a date for a hearing straightaway. If it's more complicated, you may go through several stages before getting to the full hearing, including:

✔ **Case management discussion:** Often a conference call with the tribunal chairperson to discuss what issue the tribunal has to decide or to discuss the procedure.

✔ **Prehearing review:** Held to make sure that you have a reasonable chance of making your case to the full hearing. At this point, the tribunal may decide that you have no reasonable prospect of winning or that your case is vexation. You may be ordered to pay a deposit to the tribunal of up to £500 before you can go ahead to a full hearing.

✔ **Preliminary hearing:** Held by the tribunal chairperson to see whether you're able to bring your claim. For example, the tribunal may look at whether you're an 'employee,' have enough service to claim, or whether the claim has been made in time.

The case may be settled at any of these stages, but if not, then a full hearing will hear all the evidence and witnesses from both sides and make a decision. You may get a judgement orally at the hearing, but you'll always get details of the judgement by post. With that judgement, you get details of how to appeal at an employment appeal tribunal.

Although the process is supposed to be less formal than a court, it can be fairly daunting, and you certainly have more chance of winning if you have someone with you who knows how the system works and can guide you through. Don't go it alone if you can avoid it.

Getting Help

Apart from CAB and the Law Centres, you can take advantage of several other sources of help:

✔ **Advisory, Conciliation, and Arbitration Service** (ACAS) can give advice on your rights at work. Contact ACAS through the Web site at www.acas.org.uk or through Equality Direct at ACAS 08456-003-444.

✔ **Disability Rights Commission Helpline** on 08457-622-633 can provide help on your rights as a disabled person.

✔ **Women and Equality Unit** Web site at www.womenandequalityunit.gov.uk can help on equal pay.

✔ **Equal Opportunities Commission** is at www.eoc.org.uk and can provide advice if you think you aren't being given the same opportunities at work as your colleagues.

✔ **Commission for Racial Equality** at www.cre.gov.uk may also be able to offer advice if you think that your employer is discriminating against you because of your ethnic background.

The big three commissions – Equal Opportunities, Racial Equality, and Disability Rights – are to become one: The Commission for Equality and Human Rights. The Government has not yet decided when the change will happen, but it may be around the end of 2006.

Chapter 10

Being Your Own Boss

● ●

● ●

*A*t some time or another, most people have thought about how good it would be to be your own boss – no more being at the beck and call of someone else or working hard just to put money into an employer's pocket! Every year, almost 300,000 people take the plunge. If you've got a big idea for your own business, this year may be the one to make it happen.

But running your own operation isn't always a bed of roses, and the more help and advice you get on the various aspects of it, the better prepared you'll be to deal with the problems as they arise – or, even better, to take steps to avoid them arising in the first place. Working for yourself can be very isolating, as well as extremely time-consuming. You and those around you need to be aware of just how much effort it takes to become successful and that your loved ones are willing to offer their support.

Going into Business

About 300 businesses failed every week in the UK in 2005, and around a third of all start-ups don't make it past their first birthday. The ones that fall by the wayside usually do so because they've been set up on a wing and a prayer without all the necessary preparation.

Just because you've got a good idea doesn't mean that it will fly without a lot of research and planning. If you really want to work for yourself, talk to one of the organisations, such as the Government's small business advisory service Business Link, that can help you work out whether a sustainable market exists for your products or services or whether the competition has it sewn up already. You should also discuss how to set up your business, if you do decide it's worth a try.

The first step to setting up your business it to call *Business Link,* England's local business advice office. (If you're in Scotland, Wales, or Northern Ireland the equivalent services have slightly different names; to keep it simple, I refer to the service as Business Link throughout this book.) Business Link, the national business advice service, offers free advice and support and runs all sorts of useful courses for people starting up their own enterprises.

After you decide to take the plunge into entrepreneurship, you need to consider how you're going to trade. You can choose to go it alone as a *sole trade*r, form a *partnership* with someone else, or set up a *limited company.* These entities differ in terms of the administration involved, whether you're prepared to risk your own personal assets, and how you want to be viewed for tax purposes. You can talk to a solicitor or an accountant about the legal form your business should take, but an adviser at Business Link is also able to help. The Law Society has a list of lawyers who offer small firms a free half-hour legal consultation; contact 020-7405-9075 or go to www.1fyb.lawsociety. org.uk. You can find a chartered accountant through the Institute of Chartered Accountants (www.icaew.co.uk).

Working as a sole trader

Are you going to go it alone? You can establish yourself as a sole trader very easily. You don't have to fill out a lot of forms, and you've got only yourself to answer to.

Most people who work on a freelance basis are sole traders, doing what they know best for a range of clients, as and when those clients need their services – say, a photographer who wants to work for himself rather than an employer. You can leave your job, make up a portfolio of your work or a brochure advertising your particular skills, and market your services to anyone you think might pay for them.

As a sole trader, you make your own business decisions; you answer only to clients, and the profits (and any losses) you make are yours. If you do make losses and run up debts, you're personally responsible for those debts. If things go badly wrong, you may ultimately have to sell some possessions, perhaps even your home, to pay off your debts. Basically, as a sole trader, you're running your business on your own. If you expand, you may decide to take on other people to work for you – as employees or as freelancers on short-term contracts – but the business is yours.

Most sole traders are self-employed and are taxed as such by Her Majesty's Revenue and Customs (HMRC). You need to register with HMRC within three months of starting up. You can find more information on the HMRC Web site at www.hmrc.gov.uk or from your local tax office, which is listed in the phone book.

You have to be careful because if you're a sole trader and you do most of your work for just one client, HMRC may not accept that you're self-employed. It may decide that you're an employee of that client. Talk your situation through with HMRC if you're in any doubt.

Someone who is genuinely self-employed works under a contract for service rather than a contract of employment. You're contracted to provide services. For more on how the tax office views self-employed people, see the section 'Minding the money matters,' later in this chapter.

Forming a partnership

If you're planning to set up your business with someone else or more than one other person, you can form a *partnership*. You run the business together and share all the management decisions, risks, costs, losses, and, hopefully, the profits. In any venture where you're working with other people, you need to be clear from the outset what your goals and priorities are. A partnership may be the answer if you don't have enough money to get up and running, and you know someone who has some money to invest.

You may think that you know your prospective partner or partners very well and will have no difficulty working together, but it's often said that you don't really know anyone until you live or work with them. Many a business falls apart because partners disagree on the basic aims of their venture and find that they can't work together.

Making it formal

If you simply form an informal partnership, nothing stops one partner from making decisions and going ahead without the consent of the others. One partner can take on binding contracts without the others having their say. As a result, it's a good idea to have a solicitor draw up a partnership agreement between you, setting out how the business will be run. (Another option is to use a Business Link adviser.)

You want to address issues such as how the profits are to be split, who puts in what in terms of finance, who is responsible for what aspects of the operation, and to what extent decisions can be made by individuals and which decisions must be made jointly. This partnership agreement helps everyone know where they stand from the beginning so that you can avoid disputes further down the line. If you do set out to draw up such an agreement, any differences of opinion are likely to surface before your commit yourself.

Partners are often taxed as self-employed, but as with sole traders, this setup isn't always the case, and you should talk it over with HM Revenue and

Customs. Like a sole trader, you need to register with HMRC within three months of starting up.

Limiting the liability of the partnership

Members of a partnership are all liable for any debts their venture incurs. Partners are each personally liable so that means that they could end up selling personal possessions, perhaps even their homes, to clear their debts. If one partner can't pay their share of those debts or simply disappears owing money, the other partner or partners are left holding the bills.

You can, however, limit the personal responsibility of the partners for business debts by setting up a *limited liability partnership* (unless you're in Northern Ireland, where these partnerships don't exist). Basically, your liability as a partner in a limited liability partnership is limited to the amount of money you invested at the outset and to any personal guarantees you gave if you were borrowing money for the business. A limited liability partnership is a more complicated and expensive way to form a partnership, and you'll need the help of a solicitor or an agent who forms companies. The local Business Link can give you advice and information and help you decide whether this partnership is the right option for you.

Opting for a limited company

The other option when setting up a business is to become a *limited company*. A limited company is a private business set up in such a way that, legally, the liability of the owners for any debts it incurs is limited to their shares in the company. Their personal assets are safeguarded if the business gets into financial trouble. Limited companies have 'Limited' after their names and some people like the status that gives and feel that customers will be more impressed or confident in the organisation they're dealing with. But many limited companies are no more than a one-person organisation run from the spare room in the same way as sole traders operate.

Basically, if you set up a limited company, you and your business partners are directors of the company. You can buy a company that's already registered with Companies House 'off the shelf' with an existing name, but you may want to start from scratch and come up with your own name. Companies House is the official Government register of UK companies, and you can find more information on its Web site at www.companieshouse.gov.uk or call 0870-333-3636. Becoming a limited company is a fairly straightforward process and costs just a few hundred pounds.

The advantage for the directors is that you have a limited liability for any debts the company runs up so that you don't usually risk losing personal assets, such as your home. Your personal risk is limited to the amount of money you invest in the first place and to any financial guarantees you give to an organisation, such as the bank or individual investors when you're borrowing money to put into the business. You can raise money by allowing other people, businesses, or employees to buy shares in your business. If the company does well, your buyers make a return on their investment because they're entitled to a share of those profits – depending on how many shares they bought in the first place.

You don't usually risk losing personal assets if you form a limited company, but you do have duties as a company director. If the company goes down the pan because you haven't carried out those duties, you may become liable, personally, for company debts or be disqualified from being a director of another company.

You have to draw up a *Memorandum of Association* and *Articles of Association* to get started. These documents cover the details of how you run the business, where it will be based, and what it will do. You have to send this paperwork, along with registration forms, to Companies House before you start trading. Your solicitor or an agent who specialises in forming companies can help you through the process. An adviser at Business Link can also give you all the information you need and discuss the process with you before you make your decision about going down this path.

If you do become a limited company, you pay a *corporation tax* on your company profits and send yearly returns to Companies House with details of directors, shareholders, and finances. Your company account is audited if your turnover is big enough, but most small businesses don't make enough and are exempt.

What's in a name?

Many people opt for a limited company because they like having a business name that includes the word 'Limited'. They feel that clients will think they're better established and that it sounds more professional. It's all part of the image.

So, too, is the business name. As a sole trader or a partnership, you can operate under your own name – such as R. U. Reliable. If you decide to call yourself something else, such as Reliable Services, you have to put that name on all your letterheads, contracts, and invoices. You have to register the name of your Limited Liability Partnership or Limited company with Companies House. You can buy a company from the shelf of Companies House if one is already registered with a name that you want to use but isn't in use.

If you want to have a Web site for your company, it's a good idea to check out whether the name you're using is available as a domain name or already in use by someone else. You can check through Nominet UK at www.nic. uk or Netnames at www.netnames.co.uk. You can't register a company name that is already used by a company in operation and registered at Companies House. You can contact Companies House (0870-333-3636 or www. companieshouse.gov.uk) for more information on the do's and don'ts of company names.

Becoming a franchisee

A lot of the chains on the high street are franchises. The person who comes up with the original idea sets up the business – usually in the form of a limited company and then sells off licences to people who want to operate branches of that business. The franchisee buys the right to use the company name and logo, sell the company products or offer the company services. The franchisor – the originator of the business sets out in the contract various details of how the business is to be run; gives advice on running the operation and takes a share of the proceeds. You may find it easier to run a business this way because someone else has put all the effort into working out what will make it successful but you may eventually find it limiting because there won't be so much scope for using you own initiative or putting your own stamp on the business. You can get more information from Business Link or from the British Franchise Association at www.british-franchise.org or on 01491-578-050.

Taking on Employees

One of the most important decisions for any business owner – whether he's a sole trader, in a partnership, or operating as a limited company – is when to take on employees. One minute everything is ticking along nicely, and then suddenly you have too much work to cope with and you need help. If you take a look at Chapter 9, you can see what employees can expect from their employers and of their rights. You have to make sure that you don't do anything to contravene those rights, or you may find that your employees can make a claim against you at an employment tribunal. If the tribunal finds in favour of your employee, you can then face a bill for compensation.

Right from the moment you decide to take on a staff member, you have to stay on the right side of the law. My book on *Small Business Employment Law For Dummies* (Wiley) covers the legalities in detail. If you need to talk things over with someone before taking the first steps, an adviser at Business Link is a good place to start.

Minding Money Matters

When it comes to money and your business, there are two sides to the coin. You may want to raise finance to get your business started or to help you run it and develop it. On the other hand, you must first consider the money you have to pay out, such as tax and national insurance.

Getting money to run the business

You may not need any capital to get going simply because the business you're starting up depends on little more than your own skills. You may simply turn your spare room into the place you work from, advertise your services, and wait for the jobs to roll in.

However, few businesses need no money to get off the ground. You'll probably need to pay for phone calls, Web site setup, advertising literature, and equipment. Many people start up by doing freelance work while keeping their day jobs, use their savings, or get help from family and friends.

When the venture is a bit bigger, though, finding the money you need can be harder. Banks are often not interested in dealing with a small venture. They're looking for something more profitable to invest in. Business people often say that borrowing ten million pounds is much easier than borrowing £100,000. That's not to say that approaching the banks isn't worth it. If you're looking to borrow money at the lower end of the scale, you may be able to arrange a small business loan. Other than that possibility, you can raise cash through other methods, including grants and loans. (Business Link can advise you about possible financial help from enterprise and development agencies.) Accountants are also an important source of business advice and support and many will give free advice on the phone. You can find a chartered accountant through the Institute of Chartered Accountants' Web site at www.icaew.co.uk.

In addition, venture capital companies and individual investors are looking for good business ideas to invest in. (Check with the Business Venture Capital Association at 020-7025-2950 or www.bvca.co.uk) Business Angels are investors who have been in business themselves and have retired, but want to put something back in the form of financial backing and business expertise. National Business Angels attempts to match business ventures with angel investors – contact 0207-329-2929 or www.bestmatch.co.uk.

If you go to anyone to raise cash, whether it's a bank for a loan or an investor, they'll want to see detailed business plans. These documents set out your ideas and aims clearly and your projections for how the business will grow. You need to do your research to show that you know that a good, sustainable market exists for your goods or services and that the market has enough room for you. No matter how good a hairdresser you are, no one will be interested in investing in yet another hairdresser in a location that already has several hairdressers. The business plan should reflect your market research, your marketing plans, and your ideal location for your venture.

People need to be convinced that investing in your business is worth their while in terms of a fair return. Your business plan is your most important document, so get help to draft it. Business Link run courses and has advisers who can help with business planning or point you in the direction of funding sources.

Most people or organisations willing to give you business funding will want personal guarantees from you about how much money you're putting up yourself. Even if you're planning to trade as a limited company with limited liability for business debts, investors may expect you to give additional guarantees that you'll put in more that just your original investment in certain circumstances. You may have to adjust your ambitions to fit the amount of funding you're able to raise. Don't leave yourself in the position where you may lose your home and leave your partner and dependents without a roof over their heads. If you're going to take that kind of risk, everyone involved has to be convinced that the gamble is worth taking.

Paying out

After you're trading and getting paid for your work, you have to start paying out. How you're taxed depends on how you set up your business and how you run it. If you're set up as a sole trader or a partnership, whether you're taxed as self-employed or as an employee depends on how your work is organised. You're likely to be classed as self-employed if you:

- ✔ Can send someone else along in your place to do the work
- ✔ Can work for more than one business at the same time
- ✔ Can work as and when you're required
- ✔ Provide your own tools or equipment to do the job
- ✔ Pay your own support staff if you need any
- ✔ Are responsible for your own profits and loss

You may be classed as self-employed for one job that you do but as an employee for the next job, in which case the employer is expected to deduct the correct income tax from your wages before handing them to you. You must sort out your status with HMRC within three months of starting up (although it's best to sort it out before you start trading) to be sure that you're taxed properly. At the same time, you must sort out your National Insurance, either as a self-employed person or as an employee. You can contact the local HMRC office – you can find details in the phone book, or you can find more information and contacts on the Web site at www.hmrc.gov.uk.

If you set up a limited company, you are considered a director of the company and are taxed as a company employee. The company also pays Corporation

Tax on its profits. Again, HMRC, an accountant, or the local Business Link can help you put all the necessary processes in place to pay your tax.

If you take on employees, you or the company need to deduct the correct tax and national insurance from their wages and pay that amount to the HMRC.

You must also consider *Value Added Tax* (VAT). You don't pay VAT on profits, but on the sale of goods and services. Basically, as a business, you collect VAT on behalf of the Government. No matter how your business is set up, if you have a turnover in your business of £60,000 a year or more, you have to register for VAT with HMRC. Go to the HMRC Web site at www.hmrc.gov.uk to get information or get help from your local Business Link.

You also need to consider business rates and capital gains tax. All in all, a lot of financial issues are involved in setting up and running a business. While you can deal with these issues yourself, having an accountant or financial adviser on hand to give advice and support is helpful until you're completely confident.

Getting paid on time

If you're selling goods or services as a sole trader, in a partnership, or as a limited company, you can keep afloat only as long as you're getting paid for what you do. A large proportion of the businesses that go under cite cash flow problems as the main reason for their demise. For that reason, you need good processes in place to deal with preparing invoices and chasing money that's due.

Stipulate on your contracts the terms for payment. Even if your terms and conditions of invoices don't say it, you should receive your money within 30 days; if not, the law allows you to charge interest – of the Bank of England base rate plus 8 per cent – on the overdue amount. You can also claim compensation of £40 on debts of less than £1,000, £70 on debts of £1,000 up to £9,999, and £100 on debts of £10,000 or more.

If you pay late, other companies can take the same steps against you. Don't treat your creditors as a bank.

You don't want to be in the position where you have to charge interest or chase it up because you run the risk of losing your customers. You certainly don't want to go to the time and expense of chasing your debts through the courts. You may be throwing good money after bad. The best way is to have very clear payment terms from the minute you start up. If you do a good job, give your customers that little bit extra care and attention and form a good relationship with each of them, they're more likely to stick to those payment terms for fear that you won't be available next time they need your services.

Planning for your retirement

Many business owners forget about saving into a pension fund to provide an income for their own retirement. If your business is worth a lot of money when you retire, you may be able to sell it to provide you with a retirement income. However, if you sell your business, you may be liable for Capital Gains Tax (see Chapter 3). (Seek advice from an accountant if you're planning to sell.

On the other hand, you may find that your business is worth very little without you in it. In that case, you need to plan ahead by paying into a pension or saving money in some other type of investment. If you have five or more employees, you can offer them access to some type of pension, even if it's just a stakeholder pension.

You don't have to make contributions to any pension you make available, but prospective employees may view pension contributions as a more important perk than a higher salary, enabling you to recruit the best people.

Talk to an accountant or financial adviser about pensions for yourself and your employees.

Safeguarding Your Business Assets

When you think of your business assets, you probably think first and foremost of your equipment or machinery, company cars, and so on. It's important to make sure that all those assets are looked after and insured, as well as protected by alarms and locks to cut down the risk of damage or loss. However, if you're in the business of inventing things or coming up with new ideas or you have logos or symbols that are a vital part of your business brand or image, those intangibles can be valuable assets. You can take care of most material assets, such as premises and computers, with insurance, but assets that fall under the heading of *intellectual property* are a lot harder to protect but even more damaging to lose.

Protecting your name

A rose by any other name may smell as sweet, but would your business be as successful if it was called something else? If you've worked hard to build a good reputation and your customers keep returning and sending referrals, your name is vitally important. For that reason, you don't want anyone else using it and perhaps tarnishing it by selling inferior goods or services to the ones you provide. If someone is in competition with you and tries to use the same or a similar name as yours, you can take them to court and claim that they're passing off their products as yours.

Of course, the last thing you want is to get involved in costly court proceedings, and you have to be sure that you have a good case. For example, the other company may not realise that another company with the same or similar name is doing a similar line of business. Try to negotiate before taking court action, but don't wait too long before taking action or your good reputation may be lost. Take legal advice as soon as you recognise a potential conflict with another firm.

Guarding your logos and trademarks

Often when you buy goods, you see a *registered trademark* – a symbol or logo that has been registered by that company as its own trademark. If you think about your favourite brands, you can conjure up in your mind their various logos and symbols. These items help customers recognise your products. People are searching for brands well known for quality, so logos and trademarks are important marketing tools.

If you register your trademarks, you can go to court to stop anyone else from using them, and you may even be able to claim damages as well. If you haven't registered your trademarks, you can still take legal action to stop another business from using them, but you have to prove the following:

✔ The trademark or symbol represents your good reputation.

✔ If someone else uses your trademark or symbol, customers will be confused.

✔ Your business has been damaged as a result of someone using your trademark or logo.

Register your trademarks at the Patent Office (www.patent.gov.uk or 08459-500-505). You can initially register them for ten years and then renew them every ten years for as long as you're trading.

Copyrighting your creations

You can't register *copyright* in the same way as you can trademarks. (See the preceding section for more information on trademarks.) Copyright is the exclusive legal right to print, publish, perform, film, or record literary, artistic, or musical material and to authorise other people to do the same. If you've created a piece of music or written a book, you are the owner of the copyright. The copyright exists automatically when the material becomes a physical entity – for example, when it's put onto paper. You can't copyright an idea, only the embodiment of the idea – the musical score as written on paper, for example but you have to prove that you own the copyright.

Copyright gives you say over how your material is used, – for example, whether it can be copied, performed, or broadcast – and covers music, plays, books, stories, paintings, computer programs, sound recordings, films, videos, and so on.

You can sell or transfer ownership of your copyright to someone else, and you can give someone else license to use it – as composers of music or songs do. Each time someone else uses your copyrighted material, you receive *royalties* – an agreed sum of money that's paid each time a book sells or each time your music is performed in public. Copyright terms range from 50 years for broadcasts and sound recordings to 70 years after the death of the creator of books, plays, and music.

If you do come up with something that is eligible for copyright, keep records of when it was written or produced. You may even want to keep a dated, and sealed copy in a bank box or safe or lodged with your solicitor. That way, if copyright is ever an issue, you can prove that you were the original creator, and the copyright belongs to you.

If you employ someone to come up with this kind of material as part of his job, you are the owner of the copyright unless you've agreed otherwise. You may employ someone to design computer software, for example, and you will own the copyright of that software.

If you hire someone to do a particular job – on a contract specifically for that job – and it involves a piece of artistic work, such as taking photographs or designing a Web site, that person is likely to own the copyright unless you state otherwise in the contract. Make the situation clear when the contract is being drawn up.

Protecting your designs

If your creation is some type of design, you have protection similar to copyright. *Design right* is automatic after the design exists, and you can use it to stop other people from making, using, or selling your designs or similar ones. Design right applies to a product's outward shape.

If you want stronger protection, consider a *registered design,* which covers design features like the shape or patterns on a piece of pottery. You need to apply to the Patent Office for a registered design, which lasts for 5 years and can be extended for up to 25 years. You can get more information from the Patent Office (08459-500-505 or www.patent.gov.uk).

Patenting your inventions

When you buy certain goods, you may see a patent number on them or the words *patent pending,* which means that a patent has been applied for. Patents are meant to stop someone else from making, selling, or using something you've invented without your permission. If you invent a machine for making beds, for example, the patent covers the technical elements of the invention and how it works. You can patent the following items:

- ✔ Something that's completely new
- ✔ Something that's an improvement on something that already exists
- ✔ Something already existing that has a new use

People often worry that if they do apply for a patent at some point in the process, their idea will become known to other people and stolen. But without a patent, you can't stop someone else from using your product or process for their own good. Patents protect your invention for 20 years. You can go to court to enforce it and apply for compensation if someone else has damaged your business. In that time, you benefit because no one else can make and sell your product so you can charge whatever the market will pay without competition bringing down the price. You can also sell the patent or license it out to other people to use while paying you royalties.

You can get more information about Patents and how to apply for one from the Patent Office (08459-500-505 or `www.patent.gov.uk`) or from patent attorneys who are members of the Chartered Institute of Patent Agents (020-7405-9450 or `www.cipa.org.uk`).

Closing Down Your Business

Even if your business becomes very successful, you may decide that you've had enough and want to call it a day. If you have many willing buyers, you can sell to whomever you choose.

You should take advice because the rules over transferring your business, and in particular your staff and their contracts and rights, to a new owner are complicated. As with anything to do with your business, Business Link can help, but you need a solicitor to draw up all the necessary paperwork.

If the business is really all about you and won't continue without you, you may have no choice but to simply close it down. Even then, you're faced with the problem of having to make your employees redundant. (Refer to Chapter 9 for more details of the payments you must make if employees are made redundant.)

However, most businesses close down because they run into problems. You can be very successful for years and then go into a decline simply because the market has changed and you've failed to keep that necessary one step ahead of the game. Then the contracts dry up, and the customers move on to something new and more exciting elsewhere.

Laying off staff and cutting hours

If you're facing a shortage of orders but you haven't yet decided to make redundancies, you can consider laying off employees or putting them on short-time working – where they have less than half a normal week's work and pay. Be careful, though. If nothing in their contracts allows you to lay them off or put them on short-time, you'll be in breach of contract. If you cut their wages, they can claim for unauthorised deductions from wages.

If their contracts do allow you to lay them off or cut their hours, those employees who have worked for you for at least one month are entitled to a guaranteed payment for up to five days in the three-month period following the first day they were sent home because no work was available. If the staff contract, Written Statement of Employment Particulars, or the staff handbook says that employees will be paid their usual pay if they're laid off, then you must pay them that amount. If not, then you must pay the legal minimum.

Employees who have been laid off or put on short time may leave and may be entitled to claim redundancy payments if the lay off or short-time working lasts for:

✔ Four consecutive weeks or longer

✔ A series of six weeks or more – of which not more than three were consecutive – within a 13-week period.

Making people redundant

Redundancy means that jobs are going, and therefore the people who are doing those jobs are being dismissed by reason of redundancy. Redundancy isn't the same as sacking them for disciplinary reasons. It's fair to dismiss people because of redundancy, but, as with any dismissal, you have to go the right way about it.

You have to be fair in who you decide to make redundant and go through all the necessary procedures in the correct way; otherwise, your employees can claim that they were unfairly selected for redundancy and take a claim against you at an employment tribunal. Even if you're not selecting people for redundancy but closing down your whole operation and making everyone redundant, you have to do it properly. Talk to a business adviser as soon as you think redundancies may be in the pipeline so that you know how to tackle the process.

Before you issue a redundancy notice, you must consult with your employees, even if you believe you have nothing to discuss with them. If 20 to 100 jobs are to go, you have to have at least 30 days in which to consult with unions and staff. If more than 100 jobs are to go, the consultation period has to be at least 90 days. The purpose of consultation is to see whether you can find ways to save jobs. The staff may have ideas or perhaps even want to come up with some sort of proposal to buy the business and carry on.

If you're making 20 people or more redundant, you have to notify the Secretary of State through the Department of Trade and Industry. If you don't, you can be fined up to £5,000.

People are entitled to notice that their employment is ending. (Refer to Chapter 9 for more about notice periods and redundancy payment calculations.) Most employees are entitled to a redundancy payment. How much they're entitled to depends on how long they've worked for you, how much they earn, and what age they are. The Advisory, Conciliation and Arbitration Service (ACAS) produces a ready reckoner, which shows how many weeks payment your employees are entitled to. You can find it on the Web site at ACAS at www.acas.org.uk or by contacting the helpline on 08457-47-47-47.

If you don't give employees the right notice or money in lieu of notice or don't give them written details of the calculations of their redundancy payments, they can make claims against you at an employment tribunal.

Paying what you owe

Closing down your business can be an expensive process if you have quite a few employees, and you've been in operation for some time. Add up the final payments – redundancy payments, payments in lieu of notice, and wages owed (including any bonuses and overtime to be paid and any holiday pay due).

If you can't pay your employees what you owe them, they become creditors of your business and as such are entitled to what's owed to them if enough money is left in the pot after the business is sold. Your employees become preferred creditors and should receive their money after your secured creditors, who have security such as a mortgage. You need to keep employees informed of what's going on and make sure that they know how to claim from the state through the National Insurance Fund if you don't have enough money to go around. Your employees can contact the Redundancy Payments Helpline at 0845-1450-0034 for help. See the Department of Trade and Industry's Web site at www.dti.gov.uk.

Getting Help

If you want to work for yourself as a self-employed sole trader or are thinking much bigger and want to set up a company that grows and grows, take all the good advice you can get from the vast wealth of information out there.

Most big banks provide useful brochures, packs, and leaflets on all aspects of running a business. Your solicitor and accountant, if you have them, will be helpful, but don't take petty problems to them; you have to pay for their time, and you may have more cost-effective ways of getting help and support. If you do decide to turn to your solicitor or accountant, make sure that they are experienced in dealing with businesses the size of yours. Big businesses are quite different animals from small ones.

The government runs Business Link in England and the equivalent in Scotland, Wales, and Northern Ireland, with offices in most big towns and cities, as well as advisers with a whole range of business expertise. This free service provides advice, guidance, and support on everything to do with setting up and running a business. Business Link also has a very comprehensive Web site at www.businesslink.gov.uk, which gives you most of the information you need.

Of course, Web sites can't always give you the necessary support. You can get details about the nearest office to you on the Web site or in the local telephone directory or call 0845-600-9006. In Scotland, the organisation is Business Gateway (0845-609-6611 or www.bgateway.com). In Wales, contact Business Eye (0845-796-9798 or www.businesseye.org.uk). In Northern Ireland, contact Invest Northern Ireland (0289-023-9090 or www.investni.com).

ACAS (08457-47-47-47 or www.acas.org.uk) is an invaluable source of help for businesses.

The Federation of Small Businesses has 185,000 members with 1.25 million employees between them. For an annual subscription of between £100 and £750, depending on how many employees you have, you get various services, including access to the legal helpline where you can talk to an adviser about any legal problems you have. Call 01253-336-000 or check out the Web site at www.fsb.org.uk.

The Disability Rights Commission Helpline (08457622633 and www.drc-gb.org) can help on disability issues. The Women and Equality Unit Web site, located at www.womenandequalityunit.gov.uk, can help on equal pay; the Equal Opportunities Commission is at www.eoc.org.uk, and the Commission for Racial Equality (www.cre.gov.uk) may also be able to offer advice. These big three commissions are to become one around the end of 2006: The Commission for Equality and Human Rights.

Other organisations you may find useful include

- **British Chambers of Commerce** (www.chamberonline.co.uk) provides a range of business services locally.

- **Institute of Directors** (0207 839-1233 or www.iod.com) represents individual company directors.

- ✔ **The Prince's Trust** (0800-842-842 or www.princes-trust.org.uk) offers advice and financial support for young people starting up.

- ✔ **Shell LiveWIRE** (0845-757-3252 or www.shell-livewire.org) provides advice and support for people under 30 in business.

- ✔ **Inside UK Enterprise** (0870-458-4155 or www.iuke.co.uk) brings together established firms with startups for advice.

- ✔ **Disabled Entrepreneurs Network** (www.disabled-entrepreneurs.net) provides helps for business owners with disabilities.

- ✔ **Trade associations** (020-7395-8283 or www.taforum.org) can provide assistance.

Chapter 11

Managing Without Paid Work

● ●

● ●

*I*t's not so long ago that people went into a job after leaving full-time education and stayed in that firm or in that business sector for their entire working lives. Jobs were for life. That's no longer that case. Most people expect to have two or three different careers today, and it's not unusual to have gaps in your employment record. Some lose a job through redundancy or dismissal (refer to Chapter 9) and take a bit of time off to find another. Others are forced out of paid employment by illness or to care for dependents, such as young children or elderly relatives.

If an employment gap has been forced on you, you may be entitled to financial help from the state to tide you over on the basis of national insurance contributions you've paid in the past. If that's not the case, you may be entitled to help on the grounds that you have little in the way of income or savings coming into your household. On the other hand, a big redundancy or severance package from your employer; a partner who is earning; or a reasonable amount of savings in the bank may rule out assistance, but it's worth investigating the possibilities so that you don't miss out.

You'll usually have to finance your own time out if you choose to take time away from paid work to bring up children; to retrain or study with a view to a career change; or (if you're lucky enough to be able to afford it) to do something different with your life for a while, such as travel or do voluntary work.

A whole range of benefits and tax credits are available, and the ones you're entitled to depend on your circumstances. In this chapter, I cover benefits that apply to people who aren't in employment. If you're employed but struggling on a low income or off sick or on maternity or paternity leave, take a look at Chapter 9. If you're retiring, see Chapter 12.

Claiming Welfare Benefits

The benefits system is extremely complicated. Some benefits are means-tested, which means that any other income coming into your household and how much you have in savings are considered when working out whether or not you qualify for these benefits and for how much. Some benefits are paid to you if you've made all the correct national insurance contributions in the past while you were employed (refer to Chapter 9). Others pay out for a set period of time, after which they either stop or you become entitled to a different benefit with a different set of rules. You may be entitled to claim more than one benefit at a time.

The following sections cover the basic rules. I don't include figures simply because it's impossible to tell how much of any particular benefit you may be entitled to without going into your individual circumstances in detail.

If you think you may be entitled to help, ask your local CAB to go through the figures with you. You want to be well informed before you make your application at the relevant benefits department. Look in your phone book for the CAB details or find them online at www.adviceguide.org.uk. Many people miss out on what they're rightfully entitled to because they don't know that they can claim.

Job Seeker's Allowance

Job Seeker's Allowance is paid to people who are unemployed, or on a low income and not working more than 16 hours a week, and who register with the Employment Service through the Job Centre or JobCentre Plus. (You can find details in your phone book or at www.jobcentreplus.gov.uk.) You have to be available for work and actively seeking work. If you're working or studying for more than 16 hours a week, for example, you may not be accepted as being available for work. If you're working for more than 16 hours a week, you may be entitled to tax credits (refer to Chapter 9).

Job Seeker's Allowance comes in two types:

- **Income-based Job Seeker's Allowance** is means-tested based on income and savings.
- **Contribution-based Job Seeker's Allowance** is dependent on your previous national insurance contributions.

You may be entitled to Job Seeker's Allowance based on your national insurance contributions even though you have a partner who is working, but you can claim only for yourself. You may be entitled to income-based means-tested Job Seeker's Allowance if you have a partner or a child.

You may have a problem getting Job Seeker's Allowance for the first six months if you voluntarily gave up your last job or lost it because of misconduct (refer to Chapter 9). And if you don't get out and start actively looking for another job – having interviews with the advisor at the job centre who will try to help you find work, responding to job adverts, and sending applications forms, for example – you may have your benefit stopped indefinitely. Get advice from the CAB if you have a problem claiming benefit or if it's stopped as you may have a good case to appeal.

If you apply for Income-Based Job Seeker's Allowance and you have a child living with you who has a parent living elsewhere, you have to give details of that parent unless it would put you and the child at risk. If you don't give that information, your Income-Based Job Seeker's Allowance may be reduced. You'll also be considered to have applied to the Child Support Agency (refer to Chapter 7). Any income you have from maintenance or child support from the parent is taken into consideration when calculating Income-Based Job Seeker's Allowance.

You may be able to claim a hardship payment from the Benefits Agency if you're refused Job Seeker's Allowance. Not everyone qualifies, but if you have dependent children or a sick, disabled, or pregnant partner, you're more likely to get hardship payments.

Income Support

You're likely to be entitled to means-tested Income Support if you're under 60; aren't working for more than 16 hours a week; don't have to be available for work; the amount of income coming into your household is very low; and your savings are less than a set threshold (£16,000 at the moment).

You don't have to be available for work if you're a lone parent with dependent children, are sick or disabled, or are caring for a disabled person. If you qualify, you receive an amount of Income Support for yourself and different amounts for your children, depending on their ages. If you have a partner living with you who has to be available for work, he can apply for the Job Seeker's Allowance (see preceding section) and may be entitled to an amount for you and the children.

Many factors affect the total amount of your claim, and each claimant receives different amounts depending on the circumstances. Go through the figures with your nearest CAB to make sure that nothing gets missed.

People who are on low incomes, not working, or working less than 16 hours a week but not entitled to Income Support may be entitled to a Pension Credit (see the next section and Chapter 12) if they're 60 or over. People who are working 16 hours or more and therefore can't apply for Income Support but who are still on a low income may be entitled to a Working Tax Credit (refer to Chapter 9). People with disabilities who get a Working Tax Credit are entitled to extra because of their disability.

If you're caring for someone with a disability, you may be entitled to a Carer's Allowance, but it reduces the amount of Income Support you can claim and can affect their benefits, too. (See the upcoming section 'Giving Up Work to Care for Adult Dependents'.) You may qualify if you care for them for at least 35 hours a week and earn less than £84 a week.

Even if you're only entitled to a few pence of Income Support, because of other income or savings, claim it. Don't think it's too small to bother with because it can give you a passport to other sources of financial help.

If you apply for Income Support and have a child living with you who has a parent living somewhere else, you need to give details of that parent and will be treated as if you have applied to the Child Support Agency for child support (refer to Chapter 7).

Tax and pension credits

Tax credits are a range of means-tested benefits for people on low income. The *Child Tax Credit* is paid to anyone on a low income, whether they're working or not. The *Working Tax Credit,* as the name suggests, is for people who are working and on a low income, regardless of whether they have children (refer to Chapter 9).

The *Pension Credit* is a means-tested benefit for people aged 60 or over. You can claim it whether you're working or not, and you don't have to have paid particular national insurance contributions in order to qualify. However, the amount you receive depends on the other income and savings you have.

The Pension Credit comes in two parts:

✔ The *guarantee credit* tops up your income to a guaranteed level.

✔ The *savings credit* is paid to people who have a small amount of income or savings.

You can get either or both parts, depending on your circumstances. If you are 60 or over and not working, talk to the nearest CAB about claiming the Pension Credit, or the Pension Service can help on 0800-991-234 or www.thepensionservice.gov.uk. Take a look at Chapter 12 for more on pensions.

Benefits if you're sick

If you're not earning money because you're too sick to work, you can explore a range of possibilities. If you can't go to work but are still employed by your employer, you may be entitled to Statutory Sick Pay (SSP), which is paid by your employer for up to six months (refer to Chapter 9). You may also be lucky enough to have an employer who pays extra contractual sick pay on top of SSP.

If you don't fit the rules for entitlement to SSP, you may be entitled to Incapacity Benefit instead (see the next section). Your employer should tell you why you don't qualify for SSP and how to apply for Incapacity Benefit.

If you get SSP, you may also be entitled to some Income Support or Pension Credit to top it up, and you may be entitled to help with housing costs and council tax as explained later in this chapter in the sections 'Claiming Help with Housing Costs' and 'Claiming Help with Council Tax'.

Incapacity Benefit

If you've been entitled to Statutory Sick Pay from your employer but it has run out after 28 weeks and you're still unable to work, or you aren't entitled to SSP because you haven't earned enough or paid the right national insurance contributions, you may be entitled to *Incapacity Benefit*.

Qualifying for Incapacity Benefit depends on your circumstances and national insurance contributions over the previous three years. If you qualify for it, you may get a top up of Income Support and help with housing and council tax costs. If you don't qualify for Incapacity Benefit, you may be entitled to Income Support or Pension Credit instead.

If you get SSP or Incapacity Benefit because you were injured in an accident at work or got a work-related disease, you may be able to claim Industrial Injuries Benefit. Your disease has to be on the list of recognised industrial diseases, such as asbestosis or industrial deafness, but you don't have to prove that your employer was at fault. You need good legal advice, and the nearest CAB can point you in the right direction.

Allowances if you need care

If you need help with your care or have problems getting around, you may be entitled to a Disability Living Allowance (under age 65) or an Attendance Allowance (over 65). Qualifying depends on how long you've been ill or disabled and how disabled you are. You can claim these allowances whether or not you work.

You can pick up leaflets on all these allowances from your doctor's surgery or local CAB. If you're entitled to these benefits, you receive them regardless of your other income or savings, and you don't have to have paid national insurance contributions.

These benefits don't count when it comes to working out whether you're entitled to claim Income Support or tax credits or help with housing costs.

Claiming help with housing costs

If you're able to claim any Income Support or Income-Based Job Seeker's Allowance, no matter how little, you can get help with housing costs. If you're a home buyer paying a mortgage, Income Support covers some or all of the interest you pay on that mortgage, but not the capital repayments. The mortgage interest is usually paid direct to your lender. If you're renting your home, Housing Benefit helps toward your rent.

People on low incomes who don't qualify for Income Support may also be able to get some Housing Benefit toward their rent. The amount of help is on a sliding scale, depending on income and savings. The more savings you have over £6,000 the less help you receive. You get no help if you have more than £16,000 in savings. Likewise, the more income you have, the less Housing Benefit you receive until you have too much income to qualify at all.

Other factors are considered as well, such as the number of people living with you, their ages, and their state of health and whether anyone living with you is a wage earner.

If you're a woman 60 or over or a man 65 or over and entitled to a State Retirement Pension (see Chapter 12), you may be able to get Housing Benefit. The amount of income and savings people of pension age are allowed to have, before their housing benefit is reduced or cut off entirely, is more generous than for those below pension age. The same goes for people who are disabled.

Claiming help with Council Tax

Council Tax Benefit works in much the same way as Housing Benefit (see preceding section). If you're responsible for paying council tax on your home and are on a low income – whether you're in or out of work – and have savings below the same threshold (currently £16,000), you can claim for help to pay the bill. Depending on how much income and savings you have, you may get all or part of your council tax paid. As with Housing Benefit, the rules are a bit more generous for people on state pensions and who have disabilities.

If you qualify for Disability Living Allowance or Attendance Allowance, these incomes don't count when it comes to calculating income for means-tested benefits, such as Council Tax Benefit and Housing Benefit.

Giving Up Work to Have Children

If you have a job and you have children, you should read the relevant sections in Chapter 9, which explain your rights to maternity and paternity pay and leave, adoption pay and leave, parental leave, and flexible working. If you aren't working or leave your job when you become pregnant, you aren't entitled to those payments, but you may be entitled to Maternity Allowance, depending on past national insurance contributions. You can also claim extra for an adult living with you who is dependent on you, such as a spouse. If no other income is coming into the house, you may also be entitled to some Income Support. (See the section on Income Support earlier in this chapter.)

To claim Maternity Allowance, you have to be pregnant and within the last 11 weeks before the expected week of childbirth. You also have to have worked, for yourself or for an employer, for at least 26 weeks out of the 66 weeks immediately before the week in which the birth is expected and to have been earning on average £30 a week.

If you have a partner who is working more than 16 hours a week on a low income, he may be entitled to a Working Tax Credit (see Chapter 9). If he's working less than 16 hours a week, apply for Income Support.

Child Tax Credit

If you're responsible for a child under 16 and your income is below a certain amount, you can claim Child Tax Credit. Most households with less than £50,000 a year coming in qualify for some tax credit. The amount you get depends on the number of children you have and is available whether or not you're working. If you're the main carer, the credit is paid into your bank account. It is paid from April to April, but if you have another child in that year, the amount increases. You get extra money if the child has a disability.

Child Trust Funds

If you have a child born on or after 1 September 2002, and you're getting Child Benefit for that child, your child is eligible for a Child Trust Fund account. The Government pays £250 into the account and another payment on his or her 7th birthday. Those payments have been made automatically since April 2005. You and your friends and relatives can pay money into that same account as presents or for special occasions. You can find out more about the funds from the CTF on 0845- 302-1470 or from HM Revenue and Customs on the Web site at www.hmrc.gov.uk.

Other help with children

If you get Income Support, Income-Based Job Seeker's Allowance, or Pension Credit or your income is low, you may get help with other expenses, such as dental charges and prescriptions, and you're entitled to free school meals. You may also get help with the costs of school uniforms.

If your child has a disability, you may be able to claim Disability Living Allowance from them and a Carer's Allowance for yourself. (See the next section 'Giving Up Work to Care for Adult Dependents'.) If the child you're looking after isn't yours but her parents have died or one is dead and the other is in prison or has gone missing, you may be able to claim a *Guardian's Allowance*.

Giving Up Work to Care for Adult Dependents

If you have to care for an adult – perhaps one of your parents – who is sick or disabled, you may be entitled to a *Carer's Allowance*. You have to provide the care for at least 35 hours a week, and you won't get the allowance if you're earning more than a certain amount (currently £84 a week). The person you're caring for has to have care needs and be receiving Disability Living Allowance or Attendance Allowance. (See the section on allowances, earlier in this chapter.)

If you give up work completely to provide this care and have no other income other than the Carer's Allowance, you may be able to claim more through Income Support and then qualify for help with your rent, mortgage, and council tax. You don't have to be available for work if you're caring for a sick or disabled person in order to claim Income Support.

Carer's Allowance is taken into consideration when working out whether you qualify for Income Support on top. Receiving a carer's allowance may also affect the amount of benefit the person you're caring for qualifies for.

Getting Help in Exceptional Circumstances

Sometimes you have unanticipated bills that you can't afford because you're on benefit. A system of loans and grants, called the *Social Fund,* helps people who are on means-tested benefits, such as Income Support. This fund pays out grants for funerals or maternity expenses, which you don't have to repay. It can also give you a cold weather payment if the temperature drops below a certain level.

Community Care Grants are available to people who are on means-tested benefits and leaving care so that they can set themselves up in a place of their own; or who have been homeless, in prison, or in a young offenders' institution. You may also be able to get one of these grants if it can help you stay out of care.

Budgeting Loans, which do have to be paid back, can help you buy essential items, such as furniture. And *Crisis Loans* for emergencies are paid to people who aren't getting means-tested benefits but whose income is low and they have nowhere else to get the money. You may qualify for help if you've had a fire or flood.

If your spouse dies, you may be able to claim help, depending on your age, whether you have dependent children, and whether your spouse had paid the right national insurance contributions. From December 2005, this assistance also applies to people who have registered civil partnerships (refer to Chapter 6). If your spouse has paid national insurance contributions, you may be entitled to a lump sum *Bereavement Payment* of £2,000. If you're under pension age and have children, you may receive the *Widowed Parent's Allowance.* If you're 45 or over but under pension age, you may receive a *Bereavement Allowance* for up to a year after your spouse's death. Both the allowances are stopped if you remarry or start living with someone.

Going Back to Work

Going back to work after a period on benefits can be difficult. Your benefit entitlement stops immediately when you start work again, and yet you have to be able to survive until the first pay packet comes in. However, you may be able to get *extended payments* of housing and council tax benefits for up to four weeks after you start work at the same rate as before you went back. That extension can help you avoid difficulties with the rent and council tax bills. If you've been getting help with your mortgage interest through Income Support or Income-Based Job Seeker's Allowance, you may be able to get those extended for up to four weeks, too.

You have to immediately tell the departments paying your benefits that you're going back to work.

People who are 25 and over may also qualify for a lump sum *Job Grant* if they've been receiving Income Support, Job Seeker's Allowance, Incapacity Benefit, or Severe Disablement Allowance for a few months. The Job Centre can help you claim any assistance you may be entitled to.

If you've been receiving Child Support (refer to Chapter 7) under the old rules that applied until March 2003 and you go back to work, you may be able to claim a *Child Maintenance Bonus*. You have to claim this one-time payment within four weeks of your Income Support or Income-Based Job Seeker's Allowance stopping.

Getting to Grips with the System

Not only is the range of benefits available bewildering and complicated, claiming what you're entitled to can be a bit of a nightmare. Different benefits come from different departments, and the staff in those different departments don't always know everything about the whole system, and so can't always tell you what else you may be able to claim. You have to get in touch with each department and complete the appropriate form to apply for each benefit.

Applying

The JobCentre Plus is the place to start if you're working age. It eventually deals with most claims for working-age people, but its services aren't available in every area yet. You may find your local office is still a Job Centre – without the Plus. Or you may still go to the Benefits Agency or social security office in your area.

The local authority deals with housing and council tax benefits, so go to your local council offices for those issues.

HM Customs and Revenue deals with Tax Credits, Child Benefit, and Guardian's Allowance, plus everything you ever wanted to know and more about national insurance.

If you think you may be entitled to Attendance or Disability Living Allowances, you need to contact the Benefit Enquiry Line on 0800 –882-200; to claim Carer's Allowance, call the Carer's Allowance Unit on 01253-856-123.

Because it's so complicated and because some forms can be rather daunting, your local CAB is worth a visit for information and support through the process. For benefits, and in particular the means-tested ones, such as Income Support and Income-Based Job Seeker's Allowance, you need to provide a lot of information about yourself, your family, and your financial situation.

If you don't fill in the forms properly, you may not get benefit you're entitled to. If you don't give all the correct information your benefit may be stopped.

Getting the money

Someone, somewhere, in a back room checks out your application and decides on the basis of the information that you've supplied whether you're entitled to the benefit you've claimed for and how much you'll get. You'll be told in writing what the decision is and how to appeal against it if you don't agree.

If you claim late, some benefits can be backdated, but others can't. You can get backdated Child Benefit, tax credits, Incapacity Benefit, and Carer's Allowance, but you'll get backdated Income Support and Job Seeker's Allowance only if you couldn't claim on time because the office was closed, for example. Disability Living and Attendance Allowances and Housing and Council Tax Benefits are backdated only if you have a good reason, such as being ill, for not claiming sooner.

The longest period most benefits will be backdated for is three months. Housing and Council Tax Benefits and Pension Credit can be backdated for 12 months. Check the rules before you apply and claim if you think you have a good reason for applying late.

The way you get paid also depends on the benefit. Money is usually paid into your bank or building society or into a Post Office card account. You're paid by cheque only if it's too difficult for you to open or manage an account. If you don't have a bank account, you can open a special post office account. Housing and Council Tax Benefits can be paid directly to your landlord or Council Tax account.

After you start receiving your benefits, you have to keep the office that's paying you informed about any changes in your circumstances. You may move, sell your home, or have another child, or one of them may leave school. You need to let your payment office know anything that can affect the amount of money you're entitled to.

If you don't tell the Tax Credit Office about some changes within a specific time, you may be penalised. Make sure that you know what the rules are for each benefit you receive.

If you get paid too much benefit, you usually have to pay it back. Overpayment can happen if you don't tell the various offices about changes in circumstances in time or provide them wrong information. If you lie, you can be investigated and prosecuted. If the offices make a mistake, you have the right to appeal (see the next section) against any demand for the overpayment to be paid back unless the benefit is a tax credit, in which case you have no right of appeal and have to hope that they'll admit their mistake and let you keep the money.

Appealing benefit decisions

If you think a decision to refuse you a particular benefit is wrong or that you aren't getting the right amount of money, you can appeal. You have to contact the office concerned in writing and tell them why you think they've got it wrong and ask them to take another look at your application. Keep a copy of any letters you send. You should write within a month of getting the original decision, although if the office makes a mistake in your claim, no time limit applies.

If you still aren't happy after your case has been reviewed, you can go to an appeal tribunal. You need to get your claim in within a month of the new decision. You can appeal outside this time scale in a couple of situations:

  ✔ You can show your appeal has a reasonable chance of success.

  ✔ It is in the interests of 'justice' because something serious made it difficult for you to claim within the month – for example, you were ill.

To appeal, you have to write to the office that made the decision you're appealing against. The various offices have their own appeal forms. Get one if you can, but if not, they'll accept a letter. Put down the details of the decision you're appealing against and the reasons why you think it's wrong.

At a tribunal, you can explain why you think the decision is wrong. The tribunal is made up of a solicitor or barrister, and a doctor, accountant or someone with experience of disability, depending on what expertise is relevant to the case. The department responsible for the particular benefit you're appealing about is represented, and that person presents the department's side of the case.

Tribunals usually make their decisions on the day of the hearing, and you will get written notice of that decision. Normally the tribunal's decision is final. You can appeal further to the Social Security Commissioner on only a point of law, such as:

  ✔ The tribunal misinterprets the law.

  ✔ No evidence supports the decision.

  ✔ The tribunal doesn't give a clear decision on the facts of the case.

  ✔ The tribunal doesn't give adequate reasons for its decision.

After the Commissioner has made a ruling on the case, you can appeal to the Court of Appeal, and finally the House of Lords, on important points of law.

The whole process is quite complicated, especially when it comes to appealing on points of law, and it's difficult to bring your own case without expert assistance. People who appeal without help are less likely to win their cases. Talk to the local CAB, Law Centre, or Independent Advice Centre before you start the process. They may have an adviser who specialises in benefit appeals.

Complaining about your treatment

Even if you decide not to challenge a decision made about your benefit (see preceding section), you may be unhappy about the way you've been treated by the particular benefit office – for example, you received bad advice or it's taken forever to process you claim. Write and explain and give the office a chance to explain and apologise. Each agency has a complaints procedure, so ask for information about that. If you want to take the complaint further, who you go to next depends on the department processing the benefit:

- ✔ **Local council:** Complain to the local government Ombudsman.
- ✔ **Department of Work and Pensions:** Contact your MP and apply to the Parliamentary Ombudsman.
- ✔ **HM Revenue and Customs:** Contact the Adjudicator's Office.

If you're unhappy about the way you've been treated in the benefit and appeal system and want to challenge the rules of the benefits themselves, you may have a case under the Human Rights Act (refer to Chapter 1). This area of law is new and complicated, so you really need first-class legal assistance if you go down this route.

Working on a Voluntary Basis

Voluntary work is work done for a charity or non profit organisation for which you don't get any payment other than to cover reasonable expenses. The Department of Work and Pensions can view voluntary work as taking reasonable steps to find work because you're doing something that enhances your chances of finding a paid job.

If you've retired from full-time employment and are getting the state pension or payments from an occupational or personal pension, any voluntary work you do won't affect those payments in any way.

If you're doing voluntary work while unemployed and claiming benefits such as Job Seeker's Allowance, you have to be available for work. Being available for work means that you have to be willing and able to take up work immediately. Immediately usually means that you're allowed time to wash, dress, and have breakfast, but if you're doing voluntary work, immediately usually means with a week's notice.

You're also allowed to do voluntary work without it affecting your sickness or incapacity benefits, as long as it's work for which the only payment is made to cover your reasonable expenses and it isn't work for a close relative.

Of course, if you aren't drawing any benefits of any kind and simply living on your savings, you can do as many hours on a voluntary basis as you like.

Chapter 12

Enjoying Retirement

· ·

In This Chapter

▶ Deciding when to retire

▶ Adding up what you'll have to live on

▶ Buying an annuity to give you a lifelong income

▶ Carrying on working

▶ Getting essential information and advice

· ·

*T*he law says nothing about when you must stop work and retire. You may decide you've earned enough, saved enough, and planned well enough for your future to retire in your 30s (wishful thinking!). Equally, you may well decide that you can't stand the thought of being at home all day, and that you want to carry on working as long as possible. As long as an employer is willing to keep you gainfully employed – or if you work for yourself – you can work as long as you like. There's no such a thing as a general retirement age that applies to everyone.

Making the Big Decision

The decision about when to retire is often made for you. You can *retire,* or give up work for good, whenever you want. Your company probably has an age at which it expects people to retire from the workplace, and that age will appear in your contract. If you want to retire before that time, you simply hand in your notice the appropriate length of time before you plan to leave and go several weeks later.

If you want to stay on longer, you have to negotiate, and your employer may refuse your request, in which case you have to go and find yourself another job. You can retire from one workplace and carry on working later in another.

Employers often prefer to get rid of their older workers and bring in younger replacements. These employers usually offer company pension schemes, which are set up to start paying a retirement income to employees from the specified retirement age.

Fighting age discrimination with new laws

The Government is bringing in Age Discrimination laws in October 2006, which will make it illegal to force someone to retire before 65. It would prefer employers not to specify a retirement age at all so that people can go on working for as long as they're capable of doing their jobs, but 65 will be the earliest age that can be specified for retirement.

Of course, you're still able to elect to retire earlier, and company pension schemes may still pay out earlier. You may therefore be encouraged to depart before 65, but your employer can't push you to go.

If that's the case, you have to accept your gold-plated carriage clock, smile through your leaving party, and ride off into the sunset. But you can go back to work somewhere else if you can find a more enlightened employer who appreciates the breadth of knowledge and experience you've gained over the years.

When you reach the usual retirement age in your workplace, you will be leaving your current job, but you still have decisions to make. You can take your company pension fund, use it to generate an income for the rest of your life, and stop working. You can defer taking your company pension and let it build up while you carry on earning an income from another job elsewhere. You can do a combination of both those things. If you've also reached State Pension age by the time you retire, you can take your State Pension on top of income from your company pension or defer taking one or other of them until later.

Thinking about money issues

The amount of pension income you have to live on after retirement is a big factor. If you have a company pension, you can probably start taking that pension at age 60, if not as early as 55 or even, in some cases, 50.

If you haven't paid into a company scheme, you may have set yourself up a personal pension plan. It, too, may start paying out at 60 or earlier. If you have neither of those options and are dependent on the *State Pension,* you will probably decide not to retire until you reach *State Pension Age,* which is currently 60 for women and 65 for men.

When you're approaching the normal retirement age from your current job, it's usually a good idea to sit down with an Independent Financial Adviser – or preferably take the advice of three of them – and work out what your best financial option would be given the pension provision you've made over the years. Some firms offer their employees retirement courses, including financial advice.

If you have no pension to provide a retirement income apart from the State Pension, you'll probably have no choice but to carry on working until you reach 60 (for women) or 65 (for men). If you have to leave a particular job before you reach State Pension Age and can't find another one, you may be entitled to Pension Credit (refer to Chapter 11).

Retiring early

Your employer may want you to go early – at 55, say – because the company think that younger people are more productive and cost less. You may be offered *early retirement,* where you're being dismissed or made redundant but with the incentive of a lump sum and a pension.

If your employer wants you to go, you're in a strong position to negotiate the best possible deal before you agree. If you're pushed to go before the firm's normal retirement age, and don't want to leave, you may have a good case for unfair dismissal, and you should talk to your union or nearest Citizens Advice Bureau.

This fact, along with less generous company pensions and a shortage of some skills, has prompted employers to realise that if they do let people go early, they're losing out on important knowledge and expertise. So if you've been hoping to leave early with a handsome payoff, you may be disappointed. You don't have the right to retire early unless it's part of your contract. (Refer to Chapter 9 for more on what forms part of your contract.)

If you want to retire early but it's not usual company policy, talk to your boss about the possibility. You can also discuss retiring in stages – cutting down your hours over the next few years, working part time, working flexible hours, or doing some work from home. Rather than giving up work completely, you're freeing up some time to do other things and easing yourself into retirement while your employer still has access to your expertise and knowledge of how the company works.

If none of those options exist and you want to leave before the normal retirement age in your company, you have give up your job by handing in your notice. Check the details of your company pension scheme and find out at what age you can take your pension. If you don't have a company pension scheme and can't get your State Pension until 60 or 65, you need to know that you have enough income or savings to live on until then.

Even if you can start drawing a company or personal pension at 55, think about whether you'd be better to defer it until later so that you can have a bigger weekly income in the future.

If you're off work because of long-term illness and still employed, your employer may offer you early retirement. In effect, you're just being dismissed but with a nice lump sum and pension to supplement any Incapacity Benefit you have been getting from the state. The employer is no longer holding a job open for you when you're recovered.

Accumulating Your Retirement Income

If you want to be able to enjoy retirement, you need to make sure that you can afford it. You may spend 30 years out of work, and if you're to be reasonably comfortable, you need to plan ahead.

It's never too soon to start paying into a pension. The size of the pension fund you ultimately end up with will depend on how much you pay in, when you started making contributions, and how much of your money is taken up by charges made by the pension provider for setting up and managing your pension. You may also incur charges for each transaction and for transferring out on one pension fund into another. Be very particular about checking out the charges when you're deciding which pension provider to go with.

The State pays a very basic pension that you contribute to through National Insurance contributions (NICs) while you work, as long as you're earning enough. If you want to have any more than that basic pension to live on later in life, you have to make your own additional provisions.

You may be lucky enough to accumulate a portfolio of investments you can cash in or properties you can sell or have rich relatives from whom you can inherit money, but for most people the best way of making provisions for retirement is to save through a pension.

Many people have lost confidence in pensions because a large number of company schemes closed down or failed to pay out as much as expected. Despite that loss, pensions are the most tax efficient way to save.

Understanding the State Pension

The State Pension age is currently 60 for women and 65 for men. That difference in State Pension ages is being phased out. In 2010, women will start being eligible for State Pension later, and gradually they'll catch up with their male colleagues. By 2020, both sexes will be eligible for the State Pension at 65. In the meantime, the press is full of headlines saying that everyone is doomed to work much longer because of a crisis in pension funding, and the Government can't afford for people to stop work and stop paying tax in their 60s. As life expectancy goes up, so, too, may the State Pension age, but that's some way ahead in the future.

The Government pays the State Pension to people who have worked and paid national insurance contributions after they reach the State Pension age. People are often very shocked when they find out how little they can expect from their State Pensions. Stories in the newspapers about well-heeled pensioners indulging their every whim and the importance of their spending power to the economy don't apply to pensioners who have only the State Pension to live on. In 1975, the full State Pension was worth about 22 percent of the average wage. Now it's worth about 16 percent and falling.

The State Pension, as it currently operates, has three different elements. Two different types of State Pension are no longer in use but still pay out to people who contributed to them in the past. You may qualify for money from some or all of these schemes.

- ✔ **Basic State Pension:** The amount you get depends on the number of years you've paid NICs during your working life. Working life is 49 years for a man and 44 years for a woman, starting at the age of 16. If you've paid enough NICs during that time, you get the full amount of Basic State Pension, £84.25 for a single person in 2006–2007.

  If you haven't paid enough NICs to get a full Basic State Pension, you can pay voluntary contributions to make up the difference. If you can't afford to make payments, the amount of Basic State Pension you get is reduced. If you haven't worked, you can claim on your spouse's NICs, and you receive £47.65. If both members of a couple have paid enough NICs, they both get a full Basic State Pension. You can get additional amounts for adult and child dependents.

  If you've been out of work looking after children and getting Child Benefit for those children, Home Responsibilities Protection protects you, so you have to pay fewer years of NICs to qualify for the full Basic State Pension.

- ✔ **State Second Pension:** You can get the State Second Pension (S2P) on top of the Basic State Pension. Designed to give low and moderate earners a better pension, the S2P replaced SERPS (see the next entry) in 2002. You can contract out – or leave – the state second pension as long as you join a personal scheme, your employer's scheme, or a stakeholder pension. Some of your NICs go into your chosen scheme instead of the state second pension.

- ✔ **State Earnings Related Pension (SERPS):** Started in 1978, SERPS was the Second State Pension until April 2002. If you qualified for SERPS, you still have a pension through the scheme. If you earned more than a certain amount, you built up an entitlement to SERPS. The amount you contributed to SERPS increased the more you earned.

- ✔ **Graduated Pensions:** These pensions go even further back than SERPS. Anyone who worked between 1961 and 1975 may be entitled to a small amount of Graduated Pension. If you are entitled to any, it will be paid to you with your State Pension payments.

✔ **Pension Credits:** The Pension Credit isn't a pension – it's a means-tested state benefit for people aged 60 or over. People coming up to pension age who don't have much other income and haven't yet reached State Pension Age may qualify. If you've had to retire from your job at 60 but can't get your State Pension until 65, you can claim, whether you're currently working or not. In addition, you don't have to have paid particular NICs in order to qualify, but the amount you get depends on the other income and savings you have.

The Pension Credit comes in two parts: the *guarantee credit* tops up your income to a guaranteed level; the *savings credit* is paid to people who have a small amount of income or savings. You can get either or both parts, depending on your circumstances. If you're 60 or over, talk to your nearest CAB or contact the Pension Service (0800-991-234 or www.thepensionservice.gov.uk).

It helps with your pension planning if you know ahead of your State Pension Age which elements of the State Pension you'll get and how much. You can ask for a State Pension forecast from the Pension Service (0845-300-0168 or www.thepensionservice.gov.uk).

You can delay taking your State Pension as long as you like – until you decide you really do want to finally give up work. By deferring it, you can take the money that accrues later as a tax-free lump sum or you can have a bigger State Pension later – the longer you defer the bigger it gets. After you've decided to defer, you can't change your mind, so make sure that you really can do without the money until later.

Saving through an occupational pension

When you start work for a company with five or more employees, your employer has to offer you access to a pensions scheme. The scheme may be no more than simply giving you information on how to join a stakeholder pension (see the next section), but it may mean allowing you to join a fully fledged company scheme that's already up and running. There are two types:

✔ **Final salary schemes:** Less common than they used to be, these schemes promise to pay you a certain percentage of your final salary or an average over your total period of employment. Some firms have gone bust, so not enough money has been in the pot to pay out the pensions promised.

✔ **Money purchases schemes:** Each member of the scheme pays in contributions and builds up her own pension pot. When you retire, your money is used to buy you an *annuity* – an investment that pays regular payments until you die.

Knowing how occupational schemes work

More employers are opting to set up money purchase schemes, and some are using them to replace final salary schemes. You can't be forced to join an employer's occupational pension. If your boss makes contributions to the scheme on your behalf, you miss out on those contributions if you don't join. Employers who run occupational pension schemes usually make contributions on behalf of all their employees.

As an alternative to setting up and running an occupational pension scheme, your employer may offer to make contributions equal to at least 3 percent of your wages to your personal pension plan or into a *group personal pension*. Each individual employee either arranges group personal pensions, or the employer chooses the plan for you. Group personal pensions are money purchase schemes.

Employers typically contribute an amount worth around 3 to 5 per cent of each employee's salary. That's like giving you an extra 3 to 5 per cent of wages except that you don't benefit from it until you retire. If you don't join the pension scheme, you have no right to ask for that 3 to 5 per cent in your wage packet.

Some employers are more generous with their contributions; some don't expect you to contribute at all; but most run schemes where the employees are also expected to contribute a percentage of their salary. The employer deducts that money from your salary before you get your wages.

 You get tax relief on contributions you make to an occupational pension. If you pay tax at 22 per cent on your earnings, for every 78 pence you contribute to your pension, the Government makes it up to one pound. If you pay higher rate tax on any of your earnings at 40 per cent, the Government tops up every 60 pence you contribute to your pension to one pound.

Occupational pensions are run by *pension providers* – companies that design and sell pension schemes. The scheme has to be registered with the Pensions Regulator and follow all the rules and regulations in place to protect the members who are the employees. If you're an occupational pension scheme member, you can opt out of the *State Second Pension* (see the preceding section) and have a proportion of your NICs paid into your occupational scheme instead.

Most occupational pension schemes provide for employees who have to retire early because of ill health and have a life assurance element so that if you die while you're a member of the scheme, your dependents receive a lump sum.

Employees can be elected as *trustees* of their occupational pension scheme. If you're a trustee, you have responsibility for making sure that the scheme is run properly and meets all the rules and regulations. You have the right to take time off work with pay to carry out your duties. Trustees are trained so that they know exactly what they're taking on, and the scheme has to be run for the benefit of the members, not of the business.

Building up savings

If you join your firm's occupational pension scheme, your employer also has to give you the opportunity to build up extra savings in it through *Additional Voluntary Contributions*. These contributions are what they say they are – extra contributions to enhance your pension.

If you're a taxpayer, you can contribute up to 100 per cent of your annual income into pensions, up to a maximum of £215,000 a year. If you don't pay tax, you can contribute up to £3,600 a year into a pension scheme. You can build up a total pension fund of up to 1.5 million pounds in as many pensions as you like. That amount increases to 1.8 million pounds in 2010.

Changing jobs

If you've been with your employer for less than two years when you leave, you're entitled to a refund of the contributions you've paid into the company pensions scheme, minus tax.

If you've contributed for at least two years, you can leave your money in the scheme, where it remains invested and grows (with luck) until you reach the retirement age set down by the scheme.

Alternatively, you may be able to transfer the value of what you've built up into your new employer's scheme. You may want to transfer if the new scheme is better than your old one or because it gives you fewer pensions to keep track of. You may need independent financial advice before making your decision.

Getting your hands on the money

When you eventually reach the retirement age prescribed by any occupational pension funds you've paid into, you are usually entitled to take some of the money in a cash lump sum (up to a quarter). The rest has to be used to provide retirement income. For most people, the best way to do that is to buy an annuity. Check with your occupational pension trustees because some company pensions don't give you a lump sum.

An *annuity* is a financial product that provides a regular income for the rest of your life – your pension. (See the upcoming section 'Buying an annuity.') Some people object to making contributions into an occupational pension scheme because they can't get their hands on the whole fund they've built up when they retire but have to use three – quarters of that fund to generate a regular income – usually by buying an annuity. Some prefer to put their money into other investments, properties, or other assets that they can sell on retirement and use the money as they please.

If you do decide not to join an occupational pension scheme, you'll lose out on tax relief on your contributions and on the contributions made by your employer.

Saving through a personal pension

A *personal pension,* or *private pension* as they're sometimes called, is a scheme you set up yourself. You choose the pension provider from a long list of companies, depending on how and in what you'd prefer your money to be invested and how much risk you're prepared to allow your money to take in the hope of higher growth.

The money invested grows (you hope) sufficiently to allow you to buy an annuity when you reach the age at which the plan pays out. The annuity provides you with a regular income for life – even if you live to be 110.

If you don't have the opportunity to join an occupational pension scheme, a personal pension is a good alternative. Employers can offer stakeholder pensions instead of an occupational pension, but they're also an option for someone looking for a suitable personal pension. One reason for going down that route may be that the charges for stakeholder pensions are usually a bit lower than for standard personal pensions. Having said that, though, charges for personal pensions have come down since stakeholder pensions were launched in 2001.

Some supermarkets and chain stores offer pensions. They don't manage the pensions themselves – there's a bank or insurer behind the pension that has the supermarket branding on it.

Don't put all your eggs in one basket. If you have money tied up in properties, for example, you'd probably be better to choose a pension that doesn't invest in property to spread the risk of losing out in case of a property crash.

As with occupational pensions, you get tax relief on the contributions you make to your personal pension. If you read the section on occupational pensions, earlier in this chapter, you can see how it works.

With a personal pension, your money is tied up until you're at least 50. Read the terms of your pension to see what age you can take out the money.

When you reach the age at which your personal pension pays out, you can take only a quarter of the fund you've built up in cash. The other three-quarters of the fund has to go to produce a regular income for your retirement. The income you get is taxable, along with any other income you have from other pensions or earnings.

If you're paying into a personal pension, you can opt out of the State Second Pension (see earlier section) and have a proportion of your National Insurance contributions paid into your personal pension instead. It's another case of doing the sums to work out whether you think those NICs will earn you more pension income in your personal pension or in the State Second Pension.

In the past, you may have found yourself faced with the dilemma of having to choose between an occupational pension and a personal pension. The company pension was generally seen as the best option, especially if the employer was making contributions on your behalf. The employer also bears the costs of running the pensions scheme. Personal pensions were seen as the second choice if you didn't have access to a company pension. Now you can pay into as many different pensions as you like, personal or occupational. You just can't pay any more than 100 per cent of your annual income, up to a maximum of £215,000, into pensions. Your pension may end up being an even bigger asset than your home. If in doubt about the best options, get advice. (See the upcoming sidebar, 'Getting help with retirement issues.')

As with any financial investment you should review your pensions from time to time, and if they aren't doing as well as you'd like, you have the right to transfer to a different provider. But look out for charges you may have to pay for transferring. With a stakeholder pension, you can transfer without charges.

Stakeholder pensions

You can save for your retirement through a *stakeholder pension,* which anyone can have whether or not they're employed. You can invest as little as £20 a month and stop and start contributions as and when you like.

Employers with five or more employees have to offer those employees access to a pension scheme, and a stakeholder pension is one option. However, offering access may simply amount to giving you information about the different stakeholder schemes available. The schemes are low cost and intended for people who don't have access to an occupational or personal pension. The annual management charges on a stakeholder pension must be no higher than 1 per cent.

If your company doesn't offer an occupational scheme, doesn't pay an amount equal to at least 3 per cent of your wages into your private pension and has five or more employees, it has to offer access to a stakeholder pension. Your company can make contributions to the stakeholder pension, but it doesn't have to.

Nontaxpayers can contribute up to £3,600 a year into a pension scheme, so you don't have to be working to have one. You can buy one for each of your children if you can afford it, and as nontaxpayers, they can put up to £3,600 in each year.

The same rules apply to stakeholder pensions as to occupational and personal pensions when it comes to retirement. You can take a lump sum and use the rest to generate your retirement income.

Self Invested Personal Pensions (SIPPs)

Self-Invested Personal Pensions (SIPPs) are designed to be flexible. You're in charge of what money in your SIPP is invested in. You're free to invest in all sorts of investment options, such as cash accounts, shares, bonds, government-backed bonds known as *gilts,* and even commercial property.

A lot of different SIPP providers are out there, and as a result, lots of pension providers are offering to manage investors' SIPPs. Providers include James Hay, Standard Life, Hargreaves Lansdown, and Alliance Trust.

With SIPPs, the value of your pension pot depends entirely on the level of contributions that you make and how smart your investments turn out to be. If it all goes wrong, you have no one to blame but yourself.

Like any other type of personal pension, you get tax relief on your contributions – 22 per cent if you're a basic rate taxpayer and 40 per cent if you're a higher ratepayer. You then assign your money to the investment of your choice from a list approved by the SIPP provider.

Under a SIPP your money is locked away until you reach at least 50, – rising to 55 in 2010. You also have to use at least three-quarters of the fund to provide your income in retirement.

Charges on SIPPs can vary markedly between providers. So, too, can the lists of allowed investments. Go for a SIPP that provides the right mixture of low charges and wide investment choice. You're best off getting independent financial advice.

Buying an annuity

Until April 2006, you had to use at least three-quarters of your pension fund to buy an annuity, and you had to buy one by the age of 75. Now, you have an alternative way of getting an income from that money. You can delay buying an annuity indefinitely and simply draw money directly from your pension pot – called *income drawdown*.

The rules about income drawdown, and about how much money you can draw down each year, are very strict, and many financial advisers advise that this option isn't suitable for most pensioners. In most cases, buying an annuity is still the best way to go.

How much your annuity pays out each month depends on how well the money you put into it is invested and how the investments perform. Buying an annuity is one of life's gambles. When the stock market is doing well, pensioners with annuities are richer; when the stock market is doing less well, pensioners complain of feeling the pinch.

Choosing the right annuity as a home for at least three quarters of your pension fund is a tricky business. You really do have to put a lot of work into it as your decision will dictate how well off you are for the rest of your life. It's a good idea to take independent financial advice.

The big plus point about annuities is that they pay out for as long as you live. You may end up drawing an income from an annuity from age 55 to age 105 – probably longer than you worked in the first place.

Buying an annuity is one of the most important financial decisions you can make. But many people go with the first option that presents itself. When it comes time to collect your pension fund and buy an annuity, the pension provider – an insurance company – will offer to convert your pension pot into an annuity, saving you the hassle of shopping around. But you can nearly always get a higher annuity by exercising what is called the *open market option*. You have the right to take your pension pot and shop around among the hundreds of companies out there offering annuities. The amount of income they offer can vary wildly, sometimes by up to 20 per cent. If you get your choice of annuity wrong, you may be missing out on tens of thousands of pounds.

Once you've signed up to an annuity, that's it – you can't switch from one provider to another. You can buy an annuity to provide income for a limited period of time, say five years, so that every five years or so, you can have another look around the market for a better deal.

Get independent advice on annuities and have a look at the Annuity Bureau Web site at www.annuity-bureau.co.uk, which gives you all the annuity rates on offer.

The rules of most personal, occupational, and stakeholder pensions say that you must put at least 75 per cent of your pension fund into an annuity or use it for income drawdown. That rule doesn't mean that you can't put the other 25 per cent into an annuity as well. You need to think about it carefully. If you do decide to take a cash lump sum of up to a quarter of the value of your total fund, it may be advisable to take advice on how to invest that amount, too – unless you have your heart set on a sunshine holiday and a new car!

Understanding Unusual Pension Situations

Not everyone is able to simply retire from work and live happily ever after. Some people struggle to make ends meet and have to go back to work to supplement their income or have to cash in some of their assets – usually their home – to make life easier for themselves.

Working while drawing a pension

Nothing stops you from going on working as long as you like if you can find the work. If you're going to carry on working, you need to know how it affects your various pensions. Check with any occupational and private schemes you've paid into to find out at what age they pay out. Your State Pension starts when you reach the State Pension Age of 60 for a woman and 65 for a man.

You can take your State Pension and carry on working. If you do carry on working after you reach State Pension Age, you don't have to make NICs on your earnings. However, if your work gives you enough income to live on and you don't really need your State Pension, think about deferring your State Pension. You can defer taking the State Pension for as long as you like, and by doing so, it gives you a bigger weekly pension when you do eventually take it.

Do the sums. Your State Pension, like all your other pensions, is taxable. If you take it while you're earning, you may pay more in tax than by deferring it until you stop earning. Alternatively, some people feel that 'a bird in the hand is worth two in the bush.' You may prefer to take your State Pension as soon as you become entitled to it in case you defer it and die without getting the benefit of it. You may be able to grow your weekly State Pension more by taking it and investing it than you can by deferring it. Get your calculator out.

Any personal pensions you've paid into will also have rules about the age at which you can start to draw on the fund. Again, whether or not you need to take it depends on whether you're still earning and how much you're earning. That's another case in which you need to do your calculations or get an independent adviser to do them for you.

If you reach the age at which you can draw your occupational pension and you want to carry on working in your current job, you'll have to defer taking the pension. You boss can't allow you to take your occupational pension and keep you on the payroll. That may change when the Age Discrimination legislation comes in, in October 2006, as the Government is looking for ways to encourage people to work longer. However, in the meantime, you can usually take your occupational pension and carry on working in a different job if you can find one. Depending on the terms of your occupational scheme, you may be able to defer taking your occupational pension, or take it in stages to generate some income to top up your earnings, and take the remainder at 75.

Like your earnings, you have to pay tax on your pension income. Once you reach 65, the amount of income you can have before you have to pay tax – your personal allowance – goes up from £5,035 to £7,280. It goes up again at age 75.

Using your home to generate a pension

Many people don't trust pensions and refuse to put money into them. Others don't have the opportunity to pay into an occupational scheme or feel that they can't afford to pay into a personal pension. For whatever reason, you may find yourself with little choice but to release some of the capital tied up in your home to generate an income with which to supplement your State Pension.

If you're lucky enough to have more than one property, of course, you can keep one to live in and sell the rest. You can then use the money to buy an annuity or to invest in some other savings vehicle that gives you income and capital growth. Don't forget that you're likely to have to pay Capital Gains Tax on the sale of a property that's not your only or main residence, which will significantly reduce the amount of money you have left to invest.

Alternatively, your only property may be worth enough to allow you to sell it, buy somewhere smaller, and live off the difference. This transaction has the added bonus of cutting down on bills, such as council tax and heating fuel. The difficulty is that many people seriously underestimate just how much money you need to invest to generate an income that will keep you in the retirement style you'd like to become accustomed to. The money you release from the sale of your property may not be enough.

However, the greatest difficulty comes when you don't have spare properties to sell or a big enough mansion to exchange for a two up, two down. Then the only option you may have is an Equity Release Scheme, which allows you to release some of the value of your home to produce a regular cash income while you go on living there.

With some schemes, you sell off part of the value of your home, and the money is invested to produce an income. You go on living in the property and pay rent out of the income, leaving you with a bit extra to top up your State Pension. With other schemes, you basically take out a mortgage on part of your home, the money is invested for income, you go on living there, and the mortgage is repaid when you die or go into a care home.

Be very, very careful; take advice from a range of independent financial advisers with good reputations and specialist knowledge of these schemes. You have huge potential here for getting tied up in the kind of scheme that's not right for you. Talk the decision over with one of the organisations, such as Age Concern, where the staff is experienced in the ins and outs of these kinds of plans. Find your nearest Age Concern office through the phone book, CAB, or the Web site address in the upcoming sidebar 'Getting help with retirement issues'.

Many people who struggle in retirement are entitled to some help from the state, but don't realise it. You may qualify for some Pension Credit. (See the earlier section on State Pensions, as well as Chapter 11.) You may qualify for some help with your council tax bills, for example, and a few little extras may be yours for the asking (see the next section).

Getting Extras in Retirement

There are all sorts of helpful little sums and allowances that people over 60 may be entitled to. Some you can only get if you qualify for Pension Credit. (See the earlier section on State Pensions.) Others are available for all people of a particular age.

Getting help with retirement issues

The Citizens Advice Bureau is there to give free, independent, impartial advice to anyone who asks for it. It's a charity, not a Government or local council department, and there's one in most towns and big villages (possibly part-time). Check in your phone book for the details of the nearest one or on the Web site at www. adviceguide.org. Advisers can help on benefits and most others issues you'll encounter in retirement and at work.

The Office of the Pensions Advisory Service has a wealth of information on the whole range of pensions services. Contact OPAS on 0845-601-2923 or at www.opas.org.uk.

Age Concern and Help the Aged are other charities specialising in issues to do with pensions and retirement:

Age Concern England: 020-8765-7200, www. ace.org.uk

Age Concern Wales: 02920-431-555, www. accymru.org.uk

Age Concern Scotland: 0845-833-0200 or free phone 0800-009-966, www.ageconcern scotland.org.uk

Age Concern Northern Ireland: 02890 245729, www.ageconcernni.org

Help The Aged England: 020-7278-1114, www. helptheaged.org.uk

Help the Aged Wales: 02920-346-550, www. helptheaged.org.uk

Help the Aged Scotland: 0131-551-6331, www. helptheaged.org.uk

Help the Aged Northern Ireland: 02890 230666, www.helptheaged.org.uk

(To get to the pages for the individual nations, choose the Nation Selector option on the main Help the Aged Web site page.)

Enjoying your retirement is also about doing new things you haven't previously had time to do, and many organisations can help. Try the University of the Third Age (0208-466-6139 or www.u3a.org.uk) if you want to study. The Life Academy (previously the Pre-retirement Association) (01483-301-170 or www.life-academy.co.uk/) is useful for information in the period leading up to retirement. If you're looking for an Independent financial adviser in your area, the Association of Independent Financial Advisers is on 0207- 628-1287 or www.unbiased.co.uk.

If you want to do some voluntary work in your area, try www.timebank.org.uk, www. navb.org.uk, or www.doit.org.uk, or ask at your local library if a volunteer bureau is in your area. Reach (www.reach-online. org.uk) is an organisation that puts people with managerial, professional, and technical skills in touch with organisations that need those skills, and CSV (www.csv.org.uk) is the UK's largest volunteering and training organisation.

All pensioners 75 and over are entitled to a free television licence. If you're 60 or over in the week beginning the third Monday in September, you're likely to be entitled to the Winter Fuel Payment of £100 or £200, depending on your circumstances, to help pay for heating your home. Over 80s can get up to £300. Age Related Payments help people over 65 pay for their council tax or additional living expenses, and you may be able to claim help to install central heating and have your home insulated.

You may have the right to free eye tests and prescriptions, be entitled to benefits because you need care or have mobility problems, or be able to claim your State Pension while living abroad. Most people receiving State Pensions even get a small Christmas bonus.

A lot of older people miss out on payments that would help them make ends meet because they simply don't know help is available or they're too proud to claim what they see as charity. If you have the right to assistance, such as help to pay your council tax bills (see Chapter 11), you've earned that right and should claim.

If you're retired or are approaching the State Pension age, talk to one of the organisations listed in the sidebar 'Getting help with retirement issues' to make sure that you aren't missing out on any help that you have the right to claim.

Understanding Pensions and Death

Most occupational pensions have a life insurance element so that if you die, your dependents get a lump sum, usually equivalent to a year's salary or, with the more generous scheme, maybe even two or three years salary.

You tell your pension scheme trustees who should benefit in the event of your death. If you aren't married and the person you nominate isn't your spouse, the trustees can use their discretion not to pay out the money. Most pension schemes these days, though, are less old-fashioned than they used to be and are prepared to pay out death-in-service benefits to unmarried and same-sex partners. Ask the trustees of your occupational scheme what the policy is.

Part IV
Spending Your Hard-Earned Cash

"That next door neighbour & his exotic pets! – Its escaped again!"

In this part . . .

Spend, spend, spend! If you're a consumer of any sort – whether you're shopping for food and clothes or using the services of the lawyer, the builder or the local dry cleaner – you're a lot better off if you know your rights. This part deals with getting things put right if something you've bought turns out to be faulty or if the work you've paid for isn't carried out to your satisfaction.

I also look at the bills you have to pay and what action thevarious organisations can take if you get into arrears. In an update of the old quote from Mr. Micawber, 'Annual income £23,000, annual expenditure £22,500 – result happiness; annual income £23,000, annual expenditure £23,500 – result misery!' Most people tend to spend what comes in, and few households in the UK have much savings, but when the bills can't be paid and debts are owed to credit-card companies or on loans, life can become rather miserable. Fortunately, information in this part can guide you on where to turn for help.

Chapter 13

Serious Shopping

. . . .

. . . .

*S*hopping is a serious business and not to be entered into without being fully aware of your rights – unless you want to be ripped off. Something can go wrong in just about any instance, so you need to be forewarned so that you can take precautions to avoid trouble.

Consumers are a lot savvier than in days gone by and less prepared to put up with shoddy goods and poor service. The more consumers exercise their powers and demand their rights, the more retailers and service providers have to take notice. That raises standards and drives the cowboys out of business.

Shopping by the Rules

If you abide by a few simple rules of shopping, it'll save you a lot of problems.

When shopping, be it on the high street, from a catalogue, over the Internet, or from a street market, or at home, trade with people who have a good reputation. A trader's reputation is very important to his business, and he can't afford to tarnish it by selling goods or services that aren't up to scratch or by refusing to do the right thing by his customers if things do, inadvertently, go wrong.

If something seems too good to be true, that's usually because it is. You just don't get something for nothing, and you get what you pay for. So if that watch with the well-known name is very cheap, that's likely to be because it's fake or it's fallen off the back of a lorry. Be realistic.

Shop around. If one shop is offering a special deal on something or you get points on your loyalty card, that doesn't mean that you can't get the same thing cheaper or better quality elsewhere or that you'll get good service if things go wrong.

Be sure you really want something before you buy because you have no right to a refund if you simply change your mind. The retailer may have a policy of giving refunds, but that's not always the case.

If you keep these points in mind and go armed with the information in this chapter, you'll be shopping smart.

Buying New Goods

It's a consumer society. Not only do people have the spare cash to spend, there's also more to buy. People are also time poor, so there's no time to have things repaired. When things stop doing what they're supposed to do, they're abandoned to the landfill site and a newer model purchased.

Things change and develop more quickly, too. No sooner have you bought a new mobile phone than a newer and better one with more bells and whistles on it comes out – or so the relentless advertising would have you believe. Regardless of the pleas of environmental organisations that society is depleting valuable resources and creating unmanageable amounts of waste, everyone keeps on buying new goods.

When it comes to your rights, there are a whole raft of them. Some of them apply to second-hand goods as well as new goods, and most apply no matter where you shop. UK law provides basic consumer protection, and on top of that, some traders follow codes of practice that give added protection.

Understanding the law

Under the Sale and Supply of Goods Act 1994, the law says goods you buy must be

- ✔ **Of satisfactory quality,** so there should be no defects – even minor ones – and they should be safe, durable, and have a satisfactory appearance and finish.
- ✔ **Fit for their purpose,** so they should do the job they're designed to do or that you have stipulated that you need them to do.
- ✔ **As described,** so if it says it's a yellow kettle with a whistle, it has to be a yellow kettle with a whistle.

If you get the item home and discover that it fails to meet one or some of these criteria, you have rights to have the situation put right. You need to decide what would be a satisfactory outcome and go back to the retailer. A satisfactory outcome depends on what the problem is.

If you reject the goods quickly enough, you're entitled to a full refund. If you delay, you may be entitled only to compensation to cover the costs of repairs. You don't have to take a replacement, a credit note, or a free repair if you don't want to, but you may decide a replacement is exactly what you want.

If the item is what you wanted but with minor faults – perhaps small dents or scratches, because the box has been dropped – you may well want the same item without the faults or be happy to accept some money back in compensation.

If the fault is more serious, as in a missing or broken part, you may be happy with a replacement that's intact. If the retailer can't replace it with exactly the same item, you may be happy with a similar one, made by a different manufacturer, or you may want your money back. The retailer may offer you a repair, but you're unlikely to be happy with a repair on a new item and will probably want a refund.

If the item isn't fit for its purpose, is that because the particular one you've got is missing a vital part by accident? In that case, a replacement would be fit for its purpose, so you may want a replacement. But if it says you can do something with it that you discover can't be done, you'll want it replaced with a different model or to have your money back so that you can buy a different model elsewhere.

If you've bought something that's described as something it isn't, there's no point in accepting a replacement of the same item.

Think carefully about what you want the retailer to do. A reputable retailer will be fully aware of the rights of customers and will be happy to put things right by giving you the replacement or refund.

You're more likely to run into problems if the retailer is one who simply ignores customers' rights and refuses refunds or replacements regardless of the problem, or if you have a fundamental disagreement between you about the nature of the problem in the first place.

Some retailers will tell you that it's not up to them to sort out the problem with faulty goods – that it's up to the manufacturer – but that's not true. However, what you consider unsatisfactory quality may be perfectly satisfactory in the eyes of the retailer. You may then need the opinion of the Trading Standards Officer or the consumer adviser.

If you do have a problem with the retailer, check out your rights with your local authority Trading Standards Department. You can find the contact details in the phone book or through www.tradingstandards.gov.uk. The new phone and Internet-based consumer advice service Consumer

Direct (08454-040-506 or www.consumerdirect.gov.uk) is now operating in most parts of the UK. Often, just being able to tell the retailer you've taken advice and you know what your rights are is enough to get action.

Knowing when you haven't a leg to stand on

In some situations, you won't be able to demand a refund or replacement, even if one of the criteria in the preceding section applies.

If you've examined the goods before you bought them and you should have noticed the fault or the shop staff pointed it out to you, you can't complain about it later. You accepted the goods with the fault, and that's what you paid for.

If you damaged the goods yourself, you can't expect the retailer to replace or refund them.

Contrary to what many people think, the retailer is under no obligation to give you a refund, replace something with something else, or even give you a credit note if none of the three criteria apply. If you simply don't like the item when you get it home, you're stuck with it, unless the retailer changes or refunds it out of the goodness of its heart.

Applying codes of practice

Some traders you deal with are members of trade associations and have codes of practice, which, although not legally binding, the members have signed up to. Often, customers will have extra protection under the codes, over and above the protection the law gives them. When you buy something, such as a new car, from a trader, look at the literature or in the window for the symbol of any trade association the trader belongs to. You can get a copy of the code of practice and contact the trade association if you have any dispute with the trader that you can't resolve. Some associations have mediation or arbitration services you can agree to use to resolve the problem.

Getting a satisfactory result

It's impossible to address all the situations that may arise in one chapter, but the following sections can help you decide what you should do in your own particular case and what redress you can ask for.

Rejecting the goods

You can reject the goods if they're not of satisfactory quality, not as described, or not fit for their purpose. By rejecting them, you're ending the contract with the seller. At that point, you have the right to get your money back or to agree to some other solution. But if you accept the goods, you lose that right. If you notice a problem, take them back as soon as possible.

You are allowed a reasonable time to examine the goods, but there's no legal definition of what's reasonable. If you know you won't be able to get back to the shop for a few days, phone and let them know what the problem is and that you want a refund. The longer you keep goods, the more difficult it can be to prove that they were faulty when you bought them.

Sometimes you'll buy goods from a sample – perhaps you order a sofa based on one you've seen in a shop, to be covered with fabric that you've chosen from a batch of samples in the shop. The sofa has to comply with all the criteria in the same way as any other goods you buy. If not, you can reject it.

Accepting the goods

You will be taken to have accepted the goods if you keep them for a reasonable time after you take them home or have them delivered, without letting the retailer know that you've rejected them. A reasonable time means a reasonable time to examine what you've bought – to make sure it hasn't got faults, is likely to last, and is safe.

What would be a reasonable time in which to examine an item of clothing is likely to be a lot shorter than a reasonable time to examine a car, for example. Don't get things home and allow them to lie around in a box for weeks before making sure that you don't want to reject them.

Taking goods back

Take the goods back as soon as possible after you've decided to reject them. You should have your receipt as proof that you bought the goods from that particular retailer in case the staff member disputes it. However, the law doesn't say that the retailer has to give you a receipt, so you can enforce your rights without one. You may have other ways of proving the product you bought came from a particular shop – a carrier bag, for example, a witness who was with you at the time, a label that shows it came from that shop, or simply your own word.

If the shop won't act because you don't have the receipt, talk to the Trading Standards Department. If it's difficult for you to get to the shop to return the goods, try to arrange for the retailer to pick them up, or that you post them and the retailer pays for postage and packing.

Getting a refund

If you reject the goods quickly, you're likely to be entitled to a full refund. Don't be tempted to go on using the goods or repair them yourself, or you may lose your right to a full refund.

If the retailer doesn't offer a refund but offers a replacement or repair instead, you may not have to accept that. Ultimately, if the retailer sticks to its guns, you may have to get the court to decide whether you should be given a refund. You may be willing to go to that trouble over an expensive item like a leather sofa, but it's not worth it for the price of a toast rack. Enlist the help of the Trading Standards Department, a consumer adviser, or any trade association the retailer belongs to.

Getting a repair

Under The Sale of Goods Act 1994, you may be able to ask for a replacement or free repair if something goes wrong within six years (five in Scotland) and it's reasonable to expect that the item would have lasted that long.

You can probably spot the potential for disagreements here already. You may expect a pair of shoes to last for six years, but I doubt that the retailer would accept that as reasonable – if it's still in business. But the seller is only responsible if the item went wrong because of some defect that was present at the time the item was sold.

Under The Sale and Supply of Goods to Consumers Regulations 2002 – which give you protection anywhere in the European Union if anything is wrong with goods you buy – if a fault appears within the first six months, it's assumed that it existed at the time it was sold, unless the retailer can prove otherwise. So, for the first six months, it's not up to you to prove the goods were defective when you bought them. If a fault appears within the first two years (or one year, if they were second-hand), you can ask the seller for a free repair or for a replacement. If that's not possible, you should be given compensation or a refund.

Claiming compensation

If it's too late to demand a refund and you can't get a free repair or a replacement, you may be entitled to compensation, which isn't the same as a refund. Compensation usually amounts to the cost of repairs.

Say that you've had your sofa for a year when the material starts to develop holes. You're unlikely to get a full refund – after all, you've used the sofa for a year – but it's reasonable to expect it to have lasted a lot longer. If the retailer can't give a free repair or a replacement – perhaps because he no longer sells furniture – your compensation may amount to the cost of having the sofa recovered, plus the cost of transporting it to and from the repair shop.

If the retailer refuses to pay the compensation, you may have to take a case against it in court.

If the goods were dangerous or faulty and injured someone or did some damage to other property, you can claim extra compensation to cover that as well. That compensation may be on top of a full or partial refund because the goods weren't of satisfactory quality. (See the section on unsafe goods, later in this chapter.)

Accepting a credit note

If a shop gives you a *credit note,* it means that you can choose an item to the value of the note, at a later date, when something you want is in stock. If you're entitled to a refund, replacement, repair, or compensation, you don't have to accept a credit note. You can insist on your rights.

If you do accept the credit note, you can't change your mind later and ask for a refund.

If you think you may change your mind, before you buy, arrange with the shop staff the terms on which you can bring the item back and whether you'll get a refund or a replacement item. Get it in writing if it isn't usual shop policy. Otherwise, the best you can hope for is that the manager will agree to give you a credit note to use at a later date. You may have a time limit in which you have to use it – and some time limits are very strict. In fact, one large chain store says that credit notes have to be used the same day.

If you're given a credit note, use it quickly. What's on sale at £10.99 today may cost £12.99 next week, so if you delay, you may get less for your money.

Cancelling an order

If you've ordered something, such as a sofa, but it doesn't turn up when you expect it, that doesn't mean you can reject it. It should be delivered within a reasonable time, but what's reasonable depends on the item and other circumstances, such as the difficulty the trader has had in getting the material you ordered.

If you stipulated when you put in your order that it had to arrive by a particular date – for example, because it was for a specific occasion – and it doesn't arrive on time, you still don't have the right to reject the goods. But you may be able to take action against the trader for compensation because the terms of the contract you made with them have been broken.

If the goods you order don't turn up within a reasonable time, or by the date agreed, contact the retailer again and set another date. Put it in writing and say that it must be delivered by that date – that *time is of the essence.* If that phrasing doesn't get the desired result, you can ask for a refund, compensation, or discount. The compensation should cover any loss of earnings if you've stayed in waiting for deliveries that didn't happen.

Buying on the doorstep

If you buy goods from a seller on your doorstep, you have the same rights as when you buy from a shop. But because sales people in the past have sometimes applied pressure-selling techniques to get people to buy, you do have the right to cancel within seven days and get your money back if the goods cost more than £35 – unless you signed a credit agreement at home. You can't cancel if you asked the company to send a salesperson to your home, if the goods are perishable, or if they were bought at a home party sale.

You can also cancel your order and ask for your money back. This step is a bit of a minefield, though. The retailer will argue that the goods are being made and materials have had to be paid for. If it's obvious, though, that the goods you're ordering are for Christmas – because you're ordering from a Christmas catalogue or shop, for example – then if they're not delivered in time, you can cancel and ask for a full refund. You may have to go to court to get the refund. If the trader belongs to a trade association, enlist its help.

Guarantees

Most household items you buy these days come with a free guarantee from the manufacturer. In it, the manufacturer sets out what it will do if problems arise. In most cases, you can have a repair or replacement if the item goes wrong within the first 6, 12 or 24 months. Usually, repairs and labour charges are covered for a certain period of time after which you may get a repair but have to pay for labour. Read the small print.

At the time that you buy the item, you may be offered the chance to pay for a longer guarantee. Think about the rights you have to redress from the seller before spending money on a guarantee that may offer you no additional protection over the protection you have in law for free.

Retailers sometimes hide behind the manufacturer's guarantee and claim that if something goes wrong, it's up to the manufacturer to put it right. Your rights under the guarantee are in addition to your rights to a refund, repair, or compensation, not instead of. Your beef is with the retailer. Your guarantee may give you a backup if the retailer digs their heels in, however.

Extended warranties

Guarantees are usually free from the manufacturer. *Warranties* are basically insurance policies to cover repairs that you have to pay for. When you buy an item like a washing machine, the retailer may offer you a warranty. You may be able to buy one to cover you for up to three years. Usually, they offer you similar terms to the free manufacturers guarantee, but you're paying.

Be careful of extended warranties. Retailers usually get commission from the companies providing the warranties, so they tend to push you to sign up. You may be paying for protection you already have from the retailer or the manufacturer, and warranties always have limits on what they cover. The most likely things to go wrong are rarely covered. Warranties can also work out to be very expensive – you can pay half as much again as the item cost in the first place. However, warranties can be useful if you can't get redress from the retailer because they've disappeared or are too far away for it to be practical to enforce your rights.

Under the Supply of Extended Warranties on Domestic Electrical Goods Order 2005, you have the right to cancel an extended warranty within 45 days of the agreement being signed if you decide you don't want to go ahead. So read the small print carefully and weigh up the pros and cons.

You may be able to buy peace of mind more cheaply direct from an insurance company. Some sell policies that cover all your household appliances. Don't be pushed into signing up for a warranty. Do some research into alternatives first.

Buying In Person

Going out and about, checking out what's available, comparing prices and quality, trying on, trying it out, choosing, paying, and bringing it home – it's all part of the shopping experience. There are all sorts of places to do it, too, and it's the favourite weekend pastime in the UK. Believe it or not, recent research shows that the love of shopping goes for men as well as women. It's amazing what men will say to keep the peace when a market research company questions them while out shopping!

All the rules about buying new goods (see preceding sections) apply wherever you go to shop in person – unless you're buying from private individuals or at auctions. But you won't always be buying new goods. Some of the things you buy may come with faults built in, and you may be tempted by sales or buy while you're on holiday abroad. The following sections look at how the law applies in those circumstances.

Buying second-hand goods

If you go to a retailer selling second-hand goods, you're entitled to the same protection as with new goods. They should be as described, fit for their purpose, and be of satisfactory quality. However, you wouldn't expect second-hand clothes to be in the same condition as new clothes or a second-hand computer to have all the functions a new one might offer. Check second-hand goods out and test them thoroughly before you buy.

If you're buying a second-hand car, you can expect it to be roadworthy and that the mileage you see on the clock is accurate. If it's described as having had 'one careful owner', it should be as described. The price should reflect its quality and condition. The only way to know whether you're paying a fair price for a car in that condition is to compare the prices of others of the same quality in a similar condition – on sale at other garages, for example, or by checking the prices suggested in one of the car magazines.

A little bit of haggling can save you money when it comes to second-hand goods. They're only worth what someone else will pay for them, so if there aren't many potential buyers around, you can bag a bargain.

If something does go wrong, you have the same right as with buying new goods to reject the goods and have your money refunded, the item replaced or repaired, or claim compensation. Second-hand goods should be safe, and you'll be entitled to compensation for injury or damage if they aren't. If you come across a trader selling second-hand goods that aren't safe or are faulty, contact you're local Trading Standards Department. Officers will be able to take action to stop rogue traders.

The retailer may give you a free guarantee on your second-hand goods, but they will usually be outside the manufacturer's guarantee. The retailer may also offer you the chance to buy a warranty in case repairs are needed.

Make sure that any warranties you pay for give you additional protection to the protection the law gives you, or you may be wasting your money.

Buying privately

You have very little protection from the law when you buy from a private individual – whether the goods are new or second-hand. Your contract is with the seller, who must sell only goods that belong to him and that are as described; and, if the item is a car, it must be roadworthy. As you can imagine, most private sellers will be advised not to give an item too much of a description beyond the purely factual, such as 'Vauxhall Corsa, black, two years old, for sale.'

If a car turns out to have a mileage on its clock (odometer, to give it it's correct title) that isn't accurate (the clock has been wound back, or the car has been *clocked,* as they say in the trade), you would have a case for getting your money back because the seller would knowingly have led you to believe something false in order to persuade you to buy. Clocking cars is an offence, as is selling an unroadworthy car. If you suspect that someone has sold you something that doesn't belong to them or that an offence has occurred, talk to your local Trading Standards Department.

Many people sell goods privately these days at car boot sales. Again, they should sell only what they own. If they're traders rather than private sellers, it should be very clear from the details on their stalls. Car boot sales have become magnets for dodgy traders selling illegal pirated copies of DVDs, CDs, videos, and fake copies of well-known brands of items, such as t-shirts, watches, and perfumes. If items are copies, it should be made clear; otherwise, they're counterfeits, and Trading Standards Officers have the power to seize the goods and prosecute the traders.

When goods are stolen, they still belong to the original owner. When they're found, a court can order that they're returned to the owner or the value of them is paid to the owner in compensation. If you happen to buy something that was stolen, you may have to return it or pay the owner compensation, even if you paid a fair price for it. You can try to claim the money back from the seller.

You'll usually have no comeback at all if the goods you buy privately turn out to be faulty, so check and test them thoroughly before you buy. In the case of private sales, the watchwords really are 'buyer beware.'

If you'd like to buy from a private seller, check out the local papers to see whether the same telephone number crops up fairly often. Someone may be posing as a private seller but in reality trading, in which case you have more consumer protection, but the seller is breaking the law.

Buying at auctions

If you buy new goods at an auction, you have the same rights as you do if you buy new goods in a shop. If you buy second-hand goods, you don't; these goods are usually *sold as seen,* which means just what it says.

Check the goods on offer very carefully and be sure that you know exactly what you're getting before you start bidding.

Sellers should only sell things that belong to them, but if any problem arises, you have to take it up with the seller; the auction house doesn't have to give you the seller's details – another case of buyer beware.

Buying seconds

Sometimes shops will offer *seconds* for sale. These goods are new, but come with an inbuilt fault that is usually a cosmetic fault – a flaw in the weave of material or a glaze finish that's not perfect. These items shouldn't be sold as perfect goods. If they are sold as perfect, you can reject them because they're faulty. As long as it's pointed out to you or you should have seen that the item had a fault – perhaps because of the notices on the label – you can't later go and claim a refund because of that fault. If another fault wasn't pointed out and it was reasonable for you to miss – a hole perhaps, which wasn't the reason that the goods were being sold as imperfect – you can reject the goods.

If the retailer is selling damaged goods that were perfect but have been damaged while on the shelves, it should be made clear to you, too, before you buy. Again, you can't later reject the goods on the basis of a fault you knew existed when you bought the item.

Buying in sales

When you buy goods in a sale, you have exactly the same rights as when you buy them at full price. Shops sometimes display signs that say you can't return sales goods or that no refunds will be made on sales goods, but those policies are illegal. You have the same rights to reject and return faulty goods for a refund as you do at any other time.

Buying from market stalls

When you buy from market stalls, you have all the same rights as when you buy from any other trader. You enter into a contract with the seller, and the law protects you. The trader's stall should have the trading name or name of the company and contact details. If you have a problem, you should be able to contact the trader even if that stall isn't in the market the next week.

Only buy from stalls where traders have their details displayed and who have a good reputation. If you notice a problem, find the market supervisor. The local authority can tell you how, and who to talk to, or contact the Trading Standards Department.

Buying abroad

How is it that what seems like a must-have item when you see it on sale on holiday never seems to live up to its promise when you get it home? Attics and charity shops up and down the UK are full of sombreros and straw donkeys that don't quite fit in with the climate and decor. There's not much you can do about poor shopping decisions, but what happens if you've spent a lot of money on something that turns out to be faulty when you get back?

Your rights depend largely on the laws of the country you bought the item in. If you've bought from somewhere in the European Union, then your rights are more or less the same as those described for the UK because consumer law in EU countries comes from the EU. The same isn't necessarily true for the rest of the world.

Buying with credit

If the seller arranged credit for you or if you pay by credit card, you may be protected under the Consumer Credit Act of 1974 on goods or services that cost over £100 and under £30,000. The card or credit company, as well as the seller, is liable for any breach of contract – even if you didn't pay the whole amount by credit. So if anything goes wrong and the seller refuses to put it right, you can claim against the card company instead (or as well).

The same applies if the retailer or supplier goes bust, and you've already paid in full or paid a deposit. You can claim it back from the card company. This equal liability may also apply if you buy goods abroad, and the credit card was issued in the UK.

This rule applies to credit cards, but not to charge cards, such as American Express or Diners Club, or to debit cards, such as Delta or Maestro. It's unlikely to apply to private sales as private sellers won't be equipped to accept credit cards or to arrange credit for you.

If you may be tempted to spend on something expensive while you're away, check your rights before you go. Even if you're well protected by the laws of the country you buy in, think about the practicalities. You can get carried away when the sun's high and the wine's flowing, but are you really going to be able to take something back and get a refund if it all goes wrong? Make sure that you check and double-check that you're buying what you think you're buying and that it's not likely to fall apart as soon as you get through passport control.

In addition, think about any duties and taxes you may have to pay. In some countries, you may have to pay to take certain items out, and you may also have to pay import duty when you get back to the UK. Get information before you go from your local consumer advice centre or Trading Standards Department. Depending on the problem and on the cost of the item, you may have additional protection if you use your credit card to pay. (See the sidebar 'Buying with credit'.) The rules are different if you buy from abroad through mail order or the Internet.

Buying Remotely

The high street traders are worried. More and more people are shopping remotely. Even before the age of the Internet, mail order made shopping easier, and as people become increasingly time poor, they look for ways to avoid that time-consuming pursuit called shopping.

Buying through mail order

Flick through a catalogue, see something you like, phone in your order or do it online, and wait for it to be delivered. It's so easy. The drawback is that the thing may not be quite what you expected, or it may not fit, so you need to know your rights.

Because you're buying new goods you have all the same rights as you do if you're buying new goods from the shops. (See the section 'Buying New Goods,' earlier in this chapter.)

You also get protection under The Consumer Protection (Distance Selling) Regulations 2000. These regulations cover transactions where you and the seller don't come face to face, and they apply when you buy from any European Union country.

Before you buy, you should have all the details of the seller's name and address, of the price of the goods you're ordering, and of your rights to withdraw your order. All that information will normally be in the catalogue or on the order form.

You also have the right to:

- ✔ A written confirmation of your order
- ✔ A cooling-off period of seven days in which you can change your mind and cancel your order
- ✔ Delivery within 30 days unless you agree to a different delivery period
- ✔ Any money back that's been taken from your credit or charge card through fraud
- ✔ Opt out of receiving any advertising e-mails
- ✔ Not receive unsolicited goods and services with demands for payment

One thing to remember is that these regulations don't cover holidays and travel tickets, financial services, or things like milk that you may have delivered to you every day.

You have added protection if you buy with a credit card or credit agreement arranged for you by the mail-order company. (See the sidebar 'Buying with credit.')

Problems may arise if something is delivered to you in less than perfect condition. If the supplier can't prove that the item was in perfect condition when it left its premises, you can ask to be reimbursed. If the supplier can prove that the item was in perfect condition, you will have to claim against the carrier. If the carrier is the Post Office, you receive a sliding scale of compensation if you can prove your case, but the amount you get may not cover your loss.

Companies that are members of schemes or trade associations such as the Mail Order Protection Scheme (MOPS) usually agree to replace goods free of charge if they're damaged in transit – which is a very important consideration!

MOPS also cover things you buy through advertisements in magazines or newspapers. Make sure that the advertisements carry the logo on the ad and keep a copy of the ad in case things go wrong. You can find more information near the end of this chapter in the section 'Buying through adverts.'

Buying over the Internet

When you buy goods over the Internet, you have the same rights as when you buy in a shop, as long as the seller in based in the UK. The Consumer Protection (Distance Selling) Regulations apply, too, if you're buying from an EU country (see the earlier section 'Buying through mail order') because you're not buying face to face.

You can also cancel your order up to seven working days after you've received your goods and get your money back unless they were perishables that have gone off; were software, audio or video recordings that have been unsealed; or were made to order. That right to cancel does give you quite a bit of protection, but some rights don't apply to goods bought through online auctions. The Internet is a big place, and it brings its own range of problems.

Many of the firms trading on the Internet are based outside the UK, so you're buying from abroad. (See the section 'Buying abroad,' earlier in this chapter.) Buying abroad means that the laws of the country you're buying from apply, and you may have less protection than under UK law. You also have the difficulty of sending goods back if they're faulty or not as you'd been led to believe. Even if firms are located in the UK, tracking them down can be difficult if you need a refund or to send something back.

Buy from a reputable trader – preferably one that has signed up to one of the online codes of practice that have been set up. These codes set out your rights as a customer and set standards for the firms to comply with. The Alliance for Electronic Business has a scheme called *Trust UK*, which sets out the minimum standards for codes of practice. Traders can display the Trust UK logo on their Web site if they have signed up to a code that meets those minimum standards. Have a look at the Trust UK Web site at www.trustuk. org.uk, which explains what protection this scheme provides. The whole idea of the scheme is to make sure, as far as possible, that

✔ Your privacy is protected.

✔ Your payments are secure.

✔ You'll have details of what you've agreed to and how to cancel if you need to.

✔ The goods should be delivered within the agreed period of time.

✔ Problems will be sorted out no matter where you live.

The other regulations that apply to online shopping are the Electronic Commerce Regulations 2002. Under these regulations, traders who sell or advertise goods online must:

✔ Provide you with information including the full name of the business, contact details, prices, delivery charges, and taxes

✔ Acknowledge your order promptly

✔ Give you the chance to change your order

If traders don't comply with the regulations, you may be able to cancel your order, get a court order against the firm, or sue for damages if you've suffered loss because of it.

One of the big bugbears of the Internet for many people is the amount of unsolicited 'junk' mail or 'spam' e-mails that they get from firms advertising goods or services. If you get these kinds of e-mails and you haven't asked for them, the Electronic Commerce Regulations say that you should be able to identify them as *spam* without having to open and read them, so you can block them. If you get that kind of material by e-mail and it doesn't indicate that it's unsolicited, talk to the Trading Standards Department at your local authority.

Dealing with Issues

No matter how seriously you take your shopping, you'll have issues to deal with from time to time. The main problem is that often things just aren't what they seem, and you're left with a fake (having been ripped off by a scam), with something that looked perfectly innocent but created chaos, or with something you simply didn't ask for in the first place. This section attempts to address all those little problems that leave you with egg on your face.

Faking it

Who could blame you for being taken in by some of the fakes that are around at the minute? They're very convincing! Just about anything that can be counterfeited will be counterfeited, from cigarettes and perfume to watches and designer bags and clothes. The top brands are very prone to it because their goods sell for large amounts of money and so the fakers can make large amounts of money.

The only real protection you have is to be very suspicious. Buy from reputable dealers so you can be sure they have bought their stock direct from the manufacturer. If you're planning to buy something expensive, expect it to be expensive. Find out how much it costs from reputable dealers, and if you find it elsewhere, at least ask yourself why it costs less. If famous brand goods turn up somewhere you wouldn't expect to see them, that's usually because they've borrowed the brand name and attached it to inferior items.

Some people see no problem in buying counterfeits of the real thing because they're so much cheaper. But they will be inferior quality and can be downright dangerous. Some people don't realise that they're being ripped off and think that they're getting the real thing at a bargain price. Something as seemingly innocuous as fake perfumes can contain chemicals that can sting, cause breathing problems, irritate eyes, and even bring on asthmatic attacks or allergic reactions. Fakes of expensive toys may have eyes and buttons that come off and choke a child.

Counterfeiting is illegal. If you're suspicious, contact the Trading Standards Department at your local authority. Officers can seize counterfeit goods and prosecute the sellers.

Spotting a scam

More scams are connected with services than with goods. (See Chapter 14 for more on services.) However, the kinds of goods that are usually the subject of scams are things like sets of leather bound books that you can buy in parts. The very convincing letter drops onto your doormat, making an intriguing offer at what seems like a very reasonable price. All you have to do is to send some money now and the rest in monthly instalments. What the letter doesn't say is that once you've sent off your first cheque and its been cashed, you'll never hear from the firm again, and the goods you've ordered will never arrive.

Check out any company very carefully and be sure that you're dealing with a reputable firm before you ever send any money up front. A reputable firm lets you see the goods it's offering first before you pay. Many of these scams are run from abroad and use box numbers. If you have only a box number, returning goods and getting a refund will be difficult, even if the goods are genuine. If you're buying from abroad, don't forget you may have less protection than you do if you're buying from a UK-based company. Throw the letter away and save yourself a headache.

All of the preceding advice also goes for letters telling you you've won a prize and that you should phone a given number to claim it. More often than not, the only prize you'll end up winning is a big phone bill. The number you're given to call will be a premium-rate one that costs you a fortune and nets the sender of the letter a tidy sum from each caller.

Buying through adverts

Flick through your daily newspaper or any magazine, and you'll see adverts of all shapes and sizes for goods of all description and some that defy description. Some come with order forms that you can cut out and send away – with your cheque – and have the items delivered by mail order.

If you make purchases in this way, you have all the rights you'd normally have when buying by mail order (see the section on mail-order earlier in this chapter) but you always run the chance that some of the ads may not be genuine and your cash may vanish.

To make sure that you're protected, don't send any money unless the ad has the MOPS logo. If the newspaper or magazine belongs to the MOPS scheme, you can reclaim any money you send if the firm goes bust and your goods don't turn up. Always keep a copy of the advertisements with details of the paper or magazine you found it in and what date.

The ads that may present a problem are the small ads in papers, in newsagent's windows, dropped through your letterbox, or sent by post that turn out to be scams. If you ring a number because you want to buy something that's advertised, be very suspicious if you're asked to send money in advance of getting the goods. You may find you send the money, receive nothing, and when you try the number again, it's been disconnected. Ads for 'Get rich quick schemes,' which ask you to send an amount of money for a book or a starter pack that will help you start off on a new career, are quite common and rarely deliver.

If you do get stung through an ad, make sure that you contact the publication that carried it so that it can refuse those ads in future. Also contact the Trading Standards Department at your local authority. If you think that certain ads in newspapers, magazines, on radio, or television are misleading to customers, or sales promotions are unfairly run, contact the Advertising Standards Authority (ASA) on www.asa.org.uk or call 020-7492-2222. ASA may also be able to help you if goods you have ordered through an ad don't turn up.

Getting Compensation for Unsafe Goods

The General Product Safety Regulations 1994 say that all suppliers have to supply safe products. That law covers new and second-hand goods, and on top of that, other laws cover specific products: toys are covered by the Toy

(Safety) Regulations 1995 and have to carry the 'CE' mark; furniture is covered by the Furniture and Furnishings (Fire) (Safety) Regulations 1988, which sets out fire safety tests; and fireworks have to be authorised by the Health and Safety Executive.

People rarely get hurt by goods they buy these days, partly because more product recalls occur. Companies value their reputations, and so, at the first whiff of an unsafe product, they recall them, and they disappear off the shelves in record time. But if you do buy something that injures you or damages something, you have rights to compensation.

If your washing machine goes on fire and the clothes in it are lost, you can claim from the retailer for the machine and the clothes. But the manufacturer or the importer is also responsible under the Consumer Protection Act 1987. So if your washing machine sets your house on fire and causes damage of more than £275 or injures someone, it's the manufacturer – or the importer, if the manufacturer is abroad – you need to go after. If the retailer you bought the item from can't tell you who the manufacturer or the importer is, you have to pursue the retailer.

To claim against the manufacturer or importer, you have to prove that the product:

- ✔ Was defective and not just of poor quality, which is covered by the Sale of Goods Act and is the retailer's responsibility.
- ✔ Caused the injury or damage.

You can only claim if:

- ✔ The damage amounts to at least £275, or your claiming compensation for injury of more than £275.
- ✔ You bought the item less than ten years ago.

The item itself isn't covered by the Consumer Protection Act – only the injury or damage. You'll have to claim against the retailer for the item. You may have to call in independent experts to show that the item was defective and caused the damage, and you'll need specialist help from a personal injury lawyer if you're claiming compensation for injury. The claim can include amounts for loss of earnings, as well as pain and suffering. Your nearest Citizens Advice Bureau can suggest a solicitor in your area who specialises in personal injury, or contact the Law Society (0870-606-6575 or www.lawsociety.org.uk) for some names.

Buying food

The Consumer Protection Act also covers food. In most cases, you get something like a loaf of bread home and discover it's mouldy, so the shop simply apologises and replaces it.

Under the Sale of Goods Act, you have rights to a refund or replacement because the bread wasn't of satisfactory quality. But if food you buy turns out to be contaminated, you may be able to claim compensation under the Consumer Protection Act.

Contamination may be by bacteria that causes food poisoning or by something that shouldn't be there, such as glass, which can hurt someone. You can claim against the manufacturer for compensation if someone is sick or injured because the food wasn't safe.

Keep any evidence, such as food wrappers, and if someone has been ill, get a letter from your doctor as proof. If you're ill because of something you've eaten in a restaurant, see Chapter 14.

Getting Something You Didn't Order

It's always nice to get a present through the post – except when it's *unsolicited*, something you don't want and didn't order from a company you know nothing about.

Under the Unsolicited Goods and Services Act 1971, it's an offence to send you goods you haven't ordered and then demand that you pay for them. If you receive goods in this way, you can keep them as an unconditional gift or dispose of them, and you don't have to pay for them or return them. If you do get a demand for payment, talk to your local Trading Standards Department at your local authority.

If you've ordered something or agreed to buy it, it's not unsolicited, and you have to pay for it. If you've ordered something and the wrong thing is sent, again, that's not unsolicited. You have to pay for it or send it back.

Returning presents

If you get something you didn't order because someone else has bought it for you, the person who buys the goods has the rights that have been described in this chapter. So if you give something as a gift, it's you (not the person whose birthday it is) who can take the item back for a refund or replacement.

Under the Third Party to the Contract Act, if you don't want to have to deal with any potential problems yourself, when you buy, explain to the shop staff that it's a gift and get its agreement to deal with the gift's recipient. The shop must then write the name of that person on the receipt or invoice.

Going Out of Business

If you've ordered something and paid in full or part up front, there's always a chance that the supplier can go out of business before you get your goods. If the company you were dealing with was a limited company, you may get some or all of your money back once the receiver or liquidator appointed to deal with the company's affairs has worked out how much money is left to pay customers' claims. Talk to your local Trading Standards Department about how to find out who has been appointed as receiver or liquidator.

If the supplier was a sole trader, or in partnership with someone else, but not operating as a limited company, you can sue them for your money. It would be best to do some sleuthing work first to find out what the chances are that they'll be able to pay; otherwise, you may be throwing away good money.

Check to see whether the firm was a member of a trade association or a member of the Mail Order Protection Scheme. Associations may have schemes that cover customers if their members go out of business.

Getting Help

Trading Standards Departments at local authorities have officers who enforce the consumer laws and regulations. You can find details in your phone book or at www.tradingstandards.gov.uk. The Trading Standards Institute Web site at www.tsi.org.uk has more detailed information about your consumer rights throughout the UK.

If you want quick information or advice over the phone, call Consumer Direct at 08454-04-05-06 or check on their Web site www.consumerdirect.gov.uk. Of course, your local Citizens Advice Bureau (details in the phone book) or a specialist consumer advice centre, if one is near you, can help, too.

Chapter 14

Paying Someone Else to Do the Work

In This Chapter

▶ Getting the best work for your money

▶ Resolving the problems that invariably crop up

▶ Knowing where you stand with service providers

▶ Getting help to deal with disputes

Given time, everyone can probably learn to do their own building work and dry cleaning, buy and sell houses, cut their own hair, and repair the burst pipes. But most people have jobs to do, so they usually pay someone else to do those things and many more chores. Society is buying services.

Services are everything from legal and accountancy services, work carried out by surveyors and estate agents, jobs done by garages, builders, and plumbers – right down to the service you get in restaurants and when you leave your coat in the cloakroom. (Public services, such as education, health, and transport, are services, too, but they're subject to different rules and regulations – refer to Chapter 5.)

You probably assume that people who advertise those services already know how to do what everyone else hasn't yet had time to master, so you're willing to pay to have the job done. You enter into a legally binding contract, which gives you basic legal rights.

As long as you're paying for services, you have the right to expect them to be carried out with care and skill and to be put right if they aren't satisfactory. You also have the right to claim compensation for damage or injury if something goes seriously wrong. It's the firm that supplies the services that is responsible for sorting things out.

With luck, everything goes swimmingly; the work is done according to the terms of the contract; the charges are as they were set out to be before the work started; and you're delighted with the end result.

But it doesn't always work out like that, of course. However, with a few precautions, a bit of homework, and the information in this chapter, you should be well placed to help the process come to a satisfactory conclusion or to get things put right if they don't go quite as smoothly as you'd like.

Although I can't go into every kind of service you may want to use, I touch on a few of the main ones. I include things like postal and phone services and gas and electricity supplies where you have the automatic right to small amounts of compensation if supplies aren't delivered as set out in the terms of your contract.

Getting the Basics Right

Sometimes it's clear that you're ordering services rather than goods. Hairdressing, plumbing, estate agency, and legal services are *services*. *Goods* are the kinds of thing discussed in Chapter 13 – toys, furniture, and cars.

But sometimes the two come as part and parcel of the same contract. If you put your car into a garage for repairs and it has to have a new exhaust, goods are also involved in your contract, so both areas of law apply. Whatever the service you plan to use, the following sections apply.

Getting the best possible service

The key to getting the best possible service is to be closely involved. Find out, if possible, exactly what work has to be done. Be very clear how it will be carried out, such as what materials will be used and when the work will be done by. If possible, get precise figures as to how much it will cost.

Estimates are just that – estimates. You'll invariably end up paying more. Get a quote with all the details of prices and labour charges written on headed paper and don't sign a contract without it. You may still end up paying more money, but only with your agreement and if there's a good reason for the increase, such as additional work to do.

The more professional looking the outfit you trade with, the more professional looking the job done is likely to be. Look for trade association logos. Traders who are members of their relevant trade associations have to comply with the code of practice, and a dispute resolution service is usually available if something goes wrong. (See the section 'Resolving Issues Using Third Parties,' later in this chapter.)

Try to get recommendations when looking for someone to provide you with a service and take the time to check out the standard of the work they've done. Good trades people are happy to give you contact details for previous customers so that you can see their work for yourself. The best people are always busy because they're in demand. It can pay to wait until they become available.

Sometimes a contractor isn't able to give you exact dates and prices because, until the work starts, it's impossible to tell how much needs to be done. In those circumstances, try to get maximum figures so that you're aware of the most the job is likely to cost and the best possible estimate of how long it will take. Make sure that nothing proceeds without your knowledge and agreement. That way, you're able to keep control of the purse strings. The vast majority of complaints are about costs spiralling out of control.

Sorting out the contract

The contract contains the detail of what you're signing up to. A verbal contract is just as binding as a written one, but it's much easier to be clear about exactly what was agreed if it's in writing.

What's in the contract depends on the type of work to be done. A contract for building work or car repairs contains information about the materials that will be used, the times by which various stages of the work will be completed, and the payments you'll make and when.

Whether it's in writing or verbal, the contract is legally binding, and you have the right to the services in the contract. If the trader doesn't deliver, you can ask for the problems to be sorted out or call in a second trader to put things right and claim the costs from the first. If all else fails, you can take legal action.

You also have the right, under the Supply of Goods and Services Act 1982 – or under common law in Scotland – to have the service carried out with reasonable skill and care. If no exact dates and prices are in the contract, you can expect the work to be carried out at a reasonable price within a reasonable time. Of course, 'reasonable' is a word that can cause more disputes in UK law than just about any other because it crops up everywhere and is never clearly defined. But if you make a claim against a supplier saying that a job took too long or was too expensive for the amount of work done, and the dispute ends up in court, a judge will often base a decision on what another supplier would have done in the same circumstances.

Be sure when you sign any contract for services – or any other contract, for that matter – that you understand and accept all the terms. It's quite common to find clauses that attempt to limit the trader's liability if things go wrong or to exclude liability in certain circumstances. Once you've signed it and agreed with its terms and conditions, arguing it later can be difficult. In a court dispute, you'd have to argue that the contract was unfair under the Unfair Contract Terms Act 1977 and the EU Unfair Terms in Consumer Contracts Regulations 1994. What is seen as fair or unfair depends on the circumstances of each individual case. If you do think a trader is hiding behind an unfair clause in the contract, get advice.

Cancelling orders

After you've signed a contract, you have to go ahead unless you've signed in circumstances that give you the right to a cooling-off period or the contract itself gives you a cooling-off period in which to change your mind. Read the small print before signing.

If you aren't on the trader's premises when you agree to buy their services, you have the right to cancel. So, for example, if you've signed up on your doorstep with a salesperson who visited you without your request, you'll automatically have a cooling-off period of seven days. (See the sidebar 'Signing up on the doorstep' for the details.) And if you buy over the phone or Internet without a face-to-face discussion, you have a seven-day cooling-off period.

If you have a face-to-face discussion with the trader and you then sign a credit agreement – in your own home or anywhere else away from the trader's premises – for something costing more than £35, you have five days after you receive your copy of the agreement and details of your cancellation rights in which to change your mind.

Signing up on the doorstep

If you buy services from someone who turns up on your doorstep – selling you double glazing, for example – you have the same rights as when you buy from a shop. You have the right for the work to be done in a reasonable time, at a reasonable price, and with reasonable care and skill. This is the contract even if it's not written down.

If, in the cold light of day – once the salesperson has gone – you decide that you don't want the double glazing, you have the right to cancel the order as long as you do it within seven days.

Some contracts may give you longer than that to cancel. Even if some of the work has been done by the time you cancel, as long as it's within that 'cooling-off' period, you can get your money back – but you'll have to pay for the work that's already been done.

However, you can't cancel agreements for new building work; for services that cost less than £35 unless you signed a credit agreement at home; or for services if you asked the seller to come and visit you in the first place.

In any other circumstances, you can't just cancel because you've changed your mind or found another builder or trader who will do the work more cheaply. You may be able to cancel once the work is underway if the trader does something that breaches the terms of the contract. However, you usually have to pay for any work done up to that point, and cancelling contracts in this way can lead to all sorts of expensive legal action as both sides wrangle over what's gone wrong.

Using Everyday Services

This section looks at some of the most common services you're likely to call on. The bottom line is the same in each case. The contract between you and the service provider is legally binding, so you have the right to the service defined in that contract – written or verbal – and you have the right to have the work carried out with reasonable skill and care.

If things go wrong, you have to give the trader the opportunity to put it right and then call in a second trader to sort out the problem at the expense of the first. If it all goes pear-shaped, you should try any dispute resolution schemes on offer before taking legal action. Going to court for your money back or compensation should be the last resort.

Building work

Building work always takes longer and costs more than you were led to expect by the builder. That's just the way it is! Well, it doesn't have to be that way if you do your homework and keep a close eye on the way the project is progressing.

Decide how you're going to go about getting the job done. You may hire an architect or structural engineer to manage the project, in which case your contract is with them, and they will hire the other builders. You may hire a building firm, which then hires any plumbers or electricians needed, but your contract is with the original building firm. If you hire a subcontractor to put in double glazing while you're having an extension built, you'll have a contract with both the builder and the double-glazing firm. If you hire the trades people individually, you'll have contracts with each of them.

Only go for firms with good reputations. Ask family, friends, or people whose judgment you respect. Or try your local builders' association or trade associations such as the Federation of National Builders (020-7242-7583 or www.findabuilder.co.uk) or the National Federation of Builders (0870-898-9091 or www.builders.org.uk) for firms on their list of registered members. Ask the builders for references and contact details for people who've already had work done so that you can check that they were satisfied with the service they received.

If you're thinking of choosing a particular building firm, ask to see all its different insurance policies that will cover the work and the people employed on it. The firm must have a policy to cover employees for injuries, but it should also have policies that cover injuries to you or members of the public and any damage caused as a result of the work. Pick a builder who has a policy that covers the quality of the work and gives you protection if it goes bust.

Get written quotes from several firms. Get everything in writing with details of the materials to be used and the timescales involved. Go for a builder who doesn't expect you to pay for the work up front. Agree to pay for the work in stages. You pay a certain amount when each stage is completed to your satisfaction. Don't sign anything to say work is to your satisfaction until you've checked it out fully and don't pay the final amount until you have had time to check out that it is all satisfactory.

If you pay by credit card or credit agreement arranged for you by the builder for work costing between £100 and £30,000, the credit company may be liable for anything that goes wrong if the builder refuses to put it right or goes out of business.

If someone turns up on your doorstep offering to resurface your driveway or repair your roof, because they've been doing work in the area and noticed your home looks in need of attention, refuse the help. It's likely to turn out to be an expensive exercise, and the work may be of poor quality. The person may also disappear with your money before you've had time to check that the work is satisfactory. When you try to get things put right, more often than not you'll find that the person vanished into thin air. Get a reputable builder in to check whether repairs are needed and to give you a written quote.

If, despite all your best endeavours, things still seem to be going wrong, you must give the builder or plumber, double glazing installer, or gas fitter the opportunity to put things right. It may be that they're taking an unreasonable length of time to do the work, or the tiles are uneven, or the plaster is falling off the walls. Here's what to do:

1. **Ask the person or company to put things right.**

2. **If the person or company doesn't comply, tell it the problem in writing and what you want done about the issue.**

3. **If you still see no action, get a second opinion and quotes from two or three other firms for the cost of finishing the job.**

   This step shows you mean business.

4. **If Step 3 doesn't get the desired result, you can get the work done and reclaim the expense from your original builder.**

5. **If you haven't already paid the first builder for the work, you can pay the second instead.**

   If you've already paid the first, you then have to try to get from them the cost of paying the second builder.

If goods supplied by the builder are the problem, you can ask for a refund, replacement, or repair, depending on the problem. Chapter 13 explains all your rights when it comes to goods.

You may be entitled to compensation because the trader has taken an unreasonable length of time to do the work or the work hasn't been done with reasonable skill and care; damage or injury resulted from the work; or you've been left out of pocket because you had to hire someone else to rectify faults.

Sorting out problems with builders can be very tricky. You have to think about what's reasonable. It's not reasonable to take two months to put up some shelves, but you can't expect an extension to be finished in two weeks. If you do get caught up in a dispute, you may need to get another expert opinion about the work.

Take photographs and keep a diary if trouble's brewing. You may need them as evidence if the dispute can't be resolved in any other way than through the courts.

If a trade association offers an arbitration scheme to sort out the problem, try it and use court action as the last resort. See the section 'Resolving Issues Using Third Parties,' later in this chapter, for more on resolving disputes.

Moving house

If you don't want to stay put and have the builders in, you may decide to move. Buying, selling, and moving involve paying for a lot of services so here are the main things to look out for.

Estate agents

On the list of professions everyone loves to hate, estate agents usually figure near the top. In days gone by, when you traipsed off to see your ideal home and discovered that it was in reality a rundown hovel and your time had been wasted, that dislike may have been justified. But estate agents have been forced to clean up their act.

When you're selling your home and using an estate agent – solicitors can act as estate agents and sell property in Scotland – under the Estate Agents Act

1979, they have to act in your best interests and make sure that both you and your potential buyers are treated fairly and honestly. They also have to be prompt about it.

Under the more recent Property Misdescriptions Act 1991, it's illegal for an agent to lie about the details of a property, so if it says a room is 8 x 10 feet and you discover it's 7 x 9 feet, the agent can be prosecuted. And the Supply of Goods and Services Act 1982 (see the earlier section 'Sorting out the Contract') means that you have the right to a reasonable service.

Apart from those specific laws, the law of contract covers you. If you sign up with an agent to sell your home, you're signing a legally binding contract. That means that you have to keep your side of the bargain, too, and pay the agreed price for the service delivered.

Make sure that all the details of the services you expect are in the contract. Not all agents offer the same services, so shop around for the service you want. There are no hard and fast rules about how an agent should go about finding you a buyer, so if you want your property advertised on a Web site or in particular papers, find one who is equipped to do that.

When you're choosing an agent, go for one that is a member of a trade association, such as the National Association of Estate Agents (01926- 496-800 or www.naea.co.uk) or the Royal Institution of Chartered Surveyors (0870-333-1600 or www.rics.org.uk). Both associations have codes of practice that agents must follow and can help sort out problems if things go awry.

You can sign up with one agent on a sole agency basis; with two on a joint agency basis, if both agree; or with several agents on a multiple agency basis. The one who comes up with the buyer gets the fee, and you have more than one bite of the cherry, but using multiple agents will probably cost you more because the percentage fee charged will be higher.

If estate agents and their clients come to blows, it's usually because the charges haven't been spelled out from the beginning. Agents usually charge a percentage of the sale price of the property as their fee, but you need to be clear what's included in that fee. If you want For Sale boards outside your home, find out whether they're included in the fee quoted or if you have to pay extra. Are press photographs part of the deal? Before you choose an agent, you must be given information about their services and fees and about any services they offer buyers.

You have to be told promptly about any offers that come in from potential buyers unless you've told the agent not to pass them on to you. You have to be told of any services the agent is offering your buyer, such as arranging a mortgage for them. It's illegal to mislead buyers or sellers in any way. If the agent has any personal interest in the property, you have to be told straightaway.

Be careful about the terms of the contract you sign. Go for a no-sale, no-fee agreement. Otherwise, you may end up paying the fee, even though the person who eventually buys your home had no dealings with the agent.

If you're not happy with the service you're getting from your agent, take your home off their books and contact the manager or owner of the business to get any problems resolved. If that measure doesn't sort things out, refer to the last section in this chapter, 'Resolving Issues Using a Third Party.'

Soliciting help

Whenever you need a solicitor, reduce the possibility of disputes and problems by choosing one who is experienced at the work you want done. Don't ask your divorce lawyer to buy and sell your house for you. If a property expert isn't in the firm, go elsewhere. Ask your nearest CAB (see the phone book) for solicitors who specialise in buying and selling property.

The solicitor's job is to gather all the information you need about the place you're buying and handle all the paperwork involved (refer to Chapter 3). You're entering into a contract with a solicitor in the same way as you do when you buy any other services, so the same rules apply. Know exactly what you can expect for your money and for what you're required to pay extra.

If the whole process seems to be taking an inordinately long time and isn't being done with reasonable skill and care, talk to the head of the law firm. If you have to complain, the Law Society (0870-606-6575 or `www.lawsociety.org.uk`) is the organisation that regulates the work done by solicitors. The Law Society can also get you information on solicitors in your area and their areas of expertise.

When the job has been done, your solicitor has to give you full details of where all your money has gone, of all the work that's been done, and of all the charges.

Surveying the scene

After you find the new place of your dreams, you need a survey. Mortgage lenders also need a valuation report to tell them that the property you're buying is worth the money, or they won't lend it to you. Lenders use a surveyor from their own list for that report. You'll come into contact with a surveyor if you decide that you want a more extensive survey done on the property, such as a homebuyer's report or a structural survey (refer to Chapter 3).

When it becomes compulsory for sellers in England and Wales to provide all the information about the home they're selling in a seller's pack (refer to Chapter 3), the pack will have to include surveys.

If you don't have your own survey done and it later turns out that the property has defects, taking a case against the seller will be difficult. You will have bought second-hand goods from a seller who was only legally obliged to own the property being sold and not to describe it as something it wasn't. If you're in that situation, take legal advice.

If the surveyor misses some important fault while doing the survey, you may be able to claim compensation. It will be a question of proving that the work wasn't carried out with reasonable care and skill. If you've paid for a full structural survey, which is the most comprehensive and expensive type of survey, you would expect that to throw up more information and go into more detailed checks on the property than a simple valuation report, which is just meant to reassure the lender that the property is worth the money they want to offer for it.

Some surveyors' reports say that they don't inspect covered areas or places that they can't get to reasonably easily, and so they won't report on those items. They're limiting their liability if something goes wrong, but those types of clauses have to be fair and reasonable. In a dispute, a court may decide that they're not under the Unfair Contract Terms Act. (See the section 'Sorting out the contract,' earlier in this chapter.)

Some defects make little impact on the price of a property. In that case, the amount of compensation you can claim may be so small as to make it not worth claiming – even though the repairs cost you a small fortune. You'll probably need a solicitor to help you with your case, and you're also likely to need the opinion of another surveyor. All that will be expensive. If you lose your claim, you'll end up further out of pocket.

Try to avoid problems by choosing a surveyor who comes recommended and has a good reputation in the first place. Your solicitor can probably make suggestions. Check which professional body a surveyor belongs to. The Royal Institution of Chartered Surveyors (0870-333-1600 or www.rics.org.uk) has a dispute resolution scheme that can help you settle a dispute with your surveyor.

Hiring the man and the van

If you hire a van and move house yourself, you have no one else to blame if something gets broken. If you hire a removal company, it has to carry out the service with reasonable skill and care. If it doesn't, you can claim for the items broken or lost and for any damage caused. However, don't forget to read all the small print in the contract.

Some firms may have clauses in their contracts saying that they'll be liable for only a certain amount of damage and offer you insurance for anything above that amount. If you don't take out the insurance and the company won't pay up, you'll have to sue them. Given that you signed the contract in the first place, you'd have to argue that it was an unfair clause in the contract, and the court may disagree with you.

To avoid additional problems:

✔ Make a full inventory of everything in the old house that should end up in the new one.

✔ If you pack your belongings yourself to save money, you'll have a harder time blaming the movers; they may argue that your packing wasn't up to scratch.

✔ Have up-to-date valuations of your precious belongings so that no one can dispute what something was worth if you do have to claim.

✔ Choose a reputable firm – recommended by someone you trust, if possible – that belongs to a trade association, such as the British Association of Removers (01923-699-480 or www.removers.org.uk).

✔ Have someone at both ends of the moving chain to oversee the operation. People are more careful when they know you're watching!

Utility suppliers

You use utilities like gas, phone, water, and the post everyday and rarely give them a second thought until something goes wrong. In certain situations, you have the automatic right to compensation if things do go wrong.

Electricity

If you think you're paying too much for your electricity, you have the right to change suppliers. If someone calls at your home asking you to change supplier, you don't have to agree. Be careful that you know what you're signing, or you may find that you've changed suppliers without realising.

If you're unhappy about any aspect of your supply – you think one particular bill is inaccurate, or you have a complaint with the service – as with any other service you pay for, you must talk to the company and give them the opportunity to sort out the problem. If you can't get a satisfactory result, contact the users' watchdog energywatch (0845-601-3131 or www.energy watch.org.uk) for advice and information – or the General Consumer Council in Northern Ireland (0845- 600-6262 or www.gccni.org.uk).

The government regulator for electricity is Ofgem (Office of the Gas and Electricity Markets), or Ofreg (Office for the Regulation of Electricity and Gas) in Northern Ireland. Ofgem makes sure that suppliers comply with the law, and it has set out guaranteed standards of performance. If companies don't meet those standards, you may be entitled to compensation.

You receive a fixed sum for power cuts caused by technical breakdown and negligence, but nothing if bad weather is the cause. If an engineer doesn't keep an appointment with you or if delays in dealing with some of your problems and complaints occur, you're also entitled to compensation. The amounts are small – from £20 to £50 – but they're usually automatically credited to your next bill. You can get details from energywatch or your supplier.

You may also be entitled to discounts, as well as various rebates and voucher schemes, from your supplier for paying by direct debit. Ask your supplier for the details of any scheme it runs. If you can get better prices and deals elsewhere, switch.

Gas

Gas suppliers operate in the same way as electricity suppliers (see preceding section). You can switch for better deals. Ofgem and Ofreg regulate these suppliers, and you may be entitled to compensation if they don't meet certain standards, such as missing appointments without giving you 24 hours notice.

Gas suppliers have to meet standards of care for older, disabled, or sick customers. Check with your supplier for the details. If you have any problems, contact energywatch (0845-601-3131 or www.energywatch.org.uk) or the General Consumer Council in Northern Ireland (0845-600-6262 or www.gccni.org.uk).

Water

Ofwat (0121-625-1300 or www.ofwat.gov.uk) regulates water companies in England and Wales. The Water Industry Commissioner (0845 6018855 or www.watercommissioner.co.uk) covers Scotland, while the Water Services Office of the Department of the Environment (02890 254754 or www.doeni.gov.uk) is in charge of Northern Ireland.

These bodies are responsible for making sure that you receive good quality and efficient services. All water companies are required to have codes of practice setting out the services that they offer with details of charges and advice on what to do in an emergency or if you have a complaint. Codes also cover dealing with leaks. Ask your supplier for a leaflet on the code.

Under the Water Industry Act 1999, you can't have your water supply disconnected, and you may be entitled to small amounts of compensation (up to £20) if your supply is interrupted for more than 12 hours, or if it takes longer than you were told to get your supply back on again. You may also be entitled to compensation if your home is flooded by sewage.

Postal services

If you have a problem with your postal service, complain first to the Royal Mail or any other service provider you've used, such as Parcelforce. If you can't get your complaint resolved, contact Postwatch – the consumer watchdog – on 08456-013-265 or www.postwatch.co.uk.

If something has gone missing in the post, you may be entitled to compensation, but the amounts paid out are small and may not cover the value of the item. If you're posting something that you can't afford to lose, check out the different postal services and how much compensation you'd be entitled to before you decide to go ahead. You may need to take out insurance or opt for a different delivery service.

Communications

As with the rest of the utility providers, communication services, such as phone, Internet, and television, have a watchdog as well. Ofcom (020-7981-3040 or www.ofcom.org.uk) can deal with complaints about providers, but, as with all other services, you should try to resolve those issues directly before contacting Ofcom.

Telecommunications companies have codes of practice, and in some circumstances, you have the right to compensation for poor service, such as the failure to repair faults within certain time periods. Ask your supplier for details.

Garages

Garages can be another constant source of grievance with customers. Part of the problem is that most people have little idea of how cars work under the bonnet. If something goes wrong, they take the expert's word for it, and sometimes it turns out not to be true.

If you find a garage with reliable staff who know what they're doing and don't overcharge you, just hope that it never goes out of business.

When you take your car in to have work done, you pay only for work you authorise. Predicting what needs to be done up front can be difficult. Make sure that you know what you've agreed to and get it in writing. Make it clear that if extra work is needed over and above that amount, you must be contacted to give the go ahead.

Agree on the price beforehand, too. If you don't, the law says that you have to pay a reasonable price for the work done, and a dispute may develop. If you feel the price is too high, you'll have to prove that it was unreasonable, which will mean getting quotations for the same work from other garages.

You may be forced to pay up in order to get your car back even though you're in dispute over the bill. Make it clear – in writing – that you're paying under protest. You have to protect your rights to take your car away and check out the repairs and to try to get the bill reduced later.

If you belong to a motoring organisation, such as the AA or the RAC, it may be able to help.

If you have repairs done and the car conks out again soon after, you may be entitled to compensation if you can prove that the garage was at fault. The amount of compensation usually covers the costs of further repairs. You may also be entitled to more compensation on top of this amount if you've had expenses that were predictable, such as the cost of hiring another car while yours is off the road.

You can't just paint the town red and run up big expense bills and expect the garage to pay. You have to do what you can to keep the expenses to a minimum.

While your car is in a garage, the garage has to take care of it. If your car is damaged at the garage, the garage is responsible, and you should be compensated. Sometimes you'll see notices saying that the garage isn't responsible for any damage to vehicles left in their possession. These terms are likely to be unfair under the Unfair Contract Terms Act and the Unfair Terms in Consumer Contracts Regulations, which are explained in the section 'Sorting Out the Contract,' earlier in this chapter.

Look for a garage that is a member of a registration scheme run by the Trading Standards Department of your local authority. You can find contact details in the phone book. Check out whether a garage is registered before you use its services. If it's registered, the garage will have signed up to codes of practice on standards of work and how to deal with customers and complaints.

Hairdressers

Hairdressers are like any other service providers. They have to use reasonable skill and care. However, anyone can set up as a hairdresser in the UK without qualifications or training, so there's no organisation to take action on behalf of the badly treated customers of incompetent hairdressers. As a result, some incompetent hairdressers are out there.

Using the principle that prevention is better than cure, avoid as many problems as possible by choosing a hairdresser with a good reputation and who is registered with the Hairdressing Council (020-8771-6205 or `www.hair council.org.uk`). Basically, the council is a trade association, and it can offer you advice and information and help to resolve disputes with its members.

If you have a dispute with a salon that's not a member of the council and you can't resolve it, your only option is to go to court. Take pictures, get second opinions, and gather medical evidence of any injuries. A *trichologist* – a specialist in the care of the hair and scalp – can help you with serious hair and scalp problems. If you need to contact one, go through The Institute of Trichologists (08706-070-602 or `www.trichologists.org.uk`. Not all of those who profess to be trichologists are qualified, so by contacting the Institute, you can be sure to find the genuine article.

Dry cleaning

Dry cleaning is another case where you should go to a reputable, recommended establishment and become friends with them. If a dry cleaner has a notice saying that it accepts no responsibility for any loss of damage to goods you leave with them, don't use them. The company can't hide behind this kind of notice, but why would you want to deal with a firm that tried to?

Dry cleaners have to take reasonable care of your property and clean your clothes with reasonable care and skill. If they lose or damage your belongings in the process, you may be entitled to compensation. Bear in mind, though, that some stains can be difficult to remove, especially if you can't tell the cleaner what caused them and they've been there for a long time. To give the process the best chance:

- ✔ Take the clothes to the cleaner as soon as possible.
- ✔ Discuss with them what caused the stain and how long ago.
- ✔ Examine the finished product before you pay and leave.
- ✔ If the stain is still there or other damage, such as shrinkage, has occurred, return the garment, complain, and give the cleaner a chance to put things right.
- ✔ If that doesn't work put your complaint in writing spelling out what you want done.
- ✔ If the cleaner is a member of the Textile Services Association (020-8863-7755 or `www.tsa-uk.org`), enlist that organisation's help.
- ✔ If the cleaner isn't a member of the TSA or if you don't want to use the TSA's arbitration service, you will have to go to court for compensation.

Engaging in Leisure Activities

It's not just those everyday services that you can run into difficulties with. Even when you're off duty, you can't afford to be off guard. Firms that supply leisure services are under the same legal obligations to make sure that they use reasonable skill and care – and their contracts have to be fair and reasonable, too. You don't have to put up with being ripped off when you're supposed to be having fun any more than you do if you're at home or at work.

In any case where you can claim compensation, you may find that the restaurant refuses to pay up, and you have to take it to court. The amounts are likely to be under £5,000, so you can use the small claims process at the county court, described in Chapter 1.

Eating out

The list of things that can go wrong in a restaurant is almost as long as the average menu. When eating out, it pays to be well informed.

The food

If the food in a restaurant isn't good, reject it and ask for a replacement or refuse to pay for it, just as you would with any goods that weren't fit for their purpose (refer to Chapter 13). If you pay for the food, you'll have accepted it, and getting your money back will be difficult. It will also be hard to convince the restaurant that you were unhappy because you didn't speak up at the time.

If you do decide not to pay for something, ask to speak to the manager and explain the problem. Give him the chance to put things right. If you decide not to pay for some of the food that wasn't acceptable, you have to pay for the rest that was acceptable and that you did eat. You must also pay for the drinks you've had.

If the food makes you ill, contact your doctor immediately. Unless several people are affected, proving that a particular restaurant made you ill can be difficult. However, if you have enough medical evidence, you can claim compensation for pain and suffering, as well as any loss of earnings or other expenses you incurred. You'd also expect a refund of the cost of the meal.

You should also contact the Environmental Health Department at your local authority or the local authority for the area the restaurant is in. You can find details in the phone book.

The service

Handling service problems can be harder to deal with than food issues (see preceding section). Speak to the manager or the headwaiter and try to come to an agreement about how much you're willing to pay. Pay the bill for the items that were acceptable. If the food when it arrived was fine and the drinks were okay, you should pay for them but decide on an amount you'll deduct for poor service. You may decide not to pay the discretionary service charge or to deduct an amount from the bill that's equivalent to the compulsory service charge.

Explain why you're not paying the full bill. Leave your name and address so that the restaurant can claim for the rest if it doesn't agree with the amount you deducted. If you decide to pay the whole bill, rather than have the discussions at the time, make it plain that you're doing so under protest. Put that statement in writing and try to claim some of the money back later.

If the waiter drops a bowl of soup or a ladle of cream in your lap and you can prove that he wasn't taking care while serving you, the restaurant is responsible for the cost of the cleaning. If you are injured as a result, you may be able to claim compensation.

The booking

If you decide not to go to a restaurant you've booked, you're breaking a contract you've made. Cancel as far ahead as possible. If you cancel at the last minute, the restaurant may have a hard time filling the table, which causes it to lose money. The restaurant can even sue you for that loss. Obviously, a lawsuit isn't likely to happen if you're talking about the local pizza joint, but if you booked an expensive restaurant for several people and simply didn't turn up, the loss may run into hundreds of pounds, which the restaurant may be tempted to pursue. The restaurant has to make reasonable efforts to fill the table you vacated, and if it does, it can't claim the money from you.

Many restaurants ask for credit-card numbers when they take bookings so that they can deduct a sum to cover their losses if you cancel late in the day.

If you book a table and turn up to find that one isn't available, the restaurant is breaking the contract. You can claim for any losses you incur, such as the cost of travelling there, as well as for the disappointment and inconvenience. How much you claim depends on the circumstances, such as whether it was a special occasion and how much trouble you had finding somewhere else to eat.

The charges

Restaurants have to display cover and minimum charges and any compulsory service charges on the menu so that you can accept them before you order. If the charges aren't listed, you can refuse to pay them. Talk to the Trading Standards Department at your local authority if you don't see the charges listed, because the restaurant is breaking the law.

The tip

You don't have to leave a tip. If no service charge is included in the prices on the menu or added onto the bill, you may want to leave an amount of around 10 to 15 percent of the total as a tip. But when a service charge already appears on the bill, it's entirely up to you whether you want to leave any more money. Some restaurants leave a blank space on the credit-card slip for you to add a gratuity, even though a service charge is added to the bill. You don't have to add more. If you decide not to, draw a line through the space so that it's clear to the card company what you intended.

The coats and bags

If you hand over your coat to the waiter, the restaurant has to take reasonable care of it. If it's lost or damaged, the restaurant has to prove that it did take reasonable care; otherwise, you're entitled to claim the value of it.

Some restaurants don't allow you to hand over your possessions into their care and display notices saying that they can't take responsibility for them. Under the Unfair Contract Terms Act, you may be able to challenge that as being unfair in your circumstances. Take legal advice if this situation happens.

Going on holiday

Holidays and travel are services, and so anyone providing those services is under the same legal obligations as anyone else providing a service. The suppliers have to use reasonable skill and care, and the laws regarding contracts apply. But things can go wrong. The holiday you book isn't anything like the one that was described in the brochure, or the hotel wasn't of the standard you expected. Or the flights were delayed or cancelled, and your luggage didn't turn up.

As with any other service you book, do your best to prevent problems rather than having to cure them afterward. Book through reputable companies and know exactly what's in the contract before you pay. Read all the small print, no matter how tedious it seems.

The biggest problem with holidays and travel is that you have to pay for them in advance. If something does go wrong, you have to be reimbursed for some or all of your money, rather than being in the position where you can withhold payments until things are put right. That's all the more reason then to be sure that you know what your rights are.

For more on holidays, travel, and your rights as a paying customer, see Chapter 17.

Buying timeshares

One of the things you may be tempted to do while on holiday is to invest in a timeshare apartment. If you buy a *timeshare,* you buy a share in an apartment, which gives you the right to spend a specified length of time there each year. The sun, sea, and sand seem so alluring when away from home, and the sangria can go to many a traveller's head. The next thing you know, you're signing up to two weeks a year in the same resort and the same apartment for the rest of your life. It's only when you get home that you realise you've spent money you didn't have on a place in the sun that you don't want.

Because so many people complained about being pressured into buying timeshares in the 1980s, the Timeshare Act 1992 was eventually put on the statute books. It says that if you do sign a contract to buy a timeshare, you must have a 14-day cooling-off period in which to change your mind. However, that period applies only if either you or the seller signs the contract in the UK or the contract is subject to UK law.

The Timeshare Act 1992 also says that you have a 14-day cooling-off period if you pay for the timeshare with a credit agreement, and you also have to be notified of that cooling-off period.

If someone tries to refuse you the right to change your mind in those circumstances, they're breaking the law. They're also breaking the law if they try to get you to sign the contract without giving you notice about your rights to change your mind.

If you have a cooling-off period and you cancel within that time, you have the right to get back any money you've paid in connection with that contract.

Get legal advice before signing any timeshare contract. If you sign outside the UK, you probably won't have any protection under UK law.

If you buy a timeshare in the European Economic Area, you do have a ten-day cooling-off period. You can't be asked to pay deposits until the cooling-off period is over, and you have to be given a written contract with the basic information about the timeshare in your own language.

These rules about cooling-off periods don't apply to holiday or vacation clubs where membership of the club isn't linked to any particular property; to timeshares lasting less than three years; or to floating timeshares on houseboats or narrow boats, for example. You don't have a right to a cooling-off period if you're buying a timeshare from an individual owner who is selling theirs. If you're considering buying a timeshare, take legal advice.

If you do have any problems relating to timeshare, contact the Trading Standards Department at your local authority. You can find contact details in the phone book. You can also contact the Timeshare Consumers' Association (01909-591-100 or www.timeshare.org.uk) for advice and information or the Association of Timeshare Owners' Committees (0845-230-2430). The Organisation for Timeshare in Europe (00322-533-3069) can also give advice and information.

Filling in your spare time

If you have any time to yourself after dealing with the builder and the garage mechanic, you may need to relax. Playing sport, going to the gym, studying at a night class – they may seem like areas where you'd be free from worry, but you still have rights.

If you sign up for any kind of leisure activity, read the small print of the terms and conditions. You and the service provider are signing a legally binding contract. You have the right to expect the service to be provided with reasonable skill and care. You may find clauses in the terms and conditions that try to limit the liability of the provider if things go wrong.

If you're joining a gym, for example, you expect the gym owners to take reasonable care to see that you aren't injured by faulty equipment or poorly trained staff. If you go swimming, you expect that the pool is cared for so that you don't get some health-damaging bug from the water. Evening classes should deliver a reasonable standard of teaching. Sports clubs should take care to see that you aren't injured through their negligence.

Check that gyms and clubs have insurance and exactly what that insurance covers. If something does go wrong, you should make your claim against the club, which then claims on its insurance policy. If the contract contains clauses that limit the club's liability, they may be unfair under the Unfair Contract Terms Act; take legal advice.

Some sports clubs expect you to take out your own insurance to cover you for injury and to cover other people in case you cause them injury through your negligence. Check when you join. If you play sport as an individual rather than through a club, you should have insurance to cover those possibilities. Always check to see that you're fully insured.

Check your home contents insurance. Some policies already give you the cover you need for your sporting activities. For example, you may be covered for hitting someone over the head with your stray golf ball.

Resolving Issues Using Third Parties

In any situation where you have a dispute over services and you can't resolve it with the supplier, consider calling in a third party to help. Court action should be your last resort.

Many different bodies and trade associations offer dispute resolution services, such as conciliation, mediation, or arbitration. Many are free to customers and have to be worth a try rather than going through the stress and expense of legal action. In addition, various Ombudsman schemes can help once you've gone through the suppliers own internal complaints procedure. Your Citizens Advice Bureau or Trading Standards Department can give you details if one of the associations is relevant to your dispute.

Getting help from Trading Standards

Local authorities around the UK have Trading Standards Departments that enforce the law in most situations involving the supply of goods and services. These departments are a good first port of call, and you can get their details from the phone book or at www.tradingstandards.gov.uk.

The new phone and Internet-based consumer advice service Consumer Direct (08454-040-506 or www.consumerdirect.gov.uk) is operating in most parts of the UK.

Likewise, the Trading Standards Institute Web site at www.tsi.org.uk has a wealth of information. Often, just being able to tell the supplier that you've talked to a Trading Standards Officer can be enough to get the situation resolved.

Calling in environmental health

Environmental Health Departments are also attached to local authorities and deal with anything to do with the provision of food in restaurants and cafés. You can find their contact details in the phone book under the name of the local authority.

Enlisting the help of trade associations

Trade associations are often very useful bodies to contact in the event of a dispute. I list several associations throughout this chapter, and many more cover all aspects of the service supply industry. You can get details of relevant associations at www.taforum.org or ask your Trading Standards Department.

If you hire a trader who is a member of a trade association, you can call on the association to help if things go wrong and you've reached an impasse.

Many trade associations draw up codes of practice for their members and offer dispute resolution services. They may offer to conciliate an agreement between the two sides in the dispute or mediate while the two parties come to their own agreement.

Others offer arbitration schemes where they come up with a solution that is binding on both parties. If you agree to go to arbitration, you usually sign an agreement saying that you'll abide by the decision whether or not it's in your favour. If you agree to go to arbitration and the decision is binding, you can't then go to court in the hope of getting a judgment in your favour.

Calling in the lawyers

If the service provider isn't a member of a trade association or refuses to go to arbitration, you may have no choice but to take legal action. If you're claiming an amount of money under £5,000, you can take your own case through the small claims track at the County Court. However, a letter from a solicitor may be enough to resolve the case, as the supplier will realise you're serious about your claim.

If you do hire lawyers, choose ones with the expertise you need. If you're claiming compensation for injuries, for example, you need to hire a solicitor with experience of personal injuries. Ask your nearest Citizens Advice Bureau for names of suitable solicitors or check with the Law Society (0870-606-6575 or www.lawsociety.org.uk).

If you do have to resolve your case in court, you can find more information on how the court system in the UK works in Chapter 1.

The laws may be slightly different in England and Wales from Scotland and Northern Ireland, so explain where you are when you talk to any of the organisations listed in this chapter.

At the end of the day, it's a waste of money going to court to pursue a claim against a supplier who can't pay up. Check that the firm is still in business and has assets. Otherwise, you may win your case, but still not be able to collect.

Chapter 15

Borrowing Money

*M*ost people need to borrow money at some time or another. If you add up what everyone in the UK owes on various mortgages, loans, and credit agreements, it comes to somewhere in the region of 1 trillion pounds.

That debt has purchased homes and cars, holidays and furniture, school uniforms, and birthday presents. The payments go to banks and building societies, card companies and department stores, and finance and insurance companies. And just about every time you make a repayment on what you owe, someone else comes along and offers to lend you more or to increase the amount you can borrow on an agreement you've already got.

Society is living on borrowed money. That's fine while you can afford to pay back what you borrow. The trouble arises when you can't keep up your agreed payments.

Understanding Basic Borrowing Principles

The terms and conditions you sign up to when you borrow and your rights are in the small print, but most people don't read the small print or take on board all its complexities if they do. Before you sign on the dotted line, it's as well to know what you're letting yourself in for legally and what can happen if you find yourself getting into arrears with your repayments and facing a mounting debt.

All sorts of establishments offer loans. Most people arrange personal loans through one of the mainstream lenders, such as the banks or building societies. People who find it difficult to get loans from those mainstream lenders usually locate other lenders willing to lend them money, but at a higher interest rate.

Secured loans

Very few people can afford to buy their homes without a mortgage. A mortgage is a *secured loan*. You borrow money specifically to buy a particular home. The lender will insist on having some assurance that the property you want to spend the money on is worth what you're offering to pay for it and so will want a survey – done by a surveyor approved by the lender. The lender then agrees that it will lend you money – usually up to 90 or 95 per cent of the value of the property – and that money will be secured against the property. That means that if the property is sold for any reason, the lender has to be repaid out of the proceeds of the sale.

Alternatively, if you don't keep up the agreed repayments on the money you've been lent, the lender will be able to take court action to repossess the property, evict you, and sell the place in order to get its money back plus any arrears that you owe. That's a secured loan.

Other loans can be secured against your property if you agree or if a court makes an appropriate order. You can ask your bank for a further loan to build an extension or make some home improvements, and that loan can be secured against the property, too, if enough equity is in it. Someone else to whom you owe money can ask a court to make a *charging order* against your property, meaning that when it's sold, that someone has to get his money back out of the proceeds. Loans can be secured against other types of property, too, such as shares or trust funds. You may borrow money to buy a piece of machinery and agree that the loan should be secured against that machine.

Secured loans are usually cheaper than other loans in terms of the interest you have to pay on the money you borrow because the lender has less risk of losing money. You can't sell the property without a secured creditor knowing about it and disappear with the money.

Unsecured loans

Unsecured loans aren't secured against any particular property of yours. You may ask the bank for a loan to go on holiday. The interest on the loan will be higher than on a secured loan, and you'll agree to make certain repayments.

If you stop making those payments, however, the bank doesn't have the security of knowing that it can get the money back from the sale of your home. The lender can take other legal steps to get the money back, as you can see in 'Facing court action,' later in the chapter, but it can't force the sale of your home.

Sometimes when people are in debt and can't repay their unsecured loans, lenders offer to give them a secured loan at a lower rate of interest to help them out of difficulty. Be very careful and take advice before going down that path. You may find yourself unable to keep up payments on that new secured loan later down the line and, because it's secured, face the possibility of losing your home.

Overdrafts

Sometimes you need a sum of money for a very short period of time and the temptation is to simply overdraw on your account rather than go to the hassle of taking on a loan from the bank. Don't. The charges can be very high. Arrange an overdraft with the bank instead and save yourself a lot of money.

Getting a Mortgage

If you're buying a home, you're likely to need to borrow money. *Mortgages* are loans that are specially designed for home purchase. You can borrow a large proportion of the value of the property you want to buy – usually up to 95 per cent, although some lenders at some times will consider lending the whole amount. That loan is secured against the property, and if you don't keep up your agreed repayments, the lender can take steps to repossess and sell the property to recover the amount of the loan and to have you evicted as explained in the section 'Repossessing Your Home,' later in this chapter.

You arrange to pay your loan back over a long period – usually up to 25 years, although if you can afford to clear the debt quicker, you can arrange to pay it off over 15 or 20 years. You pay interest on the loan. The interest rates can vary depending on how the Bank of England base rate varies so they can go up as well as down. You may be able to get a deal that offers you a fixed rate of interest or a discounted rate for a period of time.

The mortgage can be set up as a *repayment mortgage* where you pay back an amount of interest each month plus an amount toward the capital you've borrowed. It can be set up in such a way that you pay interest only back to your lender, but if that's the case, you need to be sure that you can pay all the capital you've borrowed off at the end of the mortgage term. Unless you're expecting to inherit a lump sum to cover it, you will need to arrange to make regular savings into an investment of some sort – such as an *endowment policy* or a *pension plan* that will pay out enough when you need it.

People have been sold savings plans in the past that didn't pay out enough to cover their mortgages when the loan had to be repaid. Take advice from at least three independent financial advisers before you decide on the most appropriate way to save to repay your loan.

The process of finding the mortgage that suits you best and of deciding how to repay it is very complicated. In addition to independent financial advisers, talk to a range of mortgage brokers.

Getting Credit

If you have money in your bank or building society account, you're *in credit.* You can do what you like with that money – it's yours. If you buy something *on credit,* someone else pays the retailer for it, and you owe the lender the money – usually with interest. You've borrowed and are in debt to the lender. The word *credit* may be used for both those situations, but it has very different meanings.

Borrowing or taking out credit can be a very useful tool for managing your finances. It allows you to buy things now and pay for them over a period of time. That setup can be to your advantage if the item is cheaper now than it will be in the future, or if it's something you really need but couldn't afford without spreading the cost over the coming months.

Credit can get you into trouble in the long run if you find later that you can't afford to pay back the money you borrowed in the amounts you agreed to.

Credit agreements

Thousands of sources of credit exist. You probably get credit offers dropping through your letterbox several times a week. If you go into a shop to buy something, the chances are you'll find that you can apply to pay for it on some sort of credit agreement. The choice is enormous, but so is the risk of confusion. Here are a few of the pitfalls to be wary of:

✔ **Buy now, pay later:** This type of credit agreement usually allows you to buy today and either pay in a lump sum in 6 or 12 months time or to start paying in instalments then. The small print may reveal that if you don't pay in full by the due date, you'll be charged interest on the total amount of the money from today's date. It can work out to be a very expensive purchase. People often forget to pay by the due date or find that a year hence, they simply can no longer afford what seemed so affordable 12 months previously.

✔ **0% finance:** The small print usually reveals that you can have the loan interest free for a few months after which you start paying interest – at a much higher rate than on other types of loans. It can be better to take out a credit agreement on which you pay interest for the whole life of the loan but at a lower rate.

✔ **Discounts:** Store cards and other credit agreements sometimes offer you substantial discount off various items if you sign up today. Beware because these cards carry high interest charges. If you don't pay the bill in full by the due date, you may end up paying more in interest than if you had bought the goods using your ordinary credit card.

When it comes to credit, the old adage applies – if it sounds too good to be true, then it probably is. Check all the figures and make sure that you know exactly what you'll pay back, how often, and over what period of time. Once you've signed, it's usually too late to change your mind. Your rights to cancel are limited and are explained in the upcoming section 'Cancelling a Credit Agreement.'

Always ask what the total cost is that you'll end up paying. If more people did that, more people would walk out of the shop empty handed. Who wants to be paying twice as much for a new sofa as the ticket price or still paying for that cashmere jumper long after it's gone to the charity shop?

If you buy something with most types of credit, it belongs to you. The credit company pays the seller, and you repay the money borrowed to the credit company. The credit company can't claim that item from you without a court order if you don't keep up the repayments. However, it can take legal action to get its money back if you fail to repay what you borrow, and eventually that item can be seized by bailiffs to sell to repay the loan.

Depending on your flexible friends

You may well have two or three of the 1,500 or so credit, debit, charge, and store cards available, in your wallet at the moment. They're such a convenient way of paying for things that you can easily fool yourself into thinking that you're not spending your own money. You have to keep a careful tally of just how much you're putting on your plastic, or before you know it, you've overstretched yourself.

Here are the various types of cards available and how they work:

- ✔ **Debit cards** are just pieces of plastic that save you from writing a cheque each time. The money comes out of your bank and into the coffers of the retailer within three days of purchase.

- ✔ **Credit cards** give you the flexibility to shop for items using your card instead of paying cash and then just pay one amount to the card issuer by a particular date each month. The card company does the rest of the work and distributes your payment to the retailers you've bought from. If you don't pay the card issuer the full amount you owe each month, the retailers still get their money. The card company pays them and charges you interest on the amount outstanding on your bill.

 If you can pay off the full amount by the due date each month, credit cards are very useful. If you can't pay each month in full, shop around for a card with a low interest rate, no annual fee, and up to 56 days between making your purchase and being charged interest.

- ✔ **Charge cards** are similar to credit cards, but with the fundamental difference that you have to clear the entire outstanding amount by the date payment comes due. No agreement allows you to pay off some of the bill and have the rest on credit. If you do fail to pay the full amount by the due date, interest rates charged on the outstanding amount can be very high. Some retailers don't accept charge cards, such as Diners Club and American Express, because the commission the card companies charge the retailers is higher than for using credit cards. So you may find your charge card is refused, and you have no right to insist that the retailer takes it.

- ✔ **Store cards** work in more of less the same way as credit or charge cards. You need to read the terms and conditions carefully. These cards are branded with the name of the store and sold to you by the store staff. You can only use your store card to buy goods from branches of that particular store. One of the ideas is to keep you coming back to buy from that store. Even if you don't have the money, you can use the card.

At the time that you sign up, you're likely to be offered discounts on your first few purchases but if you don't pay off your bill in full by the due date, the interest rates are likely to wipe out any savings. Store cards are expensive, and if you do pay interest each month, your goods will cost you a lot more than the price on the label.

 Store cards charge high rates of interest. Chop them up and stick to your credit card.

If you pay by credit card, you're protected under the Consumer Credit Act of 1974 on goods or services that cost over £100 and under £30,000. The card company, as well as the retailer, is liable for any breach of contract. So if anything goes wrong and the retailer refuses to put it right, you can claim against the card company instead or as well. (Refer to Chapters 13 and 14 on your rights when buying goods and services.) The same applies if the retailer or supplier goes bust, and you've already paid in full or made a deposit. You can claim it back from the card company. This equal liability may also apply if you buy goods abroad, and the credit card was issued in the UK.

Applying for credit

If you're borrowing from someone other than family or friends – which can bring its own sorts of problems – make sure that the lender is licensed by the Office of Fair Trading.

Most credit agreements for £25,000 or less are covered by the Consumer Credit Act 1974 and are *regulated agreements,* which means

- ✔ The agreement should include information about the amount you're borrowing, the length of the agreement, what you have to pay and when, your rights to cancel, and all the various charges, including the interest rates and APR – the Annual Percentage Rate – which is the annual cost of the credit after interest and all other charges have been added together. If any of this information is missing, the agreement may not be enforceable.

- ✔ You have to be given a copy of the agreement, which is only binding after you and the creditor have both signed it.

- ✔ You should be told what happens if you don't keep up the payments.

- ✔ If you ask for other documents or statements, they should be sent to you.

Check that it says on the document that it's regulated before you take on the loan. If the loan isn't regulated and the lender isn't licensed, you run the danger of falling into the hands of a loan shark. They can be quite ruthless when it comes to extracting money from people who get into arrears, and interest rates can be eye-wateringly high – in the thousands of per cents.

Because so many different credit options are around, you can be forgiven for thinking that if you ask for credit, you should get it. No lender has to agree to give you credit or lend you money. Not only that, but you don't have the right to be told why you've been turned down. If you have a poor record of being in arrears with your payments, you're likely to have any applications for credit refused.

Understanding the real cost of credit

Before you take out any type of credit or buy anything on credit, follow these steps:

1. **Work out what you can afford to repay each month on top of your existing outgoings.**

2. **Look at the same item in different shops, as well as the different credit deals on offer, and compare total costs.**

3. **Ask for a written quotation before you sign anything.**

4. **Think about using your credit card instead or consider a bank loan – it may work out cheaper in the long run.**

The best way to compare deals, apart from APRs and interest rates, is to find out exactly how much you'll have paid by the time you make the final payment. Then you can decide whether you'd prefer to pay £300 in total over three years or make bigger payments and pay a total of £250 over two years.

If the someone who sold you goods or services arranged finance for you, the finance company is equally liable for any breach of contract on the part to the supplier in the same way that credit-card companies have equal liability. If the goods or service cost at least £100 and less than £30,000 and something goes wrong, you can claim against the company instead of, or as well as, the supplier. This protection is particularly useful if the supplier goes out of business and you've already paid some or all of the money. If you arrange your own loan through the bank or building society, they don't have equal liability.

Cancelling a credit agreement

When you sign a credit agreement, you have to be given or sent a copy that explains your rights to cancel. Any rights you do have to cancel run from the date you sign the agreement until five days after you receive the copy that explains your cancellation rights. If you sign and get a copy of the agreement at the same time, then the clock starts ticking straight away, and you have a five-day cooling-off period in which to cancel.

Cancelling a credit agreement isn't always easy, so make sure that you're sure before you sign on the dotted line. You may have the right to cancel if:

✔ You talked to the seller about it face to face and not just over the phone.

✔ You signed the agreement somewhere other than on the seller's premises.

Even if those two conditions apply, you can fall at other hurdles. If the goods have already arrived within the cooling-off period, you have to be able to send them back in their original state. That counts perishable goods out, and if you've had new windows installed, for example, they can't go back. You may be able to cancel the credit agreement, but you'll still have to pay the seller for the merchandise.

If you haven't had a notice of your cancellation rights, the agreement can't be enforced, and you may still have the right to cancel if you've signed but the creditor hasn't. If you want to cancel, put everything in writing and keep copies of all the letters you send.

Your agreement may have cancellation rights over and above those that you have in law. They should be included in the agreement. You can cancel a credit card at any time by writing to the card company.

Deciding to lend or not to lend

Some lenders use a point scoring system to work out whether or not to accept your credit or loan application. Basically, they have a whole list of questions they ask you to answer, and they feed all the information into the computer. Each reply generates points, and the computer comes up with a total points score. If you're under a certain pre-ordained number of points, you aren't considered creditworthy, and you get turned down. The lenders set their own limit on the degree of risk they're prepared to take that the money will be paid back; if you're below a certain point, the risk becomes too great, so they say no. Having a poor credit record is likely to lead to a no.

Other lenders use information held on file about your borrowing and repayment records to decide whether to lend more money. This information is held on file by credit reference agencies.

Under the Consumer Credit Act of 1974, you have the right to see any information held about you on your credit files. If someone turns you down for credit or a loan, write within 28 days asking for details of any credit reference agency that was used to supply information on you.

It isn't the shopkeeper who makes the decision as to whether you can have credit. It's the finance company that decides. The shopkeeper will simply be given a yes or no answer and probably won't even know how the decision is made. Don't take it out on shop staff no matter how offended you are. Ask them to find out whether a credit reference agency was used and apply to the agency for a copy of your file.

Credit repair companies offer to remove details of bad credit records from your files. A bad credit record can't be removed from your file – mistakes and incorrect information can, and you can do that yourself without paying one of these companies.

Your file won't have details of your bank accounts, but it will have information about any credit you already have. A poor payment record and any judgements against you in the County Court for debt appear, along with details about whether you've gone bankrupt or had your home repossessed. Your file also includes details of any other prospective lenders who have asked to do a credit check on your file.

You may be refused credit because of a poor payment record. The information is usually held for six years, which can make it difficult to get a mortgage or loan. As time goes by, if you keep current with any payments on any credit agreements you're still operating, your record will improve again. Some lenders do agree to lend to people who seem to be high risk, but they charge higher rates of interest.

Another less obvious reason for refusing to give you credit is that there's nothing about you on file. Lenders may decide that because they can't tell from your past record what kind of a risk you are, they aren't prepared to take the risk. If you feel this clean slate puts you at a disadvantage, try talking to your bank about taking one of its credit cards, which will establish a credit record.

Dealing with Serious Debt

As soon as you borrow money, through whatever kind of agreement, you're in effect *in debt* – because you owe that money back. There's no problem while you have enough income to pay the instalments you agreed on when you borrowed the money. The trouble comes when you can no longer meet your payments in full or on time, and the arrears start piling up. If you're in that situation, you're *insolvent*.

Don't bury your head in the sand because things are only likely to get worse. Contact any lenders you have difficulty paying as soon as you realise there's a problem. Lenders are usually very keen to make it possible for you to keep on making payments, and you should be able to reach an agreement to pay a reduced payment you can afford for a while until your finances recover.

Most people enjoy their incomes to the full, with little planning for what would happen if things changed and they no longer had that income. Few people earn so much that they can save for that proverbial rainy day – especially if it turns out to be several rainy months. People who get into serious financial difficulties usually do so because of a significant change in their circumstances. Losing a job through unemployment or illness, or splitting up with a partner, are the main reasons why people find they simply can't keep up with all their repayments. Sometimes the household finances are based on two partners earning, but one then has to give up work or stop work temporarily, perhaps to take care of a relative or to bring up children. When something like that happens, it's amazing how quickly the debts can pile up.

Of course, you can get into serious financial trouble simply because you take on one debt too much. It can all be ticking over quite well, and just one added temptation can lead to the whole house of cards tumbling. The amount of income may well not change, but it may simply not be able to stretch to cover all your commitments.

The longer you ignore the situation, the more difficult it will be to extricate yourself from it. Act as soon as you know there's a problem or likely to be a problem, and if you can't deal with it yourself, don't be afraid to ask for help.

Assessing the gravity of the situation

Do as much preparation as possible before you seek help by gathering all the information you have about your income, your outgoings, and all the debts you owe on your mortgage or rent, credit and store cards, bills, and credit agreements. No piece of information is too small to include. Put everything on paper and gather up all the relevant paperwork, such as the original agreements and statements with account references and total sums owing. Now follow these steps:

1. **Add up your income.**

   List any income coming into your household from salaries, bonuses, overtime, benefits or tax credits, Child Benefit, rent from lodgers, or contributions from working children. Make sure that you list everything. Don't forget sums such as interest on savings or income from pensions.

2. **Count up the outgoings.**

   List everything that you normally spend, such as the absolute essentials like the mortgage, rent, council tax, child support, and bills. To help you work out your outgoings, go through past bills for things like insurance, electricity, phone, water, and so on. You need a full picture of how much you need to service all your essential spending.

   Then put down all your other spending on things such as travel, food, school meals, and insurance. Be honest about how much you spend on food and going out, for example. Don't forget to include things like pocket money and the television licence. You do need clothes and cleaning materials, and you will spend money on Christmas and birthday presents. Ultimately, you may have to look for ways to cut down, but list everything at this point – and be realistic.

3. **Work out how much is left.**

   Sometimes this is the easiest question to answer! It can become all too apparent that you're spending all your income on the essentials, and you have nothing left to clear your debts with. If income minus essential spending leaves some money, then you can try to negotiate with all the companies you owe money to. If your income is too low to cover all your essential spending, never mind the rest of your debts; the situation is very serious. Go straight to the last section in this chapter, 'Getting Help.'

4. **List the debts.**

   List everything you've borrowed from whatever source with details of how much you should pay each month, how much is left owing in total, and how much you're in arrears. If you're behind with the mortgage or the rent or anything else from your list of essential outgoings, such as the council tax or child support payments, put those on your debt list, too.

Acting on the information

After you've made all your lists and have the full picture of your financial situation, you can act. You may decide at this point that the situation is too complicated for you to handle alone. Some people only realise the full extent of what they've borrowed once they've got to this point. The organisations at the end of this chapter should be able to support you through the process of getting out of debt.

If you're in debt, you may have to look for ways to generate more income, such as renting out a room in your home, taking on some overtime at work or finding a second part-time job. The other option is to try to cut down your outgoings. In most households where bills are in arrears, all the outgoings have already been cut to the bone, and there's simply no more slack in the system. However, you should check that you need all the insurance policies you're paying for and think about getting rid of any store cards, which are an expensive way of shopping because the interest charges are high.

Deciding on the priorities

Your priority debts are the ones that you have to pay or face serious consequences. If you don't pay your mortgage, for example, you can have your home repossessed. (See the section 'Repossessing your Home,' later in this chapter.) If you don't pay your rent, you can be evicted (refer to Chapter 3). Those priority debts should all appear on your list of essential outgoings. If you aren't already in arrears with them, make sure that you keep paying them on time and in full. If you're already behind with your payments, these debts are the ones you need to clear first before the trouble gets any more serious.

You have to pay your rent or mortgage, or you may end up out on the streets. If you don't pay your council tax, you can be fined in court, and non-payment of fines can ultimately lead to a prison sentence. Similarly, if you have any other fines you're paying, make sure that they're on your essentials list. If you don't pay your gas and electricity, they may be disconnected eventually, so they count as essentials, too.

If you're in arrears with any of these items, they are your priority debts and should be cleared before any of your non-priority debts in the next section. Don't hesitate to get help if you're having problems paying your bills.

The rest of your debts are non-priority debts. That doesn't mean that you don't have to pay them off. You do, but the consequences of getting into arrears with them are less serious than for the priority debts in the preceding section. You can't go to prison if you don't pay these non-priority debts.

Debts on this list should include bank loans, overdrafts, credit agreements, credit or store-card bills, and catalogue shopping payments you've signed up to. If you've been paid too much of any welfare benefit and have to pay it back, this should go on the list, too.

Clearing the arrears

If you have some money left over after paying your outgoings, you may be able to draw up a repayment plan that will pay all your creditors something and clear the arrears in a reasonable time. If that's the case, most creditors will be likely to wait before taking any legal action.

If you don't have enough for this approach, tackle your priority debts first. Make sure that you don't get any further behind with them than you are already and add as much as you can to each of your monthly payments to clear your arrears in as short a time as possible. Contact each of the companies and ask how long they'll give you to clear the arrears. As long as they're cleared in a reasonable time, most creditors will accept your proposals, but what is seen as reasonable depends on the company and the type of debt.

The best approach is to come clean with them all. Let everyone know what the full picture looks like. Explain why you find yourself in your current situation and how long you expect to be in a tight financial corner. Tell them who else you owe money to and explain how much you're offering to pay each month. Ask whether they can freeze the interest on your account until the situation improves and explain that you will go back to making full payments again as soon as you possibly can.

Sometimes the companies you're dealing with are all very reasonable and accept the offers you make. If your circumstances improve, you can then go back to them and increase the amounts you pay. However, sometimes they demand that you clear the arrears more quickly than you're able to. If they don't play ball, you simply don't have the money to make reasonable offers, or you feel you can't cope with all of this yourself, get help as soon as possible.

After you come to an arrangement to clear the arrears on all your priority debts, you can think about clearing the rest. If you have any money left each month after you've tackled the priority debts, work out how much you can pay each of the rest of your creditors. You can simply offer to pay everyone the same amount each month off their arrears, but they aren't likely to accept this arrangement. What is usually more acceptable to creditors is that they get a share of your money that's in proportion to what you owe.

Work out your total debt for all your non-priority creditors and give the one you owe most to the biggest proportion of your spare cash, and so on down to the smallest creditor who gets the smallest share. If you calculate you owe £10,000 in total and you owe £5,000 to one company, that company would get half of the money you can afford each month. If you owe another company £2,000, it would get a fifth of the money you can afford each month.

What's more likely is that by the time you've made repayment arrangements with your priority creditors, you don't have any extra left to pay the nonpriority ones. You should write to them explaining that you can't pay at the moment and why and asking for the interest on your account to be frozen so that the debt doesn't get any bigger. If it's a credit-card or a store-card debt, the issuer will usually want the card back in pieces so that you can't go on using it.

You're throwing yourself on the mercy of your creditors. You have signed an agreement saying that you'll make so many monthly payments of so much each month, and you're going back on that agreement. The lenders are perfectly within their rights to start legal proceedings against you. (See the upcoming section 'Facing Court Action.') However, most won't take legal action while you're being upfront with them and they can see that you're making every effort to pay. It costs money to take you to court, and they risk throwing good money after bad.

Your nonpriority creditors are likely to accept your proposals for a few months at a time, but they'll probably want to see a full statement of your finances – showing all your income and outgoings; details of whom else you owe money to; and the amounts you're paying them. They will also want to review your payment plan every few months. If your circumstances change, you should let them know.

When you go through this process of coming to arrangements with your creditors, because they're informal, they aren't legally binding. One or more of your creditors may accept your offers to make reduced payments or to clear your arrears within a particular period of time and then later go back on that arrangement. You can take steps to make any arrangements formal under a court order. For more on this topic, see the section 'Facing Court Action,' later in this chapter.

Dealing with the red letters

Don't ignore red letters and threats of legal action. If you simply stuff them behind the clock on the mantelpiece or in the kitchen drawer, before you know it you'll be getting court documents instead.

Creditors usually don't go as far as taking legal action if they know what's going on, but if they don't have any contact with you, you may end up with a County Court judgment against you for a debt, which affects your chances of getting credit again in the future. A record of non-payment or late payments can have the same effect. Don't ignore the situation.

As soon as you decide that you're in trouble or are getting into trouble, write everyone a holding letter. This letter should explain the problem and ask them to freeze the interest on your account while you take advice and work out a payment plan. Tell them that you will be in touch again in a couple of weeks or a month and make sure that you write again within that time.

Keep copies of all the letters you write to your creditors. If they do take legal action against you, you'll be able to show the letters in court as proof that you've been trying to resolve the situation.

Facing Court Action

Ultimately, anyone you owe money to can take court action against you to get back what they're owed. People you owe money to are your *creditors*. Creditors will be happy as long as you stick to the agreement you made to pay back a certain amount, usually in monthly instalments. They only become heavy handed when you get behind with your payments and are in arrears. Even then, if you keep them informed of the situation and make arrangements to repay the arrears on top of your normal agreed monthly payments, they aren't likely to take any further legal action. Don't ignore letters from your creditors threatening legal action or any claim forms or default notices issued by the court. Get help straight away.

It isn't only your creditors who can take legal action in the courts to recover what they're owed. You can elect to go to court for an order that would allow you to lump all your debts together and pay off a certain amount each month from your total bill – in one payment to the court. This plan has the benefit of making the repayment arrangement for clearing your debts formal and binding on your creditors.

What your creditors can do

In most cases, your creditors have to get a court order before they can take action to get back what they're owed. The kind of order the court can give depends on the type of debt you've run up. Credit debts of the type discussed in this chapter are dealt with by the civil courts – usually the County Court unless the debt is for more than £15,000. (See Chapter 1 for the way the court system works.) Debts owed on your council tax are dealt with by the magistrates' court, as are non-payment of fines.

Creditors can apply to the civil courts – for a judgment against you. The judgement says that you owe a certain amount and it has to be paid by a certain date. If you pay up by that date – usually within 28 days of the judgement being made – that's the end of the matter. If you don't, then the creditor can go back to the court for another order, and the court judgement is registered against you. This means that it appears on the court register and on the credit reference file held on you by any of the credit reference agencies, making it difficult for you to get further credit.

If you appear in court and put your case along with a proposal for repaying your debt in instalments and the court accepts that, it can grant an order for you to pay by those instalments. If you don't pay the amount ordered by the given date or keep up your instalments, the creditor can apply to the court for an order to allow them to seize any property you used their money to buy – such as furniture or a car. Creditors can't take action to enforce the court judgement, even if they're unhappy about the terms of the order, unless you fail to pay, so keep records of all payments you make.

Never ignore claims or default notices that come from the courts. If you do, you'll end up with a court hearing going ahead in your absence, and you won't be there to argue your case or to come up with offers for repayment of debts that the court might accept.

You need to be in court with full details of your income and outgoings and all the other information about your debts and arrears. Your creditor may be asking the court for an order to allow your goods to be taken, or even your home to be repossessed and sold, but the court will be very reluctant to grant that sort of order if there's any chance you can clear the debts. Get help and turn up for any court hearings.

Repossessing your home

If you're a homebuyer with a mortgage, you risk losing your home if you don't keep up your mortgage repayments. The lender can take steps to repossess and sell the property and have you evicted.

The lender must go through the courts to get an order allowing the property to be sold. You will have plenty of warning that that's on the cards. No lender wants to have to take that kind of legal action, and so if you contact them with proposals for repaying your arrears within a reasonable time on top of your normal repayment, they will usually agree.

If you're in difficulties, contact the lender immediately and discuss ways the repayments can be reduced and the arrears cleared. If the lender does threaten or start court action, get advice from the money adviser at the Citizens Advice Bureau straightaway. Once the court has made a judgement against you, if you fail to pay up, that judgement can be enforced (see the next section).

Enforcing a court judgement

If, and only if, you fail to pay according to the terms of a court judgement – you don't pay in full by the specified date or you fail to keep up your instalments – your creditors can take steps to enforce the judgement. The main options are

- Applying to send in *bailiffs*
- Asking for an *attachment of earnings order*
- Applying for a *garnishee order*
- Applying for a *charging order* to be made against your property
- Taking steps to make you bankrupt

Sending in bailiffs

Bailiffs collect the money the court orders you to pay. The kind of bailiffs and their powers differ slightly, depending on the debt that they're hired to recover and the court that has made the order. If you can't or won't pay, the bailiff may be able to take your possessions and sell them at an auction to get the money to clear your debts. If the judgement concerns mortgage arrears, the bailiffs may have the power to evict you and change the locks on your home so that the lender can sell the property.

If bailiffs turn up on your doorstep, you don't have to let them in, but if there's an unlocked door or window, they can use that to gain *peaceful entry*. If they don't get in that way or you won't let them in, they can come back at a later date and force their way in. Each time a bailiff comes knocking on your door, your debt increases because it's down to you to pay his fee. How much that is depends on the type of debt the bailiff has been hired to deal with and which court has given the go ahead for bailiffs to visit.

If you have items that are worth selling to clear your debts, the bailiffs can take them. These items don't have to be things that you used the money you borrowed to buy. They do have to belong to you, though, and not to someone else in your household who has nothing to do with the debt in question.

If you do have goods that are worth selling, bear in mind that because they'll be sold at public auction, they're unlikely to fetch as much as they're really worth, so you can lose a lot of possessions to clear a fairly small debt.

If you don't have any goods worth taking for auction, the bailiffs will have to report back to your creditors that that's the case. Some creditors go through the process of sending in the bailiffs even though they know you have nothing worth selling. They may want to see that for themselves. Your bill will have gone up because of bailiffs' fees, but the creditor may then be willing to accept the repayments you originally offered to clear the debt because the other possibilities have been exhausted.

Bailiffs may also seize goods bought on hire purchase or conditional sale agreements or evict you from your property if the court allows a landlord or mortgage lender to evict you for nonpayment of rent or mortgage payments. If you're evicted and your home sold, the lender will take back what's owed, from the proceeds of the sale, and you will get anything left over.

Taking money owed out of your wages

In some cases, the court may order that money you owe is taken directly from your salary and paid to your creditors through what's known as an *attachment of earnings order*. This order may be used if you owe child support payments or if a court judgement has been made against you and you haven't paid up. If a court makes such an order, your employer has no choice but to comply with it and deduct the money before paying you your wages.

If more than one of your creditors has applied for attachment of earning orders, you can ask the court to consolidate them, and any other debts on which there is a court judgement, into one order. That way, you save having to make several payments each month yourself to other creditors, and only so much can be deducted from your wages – you have to be left with a reasonable amount to live on – which will be assessed by the court.

Garnishee orders

The court can grant *garnishee orders,* which order that someone who owes you money pays that money direct to your creditor instead of paying it to you. The court can use garnishee orders to make your bank pay over money you have in an account to your creditor.

Charging orders

If a *charging order* is made against your property, it means the amount you owe becomes secured against your home. When the home is sold, your creditor gets its money from the proceeds of the sale – after any other mortgages and secured loans or charges that have already been made are paid. Once a creditor has a charging order against your property, they – like a mortgage lender to which you are in arrears – can then apply to the court for an order that your property should be sold so that they can recover the money they lent you.

In most cases, charging orders are made against your home, but they could be made against other property you owe or own a share in, such as shares or trust funds.

Making you bankrupt

If you owe one of your creditors £750 or more and they think that you have property worth that amount, they may consider making you *bankrupt*. If two or more of your creditors know about each other and between them they're owed more that £750, they could make you bankrupt.

Creditors can apply for you to be made bankrupt for unsecured debts only if you don't appear to be able to pay. They have to show that you don't appear to be able to pay. They need to go through the procedure of trying to enforce the judgement against you for the debt by sending in bailiffs to seize goods that you own to sell.

Alternatively, they have to show that they have served you with a *Statutory Demand in Bankruptcy*. This demand requires you to pay the amount owed, offer to secure it against your property, or offer to repay your debt in a way that the creditor finds acceptable, such as in reasonable instalments. If the demand has been served and you haven't agreed to any of those options, you can be shown to 'appear unable to pay.'

In that case, a bankruptcy hearing will be held. You'll be notified of where and when. It's not too late to stop the hearing from happening, even at this stage, but you shouldn't wait until it gets this far before getting help. If you can show that you can pay or your creditor has unreasonably refused your offer to pay by instalments, to secure the debt, or to pay a reduced amount in full and final settlement, the court can refuse to make you bankrupt.

If you're declared bankrupt, a trustee is appointed to handle your affairs. Ownership of your property passes to the trustee except for the tools of your trade and household items you and your family need for basic living – such as furniture and household goods like your cooker. A new hi-fi or valuable paintings will have to go. You may be allowed to keep your car if you need it for work, or it's not worth very much. If you own your home with your partner, it can't be sold without their consent or a court order, and the trustee won't sell it unless it's worth while in terms of settling the debt.

All in all, the process is stressful and humiliating and to be avoided, if possible. You'll usually be bankrupt for a year unless fraud is involved, in which case some of the restrictions on you can last a lot longer. During that time, you can't be a councillor or a company director, and you won't find it easy to get credit in the future. At the end of the 12 months, the bankruptcy is usually automatically discharged.

Taking Your Fate in Your Own Hands

If you're insolvent and your arrears are piling up, you have three options other than coming to the informal arrangement described in the earlier section 'Clearing the arrears.' These all involve coming to formal agreements with your creditors through the courts. Rather than waiting for your creditors to take action, you can apply to the courts and start the ball rolling. In some cases, being proactive can be less stressful than waiting for someone else to act. Don't go it alone. Get help from one of the organisations listed at the end of this chapter.

Administration orders

If your total debts are less than £5,000 and one of your creditors has already applied to the court and been granted a judgement against you for the payment of the money you owe that creditor, you can apply for an *administration order*. Instead of making individual payments to each of your creditors to clear your debts, they are all lumped together, and you make one payment every month to the court itself. You can ask the court to allow you to pay back only a proportion of the total debts if it will take you more than three years to clear them. After you've paid all the money set out by the order, the slate is wiped clean, and you can start afresh. Your creditors can't chase you or make you bankrupt.

The drawback with administration orders is that the limit of £5,000 rules out many people from applying, and having an order against you is likely to affect future applications for credit. If you don't keep up the payments, the order can be lifted, and you're then treated in the same way as someone who is bankrupt when it comes to getting credit or being a director of a company.

Individual Voluntary Arrangements

An *Individual Voluntary Arrangement* (IVA) is an alternative to going bankrupt. It's suitable for people who owe around £15,000. You have to have at least three unsecured creditors. If you have any income or assets you could use to pay creditors, IVA is an option.

An IVA lasts for a set period – usually up to five years. You have to come up with a repayment proposal that is acceptable to creditors who in total are owed at least three quarters of your total debt between them. If what you're proposing gives the creditors more than they're likely to get if you go bankrupt, they're likely to agree. An insolvency practitioner has to draw up the proposal and will then oversee it and pay your creditors.

Your first step is to find an insolvency practitioner willing to act for you. Your local Citizens Advice Bureau is likely to be able to help on that score, or the local County Court will have a list of possibilities. Failing that, contact the Insolvency Practitioner Unit, The Insolvency Service, PO Box 203, 21 Bloomsbury Street, London WC1B 3QW. The practitioner's fees are included in the IVA. A problem can arise if you can't find an insolvency practitioner who will agree not to ask for the fees up front. These are usually around £3,000. You can also contact the Insolvency Service (020-7291-6895 or www.insolvency.gov.uk).

If you run a business, you'll be able to carry on trading unlike in bankruptcy. You can still be a company director and use a business name. However, if you don't keep to the terms of the IVA proposal, you can still be made bankrupt, and the costs of the IVA will be added to your total debts.

Bankruptcy

The final option is to declare yourself bankrupt. You have to petition the court to make you bankrupt on the grounds that you can't pay your debts. The main problem is that you need to have the court fee and a deposit, which come to around £460. You may have to borrow the money from family or friends.

The court will need a lot of detail about your financial situation in a statement of affairs. A judge may then consider whether an Individual Voluntary Arrangement (see preceding section) would be a better way forward. If the judge decides against an IVA, you are either declared bankrupt or your petition is dismissed because the judge thinks that you have enough assets to pay your creditors.

Once the court makes a bankruptcy order, an *official receiver* is appointed to investigate your finances, and a trustee in bankruptcy takes control of your assets. The trustee then distributes money from the sale of assets to the creditors.

You may have a sense or relief once it's all over. Once the bankruptcy is discharged, most debts are written off, and your creditors can't chase you for them any longer. The big 'buts' are

- ✔ You're likely to lose any assets that are of value that can be sold off, including the family home.

- ✔ If you have a business, it has to be sold and your employees dismissed, and you can't be a company director or trade under any other name other than the one you were using at the date of the bankruptcy.

- ✔ You can't be a magistrate, councillor, or practicing accountant or lawyer.

- ✔ You can't get credit of more than £500 without telling the lender you are an undischarged bankrupt.

- ✔ You will have a hard time acquiring a bank account of credit in the future.

- ✔ Not all the debts are written off; fines, child support payments, and secured debts can still be enforced.

- ✔ If you had joint debts with someone else (your partner, for example), that person can still be chased by the creditors.

Nearly all bankruptcies are automatically discharged after 12 months, and the official receiver involved in the case can ask for yours to be discharged earlier. However, if fraud occurred, the official receiver can apply for a restriction order. This order prevents you from getting credit, acting as a company director, or trading in a different name to the one you were using at the time of the bankruptcy for up to 15 years.

Bankruptcy isn't a pleasant process. In certain circumstances, it's the best option – such as when you have no assets to sell and none of the other disadvantages will affect you – but it's not to be opted for lightly. Make sure that you take good advice before going down this route. Talk to the money adviser at your nearest Citizens Advice Bureau.

Getting Help

When it comes to getting help with money problems, the CAB, a charity, is usually the best place to start. It's hard to deal with debt problems over the phone because they can be complex and take a long time to resolve. Face-to-face advice, information, and support are the best options. You can find contact details for your nearest CAB in the phone book or at www.citizens advice.org.uk. Sometimes you'll have to wait for an appointment with the money adviser as bureaux do get very busy, and they offer their services free of charge.

Other sources of help are Money Advice Centres and Law Centres (see your phone book); National Debt Line (0808-808-4000 or www.nationaldebt line.co.uk); and Advice UK (020-7407-4070 or www.adviceuk.org.uk).

The BBC has launched a free Debt Financial Health Check (www.bbc.co.uk/business) in conjunction with the Financial Services Authority. You enter all your financial details, and it calculates whether you're facing debt problems. It also offers free advice on how to resolve the situation. The Consumer Credit Counselling Service is another charity that offers free debt advice and debt management plans – try 0800-138-1111 or www.cccs.co.uk.

Debt consolidation companies advertise their services widely, suggesting that you take out just a single big loan to pay off all your smaller debts and then have just one payment to make regularly. You're consolidating your debts into one debt. You're likely to end up paying more because of interest charges on that loan and getting into further difficulty. Be very careful and take advice from one of the preceding organisations before considering such a move.

If you're looking for an independent financial adviser in your area, contact the Association of Independent Financial Advisers (0207-628-1287 or www. unbiased.co.uk). The group can also give you details of IFAs who can act as brokers. For a mortgage broker, try the British Insurers Brokers' Association (0870-950-1790 or www.biba.org.uk).

In addition, Credit Reference Agencies include the following:

✓ **Equifax:** 0870-010-0583 or www.equifax.co.uk

✓ **Experian:** 0870-241-6212 or www.experian.co.uk

✓ **Callcredit:** 0870-060-1414 or www.callcredit.co.uk

Part V
Getting Out and About

"Actually, my husband's an RAF test pilot."

In this part . . .

This part is all about transport. A recent survey showed that fewer young people are learning to drive, but so far, that statistic doesn't seem to have made much impact on the congested roads. Most people have the right to drive as long as they pass the test, which I explain in this part, but once you've taken to the roads, very strict rules govern how you drive and the condition of the car you're driving. Breaking those laws can result in fines, forfeiture of your licence to drive, and even imprisonment. You can find information here on the kinds of penalties you're likely to face if you commit some of the most common driving offences.

If you prefer to let the train take the strain or go by bus or plane, you have the right to a reasonable standard of service, and rules regulate what you can expect if those standards aren't reached. I also provide information about going outside the UK – the documents you may need, the items you can bring back, and how to insure yourself so that you get good medical treatment abroad.

Chapter 16

Taking to the Highways and Byways

*I*f ever there was an invention that was likely to bring people into contact with the law, it's the motor car. The law surrounding the driving and keeping of vehicles is complex and changes frequently. As the roads get more congested and cars get faster and more sophisticated, the law has to keep up. This chapter looks at the legal aspects of driving and owning a car.

Getting a Driving Licence

Once you reach the age of 17, you can apply for a driving licence. You have to pass the driving test, which is in two parts, before you can have a full licence and drive unaccompanied on public roads. While you're waiting for your test to come up and while you're learning to drive, you must have a provisional licence to drive on public roads. You can find the application form in the Post Office or take a look on the Driver and Vehicle Licensing Agency (DVLA) Web site at www.dvla.gov.uk.

With a provisional licence, you have to have 'L' plates on any car you drive, and you have to be accompanied by someone who has had a full licence for at least three years and is at least 21. Your provisional licence is valid until you are 70, but with luck and good teaching, you should pass your test before it expires.

Some people can't apply for a licence, including those who

- ✔ Have epilepsy
- ✔ Have a severe mental health condition
- ✔ Experience giddiness that is disabling, or fainting
- ✔ Have such bad eyesight that they can't read a car number plate at a distance of 20.5 metres in daylight while wearing their glasses

As soon as you have your provisional licence, you can take your driving test. If you've already learned to drive on private property, you can apply to sit for your test as soon as you have your provisional licence. You don't need a licence to drive any vehicle on private property, and bicycles and horse-drawn vehicles don't need a licence even on public roads. At 17, you can drive a moped or motorbike up to 125 cc on public roads, with a provisional licence, as long as you have done compulsory basic training in England, Scotland, and Wales. (See the upcoming section 'Travelling on two wheels.')

After you've passed your driving test, you can drive on public roads. At 17, you can drive cars and motorbikes, but you have to be 18 before you can drive small lorries, and 21 before you can drive large lorries. A young driver's scheme (not in Northern Ireland) allows you to get a full licence for large vehicles from age 18. You can get more details from Skills for Logistics (01908-313-360 or www.skillsforlogistics.org).

Your full licence is valid until you're 70 – unless you lose it for one of a variety of reasons explained in the section 'Losing your licence,' later in this chapter, or have to give it up for medical reasons. At 70, you have to apply to renew your licence every three years. You have to come clean about any disability or medical condition, and you may have to agree to a medical examination and to having your medical records read. Some drivers may have to renew their licences more frequently because of certain medical conditions.

Taking the Test

The driving test can reduce otherwise confident people to nervous wrecks. How many people do you know who pass everything with flying colours, only to have to keep repeating their driving test? It can be an expensive business because you pay fees each time.

The test is in two parts: theory and practical. You have to pass the theory before you can go on to the practical. The theory test has two parts as well, and you have to pass both on the same occasion. In part one, you have to choose the right answer from a number of choices. In part two, you have to spot the potential hazards.

After you've got your theory test under your belt, you can sit the practical part. As you'd expect, it tests your ability to drive and control the car in a normal traffic situation. You also have two questions to answer about the safety of your car.

If you have special needs, the Driving Standards Agency (DSA), which deals with driving tests in Great Britain, can make special arrangements for you. Contact the agency on 0115-901-2500 or www.dsa.gov.uk. The DSA Web site has any information you may need before sitting for your test, including details of how to apply in your area. In Northern Ireland, the department to contact is the Driver and Vehicle Testing Agency (02890-681-831 or www.dvtani.gov.uk).

If you fail your driving test the first time, you're in good company – about 1 million other people fail every year. You can try, try, and try again as many times as you like. Once you've heard those two lovely little words 'You've passed', you can throw away your 'L' plates and send off to the Driver and Vehicle Licensing Agency (0870-240-0009 or www.dvla.gov.uk) for your full licence. Make sure that you send for it within two years of passing the test, or you'll have to take it again.

As soon as your full licence arrives in the post, sign it. You'll have a driver number and be on probation for two years. If you commit an offence or offences and get six points or more on your licence during that time, it will be revoked. Points are recorded on your driver record against your driver number and held on computer by the DVLA. You can find out more about how you acquire points on your licence (have it endorsed) later in this chapter.

If you have your licence revoked, it's a case of back to square one – you'll be treated as if you've never passed a test, and you'll have to sit it over again.

Drivers who pass their test in Northern Ireland have to drive with 'R' plates (same as 'L' plates, but with the letter 'R' in red) attached to the front and back of their cars for the first 12 months. This plate shows that they're restricted and must not drive at more than 45 miles an hour.

Owning a Car

As soon as you pass your test, you'll probably want to buy your own car. Owning a car brings another raft of responsibilities. Driving safely is one thing, but the car has to be safe to be on the road, too, and you have to keep it that way.

When you own a car, you need various documents that you have to keep up to date. If the police stop you, you need to be able to produce these documents. If you can't, you have to take the following documents to your nearest police station within seven days:

- **Insurance policy:** You must have insurance. Car insurance is a legal requirement. See the section 'Thinking about insurance,' later in this chapter, for an explanation of the different types of policy.

- **Registration document:** A car has to be registered in the name of the keeper. The *keeper* is the person who keeps it, and that's usually the person who owns it. When you sell your car, you have to hand the registration document to the new owner and let the Driver and Vehicle Licensing Agency (DVLA) know that it's been sold. The DVLA has to know who to contact, if necessary – for example, in case of a speeding offence. The DVLA's address is DVLA, Swansea SA99 1BU. You can find more information on the DVLA Web site at www.dvla.gov.uk or call 0870-240-0010.

- **Tax disc:** You must pay road tax or the road fund licence, and the *tax disc* is a paper disc that must be displayed on your windscreen – passenger side – to show that you've paid. If you don't pay your road tax, it's an offence. You can pay at larger post offices. For more information, visit the DVLA Web site at www.dvla.gov.uk.

- **The MOT certificate:** If your car is three-years-old or more, you have to have it checked annually by an approved garage or MOT testing centre. If the car passes a thorough test on various aspects of safety, such as tyres, lights, and seat belts, you receive a certificate to say that on the day the certificate was issued, your car passed its test. You may need to have repairs done before you get the certificate. The tests are the responsibility of the Vehicle and Operator Service Agency (VOSA), and you can find out more from its Web site at www.vosa.gov.uk or by calling 0870-606-0440.

Driving Within the Law

After you have your driving licence, you can take to the roads without another qualified driver in the passenger seat. Whether you're driving a car you own, one you've borrowed from a friend, or a hired one, the rules are the same. If you commit an offence while behind the wheel, it's you who should take the rap.

You can't afford to break the law because if you do and get caught, you can get penalty points on your licence or be fined. If the offences are bad enough or you collect enough points, you may end up being banned from driving for a period of time or even going to jail. Don't forget what you learned about the correct way to drive. And don't forget that you have to be insured so check that any car you're driving is covered for you to drive it (see the next section).

Thinking about insurance

One of the very first things you must sort out is insurance. As soon as you're driving on the public road, you must have insurance. Motor insurance is the only insurance policy the law says you must have. If you look at Chapter 18, you can see more on the various types of insurance you can buy.

Policies can cover you and your car, as well as other road users, against damage and accident, but the very minimum you must have is a policy that covers other people for personal injuries caused by your negligence – third-party cover. That policy also covers injuries to passengers.

Talk to an insurance broker about all the different sorts of policies and the best type for you. You can find details of brokers in your local phone book or try the British Insurance Brokers Association (0870-950-1790 or `www.biba.org.uk`). The Association of British Insurers (020-7600-3333 or `www.abi.org.uk`) can give you useful information.

Once you've got a policy, your premiums will go up if you have to make a claim because your car is damaged or stolen or you injure someone or yourself. Your premiums will come down the more driving experience you have, and you will normally collect bonuses for the years in which you don't make any claims – to the point where you may be paying half or even less of what you would have been paying if you had made claims.

Even if you're unintentionally driving without insurance – your insurance company has gone bust, for example – you're committing an offence. Make sure when you hire a car that you have all the insurance you need. Your own policy may cover you for driving a hired car, but if not, you'll have to pay for insurance through the car-hire company. Read the small print of the hire agreement before you sign.

Keeping your car roadworthy

After you've got your driving licence and all the necessary documentation, you have to make sure that your car won't let you down if the police stop you. It has to be safe to be on the public road. The standard your car has to reach is set out by the Road Vehicle (Construction and Use) Regulations. These regulations cover a long list of aspects of car safety, which are checked for the MOT, including tyres, brakes, lights, wipers, number plates, mirrors, seat belts, silencer, exhaust, horn, speedometer, mileage gauge, car alarms, and child seats.

Just having an MOT certificate won't save you. You have to make sure that all aspects of your car at safe at all times, so you need to do your own checks or take your car to a garage during the 12 months between tests to keep it in tip-top condition.

Deciphering the Highway Code

You can break the law when you're a driver in all sorts of ways, and not all of them involve driving. Under the Road Traffic Act 1974, it's illegal to blow your horn while the car is stationary, and if the car is moving, you can't sound the horn between 11.30 p.m. and 7 a.m. on most streets unless there's a danger to another moving vehicle. It's against the law to park illegally or to go without road tax or a valid MOT certificate (see the earlier section 'Owning a car').

The best way of making sure that you keep up to date with the law on driving is by reading the Highway Code from time to time – and a current edition at that. You can get a copy from most bookshops or bigger newsagents or check it out at www.highwaycode.gov.uk.

The Highway Code lists the rules of the road for all road users, including pedestrians and cyclists.

Saying Hello to the Nice Police Officer

Why is it that most people feel guilty when they see a police car behind them, even when they know they haven't done anything wrong? But when the car overtakes you and indicates you should slow down and stop, it's nerve-wracking.

The police can stop a vehicle at any time and ask to see your driving licence – just because you're driving on the road. They can ask to check the vehicle's brakes, steering, and so on They can stop you if they have good reason to think that you're breaking the law or you're supervising a learner driver who has broken the law. They can also stop you if they think you were – here's a nice piece of legal jargon – 'the driver of a car when an accident occurred owing to the presence of that vehicle on the road'. That's not exactly the same as being involved in an accident – although being involved in an accident would come into that category!

The police can't stop you for a random breath test, but they can stop you if they suspect you've had some alcohol. It's very hard to argue that they didn't suspect you'd had a drink! So in reality, at any time while you're driving along the road, minding your own business, you can be stopped!

Your legal responsibilities

If the police pull you over, you have to be able to produce the requested documents, such as your licence, registration document, insurance policy, and MOT certificate. If you don't have them with you, you have seven days in which to turn up, in person, at a police station with them. You can't post them; you have to go there yourself. If you don't have your licence because you've been given a fixed penalty for a previous offence and the licence is having points added, you should produce the receipt and take the licence along once you get it back. You're likely to be arrested only if you've done something very serious, such as dangerous driving or drinking and driving. If you're arrested and taken to the police station, you're likely to be let out on bail rather than kept locked up until your case comes to court. If you're released on bail, you have to turn up at court when required or at the police station if and when told to. If you don't keep to the terms of your bail arrangement, that's another separate offence.

If you're locked up in the cells, you'll be given access to legal advice from the solicitor who is on duty that day to offer advice to people arrested for criminal offences. Take that advice. Many people don't because they think they're innocent, but failure to take advice can cause endless delays and revisits to court.

If you're on bail, see a solicitor as soon as possible. If offences are serious enough for police to arrest you, you're facing the possibility of a prison sentence and hefty fines.

Offences you may have committed

The list of motoring offences is long. In this chapter, I just deal with the driving of the vehicle. Just to give you an idea of how many ways you can break the law, here's a list of some of the most common driving offences. It's by no means comprehensive, and some categories, such as speeding, include a number of more specific offences:

- ✔ Failing to stop at a pedestrian crossing
- ✔ Failing to comply with traffic light signals
- ✔ Failing to stop after an accident
- ✔ Driving without insurance
- ✔ Driving without a licence
- ✔ Failing to produce a driving licence
- ✔ Drink driving
- ✔ Speeding
- ✔ Illegal parking
- ✔ Careless driving (driving without due care and attention or without reasonable consideration for other road users)
- ✔ Dangerous driving (if more than carelessness or bad driving are involved and there's obvious risk of danger, such as driving through red lights)
- ✔ Causing death by dangerous driving
- ✔ Taking a motor vehicle without consent (joyriding)

Using your handheld mobile phone while you're driving, including while at traffic lights and in traffic jams, is an offence. You can use a hands free phone, but you may still be prosecuted for not being in control of the vehicle or for careless or dangerous driving.

Speeding

The national speed limit is 60 miles per hour on all roads apart from motorways and dual carriageways, where it is 70. The national speed limit applies unless signs say otherwise. So in a built-up area, signs will say that the speed limit is 30 or even 20. The most common reason for getting on the wrong side of the law is exceeding the speed limit.

With the proliferation of speed cameras around the UK, getting away with speeding is much harder than it used to be. You won't get off because you didn't know you were in a 30-mile-per-hour limit when you were stopped driving at 40 miles per hour. All the court is concerned with is that the speed limit was 30 mph, and you were driving at 40 mph.

You can be charged with exceeding the speed limit shown on speed signs and temporary speeds signs at road works, for example; for exceeding the speed limit for the type of vehicle; or for exceeding the statutory speed limit for the road – for example 70 on a motorway.

If you're found guilty, your licence is endorsed with three to six penalty points, and you may be disqualified and fined.

The DVLA sends the person who is the registered keeper of the vehicle details of the offence and asks who was driving at the time. If you're the registered keeper and the driver was someone else, but you don't shop the driver to the DVLA, you'll face the penalty, and the points will go on your licence. The DVLA keeps tabs on how many points you have on your licence.

Disputing a speeding charge is difficult. It's almost impossible to prove that you weren't driving over the speed limit, especially if the police have camera evidence to prove it. In recent cases, however, a few people have been able to prove that temporary speed restrictions signs weren't erected properly or were missing completely and have had fines returned and points removed – but these cases are rare.

Parking

Illegal parking covers a multitude of sins, and because of so many rules about roadside parking and off-road parking and bylaws and parking schemes, knowing what is and isn't breaking the law is a challenge.

The absence of a 'No Parking' sign doesn't mean you can park there. Bylaws may make parking illegal, and just because you don't know about them doesn't mean you'll get off. The rules about parking meters vary from place to place, too.

Don't park where you'll cause an obstruction, such as in front of a fire station where fire engines will have problems exiting. Be careful not to break the rules about parking within the zigzag lines near pedestrian crossings. Be suspicious and read carefully any signs and notices you see. If you're unsure, find an off-street car park where the parking regulations are clearly displayed.

Don't park were it says 'No Waiting' unless it makes an exception for loading and unloading. (Loading and unloading doesn't mean nipping into the bank or picking up your dry cleaning.)

If you get a parking ticket, you can pay the fixed penalty. As long as you pay the penalty within the given time, that's all you pay, and there's no offence or conviction. If you go over the allowed time and are fined in the Magistrates' court, however, it counts as a criminal conviction, and the fine will be higher than the fixed penalty.

The registered keeper of the car may be sent the fixed-penalty notice. If you don't own up to whom was driving the car at the time, you're liable to pay the fine even if you weren't the driver.

Clamping is the motorist's bugbear. Many local authorities do allow the clamping of cars parked illegally on the streets or allow them to be taken away to a car pound. In those cases, you have to pay to get your car unclamped or released from the pound. If you feel you were clamped or removed when you weren't illegally parked, take your case to the local authority parking department.

Often people complain that no notices warned that they couldn't park where they did, or if the notice did exist, it was obscured at the time. Clampers have been accused of deliberately making notices difficult to spot so that they can make money from unsuspecting motorists.

Clamping on private property doesn't come under road traffic law. It's a service provided to the owner of the land by the clamping company, and it's up to the owner buying the service to see that it's carried out with reasonable skill and care. If you think you've been unfairly clamped on a private piece of land, take your case up with the clamping company. Talk to the Trading Standards Department at your local authority if you think clampers are breaking the law.

Drink driving

If you're found guilty of one of the range of drink driving charges, you will be disqualified from driving. Once the police have discovered that you were over the limit, you have very little chance of getting off. There are basically five drink-driving charges:

- ✔ Driving or attempting to drive with excess alcohol
- ✔ Being in charge of a vehicle with excess alcohol

✔ Driving or attempting to drive while unfit through drink or drugs

✔ Being in charge of a vehicle while unfit through drink or drugs

✔ Failing to give a breath, blood, or urine specimen at a police station or at the roadside

The police can stop and test you if they suspect you've taken some alcohol, you're in an accident, or you've committed a moving traffic offence. Even driving with a faulty rear light is enough to do it.

If you have more than 80 milligrams of alcohol in 100 millilitres of blood; 107 milligrams in 100 millilitres of urine; or 35 micrograms of alcohol in 100 millilitres of breath, you're guilty. I don't know about you, but those figures mean nothing to me in terms of how many glasses of wine or halves of beer you can drink, so if you drink at all and then drive, you're taking a risk. The maximum penalties are six months in prison and/or a fine of up to £5,000 and disqualification of at least 12 months, but you may be disqualified for longer if you've been disqualified before for drink driving in the past ten years. If you're a repeat offender and you were well over the limit, you're likely to go to jail.

It's highly likely that you'll be disqualified from driving for drink-driving offences, but you may be able to argue a special case in a few circumstances – such as having to drive in a sudden and unforeseeable emergency or someone laced your drinks. Talk to a solicitor. CAB can give you details of those who deal with criminal cases.

If you're found guilty of a drink-driving offence, you may have the period of your disqualification reduced if you agree to go on a special alcohol education programme.

Paying the Penalty

Driving offences attract different penalties. The courts can endorse the driver's licence with penalty points, issue fines, send offenders to prison, or opt for a mix of penalties. In some cases, the magistrates must impose a particular penalty – for example, in speeding cases, they must endorse the licence. They can choose to disqualify or fine the person as well. In other cases, no minimum penalty must be imposed. All cases have maximum penalties.

Points

If magistrates *endorse* your licence, they give you penalty points. Magistrates have no choice but to endorse your licence as a minimum penalty if you're found guilty of speeding and can add between 3 and 6 points to your licence, depending on the seriousness of the offence. If they decide that an endorsement isn't a stiff enough penalty because of the seriousness of the offence, they also have the power to disqualify you and fine you.

If you have your licence endorsed, the points are recorded on your driver record on the DVLA computer. The police or the courts can ask for your driver record. The offence isn't recorded on the national criminal records. Most offences are removed from your licence after four years if you send it back to be exchanged for some reason – perhaps a change of address. Drink-driving offences stay on your licence for 11 years.

Fixed penalties

Some offences have fixed penalties, such as an on-the-spot fine or a fixed-penalty notice telling you that you can pay a certain fine and/or have a certain number of points added to your licence. If you accept a fixed penalty, you're admitting guilt, but it can be preferable to a court hearing.

Unless you're sure you didn't commit the offence, and want your day in court, give the fixed penalty careful consideration. You may, though, be in the position where accepting a fixed penalty will add points to your licence and may lead to you losing it for a period of time, (in which case you may want to plead your case in court). Get legal advice.

Fines and prison sentences

If you receive a summons to appear in front of magistrates, they may decide on fines and prison sentences as penalties for more serious offences. In most cases, the sentences handed down are well below the maximum fines and jail terms. But if you're in danger of being fined or imprisoned, you should get legal advice.

Losing your licence

You can lose your driving licence – *be disqualified* – for a period of time because the magistrates believe the offence was serious enough. You can be disqualified because you're found guilty of an offence that carries an automatic disqualification. You can also lose your licence because of multiple points for offences such as speeding.

Some offences and their possible maximum penalties

It's as well to be forewarned about the consequences of breaking the law before you venture onto the roads, so here are some examples of the toughest penalties you can face:

Driving without insurance: Your licence is endorsed with 6 to 8 points, and you may be disqualified and fined up to £5,000.

Driving without a licence: If you're disqualified, you get 3 to 6 points on your licence and face a maximum fine of £1,000 or six months in prison.

Failing to produce a driving licence: You may be fined up to £1,000.

Drink driving: The maximum penalty for a charge of driving over the limit is £5,000 *and* 6 months in prison. You'll be disqualified for a year, unless the circumstances are exceptional.

Speeding: You have 3 to 6 points added to your licence and may be disqualified, depending on the seriousness of the offence. You may be fined up to £1,000, or £2,500 if the offence was on the motorway.

Dangerous driving: If found guilty, you're disqualified, fined up to £5,000, or sent to prison for up to six months.

Careless driving: If guilty, your licence will be endorsed, you may be disqualified, and you may be fined up to £2,500.

Taking a motor vehicle without consent: You may be disqualified and fined up to £5,000.

Points stay on your driver record for a set period of time if you get a fixed penalty or for however long magistrates decide. If you get a maximum of 12 points on your licence in 3 years, you lose it for at least 6 months. However, if you've previously been disqualified in the last three years, the disqualification lasts longer.

The only chance you have of avoiding disqualification is when mitigating circumstances would lead to serious and exceptional hardship. If you're in this situation, find a solicitor to argue your case.

If you're disqualified for more than 56 days, your licence is revoked, and you have to reapply for a new licence from the DVLA. You don't get your licence back automatically. You may even have to sit your test again or take a medical if the magistrates think that you're a high risk because of alcohol abuse.

If the court decides that you should be disqualified, the ban applies immediately, and you'll have to take the bus home from court. If you're caught driving while you're banned, you may well go to prison.

If you're banned from driving for more than two years, you can apply to the court to have the ban lifted early. You have to convince the magistrates that you're a reformed character. If the ban is for less than four years, you can apply after two years; if it's for longer, you can apply when half the period has expired or after five years – whichever is shorter. If you're turned down, you can apply again in three months.

Dealing with Accidents

No matter how careful a driver you are, the statistics collected by the insurance companies show that you're still likely to be involved in an accident at some time or another. So go prepared. The law says that all motorists have to take reasonable care to avoid loss, damage, or injury to other road users. If you don't take reasonable care or you're negligent and cause injury, damage, or loss to someone else, you will have to compensate them.

You can also be prosecuted if you've broken the law – for example, your dangerous driving caused the accident.

So that you can pay compensation if anyone else claims against you, you must have insurance. For more on insurance, see the section 'Thinking about insurance', earlier in this chapter, and Chapter 18.

If an accident occurs because you become ill at the wheel – for example, you had a stroke or a heart attack – you're unlikely to be prosecuted for the way you were driving, but you may still be liable for compensation.

The most basic piece of advice to anyone in an accident – apart from not screaming and shouting at the other drivers! – is the one that's most difficult to put into practice: Don't say sorry! In fact, don't say anything that may be taken as an admission that the accident was your fault. Your insurance company will want to sort out who was to blame and, if each party was partly at fault, who should shoulder what proportion of the blame. It won't be very happy with you if you've gone around saying, 'It was all my fault, I'm so sorry' – even if that was the case. If someone is injured, you'll probably want to say sorry to comfort them, but don't! Sorry may be taken as 'Sorry, I'm to blame', rather than 'I'm sorry you're hurt.'

Reporting the accident

Unless the incident is a minor prang, call the police. The police don't have to turn up if no one is injured and there's not much damage. If they do turn up, they'll want all the details of the drivers, vehicles, and the owners of the vehicles (if they weren't driving). They'll ask for all relevant documents, such as licences, registration documents, insurance, and MOT certificates. If you don't have these items with you, you'll have to take them to a police station within seven days.

The police may ask for statements from everyone. Bear in mind that copies of anything you say will be sent to all the insurance companies involved and if any legal action is taken, you could say something that incriminates you later. You don't have to make a statement there and then, but you do have to give your name and address.

Write everything down: the registration of any other cars involved or that may have contributed to causing an accident; the names and addresses of other drivers and witnesses; and insurance details of the other drivers.

The cars shouldn't be moved until a sketch has been made of the accident site showing where each car involved came to rest. The police normally do this sketch when they arrive at the scene. If they don't show up, do it yourself or take photos. Show all the road signs, road widths, the damage to the vehicles, and weather conditions. Don't leave anything to memory. You have just been in an accident, which is stressful, so you're likely to forget important details.

If the police didn't arrive at the accident scene, report it as soon as possible, but definitely within 24 hours. If you don't, your licence can be endorsed for failing to report an accident. You have to report the accident in person at a police station rather than over the phone. The only circumstances in which an accident doesn't need to be reported to the police is one in which no one was injured, and everyone gave all their particulars, including their insurance details, to anyone else involved who was entitled to ask for it.

As soon as you can, write a full description of what happened from your point of view and call your insurance company. Check your insurance policy. Most say that any accident, no matter how minor, should be reported to the company within seven days. If you don't contact your insurance company within the time limit on the policy, you may find yourself without insurance for that particular accident and for any later ones.

Even If you're not making a claim on your insurance policy for repairs to a damaged vehicle or for injuries and no one else is claiming against you, you must let your insurance company know it happened. If you don't and your insurers find out at a later date, they may refuse to pay out on any future claims.

If you're driving a hire car, you must let the car hire company know as soon as possible. If you're insured through the car-hire firm, it will deal with the accident through its insurers.

Leaving the scene of an accident

If your car is involved in an accident, you have to stop unless no damage or injury occurred. You must stop if a person or an animal (apart from a cat) is injured or another car or property, such as a fence, wall, hedge, street signs, or buildings, is damaged.

You must to stop long enough for other people involved to take your details. You have to give your name, address, vehicle registration number, and the details of the car's owner (if that's not you). You don't have to give other motorists your insurance details or your driving licence, but it's only reasonable to give details of your insurance company and to get insurance details of the other drivers involved so that the case can be resolved by the insurers.

If you don't stop, you can be charged with failing to stop at the scene of an accident; failing to report an accident; and failing to give your particulars, all of which can result in your licence being endorsed.

Making the claims

If you're injured in an accident, you can claim for your injuries or for damage to your car if you have a fully comprehensive insurance policy that covers you and your car or if you can show that someone else was to blame and claim from that party.

If you were at fault and only have a third-party insurance policy, you're out of luck. Other people who were injured in an accident caused by you can claim against you, and your third-party policy will cover their claims. Your policy may also cover third parties for damage to their vehicles and possessions.

Driving without at least third-party insurance is a criminal offence.

Claiming from your insurance company

As soon as you have an accident, contact your insurance company. If you have a fully comprehensive policy, you can claim from your insurer for your own loss, damage, and injury, no matter who caused the accident. You may be sent the usual pile of forms to complete, but many insurers handle this process online.

Make sure that you're honest with your insurers as to what happened. They decide, along with the insurance companies of any other motorists involved, who's to blame for the accident or whether blame is shared. Between them, they will decide which company should pay out for the damage and injury claims being made. You make your initial claim to your insurer, and your insurer will pay your claim. If you aren't to blame, your insurer gets that money back from the insurer of the person who was at fault.

In some cases, the other person may not have insurance, so you may have to take separate legal action for compensation.

Even with a fully comprehensive insurance policy, you can be out of pocket. If you claim on your insurance policy and are found to have been at fault for an accident, you may lose some of the no-claims bonus you've built up over the years because you haven't made a claim. Even if your no-claims bonus isn't affected, you're likely to find that your premiums will go up in future. If you have an excess on your policy, you'll have to pay that amount of the repairs yourself.

If you have just the basic third-party insurance that covers other people's injuries, they may still claim compensation from you for their loss, damage to their vehicle and other property, and/or injury if the accident was your fault. Without insurance, you'll have to pay out of your own assets. If you refuse to reach a settlement with the people who've been injured, they can take you to court.

Claiming from the other party

If you don't have fully comprehensive insurance, you can't claim through your insurance company. You may have a comprehensive policy, but decide that you don't want to claim on it. In those situations, you have to claim direct from the other party, and you'll have to prove that they were to blame for the accident. Their insurance company may pay your compensation if you prove your case, or it may dispute your claim and refuse to pay out. If you can't come to a settlement, you may end up taking a compensation claim through the courts.

You must report the accident to your insurer, in any case. Get quotes for several garages for the repairs to your car. Some insurers insist that you use their recommended garages, especially if major repair work needs to be done. Once you decide on a garage and have your car towed there, let the other driver know where it is so that their insurance company can send someone to look at it and agree that the repairs can go ahead. Keep a record of all the expenses you have, such as towing your car to a garage, the costs of repairs, and the fee for hiring a car during the repairs. If you're claiming for injuries, you need to talk to a solicitor who specialises in personal injury to work out how much to claim.

If the other side's insurance company agrees that its client was at fault, it may not pay the full amount of your claim. You have to decide whether to accept what it offers or pursue the outstanding amount through the courts.

If no insurance company is involved and the other driver refuses to pay the amount you ask for, you'll have to decide whether to reach a settlement or to take the case to court. If less than £5,000 is involved, you can take a case through the small-claims track of the Country Court (see Chapter 1). The alternative is to get a solicitor involved and hope that a letter from him or her is enough to persuade the other driver to pay up.

You can pay for legal assistance when you take out your insurance policy so that if you do have to go to court to claim compensation, your solicitors and court costs are covered.

Paying for hospital treatment

It comes as a shock to most drivers involved in road accidents to discover that they can be charged for any emergency medical treatment, given to any of the people involved, by a doctor who happens to be passing by. You'll get the bill from the doctor after the accident, and you can usually claim it from your insurance company or the other party's insurer if someone else was to blame. If a doctor arrives on the scene after being called from a hospital, you won't see a bill.

If anyone involved in an accident needs hospital treatment, the private hospital or the Department of Health, on behalf of the NHS, may claim some of the costs from the insurance company of the driver who caused the accident.

Claiming when a driver is uninsured or can't be traced

If an uninsured driver caused you loss, damage, or injury, and you don't have a fully comprehensive policy to claim through, you can claim through the Motor Insurers' Bureau (01908-830-0001 or www.mib.org.uk) for personal injury and damages. A similar scheme covers you if the driver didn't stop at the scene of the accident or gave you false details and can't be traced. If your claim is accepted, you pay the first £300 yourself and, if it's decided that you were partly to blame, the amount of compensation you get is reduced.

Driving Abroad

If you're planning to drive abroad, don't forget your driving licence, but also think about getting an International Driving Permit, which shows that you have a driving licence in the UK. You may not need this permit for most European Union countries, but it can be useful to carry anyway. The aim of this permit is to cut down problems caused by language differences. It can come in handy as an identity document if you lose your passport.

Traveling on two wheels

If your view is 'four wheels bad, two wheels good' don't forget that the same rules of the road apply to you as apply to car drivers, and you can be guilty of the same offences and face the same penalties.

The rules for motorcyclists are more or less the same as for drivers. At 17, you can get a provisional driving licence and ride a motorbike or moped up to 125 cc on the road without a full licence, but you must have done *compulsory basic training* (CBT) in England, Scotland, and Wales.

When you've completed your CBT, you're given a DL196, which you need to be able to take the practical motorcycle test. If you don't pass both your theory and practical tests within two years, you have to retake the CBT course. Once you pass your motorcycle test, you get a full licence, but most riders have to wait two years before they can ride a bike over 33 bhp.

As a cyclist, you're a road user, and the rules of the road apply to you in the same way they apply to motorists and motorcyclists. You can't be disqualified from riding a bicycle or sent to prison for breaking the rules of the road, but you can be fined.

You're breaking the law if you ride your bike through a red traffic light – even if you dismount and push your bike past a red light. You can push your bike across a pedestrian crossing because, for that purpose, you're a pedestrian, not a rider.

One of main advantages for a cyclist is that you can park more easily than a motorist. You can park on painted yellow lines, but you can be fined if you leave your bike in a dangerous position – on a footpath or clearway, for example. And you can be charged with being drunk in charge of a bike. The normal breathalyser rules don't apply – there's no scientific test for being over the limit in the case of a cyclist. It's down to the opinion of the police officer, but you can be fined up to £1,000.

The rules most often broken by cyclists – to the annoyance of pedestrian and motorists – are ignoring red traffic lights, riding on pavements, and not having proper lights and reflectors. You can be fined for these misdemeanours – if the police can catch you. But just because the police aren't usually quick enough off the mark or usually ignore you because they have better things to do, it doesn't mean that you don't have a duty to be considerate to your fellow road users.

Also take your Vehicle Registration Document. If you can't take the original because it's a company car or you've borrowed or hired it, you will need a letter of authority from the owner or a Vehicle on Hire Certificate (VE103B) instead.

If you're taking your own car abroad, check with your insurer whether you should have a Green Card (*International Motor Insurance Certificate*). Again, you won't need this documentation for many of the EU countries, but you do need it in other places. It simply shows that you have insurance cover for the country you're visiting, but check exactly how much cover your policy gives you while outside the UK.

Before you go, attach a GB sign to the back of your car or caravan. Don't forget that if you're driving on the other side of the road, you will need converters to attach to your headlamps to adjust the direction of the beam so that it doesn't dazzle oncoming drivers. Pack a First Aid kit, fire extinguisher, warning triangle, and spare light bulbs. They're required by law in many countries, but even if they're not, it's a good idea to have them in case you need them.

Take a spare set of keys. You can't imagine the trouble and expense this precaution can save you if you lose your first set. And breakdown cover can be a real blessing. If you already belong to a motoring organisation, you may be covered already, or it may be able to extend your cover.

Don't forget your passport and any visas you may need (see Chapter 17).

When you're in another country, you must obey its rules of the road. Find out as much as you can about the speed limits and priorities at junctions before you go. If you break the law in some countries, such as France, you can be pursued for that offence once back home in the UK.

Chapter 17

Travelling and Taking a Break

• •

In This Chapter

▶ Getting around on public transport

▶ Counting the cost of delays and cancellations

▶ Holidaying abroad

▶ Getting compensation if it doesn't go as planned

• •

*N*ot everyone drives a car, can afford to, or wants to. Given the congestion on the roads, it can take longer to travel from point A to B in some parts of the country than it did a hundred years ago, despite the advances in technology. Public transport reduces the damage being done to the planet through carbon emissions and greenhouse gases. For some or all of these reasons, more people than at any time in the past 50 years are letting the train take the strain.

It isn't just train travel that is growing in popularity. The growth of air travel has been phenomenal, especially over the past few years as the no-frills airlines have offered affordable flights, and Eastern European countries have opened up to visitors. An increasing number of people are flying, and flying more often, for a mixture of business and pleasure. Even those people who are reliant on their cars for the majority of their journeys also use public transport more often.

This chapter looks at your rights if you fly or use boats, trains, buses, or taxis and how you can enforce your rights if things go wrong.

Getting around the UK

Millions of people use the trains and buses each day to commute to and from work. Some drive to a nearby station, park, and finish their journeys by public transport; some use the system for the whole trip. Most of the public transport system in the UK is in the hands of private companies. Each company operates differently in terms of the types of tickets they issue and the frills they add to their basic service, but they're all regulated and have to meet Government targets or face losing their licence to run their particular section of the transport network.

Some companies are more efficient at meeting their targets than others. Some have fewer delays and cancellations and better punctuality records. Some have better on-board service. As with any other service you buy, you can choose to take your custom elsewhere – in theory, at least – but in practice, many travellers (commuters in particular) have little choice as there is only one operator on their route. Those differences aside, rules apply to all companies about the compensation you should receive if a service has been seriously disrupted or is poor.

In Northern Ireland, the public transport buses and trains are all run by Translink with three operating companies – Metro and Ulsterbus – operating the buses, and NI Railways operating the trains. The aim is to have an integrated public transport system so that passengers can get around the region with as much ease as possible. Go to www.translink.co.uk for more information about the system.

Buses

In London, buses are the responsibility of Transport for London, which grants licences to private operators. Elsewhere in the country buses are run by private firms like Stagecoach, National Express, and FirstBus; by one of six Passenger Transport Executives in England; or by local authorities. Local authorities are responsible for making sure that elderly people and users with disability have the services they need. They may do that by providing buses themselves or by entering into contracts with the private operators.

London bus companies can make you pay a penalty fare if you don't have a valid ticket or pass. The penalty fare isn't a fine, but a higher than normal fare. If you refuse to pay, you're asked for your name and contact details, which you have to give. If you don't, you're prosecuted and fined. You can appeal against a penalty fare as long as you do it within 21 days, whether you've paid it or not. For more information, go to the Transport for London Web site at www.transportforlondon.gov.uk or call 020-7918-4300. If you have any complaint about London buses that you aren't able to resolve with Transport for London, contact the London Transport Users Committee at 020-7505-9000.

Other bus operators don't have the right to charge penalty fares, but if an inspector comes on your bus and you haven't already got a valid ticket, you will have to pay up or leave the bus. If you want to complain about late buses or poor service, you have to complain directly to the bus company. You can find the details of the firm on the outside of the bus. Most companies have their own codes of practice that outline the service you should expect, their procedures for dealing with complaints, and any compensation you'll be entitled to if things go wrong.

Most bus operators publish information for users with disabilities and offer concessions on fares. Some buses must have ramps to help you on and off, and bus drivers must help you if you ask and can only refuse on health and safety grounds. Some areas run *dial-a-bus schemes,* which provide door-to-door services for people with disabilities. Contact your local authority for more information.

Coaches are all operated by private companies. Some of the bigger ones may operate local bus services, too, but many of them are small local firms operating a few coaches around their local area and further afield. They, too, have to make provision for travellers with disabilities. If you're intending to travel, you should phone ahead to arrange any assistance you need.

If you have a problem with bus or coach services outside London or you have complained and you still aren't happy with the result, contact the Bus Appeals Body (www.nfbu.org or 02392-814-493). If you've been injured or had something damaged, report the situation to the firm operating the service. If you don't get a satisfactory solution and want to claim compensation, get legal advice. If you're claiming compensation for a personal injury, it's very important to talk to a solicitor with experience with those sorts of claims. Contact the Law Society for details by visiting www.lawsociety. org.uk or by calling 0870-606-6575.

Trains

Each train-operating company must produce a passenger's charter that tells you what standards of service you can expect and how to complain. The charters have to be approved by the Rail (www.rail-reg.gov.uk or 020-7282-2000.

You will be committing an offence if you get on a train and intend to travel without paying. Some train-operating companies in some areas are allowed to charge penalty fares if you don't have a valid ticket or pass. If the fare you should have paid is £5 or less, the penalty is £10. If the normal fare is more than £10, the penalty is double the fare. If an operator is allowed to charge penalty fares, plenty of notices around the station should make that clear. If you're caught and charged a penalty, you can appeal in the following cases:

✔ You don't think enough notices were posted.

✔ English isn't your first language, or you couldn't read the notices because of a visual impairment.

✔ You couldn't buy a ticket because of long queues at the ticket desk or malfunctioning machines or because you couldn't use the machines because of a physical disability.

In other areas, train operators can't charge penalty fares, but they're within their rights to charge you the full standard or first-class fare if you have the wrong ticket or no ticket for your journey. Some special offer or discounted tickets are valid only for particular trains or at certain times of the day. Check the terms and conditions before you travel.

Rules govern paying compensation to passengers when serious delays or cancellations occur. Different companies may offer you better compensation through their passenger charters, but the rule is that you must be given at least 10 percent of the value of your ticket if the train is more than an hour late. If a severe delay causes you to decide not to travel on the train you've bought a ticket for, you can have your ticket refunded. If you have extra expense in getting to your destination – maybe you have to take a taxi home when the train does finally pull into your station because there's no connecting service – you can claim a refund of the taxi fare. Get a receipt; you will need it to make a claim.

If you're a traveller with a disability, contact the train operator to arrange any assistance you need. The train-operating companies and the station operators must have policies on providing facilities for passengers with disabilities. Ask them for information or contact your local authority or local Passenger Transport Executive. You can find contact details in the phone book.

A person with a disability can buy a railcard that allows that person and one other adult travelling with him a discount of a third on the price of tickets. You can apply at your local station or, if you already have a card, you can renew it by phone – see www.disabledpersons-railcard.co.uk or call 0191-218-8103.

If you have any complaints about the train service, you must complain to the company operating the train. Complaints about a station should be directed to the company operating the station, which may be the train company or Network Rail. The guard on the train or the person on duty at the station can give you details. Write to the relevant company, enclosing your ticket if possible or some other proof that you bought a ticket. If you don't get a satisfactory result, contact the Rail Passenger's Council – 0207-505-9090 – or go to its Web site at www.railpassengers.org.uk. You can also complain to the Rail Passengers' Council about the National Rail Enquiry Service (08457-484-950), which gives information about train times and fares.

If you're injured or have your property damaged, you may want to claim compensation. If a personal injury occurs, get legal advice from a solicitor who specialises in those sorts of claims. The Law Society can point you in the right direction – go to www.lawsociety.org.uk or call 0870-606-6575. If you think there may be a safety problem on the service you've been using, contact the Health and Safety Executive on www.hse.gov.uk or call 020-7717-6533.

Underground services

The situation in London is slightly different from other underground train services. In London, Transport for London has responsibility. Penalty fares apply in the same way as they do for buses (see the section earlier in this chapter). If you think you shouldn't have been charged a penalty fare, you can appeal. Ask at the underground station for details. If you want to complain about a penalty fare or anything else on London Underground services, contact the Customer Service Centre – www.thetube.com or 0845-330-9880 – and ultimately the London Transport Users' Committee at www.ltuc.org.uk or 0207-505-9000.

Underground services outside London are the responsibility of the Passenger Transport Executive for their area. You can find contact details in the phone book. You can't be charged penalty fares outside London, and if you have any complaints, go direct to the company operating the underground service. You can find the details on the underground trains and in the station.

Taxis

Local authorities regulate taxis and minicabs, except in London where the Metropolitan police are responsible. Drivers can't refuse to take guide dogs, hearing dogs, or dogs accompanying passengers with epilepsy or a physical disability. The dogs have to travel free.

If you have a complaint about a taxi or minicab service, take the licence number of the car and complain to the local authority or to the Public Carriage Office of the Metropolitan Police by calling 0207-941-4500.

Never take a trip in an unlicensed minicab. You have no way of tracking down the driver if something goes wrong. Always go for a licensed taxi or minicab.

Going Further Afield

If you're intending to venture a bit further from home, the choice is likely to be Eurostar, the tunnel, ferry, or plane. If you're driving abroad, refer to Chapter 16. What applies to other train journeys (see the section 'Trains' earlier in this chapter) also applies to Eurostar, which just leaves boats and planes. This section deals mainly with package holidays and air travel because that's the area to which the law gives most protection.

With the advent of the Internet, more people are making their own bookings for both travel and accommodation. In cases where you use a travel agent and a tour operator, you have some protection, through codes of practice, agreements made by international carriers, and different European Directives, to help you if things go wrong.

If you book everything yourself, bear in mind that you won't have as much protection. You may find yourself without accommodation you thought you'd booked or stranded if a ferry operator or airline went out of business. Even worse, the hotel may go bankrupt after you've paid. Not only would you have to book again, with all the extra costs involved, but you may not be able to use the original flights, which are rarely refundable.

Buying a package holiday

A *package holiday* is one where you pay an inclusive price for your travel, hotel, and any other services, such as transfers and car hire. Holidays of this sort come under the Package Travel, Package Holiday and Package Tour Regulations 1992 (see the upcoming section 'Making the booking'), as well as contract law.

If you're booking a package holiday, it's vitally important to read all the small print before you sign the booking form or press Send on your e-mail booking. You're making a legally binding contract with the tour operator organising your break, so you need to know exactly what to expect and what you're signing. Even if you book through a travel agent, the contract is between you and the tour operator. If things go wrong with the holiday, it's the tour operator you have to complain to and possibly make a claim against. However, your travel agent has to help you with your complaint by advising whether you really do have a cause for complaint and on how to write your letter.

If the travel agent doesn't do a good job and gets the booking wrong, you can complain to the agency about it and make a claim against it if necessary. However, you can't blame the travel agent if she books the holiday you wanted, and the holiday goes wrong.

If a tour operator provides air travel as part of your holiday package, you have the protection of the Air Travel Organisers' Licence (ATOL). You won't lose money or be stranded somewhere because someone in the chain goes out of business. When you book a holiday, make sure that the organisation you book with has an ATOL. The ATOL logo and number appears on all the stationery and invoices.

Making the booking

Book through a member of the Association of British Travel Agents (ABTA), the association for both travel agents and tour operators in the UK. ABTA runs a scheme to protect you if one of its members goes bust, and it also sets standards of service for its members. You can contact ABTA at www.abta.com or 020-7637-2444.

The Association of Independent Tour Operators (AITO, www.aito.co.uk or 020-8744-9280) also has a scheme to make sure that you're protected if you book through one of its members. Its mediation scheme can settle customers' disputes.

If a tour operator makes minor changes to your holiday after you've booked, you can't do much about it. When you read the terms and conditions in the brochure, you'll usually find a clause allowing for minor changes, such as changing your flight time. If you see bigger changes, such as changing your holiday resort, your hotel, or airport, under the Package Travel, Package Holiday and Package Tour Regulations 1992, the tour operator has to tell you as soon as possible. You may be entitled to cancel and get a refund or to go ahead with the break but ask for compensation. If you do cancel and it costs more to book another similar holiday, you may be able to claim the difference in costs from the first tour operator.

Knowing what to expect when you get there

The holiday described in the brochure is what you're booking, so that's what you're legally entitled to. In days gone by, you were likely to arrive at your chosen resort and find the hotel was still being built or the photo that had attracted you was years out of date. Descriptions in brochures have to be accurate. If it says the hotel is away from the nightclub area, it has to be away from the nightclub area.

Apart from the right to the service described in the brochure, you also have rights that have come about because of claims that have succeeded in the courts in the past. For example, you have the right to the standard of room that it's reasonable to expect given the price you're paying. In other words, if you pay for a five-star holiday, you shouldn't have to put up with the kind of accommodation you'd expect in a two-star hotel.

You're also entitled to any extras that you've asked for and the tour operator has confirmed. So if you've asked for a sea view and it's listed on the confirmation form, you're entitled to a sea view.

If things do go wrong and you don't get what you thought you were booking, or what you can reasonably expect given the terms of the contract, you can claim compensation from the tour operator.

Complain immediately. Something may be done to salvage the situation, such as changing you to a different hotel. If you wait until you get back home, proving that you were unhappy will be more difficult, and the tour operator may argue that you did nothing to reduce your loss, so you may end up with less compensation. (For information about making compensation claims and locating helpful organisations, see the section 'Getting Help When Things Go Wrong,' later in the chapter.)

Being an independent traveller

Many people are used to booking their own transport over the phone or the Internet. If you're one of them, you just need to be aware that if you do book that way, you have none of the protection that booking through ABTA or AITO and a tour operator gives you (see preceding section). If a ferry operator or airline goes bust, you have to pay for your own transport home. You should think about travel insurance to cover you if something does go wrong. (See the section 'Insuring yourself,' later in this chapter.)

Booking flights

Apart from the cost of the flight, you have to pay various taxes, such as air passenger tax. Be careful when you're booking; you want to know the full cost of the flight, including the taxes.

Some online sites offer you insurance for each flight you book. If you don't want it or already have insurance, you may need to remove it from the booking instead of adding it on. Don't get caught out. Other sites charge a large premium for using a credit card rather than a debit card.

In most cases, unless you have an open ticket, you can't get a refund of an airline ticket if you find that you can't travel. Read the terms and conditions carefully before you sign on the dotted line or press the Send button on your e-mail. You may be able to get a refund of some of the taxes. If your flight is delayed or cancelled or you aren't allowed to board because the flight has been overbooked, you may be entitled to refunds, alternative flights, free assistance, overnight accommodation, or compensation. (For more detail, see the section 'Dealing with cancellations and flight delays,' later in this chapter.)

Using the no-frills operators

The budget airlines have become known as *no frills* because, quite simply, they offer no frills or, if they do, you have to pay for them. You pay for your seat in the ticket price, and if you want food or refreshments while you're on board, you have to pay extra. Some airlines are very strict about the amount of baggage you can take on board, and some now charge you for the bags that you check in.

Make sure that you read the terms and conditions when you're booking so that you know exactly what to expect. Usually, you don't have tickets, so you need to take along a printout of your booking confirmation along with ID containing a photograph, such as your passport.

Despite the protests of the budget airlines, you have the same rights to refunds, assistance, and compensation for delays, cancellations, and bumps off a flight as you do with the full-cost airlines. (For more details, see the section 'Dealing with cancellations and flight delays,' later in this chapter.)

You may be able to book a particular seat when you book your ticket. Families should think about booking with an airline that will confirm seating in advance. If you're taking a long flight, don't just shop around for the best deals – check out the legroom. Airlines vary on the amount of space you get – anywhere from 29 to 34 inches. The extra legroom may be worth the extra ticket cost.

Booking accommodations

If you book your own accommodation rather than going through a travel agent or tour operator, you won't have a tour guide to assist you if you find it's not what you expected. Your contract is with the hotel or guesthouse, so you'll have to complain directly to the owner or manager. In theory, you may be able to get a reduction in the price to compensate, but if you're abroad and your language skills aren't up to the negotiation, you may find that it's best just to cut your losses and move on. You also run the risk that the hotel may have resold your room, changed ownership, or gone bankrupt since you made your payment.

If you book a hotel and the hotel accepts your booking, you've made a legally binding contract. The hotel agrees to provide accommodation for the specific dates at a certain price, and you agree to pay for it. Under the Supply of Goods and Services Act, hotels in the UK also have to provide their advertised services.

If a hotel has a brochure that says it has spas and a pool and they're closed when you arrive, you can claim compensation or ask for a reduction in the bill to make up for the disappointment. The disappointment will be greater if you booked that hotel specifically because you wanted to make good use of those facilities. Take photographs and keep receipts if you pay to use similar facilities elsewhere. You may need evidence of that sort to back up your claim if you have to take legal action.

Hotel owners also have a duty to look after you and your property while on their premises. If you're injured or your belongings are stolen because of their negligence, you may have a claim against them. They may try to limit their liability for stolen property by displaying a notice that says they won't be liable for any more than £100 in total, but if you can prove that they or their staff has been negligent, you may be able to make a higher claim. Take legal advice. The Citizens Advice Bureau (CAB) can help you. (You can find their details in the phone book.) If you've been injured, you need to talk to a solicitor with experience of personal injury claims, and the CAB can point you in the right direction.

Packing your bags

Baggage can be a problem only when you're travelling by air. On most other modes of transport, you can put your belongings where you can keep an eye on them. Problems arise only if you forget to take them with you when you arrive. When it comes to flying, travel light, and then you won't have those nail-biting moments waiting for your baggage to appear on the airport carousel.

Check the baggage allowances; most airlines charge you if you go over their allowance. If you take only cabin baggage, remember to check what size or weight of bag you can take on board. Also make sure that you don't have any banned objects in that bag, such as knives, scissors, or even eyebrow tweezers.

If you do take baggage to be checked in, make sure that it locks and is well marked. If the bag doesn't turn up at your destination or is damaged or delayed, you may be entitled to compensation under the terms of the Montreal Convention explained later in the chapter in the section 'Handling Lost Baggage.'

Never put your home address on your baggage labels – just your name. Don't announce to an enterprising thief that you won't be at home for the next fortnight.

One budget airline now charges passengers for any bags they want to check in. The idea is to reduce the amount of time taken to load and unload baggage, and so reduce the chance of delays. The airline claims that fares have come down by a similar amount to the baggage charge. How long before others follow suit?

Going by boat

The EU directive on delays, cancellation, and denied boarding doesn't apply to travel by boat. However, if you're travelling by sea as part of a package holiday, the Package Travel, Package Holiday and Package Tour Regulations 1992 do apply, so read the section 'Booking a package deal,' earlier in this chapter. The EU has strict regulations about health and safety, but standards may be much lower in more adventurous destinations. You also have a legally binding contract and the same rights as you do when buying any other service to expect the supplier to take reasonable care and use reasonable skill. If you think the service doesn't meet a reasonable standard given what you've paid, you can make a claim against the operator.

If you book through a travel agent and tour operator who is a member of ABTA or AITO, you have extra protection if the operator goes out of business.

Read the small print. You're very unlikely to have any rights to a refund if you don't travel. You don't have an automatic right to compensation if your baggage goes missing or is damaged because it is usually in your keeping while on board. However, if you hand it over to be stored for the duration of the journey, you have the right to expect it to be treated with reasonable care and skills, so if it is damaged or lost, you may be able to claim compensation.

Cancelling your plans

Whichever mode of transport you prefer, make sure that you know what rights you have to cancel before you book. Often, your rights depend on the type of ticket you've bought. Some flight tickets are open and you can cancel and travel on another date, but these tickets are the most expensive ones. Others types of tickets don't allow you to cancel. If you don't travel, you don't get anything back apart from a proportion of the taxes you paid. You can cancel and get a refund for many train tickets, but you may not get back the full amount.

With package holidays, you may be able to cancel and get some of your money refunded if you do it by a certain date, after which the amount of refund goes down. The closer to the day of travel you cancel, the less likely it is you that you'll get any refund. You may be able to cancel if you're ill or a relative dies, but not if you change your plans for any other reason. If you do have to cancel, check whether your travel insurance may cover you.

Don't leave home without travel insurance in case of medical emergencies, which can be extremely expensive. (See the upcoming section 'Insuring yourself.')

When you make hotel bookings, you're usually asked for a deposit or your credit-card number. If you cancel, the hotel is entitled to keep the deposit or to take money from your card to cover admin costs. The manager has to try to re-let your room, but if he can't, the hotel may claim its lost profit from you, which may be a high proportion of the total bill. If you do have to cancel, do it as far in advance of the booking date as possible. The longer the hotel has to re-let the room, the less chance you'll have to pay.

Big busy hotels are much less likely to claim from you than small, out-of-the-way places with few passers-by.

Taking Travel Precautions

To get the most out of your travel experiences, take a few precautions before you go. There's nothing worse than something going wrong when you're away from home, but knowing that you have good insurance and have made contingency plans in case you fall ill, for example, can give you peace of mind. There are some eventualities that you can't take precautions against, such as having your flight cancelled or your bags going astray, but knowing your rights in those situations can take the sting out of the tail.

Insuring yourself

When you make a booking, your tour operator, travel agent, and sometimes the airline will offer you insurance. That policy may not be the most suitable one for you. You may need better cover, so read the terms carefully. You can buy travel insurance from most big insurers, as well as firms that specialise. You can also buy an annual policy that covers you for all your travel during the next 12 months.

The main advantage of taking the insurance offered by the travel company is that the company can usually get payments for you, if necessary, more quickly than you could if dealing with another company.

The most important aspect of your travel insurance is the cover it gives you if you get ill or have an accident while abroad. If you need medical treatment, you want to know that the bills will be paid. Your policy should also cover the costs of bringing you home if you're ill or die; loss of money and your possessions; and cancellation. Most policies are strict about the circumstances in which they'll pay out if you have to cancel and won't cover you if you just change your mind about going.

Getting ill abroad

In EU countries, you have the right to emergency medical treatment if you fall ill. These countries have an agreement with the UK. You can find a list of countries that offer UK citizens free healthcare at the Department of Health Web site (www.dh.gov.uk) or by calling 020-7210-4850. In order to be able to claim healthcare while abroad, you need a *European Health Insurance Card* (it used to be an E111). You can pick up the forms from your doctor or at the post office.

However, the European Health Insurance Card won't be any use to you outside the European Economic Area or Switzerland. In most other countries, you'll have to pay, so you should make sure that you have appropriate travel insurance to cover the bills. (See the section 'Insuring yourself,' earlier in this chapter). You need to be sure that the insurance covers the cost of getting home, if you need to be brought back to the UK for medical treatment.

The Department of Health has all the information you need about the risks in particular countries from specific diseases, including up-to-date information on the latest health scares. It also tells you what vaccinations you need to travel to various countries. (You can also check with your doctor, travel agent, or tour operator.) If you do need particular vaccinations, you have to provide proof that you've had them when you get to passport control at your destination. You also need to plan ahead as you may need some vaccinations a certain time before you travel.

Dealing with cancellations and flight delays

Under European Union Regulations established in 2005, you're entitled to compensation if you aren't allowed to board a flight you've booked or it's cancelled or delayed for a certain length of time. The regulations apply to any scheduled, budget or chartered flight within the EU and to any flight arriving or taking off in the EU on a European airline. However, the airlines have the get-out clause that the rules don't apply if the problem was beyond their control – for example, as a result of severe weather conditions or an air-traffic control decision.

If the flight is delayed for a certain time, you should get free assistance from the airline, including meals and refreshments. This assistance applies if a short-haul flight is delayed by two hours or more; a medium-haul flight is delayed three hours or more; or a long-haul flight is delayed for four hours or more.

If the delays are longer, you may also have the right to cancel your flight and receive a full refund. If you've already travelled some distance to get to the airport – say, flown from Belfast to Heathrow to catch the seriously delayed flight – you should be able to get a refund of the costs of that journey and a free flight back to Belfast. If the flight was part of a package holiday, you'll be refunded the value of the flights, not the whole holiday, so cancelling probably isn't the best option. If you have to wait until the next day before flying out, you should get free hotel accommodation and transfers to and from the hotel.

If the flight is cancelled, you can receive a refund of the unused ticket and for any other legs of the journey you've already made and a free flight back to where you started. Or you can accept a different flight to your destination at the first possible opportunity or at a later date. Refunds are of flight tickets only and not for hotel accommodation. If you do decide to take the earliest possible alternative flight, you should get the meals, refreshments, and phone calls.

If you aren't allowed to board your flight because no seats are available, you're entitled to compensation. The amounts are set out in the regulations: £172 for a short-haul flight; £275 for a medium-haul flight; or £412 for a long haul-flight. Airlines usually ask for volunteers to give up their seat in those situations in order to avoid as much inconvenience as possible, but sometimes you aren't given the choice. In addition to the compensation, you have the right to cancel and get a refund or to take an alternative flight.

Handling lost baggage

Under the Montreal Convention, if your baggage is lost, damaged, or delayed on an international flight, you're entitled to compensation. You can claim a maximum of around £820. That amount may not be enough to cover what you've lost if you have a suitcase full of designer-label clothes, jewellery, and cameras, so you may want to claim on your travel insurance as well. However, your insurer gives you only the resale value of any item, not the cost of a new one. You're better off leaving expensive items at home or, if you must take them with you, carry them in your hand luggage.

If your baggage is delayed, you're also entitled to compensation of up to £820 so that you can buy essentials to use until it's delivered to you. If your baggage isn't at the airport, contact a member of the airline staff immediately. You'll be given a reference number, which you need in order to make a claim. If your baggage is damaged, complain to the airline as soon as you discover the problem, but you must claim within seven days.

Getting Help When Things Go Wrong

You can turn to many people if you have a complaint and can't get it resolved. (See the preceding sections for your particular concern.) The general rule is that you should complain as soon as a problem becomes apparent and to the firm operating the service you're complaining about. You need to give them the opportunity to put things right before you go any further.

If the problem is with a package holiday, complain straight away to the tour operator who may be able to resolve the situation to your satisfaction straight away – by moving you to another hotel, for example, to avoid spoiling the whole of your holiday. If you do accept some reasonable solution to your problem, leave the way open to claim compensation when you get home. Write to the tour operator and give a copy of your letter to the company representative at your resort, saying that you accept the new hotel but that you'll be claiming for the inconvenience and the part of the holiday that was ruined. If the new hotel isn't the same standard as the one you originally booked and paid for, you'll want compensation for the difference. You may decide when you get home that it's too much trouble, but at least you've left yourself the option.

The tour operator is also responsible for the services you get from the suppliers the tour operator has booked. So if you come down with food poisoning because of hotel food, you can claim compensation from the tour operator rather than the hotel. Of course, if you go out to restaurants of your choice and get food poisoning, the tour operator isn't liable.

If you have a problem and can't resolve it with the tour operator, contact ABTA (020-7637-2444 or www.abta.com) or the Association of Independent Tour Operators (020-8744-9280 or www.aito.co.uk).

Making a Claim

Neither ABTA nor AITO can intervene directly in a dispute, but both organisations have arbitration schemes, which are normally better ways to resolve a dispute than going to court. However, if you contact ABTA or AITO and still aren't satisfied, you can make a claim for compensation through the courts. ABTA and tour operators tend to offer you compensation for the part of your holiday that went wrong rather than taking the view that, because part of it went wrong, all of it was spoiled. The organisation will fight tooth and nail – and usually successfully – exorbitant claims from people they think are just trying to get a free holiday.

You need to think very carefully before putting in your claim about how much compensation you want. Be reasonable. If you had to put up with a poor standard of hotel for two days until the tour operator managed to move you to accommodation of a similar standard to that you booked, did those two days really ruin the whole of your two-week stay? On the other hand, if you wanted a poolside holiday but the pool wasn't available, and no alternative pool was made available for two weeks, that problem may indeed have ruined your whole stay.

You may need some legal advice to help you put a figure on your loss, taking into account loss of enjoyment. If you have just one holiday a year, that loss of enjoyment may be valued more highly in financial terms than if you take two or three breaks a year. If you're claiming up to £5,000, you can use the small-claims track at the County Court. Chapter 1 has more details of how the system works.

Thinking about Other Travelling Tips

Here are a few other odds and ends to think about before you set off on your holiday:

- **Mums-to-be should check with the transport provider about their rules on carrying pregnant women.** Most airlines will refuse to take women who are more than 36 weeks pregnant. (Some airlines refuse women even earlier in the pregnancy.) Don't forget that you'll have to be within their time limits on the way back from your destination, as well as on the way there. Take a doctor's letter proving the date the baby is due and check with your doctor that you're safe to travel. Your travel insurance company will need to know, too, or the policy may not be valid.

- **If you're travelling with children, you may be entitled to free or reduced fares or accommodation.** Children usually travel free up until a certain age – for example, up until the age of five on most trains in the UK – and then get discounts. You can buy a family railcard, for example, that will allow the whole family, or one parent and one child, to travel together at discounted rates. Check with the transport operator or the travel agent when you're booking a package holiday. Some hotels will take babies or young children for free if you book a family room. If you're travelling abroad, your children will need their own passports unless they were already on your valid ten-year passport before October 1998.

- **If you're travelling with disabilities, notify any transport operator in advance what your requirements are.** Most make the arrangements for free, but at least one of the budget airlines charges for the use of a wheelchair to take passengers from the check in to the departure gate. For rail travel, you can buy a railcard that gives you and an accompanying adult discounted fares (See 'Getting around the UK,' earlier in this chapter.)

✔ **Be aware of the restrictions on the amount of alcohol and cigarettes you can bring back from other countries.** Restrictions on the amounts you can bring in from many EU countries have been dropped but restrictions do still exist for some of the newer member states, such as Estonia and the Czech Republic. Check before you go. If you're travelling back from EU countries where no restrictions apply, be reasonable! If customs officers think that you're bringing the stuff into the UK to resell, they can confiscate it. You're likely to be stopped and questioned if you have more than 3,200 cigarettes or 90 litres of wine, for example. If you're travelling from a country outside the EU, you can bring in 200 cigarettes and a bottle of spirits without have to pay tax or duty.

✔ **Other restrictions apply on the value of other goods you can bring in to the UK, so check with the airline or ferry operator.** Apart from the rules on cigarettes and alcohol, no restrictions surround bringing in other goods from EU countries as taxes are already paid on those items. However, you can bring in only £145 worth of gifts and souvenirs from a country outside the EU without having to pay tax or duty. This amount increases to about £340 worth of gifts and souvenirs in January 2007. If you bring in valuables such as carpets, jewellery, or pearls worth more than that amount, you may have to pay tax, and you can be fined if you try to get the goods through customs without declaring them. Keep the receipts showing where they were bought and how much you paid. In addition, certain goods, such as meat products from South Africa, are banned completely.

✔ **If you're taking something of value out of the country to use it and bring it back in again, take the original receipts showing it was bought here.** Otherwise, you may be assumed to have bought it abroad and charged duty when you get back.

Part VI
The Part of Tens

In this part . . .

*E*very *For Dummies* book has The Part of Tens. This one covers ten insurance policies you may want to buy just in case things go wrong and you can't get them put right, and ten organisations that can help you sort out any disputes over your rights.

Chapter 18

Ten or So Insurance Policies That Can Give You Peace of Mind

In This Chapter

▶ Insuring yourself and your dependents against risk

▶ Understanding the consequences of going without insurance

I n some cases, you have rights; for everything else, you have insurance. The law in the UK gives you all sorts of rights. Along with rights come responsibilities. If you drive a car, you have a responsibility to drive it safely and not cause others injury. If you have dependents, you have a responsibility to take care of them. Insurance can help you to go on meeting those responsibilities, even when things go wrong, and can provide some peace of mind.

Peace of mind comes at a price. If you were to take out every kind of insurance, you'd end up paying more in premiums each month than you earn, so you do have to pick and choose. As with anything else in life, you get what you pay for. The better the policy and the more generously it meets any potential claim, the more the premiums cost you.

Deciding what insurance to buy is a balance. You have to decide what risks you're prepared to take and which ones you'd rather have insurance for. And as with everything else, the rights you have to claim on the policy are contained in the small print.

Taking to the Road with Car Insurance

After you've passed your driving test, you have the right to drive, but you must have car insurance. It's the only policy that the law requires.

If you're found driving without insurance, you're likely to get a criminal record, and you'll find it far harder and more expensive to get insurance in the future.

You can choose *comprehensive, third-party fire and theft,* or *third-party* insurance:

- ✓ **Comprehensive** insurance covers all costs if you have an accident in your car, or it's damaged through fire or theft. The insurer also pays up if the accident results in injury, death, or legal action.

- ✓ **Third-party fire and theft** covers the costs of other drivers (the third party) involved in an accident with you if you're at fault. Your car is only covered if it's damaged as a result of fire or theft.

- ✓ **Third-party** covers only the costs of other drivers involved in an accident with you if they successfully claim against you. This insurance is the most basic type you can have and still be legal to drive.

Comprehensive is the most expensive type of coverage, followed by third-party fire and theft; third-party is the cheapest option. If you can afford it, go for fully comprehensive cover. You can have a comprehensive policy that allows you to drive any car and still be covered or that allows any licensed driver to drive your car.

You can do a lot of things to keep your car insurance premiums down, such as keeping your car in the garage at night, agreeing to an excess that's higher than standard; fitting extra, approved security devices, and passing an advanced driving qualification.

Safeguarding Your Castle

Home buildings insurance covers you if your home is damaged due to an event such as fire, flooding, or subsidence. These problems can be very expensive to put right – often tens of thousands of pounds. If you're a property owner, don't take the risk of doing without buildings insurance.

If you have a mortgage, your lender will insist on buildings insurance, but you don't have to buy the policy that your lender suggests. However, if you're buying a leasehold property, you aren't required to have this type of insurance; instead, the freeholder should have his own buildings insurance in place to cover the rebuilding costs of the entire building. You contribute to that insurance through your service charges.

Your buildings insurance covers the cost of clearing the site and rebuilding your home, which may be less than the market value of your home. Get an insurance valuation, or you may overpay for your policy.

Insuring Your Precious Belongings

You can buy *home contents insurance,* which pays out if you're burgled or your property is damaged by something like a flood or a fire.

If you're underinsured, your insurer won't pay out the full value of your claim. Go through your home room-by-room and total up the value of your property. As a bare minimum, insurers reckon that a home contents policy should be set up to pay £15,000.

The best type of contents insurance to go for is new-for-old, which is the vast majority of policies sold today. This coverage means that if your television is stolen, the insurer pays for you to buy a brand new one rather than working out the current market value of the stolen model and offering to pay you that amount.

Putting the Family First

All the insurance policies in this chapter relate to covering events that can occur when you're alive – from burglary to car accident. Through life insurance, you arrange to take care of things when you die.

If you take out a life insurance policy, when you die, the person named in the policy as the beneficiary receives a lump sum. They can use the money to pay off the mortgage, the children's education, or day-to-day living costs. Without this money, your dependents may have to sell the house because they can no longer keep up the mortgage repayments.

Buying life insurance is a bit of a balancing act because the higher the payout – called the *sum assured* – the larger the premiums. What's more, as you get older and therefore more likely to die, the premiums can climb.

Life insurance comes in two main types:

- **Term insurance:** If you die during an agreed period of time – say, within 25 years – then the policy pays your beneficiaries cash. The downside is that the policy pays only if you die within the specified term. If you die a day after the term has ended, your loved ones get nothing.

- **Whole of life insurance:** As the name suggests, under this type of policy, your beneficiaries are in line for a payout regardless of when you die. Die the day after taking out the policy or 50 years hence, and your loved ones receive the money. However, the premiums are high and climb sharply as you get older. Term insurance premiums are generally the cheaper option.

The sale of life insurance (also known as *life assurance*) is big business, and there lots of little policy nuances that you need to take on board. Check out *Sorting Out Your Finances For Dummies* (Wiley) by Melanie Bien, for more information on life policies.

If you have no dependents who will need to be taken care of when you're gone, you probably don't need life insurance.

Protecting Your Income

Income replacement insurance pays you an income if you're unable to work due to ill health, injury, or, in some cases, redundancy. Because it tends to be expensive, income replacement insurance is an underused, but key, insurance. The insurer promises to pay a pre-set percentage or amount of income to you if you have to make a claim. You can live off this money to keep the wolf from the door while you focus on recuperating or obtaining a new job.

Income replacement insurance is also referred to as *income protection*. Income replacement products can be very complex, and you may need independent financial advice to help decide on the most suitable product for you.

Income replacement premiums can be high, which reflects the risks to the insurer. And the higher the amount of income you want to have coming in from the policy, the higher the premiums are.

Some income protection policies pay out only if you're injured and are unable to do any work whatsoever. Others pay if your condition stops you from doing your current job. You pay your money, and you take your choice, but the latter type of policy is more expensive than the former.

Covering Yourself in Emergencies

Critical illness insurance pays you a lump sum if you suffer a critical illness. For an illness to be considered critical, it usually has to be life threatening. For example, cancer or stroke may be considered life threatening, but a bout of gastric flu, however unpleasant, isn't. Critical illness coverage is meant to alleviate the financial burden at a time when you're at your most vulnerable and unable to work. One of the most common reasons for people being unable to keep up their mortgage or loan repayments is a critical illness.

Critical illness insurance tends to be cheaper than income replacement insurance. From the insurer's perspective, it's a one-off, short-term, financial hit rather than a long-term, sometimes open-ended, commitment.

Toing and Froing?

One surefire way to bulldoze your finances is to fall seriously ill or be involved in an accident abroad. Love it or loathe it, under the National Health Service, you don't have to pay for emergency medical treatment. However, the UK is fairly unusual in offering such 'free at the point of delivery' healthcare. If you fall ill or are injured abroad, you may not have the right to treatment if you have no way of meeting local medical bills.

This situation is where good travel insurance comes in. For a premium, the insurance company usually promises to meet medical bills if you fall ill or have an accident, to arrange for you to be flown home to the UK should you need to be, and covers you in cases of theft, or even financial loss, due to flight delays.

You don't have to purchase the travel insurance offered by your airline carrier or package holiday operator. You're bound to find a better deal elsewhere through an insurance broker specialising in travel coverage. In recent years, annual travel insurance policies have grown in popularity, and they can be a great idea if you plan to take multiple holidays a year.

In some European Union countries, you do have the right to emergency treatment because they have an agreement with the UK. Those EU countries, such as France and Germany, look after UK citizens if they need emergency treatment just as the UK does for their citizens. You can find a list of countries that offer UK citizens free healthcare at the Department of Health's Web site at www.dh.gov.uk. To be able to claim healthcare while abroad, you need a European Health Insurance Card (it used to be called an E111). You can pick up the forms from your doctor.

Helping Hands

Suing and being sued is becoming fairly commonplace. Nearly all the ads on daytime TV promise big payouts to people who have been involved in an accident. If you can't enforce your rights, you may want to sue someone for money you're owed or for compensation for damages, loss, or injury you've suffered because of their actions or negligence.

You can also insure yourself against the costs of being sued or having to sue someone else and of getting legal assistance. The market in *legal assistance insurance* is growing.

You may find that your home contents insurance policy or even your credit card automatically comes with legal assistance insurance tacked on. Check out the small print. Your home contents insurance is the policy that may cover you if someone is injured in your home and then sues you, for example.

Planning Ahead

One consequence of living longer is that the chances that you'll end up needing some sort of at-home or residential nursing care in later life are higher than ever. Care doesn't come cheap, and you can soon find that your hard-earned cash is eaten away. Therefore, insurers offer *long-term care plans*. Under this type of insurance, insurers pick up the tab for your care as long as you continue to pay a premium.

If you have to go into a care home in England and Wales, the government picks up the tab only after you've used up most of your assets. In fact, the government steps in only if you can prove that your assets are valued at less than £16,000. Scotland has different rules for paying for older people in care.

Keeping the Roof Over Your Head

Mortgage protection insurance does what it says on the tin. It covers your mortgage repayments if you can't work because you fall ill or are injured. If your mortgage loan is high relative to the value of the property you're buying, many lenders are insisting that you have this type of insurance in place.

Avoiding Debt

Payment protection insurance works on the same principle as mortgage protection insurance. If you're unable to make the repayments on your personal loans and credit debts, then the insurer steps in. However, the reasons that you're unable to make your repayments have to match the provisions of the policy, or it doesn't pay out. For example, you can't take out this type of policy and then resign from your job in a fit of pique and rely on the insurers to pay your debts.

Consumer groups claim that mortgage and loan payment protection insurance is often overpriced and has lots of built-in get-out clauses that allow the insurance companies to refuse to pay out. The watchwords, as always with buying insurance, are shop around for the best deal and check out the policy's small print.

Chapter 19

Ten Ways to Protect Your Rights

In This Chapter

▶ Being aware of your rights

▶ Understanding how to enforce them

▶ Knowing when and where to get help

This book looks at a whole range of different rights you have under UK law. You may sail through life never coming across a situation where your rights are denied you – but you'll be a very lucky and unusual individual, if that's the case. Problems usually arise when other people you come into contact with aren't aware of your rights, or your rights are in conflict with theirs.

If you do get into a tussle over your rights, you have several options. Taking court action should always be the last resort, as it can be costly and you can end up losing. The first step is to get the right advice so that you're absolutely sure of your ground; then go through all the complaints and negotiation procedures open to you; accept independent mediation by a third party to try to resolve the situation; and use an Ombudsman scheme, if one is available for your particular dispute. At any point during the process, you may decide that you'd rather forfeit your rights than get embroiled in a lengthy legal battle in order to enforce them.

If you do decide to take legal action, make sure that you understand the way the court procedures work (refer to Chapter 1, which explains the system in the UK) and that you get lawyers with the right experience to fight your corner. Be prepared to lose. If a dispute over rights ends up in court for a resolution, it's usually far from clear-cut, and the judgement may come down in favour of either party.

Many disputes that started out over fairly minor matters have ended up becoming an obsession for the people involved and have had dire consequences. There's no point in losing the shirt off your back over the height of the hedge next door. Even if you win the case, you'd never have a cordial relationship with your neighbour again. It can be cheaper to move house and move on. In this chapter, I give you some ways that you can avoid making the trip to court.

Preventing Problems in the First Place

The most effective way to protect your rights is to know what they are and to take all the right precautions in the first place. The more informed you are as consumers of all sorts of goods and services, the more power you have to protect not only your own rights but those of the wider community. Consumer power can force traders, public bodies, and private organisations to improve their standards of service.

Only do business with people who have a good reputation. Don't accept work estimates that are scribbled on the back of an envelope – get everything in writing, on headed paper, with all the terms and conditions agreed to before you sign on the dotted line.

Remember that if something seems too good to be true that's because it is and you'll have trouble further down the line. Check out your rights and discuss these with the salesperson. Let them know that you know where you stand. Get a written contract and read all the small print of the terms and conditions. Don't leave anything to chance, and you're less likely to get stung.

Getting Help from Your Local Citizens Advice Bureau

There's a *Citizens Advice Bureau* (CAB) in most towns in the UK and several in the larger cities. Each bureau is a charity run by a management committee of local people and is staffed mainly by volunteers. Many of the bigger CABs have specialist workers, such as money advisers and people who deal mainly with benefits problems or employment issues.

CABs have a wealth of information available to them, and the workers are trained to research that information and help you to work out where you stand in any given situation. Because there are often slight differences in the laws between England and Wales, and Scotland and Northern Ireland, each has its own relevant information. Bureaux offer free, independent, impartial advice. They don't charge, and they don't judge. Many people are loath to go to CAB because they assume it's a Government organisation, but that's not the case.

You shouldn't expect the advisers to sort out your problems for you. They're there to help you sort them out for yourself and give you the information, advice, and support you need. If you need help with filling in forms or you need extended support to deal with complex debt problems, you'll get it. If the CAB isn't the best place to get help or if you need more specialist help than it can offer – such as a solicitor – the advisers can point you in the right direction.

CABs are busy, and you may find that you have to sign up for a waiting list or an appointment system to get the right adviser to help with your particular problem. Whatever your problem, CAB is a good place to start. You can find contact details in your local phone book or at www.citizensadvice.org.uk.

Along similar lines to CABs, your town may have a *Law Centre* or another advice-providing organisation, such as an advice centre specialising in consumer issues or a money-advice unit that can help you with debt problems. Take a look in your local phone book for contact details of a suitable organisation, try www.adviceuk.org.uk for the details of advice services or www.lawcentres.org.uk – call 020-7387-8570 for details of a Law Centre near you.

Contacting the Trading Standards Department

When it comes to most issues surrounding your consumer rights, the *Trading Standards Department* at your local authority offices may be able to help. Its officers are trained to deal with retailers who won't give you your money back when they've sold you something faulty or who try to rip you off. The Trading Standards Officer is the person to help you get what's rightfully yours if someone is selling fake goods on market stalls or at car boot sales; dangerous toys; second-hand electrical goods; cars that have had their speedometers wound back to look as if they have low mileage; or goods that aren't as they're described.

Trading Standards officers also deal with weights and measures and people selling dodgy services, such as cowboy builders. The sale of alcohol or cigarettes to underage customers and loans and credit agreements sold by financial firms licensed under the Consumer Credit Act 1974 (see Chapter 15) are also part of their remit.

If you have a dispute with a retailer or tradesperson and you've tried to resolve it but can't, check out your rights with the Trading Standards Department. You can find contact details under your local authority in your phone book, or the CAB (see preceding section) can advise you on how to get in touch.

Traders may be members of *trade associations,* which are set up to give their members guidelines and to set standards on how they should best treat their customers. Some trade associations have an arbitration or a mediation service through which they try to resolve disputes between members and their customers. Gas installers should be members of the Corgi scheme, for example. You can contact Corgi at 0870-401-2300 or visit its Web site at www.corgi-gas-safety.com. Check on the trader's letterhead, invoices, or advertising materials for trade association logos. You can find contact details by asking the trader you're dealing with, the CAB, or the Trading Standards Department or by checking www.taforum.org.

Calling for Help on Health and Safety Issues

Health and safety at work is usually the concern of the *Health and Safety Executive* (HSE), which enforces the legislation and regulations aimed at keeping employees safe and healthy at work. If you're worried that your employer is taking risks and that you haven't been provided with a safe and healthy working environment, talk to the workplace safety representative of your union; if no union exists, you can get information from the HSE. You can check out your rights on the HSE web site at www.hse.gov.uk.

If you're setting up a business, you can get help with health and safety issues before you take on staff. The HSE Infoline is a valuable source of information – 0845-345-0055.

Environmental Health Officers also deal with workplace health and safety issues – in particular, for shops, leisure centres, pubs restaurant, and hotels. If you have a problem with food in a restaurant or with noisy neighbours – including noisy workplaces nearby – they also deal with that issue. You can contact your Environmental Health Department at your local authority. You can find the contact details in the phone book under the name of your local authority.

Taking Your Complaint to an Ombudsman Scheme

Various *Ombudsman schemes* have been set up to resolve problems. An *Ombudsman* is a person specifically appointed to investigate individuals' complaints. Ombudsman's offices deal with complaints on anything from pensions to estate agents' services, and insurance products to patient care under the National Health Service. These schemes provide an alternative to using the courts; in most cases, the Ombudsman's decision is binding on both parties. If you choose to use one of these schemes and don't like the outcome, you can't usually then go back and try for a different outcome through the courts.

Schemes cover pensions, insurance, banks, financial services, local government, Government departments and other public sector bodies, the health service, legal services, estate agents, funerals, and many more.

Ombudsmen deal with complaints that haven't been satisfactorily resolved by the public body or private sector services you're in dispute with. Ombudsmen offer their services for free, and their powers and procedures vary.

Before you can call on the help of an Ombudsman, you need to have exhausted the internal complaints procedures of the organisation you're in dispute with. You have to give them the opportunity to respond to your complaint and to investigate it fully internally before a third-party gets involved.

If you have a problem that hasn't been resolved by the people you normally encounter in the course of your transactions, ask to speak to a manager or supervisor. If you still get no resolution, ask for a copy of the complaints procedures, which usually involve contacting the regional manager and then the head office. After you go through those procedures, you can then contact the relevant Ombudsman's office. If you complain to the Ombudsman before you've gone through all the internal procedures, you're referred back to the internal procedures.

Ask the organisation you're in dispute with for details of an Ombudsman or contact your CAB for advice.

Calling the Police

If you're subjected to any kind of crime, even though it's fairly minor, you may not be able to get very far in enforcing your rights unless you've called the police. If you've had your wallet or mobile phone stolen, for example, or even had a break-in at home, the police may not visit the scene. However, unless you've reported the incident and have a reference number, your insurance company is unlikely to pay out.

In the case of a car accident, you may discover that the driver who caused the accident was uninsured or gave you false information at the scene and may never be traced. Unless the police have been involved and have a report of the accident, you may find have difficulty claiming for the damage through the Uninsured Drivers Agreement or Untraced Drivers Agreement, which is run by the Motor Insurers' Bureau. You can get more information on the Bureau's Web site at www.mib.org.uk or from the CAB.

Similarly, a *Criminal Injuries Compensation Scheme* helps the victims of crime. If you've been attacked and injured in the street and the attacker can't be found or can't pay you compensation, the scheme pays fixed sums for particular injuries. Once again, you need to report the incident to the police. You can get details of the scheme from the Criminal Injuries Compensation Authority at www.cica.gov.uk or 0800-358-3601, or the CAB can help.

Don't let crime go unreported just because you feel that nothing can be done or that the police will be reluctant to be involved. You may find it difficult to enforce your rights if you haven't reported it and recorded the details.

Using the Right Solicitor

If you've unsuccessfully tried all other avenues to enforce your rights, you may have to employ the services of a solicitor. They're usually high on the list of people you love to hate, but that's because most people feel they charge too much for the work they do. All you see is the letters that are sent and the documents that are drawn up, but you may not be aware of all the research that can go on behind the scenes.

You must have the right solicitor to deal with your case. You don't want to use the same solicitor who dealt with your house purchase to deal with your divorce if that's not their area of expertise. If you want a will drawn up, make sure that the solicitor specialises in wills and trusts. If you need a solicitor to help with a case against your employer, find a solicitor who knows a lot about employment law. If you've been involved in a criminal case, you need a lawyer who deals with criminal matters and not one who deals with personal injury and vice versa.

The Law Society has lists of solicitors and the subjects they specialise in. To locate the Law Societies for England and Wales, Scotland, and Northern Ireland, go to www.lawsociety.org.uk.

Your local CAB knows the expertise of the solicitors in the area, and often, solicitors offer a half hour initial interview free if you're referred to them by organisations such as the CAB, or they'll see you in the CAB office for a free or fixed-fee interview. Ask the CAB what's available. Also, check out your solicitor's costs before you go ahead and ask whether any free legal advice is available to you.

With luck, your solicitor sending a letter threatening legal action is enough to get the dispute resolved. But you should be aware that sometimes the other side responds by getting their solicitor involved, and then the dispute escalates – ending up in court before you can stop it.

Making a Claim at an Employment Tribunal

When it comes to enforcing your rights over work issues, *employment tribunals*, not courts, are the bodies that make most of the decisions. You may want to take action against your boss for many reasons, including the most common one: unfair dismissal. (In Chapter 9, you can see other reasons for making a claim.)

Although tribunals were set up to allow employees and employers to represent themselves, they've become very legalistic and employers usually hire solicitors. That makes it all the more difficult for you to win your case without representation. Talk to your union representative or your local CAB or Law Centre before starting your claim. You need to get advice right at the start so that you don't leave any vital information out when you fill in the forms to start the process. In most cases, you need to start your claim within three months of the event that led to it. Chapter 9 has more details on how the procedure works.

Often, you've already lost your job before you make your claim or making a claim makes it difficult to work with your employer again. Don't let the problem get that far if you can avoid it. Talk to your union or a CAB or Law Centre about your rights at work and see whether you can resolve the issue informally with your boss – with the help of the union rep or an adviser, or through the employer's grievance procedure – before it's too late.

Suing in Court for Money You're Owed

If you're owed money and the person who owes it refuses to pay up, you can use the court system to get it back. In some situations, the amount of money involved in a dispute may seem hardly worth worrying about. Certainly, if you have to resort to court action and face losing more in costs than you're owed in the first place, it can make you decide to let the whole thing drop. However, if you've checked your rights and you know that you have a good case, you can sue quite cheaply in the County Court using the *small-claims track* for amounts of less than £5,000. The kinds of cases dealt with by this system are consumer disputes, disputes about ownership of goods, accident claims, and most disputes between landlords and tenants. You can also sue for compensation for personal injury if you're claiming less than £1,000.

Because you can recover only limited costs if you win under the small-claims system, you're unlikely to want to hire a solicitor. Because of that, the procedure is simple and informal, and you can conduct your own case. But do get help from the CAB or a Law Centre before you go ahead. You can't afford to omit vital information when you're filing your claim.

If you're owed between £5,000 and £15,000, you can sue for the recovery of the money using the *fast-track system* if the trial isn't likely to last for more than a day and limited expert evidence is to be heard. If you're suing for more than small amounts, get legal advice.

Claiming Compensation Through the Courts When Something Goes Wrong

If your rights have been contravened and you haven't been able to enforce them or to resolve the dispute to your satisfaction in any other way, your last resort may be to sue for *compensation*. Suing for compensation is not the same as going to court to get back what you're owed (see the section above). Compensation is an amount to make up for loss that you've suffered because of the dispute or incident you've been involved in.

You may want to claim compensation for personal injury caused by the negligence of an employer, by someone who caused an accident, or someone who attacked you in the street. You can sue a health authority for compensation for medical negligence or because you've been discriminated against.

These cases can be very complicated, and the amounts involved vary according to the amount of loss you've suffered. The loss may be financial as in loss of earnings, but that loss may also include an amount for loss of enjoyment, for example, if you've had problems while on holiday. In addition, you can add in compensation for pain and suffering – some of which may be emotional, rather than physical, pain and suffering.

If you're going to claim for compensation, you need a solicitor who can assess the kind of figure you should be suing for and how much each of the elements of the claim may amount to. The court procedures for these kinds of claims are much more formal and protracted. These cases can go on for weeks while the courts decide whether an employer has been guilty of discrimination and how much money should be awarded to the claimant.

Index

• C •

• *F* •

• *Q* •

• *R* •

FOR DUMMIES®

A world of resources to help you grow

HOBBIES

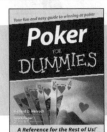

0-7645-5232-5

0-7645-6847-7

0-7645-5476-X

Also available:

Art For Dummies
(0-7645-5104-3)
Aromatherapy For Dummies
(0-7645-5171-X)
Bridge For Dummies
(0-7645-5015-2)
Card Games For Dummies
(0-7645-9910-0)
Chess For Dummies
(0-7645-8404-9)
Crocheting For Dummies
(0-7645-4151-X)

Improving Your Memory
For Dummies
(0-7645-5435-2)
Massage For Dummies
(0-7645-5172-8)
Meditation For Dummies
(0-471-77774-9)
Photography For Dummies
(0-7645-4116-1)
Quilting For Dummies
(0-7645-9799-X)
Woodworking For Dummies
(0-7645-3977-9)

EDUCATION

0-7645-7206-7

0-7645-5581-2

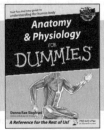

0-7645-5422-0

Also available:

Algebra For Dummies
(0-7645-5325-9)
Algebra II For Dummies
(0-471-77581-9)
Astronomy For Dummies
(0-7645-8465-0)
Buddhism For Dummies
(0-7645-5359-3)
Calculus For Dummies
(0-7645-2498-4)
Christianity For Dummies
(0-7645-4482-9)

Forensics For Dummies
(0-7645-5580-4)
Islam For Dummies
(0-7645-5503-0)
Philosophy For Dummies
(0-7645-5153-1)
Religion For Dummies
(0-7645-5264-3)
Trigonometry For Dummies
(0-7645-6903-1)

PETS

0-7645-5255-4

0-7645-8418-9

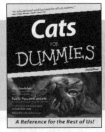

0-7645-5275-9

Also available:

Labrador Retrievers
For Dummies
(0-7645-5281-3)
Aquariums For Dummies
(0-7645-5156-6)
Birds For Dummies
(0-7645-5139-6)
Dogs For Dummies
(0-7645-5274-0)
Ferrets For Dummies
(0-7645-5259-7)
German Shepherds
For Dummies
(0-7645-5280-5)

Golden Retrievers
For Dummies
(0-7645-5267-8)
Horses For Dummies
(0-7645-9797-3)
Jack Russell Terriers
For Dummies
(0-7645-5268-6)
Puppies Raising & Training
Diary For Dummies
(0-7645-0876-8)
Saltwater Aquariums For
Dummies
(0-7645-5340-2)

FOR DUMMIES®

The easy way to get more done and have more fun

LANGUAGES

0-7645-5194-9

0-7645-5193-0

0-7645-5196-5

Also available:

Chinese For Dummies
(0-471-78897-X)

Chinese Phrases
For Dummies
(0-7645-8477-4)

French Phrases For Dummies
(0-7645-7202-4)

German For Dummies
(0-7645-5195-7)

Italian Phrases For Dummies
(0-7645-7203-2)

Japanese For Dummies
(0-7645-5429-8)

Latin For Dummies
(0-7645-5431-X)

Spanish Phrases
For Dummies
(0-7645-7204-0)

Spanish Verbs For Dummies
(0-471-76872-3)

Hebrew For Dummies
(0-7645-5489-1)

MUSIC AND FILM

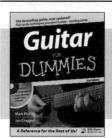

0-7645-9904-6

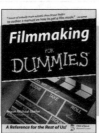

0-7645-2476-3

0-7645-5105-1

Also available:

Bass Guitar For Dummies
(0-7645-2487-9)

Blues For Dummies
(0-7645-5080-2)

Classical Music For Dummies
(0-7645-5009-8)

Drums For Dummies
(0-471-79411-2)

Jazz For Dummies
(0-471-76844-8)

Opera For Dummies
(0-7645-5010-1)

Rock Guitar For Dummies
(0-7645-5356-9)

Screenwriting For Dummies
(0-7645-5486-7)

Songwriting For Dummies
(0-7645-5404-2)

Singing For Dummies
(0-7645-2475-5)

HEALTH, SPORTS & FITNESS

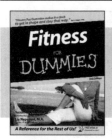

0-7645-7851-0

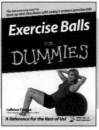

0-7645-5623-1

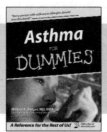

0-7645-4233-8

Also available:

Controlling Cholesterol
For Dummies
(0-7645-5440-9)

Dieting For Dummies
(0-7645-4149-8)

High Blood Pressure
For Dummies
(0-7645-5424-7)

Martial Arts For Dummies
(0-7645-5358-5)

Menopause For Dummies
(0-7645-5458-1)

Power Yoga For Dummies
(0-7645-5342-9)

Weight Training
For Dummies
(0-471-76845-6)

Yoga For Dummies
(0-7645-5117-5)

8821_p3

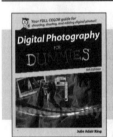